The Social Construction
of Written Communication

Writing Research

Multidisciplinary Inquiries into the Nature of Writing

edited by Marcia Farr, University of Illinois at Chicago

The Social Construction
of Written Communication

edited by

Bennett A. Rafoth

Donald L. Rubin

ABLEX PUBLISHING CORPORATION
NORWOOD, NEW JERSEY

Printed in the United States of America.

Library of Congress Cataloging-in-Publication Data

The Social construction of written communication.

  (Writing research)
  Bibliography: p.
  Includes indexes.
    1. Written communication—Social aspects.   I. Rafoth,
Bennett A.   II. Rubin, Donald L.   III. Series: Writing
research (Norwood, N.J.)
P211.S63   1988   302.2'244   88-22347
ISBN 0-89391-436-3
      0-89391-549-1 (ppk)

Ablex Publishing Corporation
355 Chestnut St.
Norwood, NJ 07648

Table of Contents

v

Chapter 1

Introduction: Four Dimensions of Social Construction in Written Communication

Donald L. Rubin
The University of Georgia

This book is about the ways in which written discourse is shaped by the social context in which it takes place. This book is also about the converse, about the ways in which writing (and the activities surrounding it) shape social contexts. Social contexts and written discourse stand in a reciprocal, mutually constructive relationship, one to the other.

Of course neither contexts nor texts carry any significance except as they are reconstructed in the minds of language users. If a writer construes a cordial relationship with the reader, then he or she will intuitively adopt a correspondingly informal style. And if a reader receives a message and construes the style as representing a cordial, informal relationship, then that reader may be disposed to respond in kind when composing a reply. The participants thus negotiate the definition of their relationship; discourse has constructed social context. To compose and to comprehend, to engage in written communication, people construct for themselves and for others the nature of their relationships, their communicative purposes, their topics, and their texts. These constructions—simultaneously and inextricably both social and cognitive, I will contend—are what people operate with and operate upon in communication.

A folk story further illustrates what it means to say that people operate on the basis of their constructions of social context. The tale, popular among people of Eastern European Jewish descent, tells of two merchants—one a young man and the other more mature—both traveling by rail from Krakow to Lodz.

"Pardon me," says the younger of the two. "What time do you have? I was in such a hurry checking out of my room this morning that I stupidly packed my watch in my valise."

The second traveler, noticing the young man for the first time, studies his chance companion a brief moment, then cries out in alarm, "No, no. It's quite impossible. I won't have it, and you must leave at once!"

"A thousand pardons," says the young man. "The train is crowded, but you needn't worry. I'll find another compartment. Just tell me before I go, what was so terrible about asking the time? Why such a fuss about an innocent word between fellow passengers traveling the train together?"

"Can't you see, don't you understand? By itself, it's not such a terrible thing to ask a man the time. But you're a nice looking young man, and one thing would lead to another: we would have started a conversation. We would be talking, and one thing would lead to another: I would discover you have no friends or family in Lodz. I would feel badly for you, and one thing would lead to another: I would invite you to my home for dinner. You would be a guest in my home, and one thing would lead to another: you would meet my daughter, Leda. You would meet Leda, and the two of you being young and both full of grace, one thing would lead to another: you and Leda would fall in love. You and Leda would fall in love, and naturally one thing would lead to another. You'd want to get married and start your own household."

The elder traveler was becoming increasingly vexed as he spoke, and here he virtually rose out of his seat and screamed, "But no, it's impossible! Leda is too young, too young and too inexperienced to get married now. So you see, you must leave at once, right now, before one thing leads to another!"

4 TYPES OF SOCIAL CONSTRUCTIVE PROCESSES

One thing does indeed lead to another. Inferences and associations lead us to construct complex ways of organizing and predicting information about social context. This is no less true for written than for oral discourse. The works collected in this volume, grounded in a considerable body of allied research and theory in written discourse, suggest four interrelated perspectives on the ways people socially construct written communication: (1) Writers construct mental representations of the social contexts in which their writing is embedded; (2) Writing as a social process or system can create or constitute social contexts; (3) Writers—in some senses *all* writers—create texts collectively with other participants in discourse communities; (4) Writers assign consensual values to writing and thus construct a dimension of social meaning. This chapter, and this book, considers each of these approaches to social construction and writing.

Representing social contexts is one type of constructive process in which writers engage. Writers formulate mental representations of the particular readers, purposes, topics, and other features that constitute their immediate communicative contexts. Indeed, skilled writing performance is enabled by the ability to mentally construct complex rhetorical plans (Flower & Hayes, 1980), and most especially by the ability to anticipate readers' responses (Rubin, 1984b). We write a letter while on vacation to our colleagues back at the office, and we try to second guess: will they know this reference to Villa Borghese or should I elaborate? On the other hand, will they think that I think them ignorant if I tell about the Swiss Guards at the Vatican? And will they be stimulated or just plain jealous if I recount the menu at the trattoria? It is this sense of cognitive representation as part of individuals' active "effort after meaning" that is most commonly associated with constructivist notions of language processing (Spiro, 1980) or social interaction (O'Keefe & Delia, 1979). The schemata that experienced and effective writers use to guide their mental representations, however, are not idiosyncratic inventions; they are instead consensually understood patterns that writers internalize, interpret, and execute. These schemata are by no means "given"; they are instead dynamically negotiated between members of discourse communities. It is this sense of socially negotiating ways of construing the world that is most commonly associated with the social construction of reality (Berger & Luckman, 1967; Gergen, 1985).

Beyond understanding social context, writers can actively define or alter it. "Pursuant to the agreement we reached in our conversation of January 15th . . ." the memo writer intones, and thus constructs an operative social context (though the reader may choose to veto it) that encompasses a specified history and that presupposes a spirit of concurrence. Writers' texts function to project, manipulate, or negotiate social relations between writers and readers. Writing can *evoke* a social setting with which readers have past experience (e.g., sitting around a camp fire to swap ghost stories) or it can *invoke* a community of interest that otherwise might have remained merely latent (e.g., physicians for nuclear disarmament). Writing can also constitute, or at least "amplify," social institutions (e.g., a business enterprise's articles of incorporation bring that enterprise into being and also reaffirm or instantiate the foundations of capitalism). These are all instances of *creating social contexts through writing*.

While writing is commonly regarded as a private, solitary activity, experience in the world of practical discourse reveals that much writing can be regarded as a corporate effort. Collaborative writing is the norm rather than the exception in many institutional enterprises—writing advertising copy, drafting legislation, issuing corporate reports. Even the novelist who invents fantasy worlds of people and events in the garret of his or her remote farmhouse in the Berkshires is likely to have incubated ideas and a sense of style in prior conversations. And if the writer hits the mark, the manuscript will pass under the successive pens of several editors. In these interactive events and in a great many others, writers can be regarded as *creating texts collectively*.

Understanding the meaning of any message or symbol system requires an appreciation of evaluative as well as denotative dimensions (Blom & Gumperz, 1972). Broad social, cultural, and political factors imprint social valence upon writing and written products (Cook–Gumperz, 1986). The ways in which individuals acquire, practice, and interpret the written word are interwoven with *assigning social values to writing*: What standards define "good" writing, and what social order gives rise to them? What moral judgments do we make about illiterate people? What world view ought writing instruction inculcate? Examples include the nature of work and authority, art and creativity, and the validity of individuality and self-knowledge.

COMPLEMENTARY PERSPECTIVES ON A WRITING EVENT

No claim is made that one could uniquely classify a writing event under any one or another of these four types of social constructive processes. On the contrary, all four dimensions are relevant to any given act of written communication. They are simply alternative and complementary perspectives on social construction. Consider the varied social constructive facets of the following very unremarkable text, a notice of a meeting issued by a school librarian to members of a parent advisory committee:

Dear Media Committee Members,
We'll have our nwxt Media Committee meeting on. . . . Here's our agenda for the meeting:

1. Discussion of the paperback books purchased from the Book Fair. (At our last meeting books for which we had no review were distributed for members to read and report on at our next meeting)
2. Discussion of next Spring's Book Fair and ways we can involve lots of students.

I hope we'll see you Monday.

This brief text presupposes a particular social perspective in which the writer represented the context for this message to herself and to her audiences. For example, the form of address ("Dear Media Committee

Members") implies that in this context the official roles of participants were more salient than any unofficial interpersonal bonds between the writer and the readers. Clearly, also, the writer recognizes differences in prior knowledge between individual readers. The material enclosed in parentheses was new and necessary information only for those who had been derelict and had not attended the previous meeting.

Moreover, the writer tacitly took into account a number of secondary audiences beyond the primary readers, the members of the Media Committee. As a member of a public school community, the librarian who drafted this notice was well aware, for example, that each classroom teacher through whose hands the paper passed was a potential reader. The school principal, prone to keep tabs on all parent-involvement efforts, was also a likely reader. And because the parent Media Committee had been established in part to protect the school against claims of moral turpitude in the library stacks, another audience was the legalistic "for the record." The resulting text reflects an effort to maintain credibility with all of these audiences.

The message creates a social context in the quite concrete sense that it provokes a congregation that otherwise would not gather. Of greater interest, the use of contractions ("we'll" twice, and "Here's"), colloquial diction ("lots"), and the repeated use of inclusive first-person plural pronouns ("we," "our") instantiates in the text a humane, collegial persona that in fact sets the tone for the group's interpersonal climate. At the same time, the message induces a sense of obligation by reminding readers that people on this committee have been expending effort, and if particular readers have not shared that burden, then by golly, "I hope [at least that] we'll see you Monday."

Although this particular document was drafted by a single author, it nevertheless bears some influences of a collective process. The writer had discussed the agenda and had solicited additional items in earlier conversations. Also, she depended upon a network of cooperating students and teachers to distribute the messages to the intended audience. And to the degree this message was addressed "for the record," the style, content, and format were all consistent with similar archival materials which circulate throughout a school.

While this writing was not intended for public scrutiny, it nonetheless exerted an influence upon, and was in turn influenced by, broad cultural values. It is good, in the consensual social ethics, for public institutions—especially those given care of minor children—to operate in an orderly fashion. To the extent that this meeting notice contributes to and reflects that order, it is good writing. On the other hand, the school librarian can be regarded as one of the chief guardians of cultural standards, especially regarding good language. The typographical error ("nwxt") becomes particularly salient and especially hard to forgive in that context. What might be passed over as a careless lapse had it been committed by the grocer becomes a subject for goodhearted—but nevertheless sincere—rebuke.

This writing event contributes in meaningful ways to maintaining fundamental social structures. It is part of the fabric that binds the citizenry to public education in middle-class America. (No doubt that fabric is considerably frayed and in jeopardy of disintegrating in the last decades of this century.) It supports a fundamental underpinning of middle-class culture: literacy is good for children. Accordingly, imparting literacy becomes bound up, in part through the offices of this simple memorandum, with archetypal roles of parenting and nurturing. Finally, the phenomenon of a written agenda promotes the notion that talk can be planned, organized, task-oriented, and rule governed. Talk, in short, can be an extension of, and controlled by, writing. Writing has awesome power, even the power to legislate talk, in this literacy-based culture.

To this point, this chapter has briefly characterized four perspectives on the social construction of written communication. I have demonstrated that in looking at any given writing event, each of the social constructive perspectives complement the others. The following sections of this chapter elaborate each of these perspectives and point in particular to the ways in which the other 13 chapters in this volume explicate these various types of social constructive processes.

If this account of social constructive dimensions of writing rings true, then it will be apparent that discussing any study of writing under one social constructive rubric rather than another is a somewhat arbitrary decision. The dimensions of social construction operate jointly in any communication event. In writing, social forces constrain the writer at the same time as the writer interprets, and therefore constrains, social forces. This book is organized around the four dimensions of social construction discussed here. The chapters are placed in sections where they best illustrate the operation of one or another of the dimensions. But each chapter will be found to provide insight about all four dimensions. That is because societies and individuals, contexts and cognitive processes, values and social structures, in the end, can only be understood in concert.

REPRESENTING SOCIAL CONTEXTS

Adapting to the Social Context

The sociolinguistic, the rhetorical, and the cognitive-developmental traditions all converge in portraying effective communication as a process of adapting to social context. The sociolinguistic perspective regards communicatively competent speakers as selecting from a repertoire of alternative linguistic varieties: registers, dialects, or languages. Speech communities embody implicit rules of appropriateness, rules for switching from one language variety to another on the basis of social contextual variables such as topic, participant role relations, and setting (Ervin–Tripp, 1972; Hymes, 1971, 1974).

The rhetorical point of view postulates that the goal of rhetorical discourse is to affect audiences, either in the agonistic sense characteristic of classical rhetoricians or in the sense of inducing cooperation or "consubstantiality" as in non-Aristotelian rhetorics (Bator, 1980; Burke, 1950). The rhetor's discourse is engendered and shaped by the "exigencies" of the rhetorical situation, which include elements of the immediate and the historical setting (Bitzer, 1968).

The cognitive-developmental view postulates that with maturation individuals become increasingly able to integrate divergent perspectives on a single event. In the realm of social development, accurate social perception requires that individuals hold their own perspectives in abeyance while predicting the simultaneous but differing social perspectives of others (Feffer, 1970). In addition, sophisticated social perception requires that individuals recognize and reconcile divergent characteristics that comprise the psychological makeup of any given individual (e.g., "ambitious but too polite to show it"; Secord & Peevers, 1974). Although empirical support is equivocal, the cognitive-developmental position conceptualizes social perceptual skill as a necessary precondition for effective communication (Flavell, Botkin, Fry, Jarvis, & Wright, 1968). In order to influence someone, or even to enable comprehension, one must accurately infer the audience's beliefs and prior knowledge.

Construing the Social Context

Each of these three perspectives—the sociolinguistic, the rhetorical, and the cognitive-developmental—portray competent communicators adapting to, and in that sense constrained by, the communicative contexts into which they implant their messages. This portrait suits writing processes as well as face-to-face speech. Studies which elicit writers' think-aloud protocols demonstrate that writers devote a great deal of attention to envisioning their readers and those readers' responses (Berkenkotter, 1981). Writers also work at a variety of other social-cognitive tasks, such as defining for themselves their communicative purposes, and indeed refining those purposes as the text evolves with new implications for rhetorical effect (Flower & Hayes, 1980). Protocol analysis studies suggest, in fact, that expert and novice writers are distinguished in large degree by the nature of their communicative concerns. Whereas expert writers construct rich representations of their audiences and use audience awareness in a productive and heuristic fashion, less proficient writers are weighed down by their obsession with their readers as rigid and petty evaluators (Perl, 1980). These conclusions are confirmed by other lines of research that show significant relationships between general social cognitive ability and writing quality (Kroll, 1985; Rubin, Piche, Michlin, & Johnson, 1984; Rubin & Rafoth, 1986b), between social cognitive ability and certain sophisticated discourse strategies in writing (O'Keefe & Delia, 1979; Pellegrini, Galda, & Rubin, 1984; Rubin, Galda, & Pellegrini, 1986), and between general writing ability and tendencies to make and use certain inferences about readers (Rafoth, 1985).

Rubin (1984a; Rubin & Kantor, 1984), has applied to analyses of written discourse the notion of communicative competence as explicated in Dell Hymes's (1971, 1974; see also Ervin–Tripp, 1972) influential work on the ethnography of communication. Drawing upon Hymes's work, Rubin posits six features of communicative contexts that affect style in written discourse: (1) channel of communication (speech or writing), (2) function of communication (narrative, persuasive, phatic), (3) participant role relations (solidarity or alienation, shared or divergent background knowledge), (4) setting (open classroom, traditional classroom, government agency), (5) topic domain (cosmology, child rearing, Woody Allen movies), and (6) discourse structure (genre, sequencing). It is possible to generalize about the co-occurrence between particular social contexts and particular constellations of stylistic features. For example, proficient writers tend to use more complex syntax for persuasive functions, simpler syntax for narrative (Crowhurst, 1979).

But such contextual-stylistic generalizations gloss over important insights about the phenomenology of social-cognitive construction. Stylistic analyses often take the definition of a social context as "given." Writers, however, *invest* meanings in social contexts. Most composition instructors have experienced the disappointment of a student submitting a moribund paper on a topic that we "knew" was of intense interest to the writer. The explanation may be that the student did not construe the assignment as a context for exploring genuine feelings (Newkirk, 1984).

An especially interesting line of research concerning the social-cognitive construction of writing, therefore, explores individualized processes of representing social contexts. In Chapter 2 of this volume, "Children's Perceptions of Classroom Writing: Ownership Within a Continuum of Control," Sally Hudson investigates a corpus of writing events in which the young writers' construction of social context differed from the a priori definition of their writing situations. These were writings in

which children apparently seized ownership of their composing—
thought of it much like the self-initiated stories and poems they often
wrote on their own at home—despite the fact that teachers were requiring the compositions as assignments tied to the official curriculum. Thus
one third-grade boy reports the context of a piece for which he claimed a
sense of ownership: "She [the teacher] made me, but I didn't really have
to and I had plenty of time" (p. 00).

Hudson's methodology here fits neatly with constructivist principles.
Student writers were interviewed and asked to identify their own ways
of categorizing features of social context—ownership, setting, audience,
purpose, degree of involvement, and genre—in which they produced
writing samples collected in their portfolios. In this chapter Hudson attends specifically to those scripts for which the writer's construction of
social context manifests what would appear to be an incongruity between contextual elements. It seems incongruous to adults, for example,
to find that children sometimes claim ownership for work to which they
attribute a school-based, evaluation-oriented purpose. In each case, the
apparent incongruities are well reconciled within the child's own mental
representation.

The inherent complexity of social-cognitive representation and its re-
sistance to simplistic taxonomic or linear modeling is likewise the theme
of Chapter 3, "Communicative Tasks and Communicative Practices: The
Development of Audience-Centered Message Production," by Barbara
O'Keefe and Jesse Delia. In this essay, O'Keefe and Delia trace the progression of their research program, beginning with an early approach
that regarded awareness of a specific audience as the critical ingredient
for formulating person-centered messages. Their more recent conceptualization attributes greatest importance to social-cognitive activity that
enables communicators to construct and integrate multiple goals for any
given communication event. In argumentative discourse, for example,
effective communicators find strategies for pursuing the main persuasive function, but they also construe the situation as one in which they
must simultaneously pursue seemingly contradictory "face" goals for
showing respect and consideration to their "target." People with complex systems of social-cognitive construction are most likely to produce
"multifunctional messages." O'Keefe and Delia relate multiple goal construction to overarching message design logics—ways of reasoning
about communication.

O'Keefe and Delia formulate their conceptions of rational goal analysis and message design logics in part in response to a research literature
that generally demonstrates *poor* correspondence between measures of
social cognitive activity and measures of communication effectiveness
(see review in Rubin, 1984b). When people are queried about their

social-cognitive constructions, it is apparent that their social knowledge often exceeds their ability to utilize that knowledge in composing messages well adapted to audience, purpose, setting, and the like. Often times we can tell that *something* is wrong with our messages, but we don't know what it is; or we may be able to identify *what* is wrong, but we don't know how to fix it (Alvy, 1973; Delia & Clark, 1977). Writers may talk eloquently about their audiences, yet fail to address them adequately in writing (Quick, 1983). Attendant to problems in understanding how individuals generate social-cognitive constructions, then, are difficult questions about how people use (or fail to use) the fruits of their social-cognitive processes in formulating messages.

In Chapter 4 of this volume, "Using What They Know: 9-, 13-, and 18-Year-Olds Writing for Different Audiences," Sheryl Fontaine reports a study designed to "look behind and beyond the essays to what writers may know about the audience but may not be using in their writing" (p. 114). Using an eclectic methodology incorporating text analyses, thinking-aloud, and retrospective protocol analyses, Fontaine demonstrates consistency between older subjects' social cognitive constructions and their message strategies. Nine-year-olds differed little from their older counterparts in representing their audiences, but they differed significantly in their failure to compose audience-adapted messages. Their social-cognitive construction of writing encompassed representational or conceptual functions, but they had not yet learned that writing can also serve social or interactional functions.

CREATING SOCIAL CONTEXTS THROUGH WRITING

A number of composition theorists reject the notion that competent writing is a matter of analyzing and adapting to social context. After all, writers cast their wares out into the public domain with no control over who will and will not become a reader, how the writer's purpose will or will not be construed. And very often writers claim that they are writing for their own private gratification, to sharpen their own insight, to purge their own demons or to tickle their own sense of aesthetics. At least for proficient writers, it is reasonable to think of writers creating contexts which invite *readers* to adapt (Ong, 1975; Long, 1980). As Edwin Black observed in "The Second Persona" (1970, p. 119), ". . . in all rhetorical discourse, we can find enticements not simply to believe something, but to *be* something. We are solicited by the discourse to fulfill its blandishments with our very selves."

Writers, then, may invoke audiences as well as address them (Ede & Lunsford, 1984). Indeed, writers may invoke a complete social context: purpose, setting, topic domain, and the rest. Bartholomae, in reference to inexperienced college writers, says, "Every time a student sits down to write for us, he has to invent the university for the occasion" (1985, p. 134). Rubin and Rafoth (1986a) go so far as to argue that writers, by employing conventional markers of spoken conversation like formulas and second person address, can even invoke orality in print. And Roth (1987) demonstrates that writers often make conscious decisions to revise their sense of audience as they are revising their texts. Sometimes effective writing is as much a matter of forging a context as accommodating to one.

Negotiating a Social Context in Writing and Reading

An easily recognizable example of creating a social context through writing is the status negotiation that often goes on between letter writers. The writer who initiates the correspondence, especially if he or she lacks institutionally conferred status, may be unsure of how to define role relations and may therefore decide to err in the direction of formality. He or she uses formal terms of address ("Dear Mr. X") and formal diction ("Please rest assured that were I not most willing to undertake. . . ."). The correspondent, in turn, takes the onus of defining the relationship as more egalitarian and sends cues to that effect ("Best regards, Herb"). The first writer acknowledges and reinforces the redefined context when next writing ("Dear Herb, Thought I'd best be getting back to you about. . . .").

In this way, writers construct context by negotiating the definition of salient social parameters. Even when the writing situation precludes much direct feedback between writer and audience, it is reasonable to think of each piece of discourse accompanied by a contract that sets forth the definition of social context within which the text ought to be interpreted. Those who read in good faith—or who are willing at least temporarily to suspend skepticism—accept that contract. Thus, one finds oneself reading all sorts of unusual material while captive in airplanes and waiting rooms. If I read a profile of a captain of industry in *Business Week*, I discern what the text presupposes about audience beliefs and values, about what counts as a significant topic of extended discourse, and about the functions played by contemporary biography. To the extent I am able, I adopt those definitions of social context temporarily. I participafe, however briefly, in the social context constructed by that discourse.

Creating Fundamental Social Structures

Now writing may effect social context, bring it into being, in a rather concrete sense. As this essay is drafted during the bicentennial anniversary of the U. S. Constitution (itself a prime example of collective text construction, incidentally), it is easy to recognize that particular writing events can have great impact on social movements—Dante's vulgate *Inferno* no less than the Constitution. Certainly the invention and dissemination of writing technologies—movable type, for example—influences how a society develops (Eisenstein, 1985). More speculative, yet of profound import, is the claim that some cultures are permeated by a literate epistemology—ways of knowing that parallel the linear, analytical, objectifying patterns of written discourse (compare Ong, 1982; and Street, 1984).

Setting aside questions of the "autonomous" (Street, 1984) effects of written language upon a culture's modes of perception and logic, there can be little doubt that complex forms of political and economic organization are made possible by virtue of written symbol systems. In Chapter 5, "From Accounting to Written Language: The Role of Abstract Counting in the Invention of Writing," Denise Schmandt–Besserat demonstrates the intertwining of social organization and writing. Thousands of years ago writing systems evolved along a dimension of increasing abstraction of graphic signs from the physical entities for which they stood. The earliest accounting system utilized tokens, discrete three-dimensional clay forms. Tokens and other early counting signs required that the object/sign representing a particular commodity/referent be repeated to designate multiple units—four ovoids, say, to represent four flasks of oil. On the other end of the evolutionary scale were pictographs, which were two-dimensional images engraved on tablets. The advent of pictographs brought forth a revolution in graphic representation; quantities could be expressed as abstractions, and the signs expressing quantification were invariant regardless of what referent they modified.

This progression in the complexity of writing systems correlates with a progression in the complexity of social organization. Plain tokens, which seem best suited to accounting for stocks of cereals and animals, appeared during the same epoch as the beginnings of farming. Complex tokens, which represented oil, bread, and other manufactured goods, coincided with the rise of cities. The creation of the state and its advanced bureaucracy was contemporaneous with the movement toward impressed and pictographic writing. Schmandt–Besserat does not speculate about the causal relationship holding between social organization and writing systems. But, of course, writing systems are components of social organization; the pressure of more complex social structures demanded the invention of more complex writing systems. And conversely, complex writing systems made possible the management of increasingly complex societies.

Creating Roles and Occasions

Writing systems and the possibility of writing in general, then, establish broad social structures. Specifically situated writing events and their resulting texts can also create social context. Sometimes writing brings forth a context in a very tangible way. Thus Hitler's *Mein Kampf* constructed roles and a world view and a rhetorical style with which a great many post-Weimar citizens indeed sought identity (Burke, 1967). But the horrible precipitating effect of this writing is a contingent historical fact. Today one reads *Mein Kampf*, understands it as an awesome discourse within a particular social context, and rejects it as pernicious and morally reprehensible.

On a much less dramatic scale, it is possible that a particular genre of essay, say the slick magazine portrait of captains of industry, such as Lee Iacocca, Donald Trump, or Carl Icahn, may fall out of favor. Imagine: A new generation of team-playing business managers rejects the cult of personality; magazine editors stop publishing biography. When stray readers in this hypothetical literary world do encounter examples of this genre, they may read intending to find flaws, or they may read with a sense of scholarly distance. Their purposes for reading are at odds with the purpose which the text presupposes. In fact, no one participates in the social context that such essays construct, no one accepts the contract that these texts put out to bid. But I am contending that social context is constructed even though there may happen to be no players willing to buy into the particular definition of social context underlying a piece of discourse. To borrow the terminology of speech act theory (Austin, 1962), writing may or may not have a perlocutionary effect on readers, but it always has the illocutionary effect of constituting an audience, a topic domain, a discourse structure, and so forth. Competent users of written language can *discern* the social context that a text presupposes; they may or may not accept the implicit invitation to *participate* in it.

This approach treats writing as human action that constructs roles. Texts bring social contexts into existence. Writers and readers who elect to don those roles and participate in those contexts are thus constituted into a *discourse community*. A discourse community may be roughly understood as a consensus about ". . . what is worth communicating, how it may be communicated, what other members of the community are likely to know and believe to be true about certain subjects, how other members can be persuaded, and so on" (Faigley, 1985, p. 238). Each writer, in every writing event, reconstitutes a discourse community.

In Chapter 6, "Discourse Community: Where Writers, Readers, and Texts Come Together," Bennett Rafoth explicates a view of discourse community and its role in composition theory. Rafoth argues that the concept of discourse community is more satisfactory than *audience*. Of particular interest is the utility of the discourse community concept in reconciling how it is that writers both construct social context in the sense I am discussing in this section, and at the same time adapt to social context in selecting contextually appropriate discourse strategies. While an emphasis on the communal aspects of writing may be regarded as discounting individual creativity, Rafoth argues that this is not so, "because individual interests do not necessarily conflict with community interests" (p. 143).

Each time they write, writers construct one very fundamental aspect of social context: they define the situation as an appropriate occasion for writing. While that statement smacks of tautology, it is clear that cultures vary considerably among themselves in norms for speech or silence, for conversational turn taking, for loquacity, or pithiness (Hymes, 1974; Scollon & Scollon, 1981). For many individuals, writing constructs contexts for expressing emotion, for cementing interpersonal bonds, for exploring self, and for consolidating knowledge. For others, writing constructs only contexts for suffering evaluation.

For novice writers, except for the self-sponsored and "unofficial" writing events of the kinds discussed by Hudson and Dyson (both this volume), it is teachers who most often impose their definitions of what is or is not going to count as a context for writing. Most teachers, regrettably, construct classroom discourse communities that are impoverished indeed. They call for extended writing only rarely, and then for very restricted purposes revolving mainly around testing (Applebee, 1981). Some teachers, surely, are more generous than others in what contexts they project as appropriate for writing.

In Chapter 7, "Writing Apprehension in the Classroom Context," John Daly, Anita Vangelisti, and Stephen Witte report a series of studies investigating individual differences in teachers' practices involving writing assignments. Teachers' own apprehension about writing predicts reliably, though only moderately, the extent to which they themselves write and also the importance they accord to writing as a classroom activity for their students. Teachers comfortable about their own writing differed from their more anxious colleagues, particularly in cultivating for their students a sense of writing as a context for self-expression. And indeed, "low apprehensive teachers' assignments were marked by greater variability in purpose and audience than were the assignments of high-apprehensive teachers" (p. 163).

Daly and his colleagues then pursue the logical extension of these studies of individual differences in the ways teachers construct writing contexts for their students. They ask, to what extent do those classroom variables presumably under teachers' control affect individual differences in *students'* writing? Their findings suggest that the amount and kind of writing instruction that students receive directly affects their attitudes about themselves as writers, and these attitudes in turn affect writing performance. In effect, a chain links teachers' feelings about writing with the ways in which they construct (or fail to construct) contexts for writing for their students, and the resulting diet of writing instruction is further linked to students' own attitudes toward writing. And in the final link in the chain, students' writing attitudes affect writing performance.

CREATING TEXTS COLLECTIVELY

When one begins to consider the notion of context in discourse analysis, interesting and productive questions about *units of discourse* quickly surface. In connected discourse, the meaning and structure of any one sentence is affected by the sentences surrounding it—the linguistic context. Structuralist grammarians in the 1950s felt little need to consider units larger than single sentences, however; a grammar that could handle isolated sentences could in principle handle connected discourse by the neat trick of simply viewing a text as a long, conjoined sentence. More recent approaches to intersentential dependencies, in contrast, identify cohesive devices or thematic structures that establish semantic rather than syntactical ties within a text. A sentence such as, "They rent their garments," takes on one meaning if it is embedded in a paragraph about Biblical mourners at the death of a patriarch, and quite another if embedded in a paragraph about American high school students at the prom.

In the case of noncontinuous discourse—that is, conversation—preceding utterances constitute an essential part of the context needed to interpret any subsequent utterance. One person's answering utterance, "Just a minute," can be interpreted only by reference to an interlocutor's preceding question, "How long does it take to prepare Coquilles St. Jacques in your new microwave oven?" One person initiates a topic, the next responds with a comment. One person states a subject, the next a predicate. One person floats a claim, the next elaborates the (confirming or disconfirming) evidence. In the context of dialogic interaction, the informative unit of discourse analysis extends well beyond a single utterance. Dialogue is constructed through collaboration between conversational partners.

Inherent Conversationality in Writing

Less apparent is the essential collaborative nature of written discourse. There are at least three ways in which writing parallels conversation as a collective production: written correspondence, joint authorship, and conversation as a resource for writing. First, it is not unusual for people to conduct conversations in writing, to correspond. Letter-writing exchanges are obvious instances of written conversation that conform in virtually every respect to the same norms for turn taking, topic shifting, and coherence that operate in spoken conversation (Craig & Tracy, 1983). Electronic messaging through computers is likewise quite amenable to conversational analysis (Murray, 1985).

More generally, every bit of writing qualifies as an entry into a universe of discourse. As we read about a topic and read within a particular discourse community (Rafoth, this volume), we internalize matters of stylistic convention, topical relevance, and even communication ethics. When we do write in even an impersonal form, such as an academic essay, it is never truly an autonomous text capable of being understood exclusively through self-reference. Instead, such an essay is a comment intruded into an ongoing conversation (Bartholomae, 1985; Bazerman, 1980; Bruffee, 1984). The person who writes that essay constructs it in collaboration with "conversational partners" also participating in that universe of discourse.

Joint Authorship

The second sense in which it is common to think of collective writing pertains to those situations in which a text is composed jointly by several individuals. Clear cases of this sort of multiple authorship include "creative" writing of advertising copy and comedy sketches, and also certain classroom exercises, in which language is first spoken within a dyad or group and then transcribed (and thereby transformed) into print. Here, interactive speech serves as an adjunct to composing processes (Rubin, 1987). But as most people discover when they attempt jointly to compose a text of any length or complexity, it is more efficient to divide the labor. Subtopics are divvied up among the collaborators (horizontal collaboration), and/or the jobs of gathering information, drafting, revising, and editing are distributed (vertical collaboration).

A great deal of document production in the worlds of government and commerce is accomplished through various forms of multiple authoring. For example, a partner at a law firm is responsible for submitting a legal brief to appeal a trial verdict. He or she begins by assigning each of several associates to research and write notes about the points of law that will be covered in the appeal. Someone must also draft a statement of the facts of the case (which are not in dispute during the appellate process). The partner will receive drafts of these legal notes, request revisions, smooth over any stylistic inconsistencies between them, and ultimately synthesize them into a single document. Whenever possible, the lawyers at each stage of composing will probably try to utilize linguistic shells ("boilerplates") located in similar briefs composed by some predecessor. Authorship of such corporately constructed documents defies clear-cut assignation. Within the official judicial system, the entire law firm is identified as author. Within the informal legal community, the brief will be attributed to the partner who coordinated it (not necessarily the same person who argues it orally in court). Within the culture of the particular firm which generated the brief, the contributions of the individual associates may be acknowledged. (Similar ambiguities in attributing authorship also plague academic discourse. An interesting convention is that increasingly adopted by newspaper editors who may assign an individual by-line to one reporter, but list at the bottom of the article names of additional writers who "also contributed to this story.")

Conversation as a Writing Resource

The third sense in which writing can be collaborative pertains to situations in which an individual's writing emerges out of a conversation. Here, talk is not an adjunct to composing, but rather accompanies writing behaviors. The impetus for writing may come from some dissonance experienced in conversation. Or ideas about what to write or about approaches to a topic may emerge in conversation (as in classroom prewriting discussions). Plans for revising the composition may be stimulated by subsequent talk (as in classroom peer response groups). The writer in these cases collaborates with conversational partners not by integrating them into some sort of corporate authorship, but by using those partners as consultants and informants. For some writing situations, it is as though the writer simply chooses to take one of his or her conversational turns on paper rather than in speech. The written word, in those cases, is very much a direct extension of dialogue.

Indeed Snow (1983) demonstrates that the very genesis of literate language lies in dialogue. Caretaker–child conversational routines surrounding early literacy events prepare the child for the demands of literate language for explicitness, elaboration of meaning, and conventionality. Similarly, Moffett (1968) and other composition theorists assert that novice writers must attain competence in dialogic (i.e., collaborative) discourse before they master monologic (i.e., more autonomous) discourse.

In Chapter 8, "Children's Use of Narrative Language in Peer Interaction," A. D. Pellegrini and Lee Galda explore the manner in which children on the brink of literacy acquisition collaboratively compose coherent conversations with peers. In particular, Pellegrini and Galda discuss production and use of narrative themes during spontaneous play. This is the talk by which children, solely by the power of their language, constitute fantasy worlds in which they can, if the language is successful, jointly participate (e.g., "That can be the bridge. And here can be the river"; "You know what I'm making? Fire demons.") These narratives appear especially frequently in ambiguous play contexts and also immediately following conflicts among peers. Children use narratives, then, as a way to make their social worlds manageable.

Narratives also function as the matrix for sustaining continuous discourse. Pellegrini and Galda report cases of narratives heading sequences of more than 30 conversational turns. Within one of these jointly composed narrative sequences, one child sustained a single monologic "text" of more than 40 utterances. Not all narrative themes introduced are so successful, however. When children use narratives or idiosyncratic "assimilative" functions, peers are unlikely to take up these themes and extended discourse is unlikely to result. When children use narratives for "accommodative" functions and adapt their themes to the ongoing conversational theme, on the other hand, collaboratively composed coherent discourse can be produced.

Although in this particular study Pellegrini and Galda do not follow children from the construction of coherence in oral conversation to the construction of coherent writing (but see, e.g., Pellegrini, 1985), Jana Staton and Roger Shuy's contribution to this volume elucidates something about the nature of that link. In Chapter 9, "Talking Our Way into Writing and Reading: Dialogue Journal Practice," Staton and Shuy claim that many forms of "real-life written communication" conform with the same conditions that engender competent oral conversational performance. Some of these conditions for authentic communication point to the inherently collective nature of text construction, for example: "meaning is interactively negotiated between speakers over time, with ample opportunities for feedback, clarification and elaboration of points" (p. 198).

Dialogue journals exemplify written conversation and engender a style that appears to be transitional between oral and written language. While dialogue journal language shares some characteristics with oral interaction (e.g., direct questions, personal and expressive functions), it exhibits other features more typical of essayist writing (e.g., elaboration, cumulative development). Of course all writing involves reading; even the garreted author of *belles lettres* must reread the words that issue from his or her own pen. But as spoken conversation consists at least as much of listening as of speaking, so is the role of reading especially apparent in dialogic writing. Responses in dialogue journals, therefore, possess strong validity as indexes of reading ability.

True dialogue presumes mutuality, some degree of role reciprocity (Habermas, 1970). In that sense, dialogue journal writing is antithetical to notions of traditional teaching in which there is considerable discrepancy in the balance of power between teacher and student. Indeed, Staton and Shuy present data indicating that typical oral discourse in classrooms is hardly dialogic; writing in dialogue journals is considerably more conversational.

In classrooms in which more-or-less open interaction between students is tolerated, teachers are not the only ones who provide scaffolding for the efforts of beginning writers. In Chapter 10, "Unintentional Helping in the Primary Grades: Writing in the Children's World," Anne Haas Dyson describes the manner in which children's writing can emerge and be supported by virtue of the children's participation in an informal social "collective." Dyson's position is that in interactive classrooms, writing is part of the flow of social events—with the same rewards of peer status and the same issues of group identity—as much as any activity in which children can find opportunities for play, teasing, boasting, and sharing.

Writing can become the particular focus of that social collective when children are displaying their own competence or monitoring the competence of their peers. Children challenge each other in "spelling duels." They comment upon and critique each others' stories and drawings. And in the particular case of receiving back teacher-graded written work, they struggle to accommodate an adult-defined label to their collectively defined sense of self.

The social collective Dyson portrays is a powerful structure within which children can engage in particular literate acts. They write stories about each other in which they work through an agenda relating to peer acceptance and affect. They comment upon each other's writings in ways that help the writers to make connections between a world constructed in orthography and a world constructed of bicycle training wheels triumphantly jettisoned or shamefully still attached. At the same time, the social collective provides a scaffold upon which children construct their sense of the general social nature of literacy. They learn what experienced writers must also relearn virtually every time they sit before a blank sheet of paper: to write is "to experience the tension between individual expression and social communication that is the living tension of language use" (p. 246).

In the social collective situation which Dyson studied, writing was naturally a beneficiary of the collaborative climate the children constructed for themselves. The children did not set out to collaborate on written discourse. Deliberately collaborative composition among young writers is, in contrast, the focus of Chapter 11, "'Let's Brighten It Up a Bit': Collaboration and Cognition in Writing," by Colette Daiute and Bridget Dalton. This study examines interaction and the texts that resulted as pairs of children worked to compose joint stories at the computer keyboard. Daiute and Dalton describe a collaborative composing process in which "the children did little checking with each other to find out if the next step was okay with the other person. The assumption seemed to be that composing was like a dance in which the students followed each other by signals in the rhythms of talk rather than by explicit cues" (p. 259).

As Dyson (this volume) points out, the effect of peer interaction on writing is not uniformly positive. To understand better the quality of collaborations that do help writing, as opposed to those that may actually undermine it, Daiute and Dalton compared the collaborative talk of successful and unsuccessful writing teams. The talk of successful collaborators, they conclude, is marked especially by evidence of cognitive conflict: negotiating and suggesting alternatives. But this conflict among young writers was by no means heavy-handed. Rather, the interaction in which conflict was embedded was playful and fun. Recall that Pellegrini and Galda (this volume) also highlight the role of conflict in promoting collective text construction. In this respect, collaborative text construction is similar to problem-solving activities conducted in many different social contexts. The most successful problem-solving groups are not those that manifest smooth and tension-free interaction. Rather, effective groups are those with sufficient solidarity to encourage and then to resolve conflict constructively (Janis, 1982).

ASSIGNING SOCIAL VALUES TO WRITING

Writing is not merely a value-neutral channel for conveying information. The three aspects of writing to which social evaluative meanings are assigned correspond roughly to (1) The uses of writing (for example, attitudes toward composing advertising copy for hire as opposed to writing "serious" poetry with no expectation of financial gain), (2) The users of writing (e.g., attitudes toward placing political power in the hands of the marginally literate as opposed to restricting power to the highly literate), and (3) The codes of writing (e.g., attitudes toward Latin-based vocabulary in academic essays as opposed to Germanic-based vocabulary: "propelled" vs. "pushed"; "cognition" vs. "thought").

Attitudes Toward Using the Written Channel

For Socrates in *The Phaedrus*, writing epitomized the alienation of rhetors from their messages, and he decried its potential for irresponsive and irresponsible human relations. Socrates notwithstanding, contemporary literacy-based cultures attribute particular credibility to the very process of written communication. The spoken word is easily retracted, but when people write, they are serious. (But see Elbow, 1985 for the opposite view.) "It's an interesting idea," we say. "Put it in writing and I'll consider it." Our belief in the authority and veracity of writing is no where more evident than in the workings of the legal system. One curious ramification is the stricture, still prevalent in most jurisdictions, against jurors taking notes during trials for subsequent use in the deliberation room. Despite the fact that jurors' recall of trial facts is improved when they are permitted to write notes, those who regulate trial procedures fear that vigorous oral debate among jurors may be silenced by the presumed credibility of what jurors might scrawl (perhaps erroneously) in their notebooks (e.g., "May a Juror Take Notes in Illinois?" 1969).

Attitudes Toward Literates and Literacies

In addition to attitudes toward the uses of writing, social valence is associated with the users of writing, more exactly with the distribution of writing abilities within a population. Historical accounts show that acquisition of literacy has always had political implications (see review in Clifford, 1984). Prior to our relatively modern espousal of universal literacy, those who possessed knowledge of reading and writing controlled the flow and exchange of information, and hence controlled community power. Often the information they controlled was God's word, inaccessible to the illiterate. Sometimes the information they controlled was economic, and the illiterate were defenseless against the tax collector's quill and ledger. The political power of literacy is most evident in the ways in which access to literacy is bestowed or withheld selectively. Tracing the lineage with which Koranic literacy in a traditionally oral culture is transmitted from teacher to student assumes a stature similar to tracing lineage in any royal family (Wilks, 1968). In slave-holding America, it is little wonder that few slave "transgressions" were so severely proscribed as book reading. And once slavery was abolished, the identical social order would be preserved for many years in the institution of literacy tests for voters.

Even in societies that do espouse the ideal of universal literacy, definitions of what is to count as writing proficiency, or decisions about who is to obtain certain kinds of writing instruction, all reveal the social evaluative construction of literacy. Compelling historical accounts show that current practices in teaching secondary and postsecondary school writing are rooted in what were the economic needs of a rapidly industrializing America toward the turn of the 20th century. America required competent scribes and clerks and bureaucrats, but the nation could ill afford the luxury of free thinkers, profound intellectuals, or ethnic nationalists. Hence the curriculum moved toward analysis of "cultured" literary texts and toward an obsession with transcriptional propriety (Douglas, 1976; Piché, 1977).

As America moves toward deindustrialization in the waning years of this century, the distribution of writing skills remains governed by economic and political considerations (Ohmann, 1985). Much public sentiment has been directed toward the plight of adult illiterates. But as authors of a recent survey of literacy among young adults conclude, few adults exhibit truly abject ignorance of how to encode or decode print. At the same time, however, few adults exhibit truly profound understanding of how to use writing for any advanced purposes. "It is clear from these data that 'illiteracy' is not a major problem for this population. It is also clear, however, that 'literacy' *is* a problem" (Kirsch & Jungeblutt, 1986, p. 5).

Most modern Americans can read and write well enough to deserve the label "functionally literate." That is, their level of literacy allows them to function within their society, but not necessarily to understand that society, almost certainly not to change that society. A number of observers (e.g., Hendrix, 1981; Levine, 1982) have speculated about the social evaluative bases by which some students are selectively provided instruction in *functional* literacy, whereas others are given access to what in contrast must be considered *full* literacy. (Certainly the contrasting term to "functional literacy" ought not be "dysfunctional literacy.") If instructing some students in "functional" writing means teaching the unanointed how to fill out applications for jobs on hamburger assembly lines or how to select the proper salutation for thank you notes, then— despite the ideal of universal literacy—the writing curriculum can be viewed as nothing other than an instrument for reproducing cultural valences regarding social status and disenfranchisement. Serious efforts to transform the teaching of writing are efforts to transform society (Freire, 1970; Shor, 1980).

Attitudes Toward the Written Code

Language variety, as a marker of social identity, serves related functions as a device by which societies display and reinforce social stratification. Although we may accept certain stylistic variations in written language due to genres, we tend to judge writing and writers according to their conformance to conventions of the written code. (Of course what counts as an inviolable convention and what gets noticed as a flagrant deviation differs from reader to reader.) The language of schooled literacy is especially conservative; it does not easily tolerate violations of conventions that, after all, often serve little communicative purpose (e.g., subject–verb agreement). Individuals who fail to conform to that code are evaluated (by those who hold institutional power and hence enforce the written code) as ignorant, slothful, or unpatriotic.

Indeed, the very choice of a people's orthography is embedded in these very same dynamics of language variety, social identity, and evaluation. In Chapter 12, "Ethnocultural Issues in the Creation, Substitution, and Revision of Writing Systems," Joshua Fishman focuses especially on differences between social-evaluative meanings when changes in writing systems are brought about through indigenous forces, as opposed to cases in which those changes are imposed by culturally alien forces. Indigenous writing systems are powerful symbols of cultural autonomy and self-regulation. And for that very reason they are at jeopardy from "global" written languages (e.g., Russian, English) that offer tangible rewards in terms of commerce and technology in exchange for that autonomy. When a language group faces a choice of accepting a new writing system or of altering an existing one, "both acceptance and rejection are sociopolitical statements and advocates and opponents will react to them as such" (p. 277).

The orthographic features which trigger social-evaluative meaning among native users of a writing system sometimes operate in ways not easily anticipated by outsiders. Fishman cites the case of vowel length and tone markers in written Navajo. On the one hand, these markers tangibly set the Navajo writing system apart from the surrounding English literature culture. The markers ought to be cherished, therefore, as preserving the integrity of Navajo cultural identity. As it happens, however, these markers are necessary only for nonnative Navajo speakers. The information they convey is redundant to native speakers, who have full control over patterns of vowel length and tone in the spoken code. From the "emic" perspective of native Navajo, therefore, these markers are nonauthentic intrusions in their writing system, and they are usually ignored.

Even in the case of a well-established writing system in a monolingual setting, social-evaluative dynamics are often unexpectedly complex. This is the case of writing performance among nonstandard dialect speakers. Speakers of diverse dialects seem to commit many of the same types of morphological and syntactical violations, though at frequencies which reflect their oral dialect patterns (Farr Whiteman, 1981). Although evidence, then, shows some dialect interference in writing, it is not of the scope that justifies the emphasis which writing instructors often place on it. The National Assessment of Educational Progress, in fact, recently reported that such violations are not a major problem in the extensive corpus of student writing which they sampled nationally for their study (Applebee, Langer & Mullis, 1987). Many educators, however, persist in ascribing the poor writing performance of nonstandard dialect speakers primarily to oral dialect features. In evaluating writing this way, teachers are, in effect, manifesting underlying and largely unintentional social biases about those groups of people who happen to speak particular dialects; writing evaluation is simply a conveniently subjective avenue for expressing those biases (Piché, Rubin, Turner & Michlin, 1978).

Of more importance than nonstandard grammatical patterns are the discourse conventions for writing (and for oral language) which are culturally linked. Since these conventions can differ dramatically from culture to culture, speakers from nonmainstream backgrounds face the task of learning new ways of expressing meaning when they learn to write (see review in Farr & Daniels,1986). Volubility as a style of discourse, for example, is a norm for middle-class Anglo households (as it is also a norm for certain minority groups, but not for others; Hymes, 1974). Volubility is a distinct advantage in managing the written code; at least in school literacy one is expected to exhaust a topic, not merely mention it. Similarly, the concrete associative style of narration typical of many inner-city black Americans is mismatched with the demands of the written code for topic-centered discourse with explicit transitions and other structural cues (Farr & Daniels, 1986; Michaels, 1986).

At present, we know little about the impact of violations of broad discourse conventions on judgments of writing quality and of writers. Quite possibly such violations are what lie at the core of those writing performances that cause teachers to throw their hands in the air and to conclude that a piece of writing is not salvageable. In response to such "nonrepairable" writing, most teachers have little recourse other than to put students to the irrelevant task of patching up cosmetic or mechanical errors.

And indeed one cannot "remediate" a difference in cultural norms for what counts as coherent discourse. A novice writer's success in learning to conform to discourse conventions from a second culture is determined foremost by the learner's affinity for the values and world view of that second culture. Just as learning a dominant culture language or a dominant culture dialect are governed in large measure by speakers' attitudes toward that dominant culture (Lambert, 1972), so is acquiring a written code most of all a function of whether the learner embraces the mainstream culture in which norms for literate discourse are embedded (see Clay, 1976; and Demoz, 1986).

Studies of contrastive rhetoric describe norms for extended discourse that may prevail in a writer's native culture and that may interfere when that writer attempts to compose in a second language and culture (e.g., Kaplan, 1966; Matalene, 1985). In Chapter 13, "An Analysis of Oral and Literate Texts: 2 Types of Reader–Writer Relationships in Hebrew and English," Michal Zellermayer uncovers systematic transformations in patterns of discourse when novels originally composed in English are translated into Hebrew, and when Hebrew novels are translated into English. Zellermayer identifies differing cultural norms for thoughtfulness and considerateness in writing, similar to Shaughnessy's (1977) notion of "the economy of reading and writing," that is, the amount of effort the reader as opposed to the writer must invest in processing text information. The Western literate tradition favors a decontextualized style in which all information needed to disambiguate meaning is given by the writer to the reader within the text. The rhetorical community in which Hebrew literacy resides, in contrast, favors more oral-based discourse strategies, such as use of formulas that recall canonical (usually Biblical) texts.

Zellermayer's analysis shows that when Hebrew texts are translated into English, their styles become more linear, more "considerate" of disparate readers' efforts to extract information. This stylistic transformation takes the form of adding explicit markers of cohesion, elaboration, and syntactical integration. Conversely, Hebrew translations of novels originally composed in English demand more "thoughtfulness" from the reader. The style is more recursive than linear, and the reader must invest more inference-making efforts to recover meaning.

Studying the works of acclaimed novelists, Zellermayer can only claim to be describing paradigmatic realizations of discourse norms. Her research in this case does not directly address sociopolitical questions of who is conferred access to the means for becoming a proficient writer within a discourse community, questions of who attains full literacy. Nor does it address questions of the political factors that sometimes determine what, in the first place, will count as the standard for proficient writing. In Chapter 14, "The Ecology of Literacy: Negotiation of Writing Standards in a Caribbean Setting," Patricia Irvine and Nan Elsasser confront just these issues of access and definition.

If it is the case—as I have asserted—that learning to write is in large part determined by one's affinity for the values and beliefs of a mainstream culture of literacy, then colonial settings will provide dramatic demonstrations of this process. In the context of colonization, such as the Caribbean setting which Irvine and Elsasser examine, imposed imperialistic values regarding literacy are rendered especially visible by the contrast to indigenous discourse norms. Eastern Caribbean students learn in their composition classes to disvalue their native Creole. Like novice writers from many nonmainstream cultures, they become obsessed with conforming to a standard written code comprised of alien ways of arguing and developing themes, as well as alien lexicon and syntax. An indigenous Caribbean literacy, in contrast, borrows discourse strategies, such as humor and metaphor, from the calypso tradition.

Transforming writing standards from those imported by colonizing cultures (and enforced perhaps unwittingly by institutions of higher education) to those that celebrate indigenous values is a matter of political as well as linguistic liberation. Irvine and Elsasser begin to sketch how literacy programs of this type might take shape. By empowering students to utilize Creole, to emulate Caribbean authors, and to draw upon calypsonian rhetorics, these programs would promote writing proficiency defined by affinity for the values of students' native culture. This stance leads inevitably to support for a politically independent Eastern Caribbean.

UNITING THE SOCIAL AND THE COGNITIVE VIEWS OF WRITING

This chapter, and the volume it introduces, treats social accounts and cognitive accounts of written communication as fundamentally complementary. Neither a social nor a cognitive focus provides by itself an adequate picture. A certain current in contemporary composition theory, however, seems to be somehow counterposing social perspectives on writing against cognitive processes. The concept of adapting to a rhetorical situation is regarded as in opposition to constructing social context imaginatively. Discourse communities presupposed in text are contrasted to communities comprised by actual readers. For example, Myers (1986) refers to a population of "[w]riting researchers who have found cognitive models restricting" and have therefore moved toward an alternative "social view" of composing (p. 596). Faigley (1986), on the way toward developing a more synthetic proposal, characterizes the social view of composing as *competing* with the expressive and the cognitive views:

> My effort to outline a social view will be on the basis of one central assumption: human language (including writing) can be understood only from the perspective of a society rather than a single individual. Thus tak-

ing a social view requires a great deal more than simply paying more attention to the context surrounding a discourse. It rejects the assumption that writing is the act of a private consciousness and that everything else—readers, subjects, and texts—is "out there" in the world. The focus of the social view of writing, therefore, is not on how the social situation influences the individual, but on how the individual is a constituent of culture. (Faigley, p. 535)

This particular version of a social perspective on writing emphasizes historical and acculturation processes. Studies of written discourse arising from this view might examine how writers negotiate what is to count as credibility or as convincing evidence, or even what is to count as an askable question, within a particular discourse community (e.g., Myers, 1985). Or such studies might examine shifts over time in what has been considered worthy of teaching and feasible to learn about writing, especially as these shifts participate in some more general contemporaneous intellectual currents (e.g., Connors, 1987).

But the cognitivist perspective that these social views of writing seem to be shunting aside is no less central to social construction. Gergen (1985) explains that social constructionism is concerned with "processes by which people come to describe, explain, or otherwise account for the world (including themselves) in which they live" (p. 286). Surely there is dynamic interplay between these processes at the community or concensual level and at the individual or cognitive level. Much work in the area of social cognition and writing examines how writers assimilate information about their communicative task and setting and formulate for themselves corresponding rhetorical problems (e.g., Flower & Hayes, 1980). Related studies inquire about individual differences in social cognitive status and their relationship to individual differences in writing proficiency (e.g., Rubin & Rafoth, 1986b).

It is understandable that the social and the cognitive views of the social construction of writing should be cast as oppositional. Cognitive approaches to composition theory and research seem to have colluded with the sorts of social approaches just cited to create this sense of fragmentation. Much work on the individual writer's composing processes makes scarce reference to the broad social and cultural contexts in which that composing takes place. (See comprehensive reviews of composing process research in Hillocks, 1986; and Scardamalia & Bereiter, 1985). Influential models of composing processes (e.g., Flower & Hayes, 1980) may recognize that writers consider their audience's dispositions and that writers draw upon their life's experience. But they rarely investigate the cultural embedding of cognitive constructs like memory and inference and what counts as sound reasoning (Scribner, 1977).

In fact, communities as aggregates, and also each individual writer, participate in negotiating a community's social construction of, say, what counts as an appropriate and effective appeal to authority. Consensual social constructions provide writers with scripts or schemata for appeals to authority (e.g., "Quote the critic for the *New York Times*"), but then it remains for the individual writer to represent mentally specific tasks (e.g., leaving a note for the baby-sitter) as calling for such appeals or not. And it remains for the individual reader to represent specific chunks of discourse as conforming or not conforming to the parameters of such appeals ("Went to movie the *Times* called riveting. Will be home early"). The discourse community constructs written communication, and the individual writer—over and over again—reconstructs it.

A social account posed in opposition to a cognitivist explanation has sometimes been invoked as a satisfying way of explaining success or failure in academic essay writing (e.g., Bizzel, 1986; see Burleson & Rowan, 1985, for a consistent claim of the primacy of conventionalized schemata over social cognition in narrative writing). According to the definitive social view, an ability to discern particulars about one's readers is not central to learning to write essays; students would hardly improve their essays were they magically made privy to their English instructor's favorite kind of omelet or preference for Joyce over Proust. Audience doesn't matter in the case of the expository essay because the essay must in fact transcend the idiosyncrasies of the actual reader. What matters is the writer's feel for what counts in the academic community as a substantive topic, as sufficient support, as taken for granted, or as a point to be established. The essay writer's success will hinge on his or her ability to tap into the consensual construction of these matters.

Accordingly, to "tap into" the social construction of an academic essay requires students, who are after all novices, to appropriate the role of someone who has collegial authority within an academic discourse community. Some theorists have therefore claimed that student essay writers are not acting "on their own," but are instead invented as essay writers by the discourse available to them for use in their appropriated role (Bartholomae, 1985, p. 145).

Even this ontologically radical position is not inconsistent with a theory of mental representation. To appropriate a role means to hold one's other potential perspectives (presumably more comfortable or natural) in abeyance. It means construing the discourse context from the perspective of that appropriated role. It means, in short, engaging in very sophisticated social cognitive operations.

Mentally representing an appropriated role is simply a different type of social cognitive operation than analyzing an agonistic audience, as in

the traditional emphasis on audience analysis. Able writers can both analyze determinant readerships and also invoke indeterminant audiences. They engage in these complementary processes in different ra-
tios, depending on how they construe or construct their rhetorical tasks.

This volume embraces chapters that represent diverse pieces of that
complex system of social construction. Some of the contributions emphasize individual cognitive representation. But they also at least imply
participation in the consensual discourse community. Other contributions focus on broad social forces of convention and conflict, but they at
least imply individual actors who negotiate through these broad forces.
As a body, the works in this volume testify to the essential interconnect-
edness, the unity, of these dimensions of the social construction of written communication.

REFERENCES

Alvy, K. (1973). The development of listener adapted communication in grade
    school children from different social class backgrounds. *Genetic Psychology
    Monographs, 83*, 35–104.
Applebee, A. (1981). *Writing in the secondary school: English and the content areas.*
    Urbana, IL: National Council of Teachers of English.
Applebee, A. N., Langer, J. A., & Mullis, I. V. S. (1987). *Grammar, punctuation,
    and spelling: Controlling the conventions of written English.* Princeton, NJ: Ed-
    ucational Testing Service.
Austin, J. (1962). *How to do things with words.* Cambridge, MA: Harvard Univer-
    sity Press.
Bartholomae, D. (1985). Inventing the university. In M. Rose (Ed.), *When a writer
    can't write* (pp. 134–165). New York: Guilford Press.
Bator, P. (1980). Aristotelian and Rogerian rhetoric. *College Composition and Com-
    munication, 31*, 427–432.
Bazerman, C. (1980). A relationship between reading and writing; The conversa-
    tional model. *College English, 42*, 656–661.
Berger, P., & Luckman, T. (1967). *The social construction of reality.* New York:
    Doubleday.
Berkenkotter, C. (1981). Understanding a writer's awareness of audience. *College
    Composition and Communication, 32*, 388–399.
Bitzer, L. (1968). The rhetorical situation. *Philosophy and Rhetoric, 1*, 1–12.
Bizzel, P. (1986). What happens when basic writers come to college? *College Com-
    position and Communication, 37*, 294–301.
Black, E. (1970). The second persona. *Quarterly Journal of Speech, 56*, 109–119.
Blom, J., & Gumperz, J. J. (1972). Social meaning and linguistic structure. Code-
    switching in Norway. In J. J. Gumperz & D. Hymes (Eds.), *New directions
    in sociolinguistics* (pp. 407–434). New York: Holt Rinehart, & Winston.
Bruffee, K. (1984). Collaborative learning and the "conversation of mankind."
    College English, 46, 635–652.

Burke, K. (1950). *A rhetoric of motives*. New York: Prentice–Hall.

Burke, K. (1967). *The philosophy of literary form*. Baton Rouge, LA: LSU Press.

Burleson, B., & Rowan, K. E. (1985). Are social-cognitive ability and narrative writing skill related? A response to Rubin et al. *Written Communication, 2*, 25–43.

Clay, M. (1976). Early childhood and cultural diversity in New Zealand. *Reading Teacher, 29*, 333–342.

Clifford, G. J. (1984). Buch und lessen: Historical perspectives on literacy and schooling. *Review of Educational Research, 54*, 472–501.

Connors, R. J. (1987). Personal writing assignments. *College Composition and Communication, 38*, 166–183.

Cook–Gumperz, J. (1986). Literacy and schooling: An unchanging equation? In J. Cook–Gumperz (Ed.), *The social construction of literacy* (pp 16–44). Cambridge, England: Cambridge University Press.

Craig, R. T., & Tracy, K. (Eds.). (1983). *Conversational coherence: form, structure, and strategy*. Beverly Hills, CA: Sage.

Crowhurst, M. (1979). On the misinterpretation of syntactic complexity data. *English Education, 11*, 91–97.

Delia, J. G., & Clark, R. A. (1977). Cognitive complexity, social perception, and the development of listener-adapted communication in six-, eight-, ten-, and twelve-year-old boys. *Communication Monographs, 44*, 326–345.

Demoz, A. (1986). Language, literacy and society: The case of Ethiopia. In J. Fishman, A. Tabouret–Keller, M. Clyne, B. Krishnamurti, & M. Abdulaziz (Eds.), *The Fergusonian Impact* (Vol. 1, pp. 343–366). Berlin: Mouton de Gruyter.

Douglas, W. (1976). Rhetoric for the meritocracy: The creation of composition at Harvard. In R. Ohmann (Ed.), *English in America* (pp 97–132). New York: Oxford University Press.

Ede, L., & Lunsford, A. (1984). Audience addressed/audience invoked: The role of audience in composition theory and pedagogy. *College Composition and Communication, 35*, 140–154.

Eisenstein, E. (1985). On the printing press as an agent of change. In D. Olson, N. Torrance, & A. Hildyard (Eds.), *Literacy, language, and learning* (pp. 19–33). Cambridge, England: Cambridge University Press.

Elbow, P. (1985). The shifting relationship between speaking and writing. *College Composition and Communication, 36*, 283–304.

Ervin–Tripp, S. (1972). On sociolinguistic rules: Alternation and co-occurrence. In J. J. Gumperz & D. Hymes (Eds.), *New directions in sociolinguistics* (pp. 213–250). New York: Holt, Rinehart, & Winston.

Faigley, L. (1985). Nonacademic writing: The social perspective. In L. Odell & D. Goswami (Eds.), *Writing in nonacademic settings* (pp. 231–248). New York: Guilford Press.

Faigley, L. (1986). Competing theories of process: A critique and a proposal. *College English, 48*, 527–542.

Farr, M., & Daniels, H. (1986). *Language diversity and writing instruction*. New York and Urbana, IL: ERIC/Institute for Urban and Minority Education and National Council of Teachers of English.

Farr Whiteman, M. (1981). Dialect influence in writing. In M. Farr Whiteman (Ed.), *Variation in writing: Functional and linguistic-cultural differences* (153–166). Hillsdale, NJ: L. Erlbaum.

Feffer, M. (1970). Developmental analysis of interpersonal behavior. *Psychological Review, 77*, 197–214.

Flavell, J. H., Botkin, P. T., Fry, C. L., Jarvis, P. E. & Wright, J. W., (1968). *The development of role-taking and communication skills in children.* New York: J. Wiley.

Flower, L., & Hayes, J. R. (1980). The cognition of discovery: Defining a rhetorical problem. *College Composition and Communication, 31*, 21–32.

Freire, P. (1970). Adult literacy processes as cultural action for freedom. *Harvard Educational Review, 40*, 205–225.

Gergen, K. J. (1985). The social constructionist movement in modern psychology. *American Psychologist, 40*, 266–275.

Habermas, J. (1970). Towards a theory of communicative competence. *Inquiry, 13*, 360–375.

Hendrix, R. (1981). The status and politics of writing instruction. In M. F. Whiteman (Ed.), *Variation in writing: Functional and linguistic-cultural differences* (pp. 53–70). Hillsdale, NJ: Erlbaum.

Hillocks, G. (1986). *Research in written composition: New directions for teaching.* Urbana, IL: National Conference on Research in English.

Hymes, D. (1971). Competence and performance in linguistic theory. In R. Huxley & E. Ingram (Eds.), *Language acquisition: Models and methods* (pp. 3–28). New York: Academic Press.

Hymes, D. (1974). *Foundations in sociolinguistics: An ethnographic approach.* Philadelphia: University of Pennsylvania Press.

Janis, I. L. (1982). *Groupthink.* Boston: Houghton–Mifflin.

Kaplan, R. B. (1966). Cultural thought patterns in intercultural education. *Language Learning, 14*, 1–20.

Kirsch, I., & Jungeblut, A. (1986). *Literacy: Profiles of America's young adults.* Princeton: National Assessment of Educational Progress.

Kroll, B. M. (1985). Social cognitive ability and writing performance: How are they related? *Written Communication, 2*, 293–305.

Lambert, W. (1972). *Language, psychology and culture.* A. Dil (Ed.). Stanford, CA: Stanford University Press.

Levine, K. (1982). Functional literacy: Fond illusions and false economies. *Harvard Educational Review, 52*, 249–266.

Long, R. C. (1980). Writer–Audience relationships: Analysis or invention? *College Composition and Communication, 31*, 221–226.

Matalene, C. (1985). Contrastive rhetoric: An American writing teacher in China. *College-English, 47*, 789–808.

May a juror take notes in Illinois? (1969). *Chicago–Kent Law Review, 46*, 223–225.

Michaels, S. (1986). Narrative presentations: An oral preparation for literacy with first graders. In J. Cook–Gumperz (Ed.), *The social construction of literacy* (pp. 94–116). Cambridge, England: Cambridge University Press.

Moffett, J. (1968). *Teaching the universe of discourse.* Boston: Houghton–Mifflin.

Murray, D. E. (1985). Composition as conversation: The computer terminal as medium of communication. In L. Odell & D. Goswami (Eds.), *Writing in nonacademic settings* (pp. 203–228). New York: Guilford Press.

Myers, G. (1985). The social construction of two biologists' proposals. *Written Communication, 2,* 219–245.

Myers, G. (1986). Writing research and the sociology of scientific knowledge: A review of three new books. *College English, 48,* 595–610.

Newkirk, T. (1984). Anatomy of a breakthrough: Case study of a college freshman writer. In R. Beach & L. Bridwell (Eds.), *New directions in composition research* (131–148). New York: Guilford Press.

Ohmann, R. (1985). Literacy, technology, and monopoly capital. *College English, 47,* 675–689.

O'Keefe, B. J., & Delia, J. C. (1979). Construct comprehensiveness and cognitive complexity as predictors of the number and strategic adaptation of arguments in a persuasive message. *Communication Monographs, 46,* 231–240.

Ong, W. (1975). The writer's audience is always a fiction. *Publications of the Modern Language Association, 90,* 9–21.

Ong, W. J. (1982) *Orality and literacy: The technologizing of the word.* London: Methuen.

Pellegrini, A. D. (1985). Symbolic play and literate behavior. *Review of Educational Research, 55,* 107–121.

Pellegrini, A. D., Galda, L., & Rubin, D. L. (1984). Persuasion as a social-cognitive activity: The effects of age and channel on children's production of persuasive messages. *Language and Communication, 4,* 285–293.

Perl, S. (1980). Understanding composing. *College Composition and Communication, 31,* 363–369.

Piché, G. L. (1977). Class and culture in the development of the high school English curriculum, 1880–1900. *Research in the Teaching of English, 11,* 17–27.

Piché, G. L., Rubin, D. L., Turner, L. J., & Michlin, M. L. (1978). Effects of nonstandard dialect features in written compositions on teachers' subjective evaluations of students and composition quality. *Research in the Teaching of English, 12,* 107–118.

Quick, D. M. (1983). *Audience awareness and adaptation skills of writers at four different grade levels.* Unpublished dissertation, State University of New York at Albany. (University Microfilms NO. DA 8325612). (*Dissertation Abstracts International, 44,* 2133–A.)

Rafoth, B. A. (1985). Audience adaptation in the essays of proficient and nonproficient freshman writers. *Research in the Teaching of English, 19,* 237–253.

Roth, R. G. (1987). The evolving audience: Alternatives to audience accommodation. *College Composition and Communication, 33,* 47–55.

Rubin, D. L. (1984a). The influence of communicative context on style in writing. In A. D. Pellegrini & T. Yawkey (Eds.), *The development of oral and written language in social contexts* (pp. 213–232). Norwood, NJ: Ablex.

Rubin, D. L. (1984b). Social cognition and written communication. *Written Communication, 1,* 211–245.

Rubin, D. L. (1987). Divergence and convergence between oral and written communication. *Topics in Language Disorders, 7* (4), 1–18.

Rubin, D. L., Galda, L., & Pellegrini, A. D. (1986). *Development of informational adequacy in speech and in writing*. Unpublished manuscript, University of Georgia Institute for Behavioral Research.

Rubin, D. L., & Kantor, K. J. (1984). Talking and writing: Building communication competence. In C. Thaiss & C. Suhor (Eds.), *Speaking and writing, K-13* (pp. 29–73). Urbana, IL: National Council of Teachers of English.

Rubin, D. L., Piché, G. L., Michlin, M. L., & Johnson, F. L. (1984). Social cognitive ability as a predictor of the quality of fourth-graders' written narratives. In R. Beach & L. Bridwell (Eds.), *New directions in composition research* (pp. 297–307). New York: Guilford Press.

Rubin, D. L., & Rafoth, B. A. (1986a). Oral language criteria for selecting listenable materials: An update for reading teachers and specialists. *Reading Psychology, 7*, 137–152.

Rubin, D. L., & Rafoth, B. A. (1986b). Social cognitive ability as a predictor of the quality of persuasive and expository writing among college freshmen. *Research in the Teaching of English, 20*, 9–21.

Scardamalia, M., & Bereiter, C. (1985). Written composition. In M. Wittrock (Ed.), *Handbook of research on teaching* (3d ed.). New York: Macmillan Education.

Scollon, R., & Scollon, S. (1981). *Narrative, literacy and face in inter-ethnic communication*. Norwood, NJ: Ablex.

Scribner, S. (1977). Modes of thinking and ways of speaking. In P. Johnson–Laird & P. C. Wason (Eds.), *Thinking: Readings in cognitive science*. New York: Cambridge University Press.

Secord, P. F., & Peevers, B. H. (1974). The development and attribution of person concepts. In T. Mischel (Ed.), *Understanding other persons* (117–142). Oxford: Basil Blackwell.

Shaughnessy, M. (1977). *Errors and expectations*. New York: Oxford University Press.

Shor, I. (1980). *Critical teaching and everyday life*. New York: South End Press.

Snow, C. E. (1983). Literacy and language: Relationships during the preschool years. *Harvard Educational Review, 53*, 165–189.

Spiro, R. (1980). Constructive processes in prose comprehension and recall. In R. Spiro, B. Bruce, & W. Brewer (Eds.), *Theoretical issues in reading comprehension* (pp. 245–278). Hillsdale, NJ: Erlbaum.

Street, B. V. (1984) *Literacy in theory and practice*. Cambridge, England: Cambridge University Press.

Wilks, I. (1968). The transmission of Islamic learning in the Western Sudan. In J. Goody (Ed.), *Literacy in traditional societies* (pp. 161–197). New York: Cambridge University Press.

Part One

Representing Social Contexts

Chapter 2

Children's Perceptions of Classroom Writing: Ownership Within a Continuum of Control*

Sally A. Hudson
The University of Georgia

I once asked Nicole, a very bright, second-grade writer, what her teacher wanted in her writing, what made it good. With an air of exasperation, Nicole shrugged, "Oh, she wants mistakes." "What?" I asked, a bit taken aback. "You know. She always says we can have all the mistakes we want in our first drafts because we can fix them up when we revise." Then she confided, "I don't make any mistakes, but to make her happy, I always go back and put in a few before I turn in my papers."

Ah, the voice of experience. We chuckle easily over Nicole's naïveté, but is that what it is? Is Nicole simply misinterpreting the directions of a teacher dedicated to teaching writing as a process? Or does she perhaps understand more of, or a different side of, classroom curriculum than we do?

Many times in their school careers, children put pencils to paper, and in the last decade, researchers and teachers have begun to examine that writing through observations of processes and analyses of the resulting products. Many theorists (e.g., Boomer, 1985; Moffett, 1985) currently support the need to *empower* students, to give them control and ownership of their writing, if it is to be meaningful. Yet few of us have asked children themselves how *they* perceive writing experiences in school. In particular, how do children view ownership of the writing they do in the classroom?

Typically, from an adult researcher's perspective, we have examined children's writing within a matrix of setting (home or school) and own-

* This study was funded in part by grants from the Research Foundation of the National Council of Teachers of English and the Graduate College of the University of Northern Iowa.

ership (self-initiated or assigned). Fiering (1981), however, proposed that the common opposition of home-versus-school writing (typically associated with self-initiated and assigned writing, respectively) clouded an important issue: Self-initiated writing may occur in both settings. Other researchers (Clark & Florio, 1982; Dyson, 1984a, 1984b, 1985; Fiering, 1981; Hudson, 1984, 1986) have supported this claim.

The present investigation is limited to children's writing in the elementary school setting, but within that setting, a wide range of ownership possibilities will be examined. In fact, I would like to propose that classroom writing can best be seen within a continuum of control, a balance of ownership tipped sometimes toward the school curriculum and sometimes away from it and toward the child. At one extreme, assigned writing, more distinctly labeled *official* writing, is in some way a response to the curriculum, here including teacher and materials as representatives of the sanctioned school curriculum. Within the realm of official writing, several levels of ownership involve *control shared* by both curriculum and child. Bissex (1980) and Hudson (1984) call such writing "invited," in that children are encouraged to write but not always required to do so in a specified manner. At the other extreme is *unofficial writing*, that which is totally initiated, controlled, and evaluated by the child or others outside of classroom roles.

Importantly, however, this study examines children's, rather than a researcher's, perceptions of this range of ownership possibilities. Researchers observing classroom writing events have typically distinguished between the *initiator* and the *composer* of written products (e.g., Clark & Florio, 1982; Dyson, 1984b). From the adult perspective, a relationship is implied between the initiator and ownership of a product. (Notice, for example, our common terminology for ownership: "self-initiated," "self-sponsored," "teacher-assigned.") In other words, the person who decides that the writing will be done is likely to control it.

Data analyzed for the present study, however, revealed that this clear-cut distinction between ownership and the notions of composer and initiator is less apparent, or simply different, for children. When children were asked to categorize their written products by ownership, setting, audience, purpose, degree of involvement, and genre, the interrelationships among these contextual factors revealed that some products, which adults might assume were assigned, were perceived by children as their own. Other products which children claimed were assigned may have been intended by a teacher as unstructured free writing, open for student choice. As a result, I would like to argue that a child's sense of ownership may more closely parallel an adult's definition of composer, rather than that of initiator. In other words, the more children write, the more freedom they have to write as they please, and the more opportunity they have to make meaning, the more likely they are to claim ownership for a classroom product, no matter who decided originally that it would be done.

The following questions then guided this investigation. Why would children claim some products to be their own when—rather obviously to the adult observer—the teacher decided, and even required, that they write? When do children perceive that they have control of their writing in the classroom setting? What does writing at each level of control—official, shared official, and unofficial—look like? What kinds of experiences enable children to sense ownership of writing in school?

Concerns such as these are on the cutting edge of much current practice and discussion supporting the notions of ownership, control, and empowerment of writing in the classroom. (See, e.g., Boomer, 1985; Hansen & Graves, 1986; Moffett, 1985; Perl et al., 1983; and the entire February 1987 issue of *Language Arts*.) However, little specific research has investigated the nature of children's products and their related, personal senses of ownership. Therefore, answers to these questions can provide new insights into children, writing, and the curriculum. They can also contribute an important perspective to the growing body of composition theory and research.

BACKGROUND

Studies of the school writing of young children support the interpretation of classroom ownership as a continuum of control. They also reveal, however, that we need broader definitions, appropriate, related qualitative research methods, and children's own perspectives of their writing if we are to achieve a clear picture of perceived ownership within the elementary classroom setting.

Four studies discussed here give an overview of the range of ownership possibilities in elementary-school classroom writing. Bloome (1984) focused on academic, or curriculum-constrained, official writing in a broad study aimed at analyzing resources for writing (pens, paper, materials, etc.) across several classrooms, grades K through 8, in an urban, all-Black school. In a very different setting, Clark and Florio (1982; and Florio & Clark, 1982) observed writing instruction in two open-concept, Midwestern, suburban classrooms where children in grades 2/3 and 6 had many choices in their learning. The researchers inferred four major functions for writing, ranging from constrained academic writing through shared control to somewhat unofficial writing to occupy free time. Dyson (1984a, 1984b, 1985; see also Dyson, this volume) observed writing occasions in a kindergarten and second-grade classroom in a

Southern city. Like Clark and Florio (1982), she found writing occasions that were both teacher and student initiated. At the other end of the ownership balance, Fiering (1981) concentrated solely on "underground" or "spontaneous literacy" (versus "directed" literacy activities) in a primarily Black, urban school. Perhaps, she suggests, her interest evolved from a "perverse delight in focusing on what had so traditionally been out of focus for teachers, educational theorists, and researchers" (p. 616). She observed unofficial writing across an extensive range of subject areas and school activities in two fifth-grade classrooms and one in the second grade.

At one extreme, then, what is official writing at the level most constrained by the curriculum? These studies raise three major points about the nature of official, academic writing. First, such writing is generally teacher initiated and teacher controlled. Official writing is assigned by the teacher for academic purposes, often for evaluation and judgment in other content areas, rather than in the ability to compose (Clark & Florio, 1982). Bloome (1984) found that when paper and pencils were handed out in the classroom, children were not typically free to do what they would like with them; what they *should* do, however, was often implied by a worksheet or the blackboard. Dyson (1984b; see also Dyson, this volume) similarly describes "boardwork," official writing marked by copying, completion, and short, text-based composing exercises.

In general, teacher control of these materials is highlighted by a second major factor: a majority of the text is preprepared by the teacher or, as Clark and Florio (1982) suggest, by publishers through commercial materials which constrain topic, format, and function of the writing to be done. As a result, most official, academic writing "eschews production of connected discourse"(Bloome, 1984, p. 99). Instead, Bloome found that "cataloguing" counted as composition from second grade on. In "cataloguing . . . like a telephone book or Sears catalog, the listing of items is not only the dominant feature of the text but is itself the substance of the text" (p. 99).

Finally, Dyson (1984b) discovered that individual children dealt with these official, teacher-initiated tasks in varying ways, some more successfully than others. Like Bloome (1984), she found that some children overgeneralized approaches they understood (such as text reproduction or copying) in order to handle ones they didn't (such as completion exercises). As a result, some children understood and handled writing tasks in ways different from those the teacher had intended.

These researchers and others (e.g., Applebee, 1984; Britton, Burgess, Martin, McLeod, & Rosen, 1975; Emig, 1971; Hudson, 1984, 1986) have found official, academic writing to be the most common writing done in school settings. Bloome (1984), in fact, observed no other levels of writing in the classrooms that he visited. In addition, he found that the dominant forms of academic writing did not change across grades, a point substantiated by Applebee (1984), Britton et al. (1975), and Hudson (1984, 1986) among others. Although older children in Bloome's study were more responsible for writing tools (their own pencils and paper), they gained no power in what they could do with them.

Beyond official, curriculum-constrained writing are levels of official writing, where children share control, where writing is officially sanctioned by the teacher but to some degree controlled by individual writers. For example, Dyson (1984b) describes "composition" as either free writing or free writing constrained by given topics. Clark and Florio (1982) identify "writing to participate in community"—primarily the negotiated development of class rules and disciplinary measures—and "writing to know oneself and others"—basically diaries—which fall into these levels. Although these are the most common types of writing espoused by process approaches to writing, we know little about how children perceive them in classroom settings.

Previous research (Britton et al., 1975; Clark & Florio, 1982; Dyson, 1984b) has shown, however, that these types of writing can be confusing to children. A notable example occurred in Clark and Florio's study; diaries were structured by the teacher but generated and composed by the children. Although the teacher stressed privacy, she would indeed read the diaries; thus, children were uncertain as to the intended audience for their work. The children's work reveals that, without direction, they subtly but quickly adapted personal writing styles to more teacher-oriented formats. Britton et al. (1975) also mention this problem of a "double audience" in much school writing. Like Nicole in the introduction to this chapter, children are at times unsure what is expected of them in official writing situations and thus must interpret such assignments as best they can.

With unofficial writing, however, children may not only share control but may also work beyond the influence of any curricular control. For example, teachers in the Clark and Florio (1982) study provided unstructured time after individuals completed classwork, thereby sanctioning writing done during that time. The children often chose to write stories, letters, and cards, and the researchers labeled this function "writing to occupy free time." The researchers were surprised that complete autonomy in materials, content, and format led these children to write in "intimate, transactional ways" rather than in more diverse forms (Florio & Clark, 1982, p. 127; see also Fontaine, this volume).

Dyson (1984b) and Fiering (1981), however, found similar transactional or interactional functions for writing produced when time was *not* specifically set aside for unofficial writing. Second graders in Dyson's study and many children in Fiering's wrote spontaneously after they had completed other work or even while they were doing it. This writing, completely controlled by the writer, was quite different from, and in fact more varied, in form and purpose than official, assigned writing. It served to keep one busy, to avoid getting in trouble for talking, and to avoid boredom. It appeared as stories, letters to friends and parents, labels, envelopes, and scribblings. It frequently involved making objects as gifts and keeping communication and friendship patterns open and sometimes ended in some sort of display or performance for the teacher or classmates (see Dyson, this volume).

By second grade, unofficial writing "appeared embedded within the social lives of the children" (Dyson, 1984b, p. 2.26). Interestingly, Dyson observed no unofficial writing in kindergarten. This may be the result, as Bloome (1984) suggests, of the teacher's control of writing materials at that grade.

Major methodological concerns arise when comparing these studies with those conducted among older writers. First, definitions may differ when dealing with the writing of young, elementary schoolchildren. For example, in his extensive study of writing in secondary schools, Applebee (1984) defines writing as "at least a paragraph in length" (p. 10), yet much writing which younger children produce, in any setting, may be shorter. Note, for instance, that much of the academic writing described in the four studies above would not have been included under this definition; similarly, children's unofficial writing is often quite brief. In a related vein, Britton et al. (1975) identify, but only minimally discuss, two function categories—practice-play and immature writing—which may be uninteresting for older students but which other researchers have expanded upon in studying younger writers (Gundlach, Litowitz, & Moses, 1979; Whale & Robinson, 1978). Thus, studies of the writing of young children must allow for broader definitions than some major studies of secondary writers.

Secondly, studies which deal with younger writers usually employ qualitative observations and/or interviews as well as product analyses. They realize, as Brandt (1986) suggests, that although texts may occur in isolation from a particular situational context, writers do not. The written products of young children, in particular, may appear meaningless to adults who do not understand the context in which they emerged.

Finally, however, many researchers, even those dealing with the writing of young children, continue to interpret their findings through a researcher's eyes. Yet, as Dyson (1984b) and Clark and Florio (1982) came to realize, children's views of curriculum may differ significantly from the views of both teachers and outside researchers. Dyson was able to discover children's adjustments to the curriculum because she both observed and talked with children in order to infer their interpretations of these school tasks. Similarly, Clark and Florio (1982) almost overlooked official, academic writing on preprinted worksheets because it is "so commonplace in our culture" (p. 125). However, students consistently grouped these materials together as a major part of their school writing (because they were produced "by machine," p. 125) and persuaded the researchers of its importance.

According to Fiering (1981), "although children often appear to use literacy in ways identical to adult use, the underlying functions may differ" (p. 615). If we are to understand a child's view of writing in school, we must ask children themselves to interpret the situation and their products for us. Such studies, designed to help us understand children's concepts of their writing, can provide a valuable new perspective on that which adults may take for granted.

THE STUDY

Participants

Participants for this study were selected from approximately 2,500 children in three elementary schools, grades 1 through 5, in a middle-class, suburban school district in the Southeast. Through questionnaires (N returned = 1394) and small-group interviews with 114 selected children, I identified 20 children who (1) revealed that they wrote often and in a wide variety of contexts, (2) demonstrated that they were sufficiently articulate to provide further information about their writing, and (3) proved to be comfortable in interactions with me and expressed an interest in sharing their writing.

These 20 children—two boys and two girls at each grade from first through fifth—were admittedly *unique cases* (Goetz & LeCompte, 1984) in that they were set apart from other children as avidly self-motivated writers who were comfortable and verbal in discussing their writing. Parents and teachers of all 20 children also agreed to participate, and I met with each parent before data collection began, to obtain both background information about the child as a writer and the parent's cooperation in the study.

Data Collection and Analysis

Between December 1983 and March 1984, these children, with help from their parents and teachers, collected their written products from home and school. I provided folders for these collections in both settings and asked participants to consider each folder as a "trash can" in which they should place anything on which the child had written.

Two important points should be noted about these products. First, they were naturally produced. No student was asked to write for the researcher or the study; as a result, products should represent writing which these children produce normally in such settings. Secondly, writing was defined as "any product resulting from the child's putting pencil or other writing instrument to paper or other writing surface." Products collected for the study thus included drawing, scribbling, words, and short sentences or fragments as well as longer papers. This broad definition was essential if all types of writing produced by these younger children were to be considered.

In a series of three meetings, the children labeled their products. Before each meeting, I reviewed and numbered the papers for easy reference. Each meeting involved six separate "stackings" of products by categories which the children named for the following contextual factors and corresponding definitional questions:

1. Ownership: Who decided that you would do this?
2. Setting: Where were you when you wrote this?
3. Audience: Who was your audience? Who saw this?
4. Purpose: What were your reasons for writing?
5. Degree of involvement: How exciting was this to write?
6. Genre: What kind of writing is this?

The child named categories and separated the papers first for ownership, re-sorted them for setting, and so forth. For example, a tape of one child's meeting was as follows: "I decided to do number 50. My teacher told me to do number 51." Then after all papers were labeled for ownership, she began again, "I wrote number 50 in my playhouse. Number 51 we did at the reading center," and so on. Thus, each product was labeled for each factor separately, rather than all at once for all six factors.

The inductive, *constant comparative* method for data analysis proposed by Glaser and Strauss (1967) best suited the goals of this study. Through simultaneous data collection, coding, and analysis, I sought to describe both the categories of the established contextual factors and their interrelationships. In order to reduce the data for analysis and reporting purposes, I thus derived category labels for the six contextual factors by summarizing and combining categories and looking for logical groupings across meetings and children. These categories were, however, "abstracted from the language of the research situation" (Glaser & Strauss, 1967, p. 107) and accounted for all category names given by the children. For example, the "audience" category of "unrelated peers" included children's labels, such as my friend, a pen pal, and Michael Jackson; the "genre" category of "fiction" included children's labels, such as story, book, tall tale, and make-believe. I also, however, returned to original interview records (written and taped) and actual student products in order to describe more clearly the children's perceptions of the contextual factors surrounding their writing.

Among other discoveries focusing on categories and their interrelationships and reported elsewhere (Hudson 1984, 1986), one odd but interesting development arose: more than 200 products out of the 2,500 from all 20 children were labeled by the participants themselves as self-initiated or shared in ownership with the teacher, despite the fact that all other factors indicated that these products had been assigned. Setting for these products was at school and purpose was simply to fulfill a requirement. Often too, the audience was the teacher, and the genre was a type of schoolwork. This apparent discrepancy in the data led to the refined research questions listed above and to the reanalysis of the data presented here.

FINDINGS AND DISCUSSION

The common dichotomy of assigned versus self-initiated writing in the classroom must be re-examined. Instead, ownership can be more clearly seen as a broad spectrum or continuum of control ranging from almost total constraint by the curriculum to almost total control by the writer. Both adults and children perceive this range; however, their perceptions of where control by curriculum or writer begins and ends may differ.

In Figure 1, five levels of control are proposed; four levels reveal a range of control within official writing (curriculum-constrained, curriculum-perceived and/or distorted, curriculum-sponsored, and curriculum-surpassed), and unofficial writing exists beyond the curriculum. In general, in this continuum each level of control reveals an adult's common view of the child's position in relation to the curriculum. To the left, the curriculum controls; all official writing is to some degree initiated by the curriculum or teacher. To the right, the child is in charge because he or she chooses to do the writing beyond the demands of the curriculum. In this adult view, control and ownership go hand in hand.

Adults examining children's products may easily agree about which written products were assigned and which ones were child-initiated (i.e., who initiated the writing) as well as about how much of the composing is done by the child versus the teacher or curriculum (i.e., who is the composer). Observations and even product analyses alone are in most cases enough to reach some degree of reliability about the place-

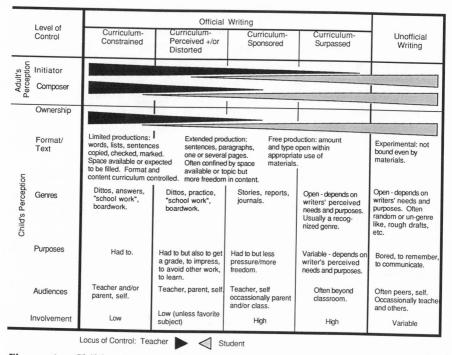

Level of Control	Official Writing				Unofficial Writing
	Curriculum-Constrained	Curriculum-Perceived +/or Distorted	Curriculum-Sponsored	Curriculum-Surpassed	
Adult's Perception — Initiator					
Composer					
Ownership					
Format/Text	Limited productions: words, lists, sentences copied, checked, marked. Space available or expected to be filled. Format and content curriculum controlled.	Extended production: sentences, paragraphs, one or several pages. Often confined by space available or topic but more freedom in content.	Free production: amount and type open within appropriate use of materials.		Experimental: not bound even by materials.
Genres	Dittos, answers, "school work", boardwork.	Dittos, practice, "school work", boardwork.	Stories, reports, journals.	Open - depends on writers' perceived needs and purposes. Usually a recognized genre.	Open - depends on writers' needs and purposes. Often random or un-genre like, rough drafts, etc.
Purposes	Had to.	Had to but also to get a grade, to impress, to avoid other work, to learn.	Had to but less pressure/more freedom.	Variable - depends on writer's perceived needs and purposes.	Bored, to remember, to communicate.
Audiences	Teacher and/or parent, self.	Teacher, parent, self.	Teacher, self occasionally parent and/or class.	Often beyond classroom.	Often peers, self. Occasionally teacher and others.
Involvement	Low	Low (unless favorite subject)	High	High	Variable

Locus of Control: Teacher ▶ ◁ Student

Figure 1. Children's perceptions of classroom writing: ownership within a continuum of control.

ment of products along such a continuum of initiator and composer (see Clark & Florio, 1982; Dyson, 1984b).

However, the traditional notions of ownership become blurred here because children, unlike adults, may perceive each type of initiation (assigned, shared, and self-initiated) within each level of control (from curriculum-constrained official writing through curriculum-surpassing writing and unofficial writing). In other words, the most constrained assignment may be seen by some child as self-sponsored while a totally self-initiated piece may be seen as constrained by curricular demands.

In general, however, I would like to suggest that while ownership correlates most closely with the initiator role to an adult, a child's sense of ownership (the third line of arrows in Figure 1) more closely parallels an adult's definition of composer. In other words, the more children write, the more freedom they have to write as they please, and the more opportunity they have to make meaning, the more likely they are to claim ownership for a classroom product, no matter who decided originally that it would be done.

I would like to discuss and illustrate each of the five levels of control identified here, focusing on children's perceptions of ownership. In order to describe each level more clearly, I will also examine the format of common texts, as well as these 20 children's views of the prevalent genres, purposes, audiences, and degree of involvement within that level of control. I make here the age-old caution that these are not distinct boundaries but merely a framework within which we can better understand children's perceptions of the ownership of their classroom writing.

Official Writing: Curriculum-constrained

From an adult's perspective, curriculum-constrained writing is usually initiated by teachers, controlled by teachers, and almost totally composed by teachers (on the blackboard or dittos) or by publishers of the materials (in texts, workbooks, or dittos). Such writing entails copying letters, words, sentences (including punishment sentences), and occasional poems; filling in words, numbers, or marks in exercises; or listing short, decontextualized answers, such as spelling words on lined paper. These are exactly those artifacts noted by both Bloome (1984) and Dyson (1984b) as boardwork, seatwork, or skills lessons. It includes the machine-produced dittos and worksheets, which Clark and Florio (1982) discussed. The children in the present study turned in hundreds of such products; however, we only labeled a few at each meeting because, like Clark and Florio's (1982) children, these children claimed they were "all alike."

Such writing is not only limited by written directions and space available on preprinted paper but also by expectations of the amount and type of space to be filled. Even when answers are written on empty paper, the teacher controls this writing. For example, on one paper in the present study, George, a third grader, wrote a list of phrases and fragments under the title "Reading." His teacher wrote back, "Not acceptable 1) Cursive 2) Complete Sentences." He and other children were also admonished on papers for being late, leaving off names and dates, or leaving out particular answers. Format as well as content is being strictly controlled here.

In the children's eyes, genres, purposes, and audiences are equally limited. Children lump curriculum-constrained writing under genre categories such as "schoolwork," "math," "boardwork," or "assignments." They also reveal their uncertainty as to its genre when they stare at such writing during data collection sessions and end up labeling it as "just answers."

Curriculum-constrained writing has almost no purpose for these children other than to fulfill a requirement imposed by someone in authority. Typically, they complete these products only because "I had to" or at best in order "to learn" in general. As Applebee (1984) puts it, there is no reason to write "beyond simple obedience" (p. 170).

The children also perceived a narrow audience for curriculum-constrained writing: the teacher and/or a parent. Sometimes a child felt that he or she alone was the audience, even when a teacher had obviously marked the paper. Writing intended only as proof of academic competence rather than as communication of meaning may simply require no "audience" per se. In our discussions, children repeatedly referred to who *saw* these products, not to who *read* them as they did for other pieces. In general, these products are to be checked and/or corrected, and their value ends there. Repeatedly, children easily grouped these products as low in involvement.

Ownership within curriculum-constrained writing. By far, children relegated most of these products to the realm of teacher control. Very few products in the curriculum-constrained range were considered to be self-initiated or shared in ownership with a teacher, *except* by first graders. The latter did include some dittos, copied words, practice spelling lists, or short word puzzles as self-initiated or shared in ownership with the teacher. One child explained that these were optional beyond regular work. Others gave no direct explanation for their sense of ownership. These products were sometimes incomplete and seen by no one but the student; therefore, children may have assumed responsibility for rough drafts, "mess-ups," or practice efforts, which were not handed in.

Another explanation may be that for first graders, even a few words of handwriting, constrained or not, may at times constitute "creation" or "composing" from their newcomers' perspectives. Thus definitions of initiator and composer begin to be blurred: if the child put pencil to paper, he or she sensed ownership. Dyson's (1984b) kindergartners saw boardwork as something they could be proud of and even give as "gifts" to significant others. By second grade, however, the children in her study, as well as mine, understood boardwork and other curriculum-constrained products as assignments.

Official Writing: Curriculum-perceived (but Distorted)

At a second level of control—curriculum-perceived but often distorted—materials or assignments still constrain children's writing, but because they compose more of the products, children may sense more control than they do for products completely constrained by the curriculum. At this level, children perceive that curricular expectations drive their production; they understand that the teacher has reasons for them to accomplish these tasks. However, children may be uncertain as to what the specific curricular demands are. When confusion occurs, children, perceiving *some* control over these products, create their own means and goals for accomplishing the work. Thus when they do claim ownership for such products, it is sometimes for reasons that distort the curriculum; they know—often impishly—that they are inappropriately taking charge.

As with curriculum-constrained products, the teacher usually initiates, requires, and evaluates curriculum-perceived products in order to measure academic competence. The major difference between products at these two levels is that here children have an opportunity to produce somewhat more extended discourse with fewer constraints. At this level, boardwork, textbook assignments, or dittos require full sentences, descriptive paragraphs, or even stories which run from a few sentences to several pages. Unlike curriculum-constrained products, however, in curriculum-perceived products there is no copying, children create and compose the majority of any piece themselves, and products are extended enough that meaning making is at least possible. However, these products are tied to specific curriculum objectives, often narrow skills. For instance, children may have to wrap their language around several spelling or vocabulary words, as did Lisa in the following piece:

I *got* sick.
He *can* got to school tomorrow.
I am a girl.
They can *fix* almost everything.
Buffy called *help*.
They have a *plan* to go swiming.
He saw a big bat!
They had *ham* for supper.
He was *glad* he got a straight A.
They have a *black* cat.

(from Lisa, grade 1)

Children also were asked to describe a setting using numerous adjectives or to use formally defined content-area words to reveal understanding. As a result, the meaning created is generally less important than the skill practiced.

Quite often such curriculum-bound writing requires or encourages a stretching of the language that results in a distortion of the curriculum goals. Frequently, as Lisa's writing above reveals, sentences derived for spelling words develop a singsong pattern (see also Dyson, 1984b), and attention to spelling (other than the words under consideration) and mechanics is minimal. Stories using spelling words may turn out acceptably, but just as often they lead to absurdity in the effort to include unrelated words. Similarly, a paragraph written simply to display adjectives or verbs often manages to do little else. Likewise, children's interpretations of formal definitions can lead to humor but questionable understanding:

vertical—straight up and down
Christa's brain is vertical.

pedastal—a base of a statue
Why don't we use Christa as a pedastal.

thrive—grows well
Go get some more thrive for Christa.

(excerpts from Darin, grade 5)

Genres and audiences listed for curriculum-perceived writing were similar to those for curriculum-constrained writing. Most products were listed as a type of schoolwork (assignment, science, or simply "work"). Even when a story appeared to have emerged fairly coherently, products at the curriculum-perceived level were more likely to be labeled as a school genre rather than as a commonly accepted category such as story or fiction. Again, teacher, parent, and self were common audiences.

Children did, however, perceive both a wider range of purposes and a more frequent sense of shared ownership with the teacher for products at the curriculum-perceived level. However, variation here—while the assignment is still so closely tied to curricular demands—may lead as much to confusion as to actual freedom. For example, it was often at this level of curriculum-perceived control that the children described by Dyson (1984b) and Bloome (1984) had difficulty interpreting a teacher's task. According to Dyson, "The children knew that school tasks must be interpreted in relation to the teacher's, rather than their own, intentions, and they were attuned to her desires" (1984b, p. 5.5). However, not all children succeeded.

For example, Dyson tells of Callie, who tried to adapt methods which she understood (copy words on the board for boardwork) to the teacher's directions to "copy either word (boat or boats) and write a story about it" (1984a, p. 250). Callie at first fails; all she does is copy. Similarly, in urban classrooms, Bloome found the production of extended discourse to be so infrequent that children often interpreted such assignments in light of what they could control—reproduction or cataloguing.

Applebee (1984) recognizes this situation as a tension that exists "between the goals which a teacher may hold for a particular assignment, and the purposes that the students may develop in the process of making that assignment their own" (p. 54). The present data suggest that as children are permitted and expected to compose more of a product, they are more likely to perceive ownership and control of it; however, as they develop their own purposes for such assignments, they may distort the curriculum goals in order to justify their efforts.

For example, although most curriculum-perceived products were again done "because I had to" and some were "for practice," children also suggested that they completed these assignments in order to "get a grade," to get a reward such as a sticker, to "impress the teacher," or to "avoid other work." They seemed to realize that by composing appropriately here they could achieve beneficial end goals. However, learning per se was not perceived as a major goal; only rarely did a child state a specific educational objective (such as "sentences to learn homonyms") as a reason for completing an assignment at this level.

These purposes reveal the attempts of children—who often do not accurately perceive a teacher's curriculum objectives for an assignment—to gain some control over this type of writing. They sense that there is more at issue here than completing an otherwise unnecessary exercise and that they *can* affect an outcome; however, they are not always aware of what constitutes success to an adult (e.g., learning objectives), only how to achieve it (create an acceptable end product).

Purposes which distorted curriculum goals were less frequently given for products at other levels of control. Instead, curriculum-constrained products were simply done because "I had to," while products which allowed children higher levels of control (curriculum-sponsored or curriculum-surpassed) often rose, as we shall see, to more meaningful purposes.

In general, children felt a low sense of involvement in curriculum-perceived products, much as they did for more constrained curricular materials. However, individuals occasionally expressed interest and enthusiasm for such work *if* it was in a favorite subject area or *if* they had managed to make the writing entertaining as did Darin in the above example. When such levels of involvement arose, children were more likely to assume some sense of shared ownership.

Ownership within curriculum-perceived writing. Again, children above first grade recognized most curriculum-perceived writing as teacher initiated. However, children in grades 1 through 3 sometimes viewed these products as shared in ownership with the teacher. Said one child, "She told me to, but I decided what." Because they were able to compose the product, children were able to feel some control. Similarly, children who specified curriculum-distorting purposes for products (to get a grade, to avoid work) were more likely to claim ownership.

Fourth and fifth graders, wiser to adult goals, generally realized that all products in the curriculum-perceived level were indeed assigned.

Official Writing: Curriculum-sponsored

Florio and Clark (1982) believe that diaries and other such curriculum-sponsored writing may be the *"cusp* of purely private and personal writing to occupy free time and the more formal and public school-oriented writing" (p. 126). Data from the present study suggest that this may be true: curriculum-sponsored writing such as journals, reports, stories, and books may be the fulcrum of the balance of ownership between curriculum constraints and complete freedom in composing (see Staton & Shuy, this volume).

Curriculum-sponsored and supported products are those inspired or initiated by the teacher, materials, or other curricular sources, but heavily infused with original composition by the writer. For example, within the parameters of a daily writing time such as Dyson's (1984b) free writing, a sanctioned genre such as Clark and Florio's (1982) diaries, or simply a given topic such as Dyson's (1984b) constrained free writing, children have freedom to write. Such free composing was quite common in the classrooms examined for the present study, unlike those observed by Bloome (1984).

In general, children engaged in curriculum-sponsored writing often fill one or more pages with text and/or drawing. They often appear to be limited more by time constraints than by curriculum demands; however, children can overcome time constraints by continuing some writing over several days or even weeks if a topic or theme attracts their repeated attention. No specific skill objectives appear to be emphasized in such writing and, as other researchers have suggested, the teacher's role is not to evaluate here but to encourage writing. For example, George's teacher, who had reprimanded him in curriculum-constrained materials, here cheers him on with readers' questions ("Where are you going with this?" "What is an 'airwolf'?" "What's your mission?") and encouraging comments ("You have a good beginning here." "Sound effects!" "Love this. Good comparison!" "Nice, freely expressed.")

The 20 children in this study recognized a wide range of genres for such writing including stories, books, reports, poems, experiences, notes, and reminders. Most of their designations match adult definitions of genres, and these designations become both more standardized to adult norms, and more varied in number, among the older children (See also Hudson, 1986; Langer, 1985; Rafoth, this volume). Some curriculum-sponsored writing retained basic "schoolwork" labels, but two major reasons for such designations emerge. If George, for example, was uninterested in a particular product, he did not call it a story or experience as he often did when he was enthusiastic about a piece of writing. Instead, said he, "It's just journal writing. It's good work but just passing time." Secondly, children in grades 4 and 5 continue to understand that writing at the curriculum-sponsored level of control is assigned and required. So, although many products are labeled with specific genres, some, like one long story that Zac did in fifth grade, are still "just a regular old assignment."

By definition, curriculum-sponsored writing, much as that which is curriculum-constrained or curriculum-perceived, is again attached to curricular demands and leads children to realize at times that it is done as an assignment, often "because I had to." However, children appear to sense a lack of pressure to perform here and instead can concentrate on meaning making. Said Danny, in third grade, "She made me, but I didn't really have to and I had plenty of time." In the fifth grade, Darin reiterates, "We had to do it, but it didn't go in the grade book." Jolie in grade 3 and Susan in grade 4 specified that the teacher "wanted" or "requested" that this writing be done, clearly distinguishing it from writing she "told me I had to do."

Children tended to enjoy this writing, and in labeling it for involvement, they explained their reasoning quite clearly. Repeatedly, they seemed to be saying, "I had to do this, *but*. . . ." Most often their exceptions were due to a sense of freedom of topic, of choices within a topic, of language or tone, or freedom from evaluation. They expressed exasperation or boredom with some pieces that were dead-end drafts.

Much curriculum-sponsored writing continues to reach only the teacher, and sometimes the child never even turns it in to the teacher. More frequently than for the previous two levels of control, however, this writing is sometimes shared with the class through reading it aloud or posting it around the room. Sadly, perhaps, children infrequently perceive parents as an audience for this writing. However, on those occasions when parents are audiences here, they serve more as readers of ideas (valentine's greetings, invitations to meetings, entertaining stories about hobbies or family activities, etc.) than as watchdogs of academic performance.

Ownership within curriculum-sponsored writing. Children perceived much curriculum-sponsored writing as being assigned. Especially in grades 4 and 5, few such products appeared as self-sponsored, although journals, free writing, stories, and reports were encouraged and supported. These older children perceived some science reports and stories as shared in ownership with the teacher, especially if a wider audience or more clearly delineated purpose was apparent to them.

Children in grades 1 through 3 were more willing to accept full or shared ownership for curriculum-sponsored writing. Again, the fact that they created most of the text themselves appears to influence their perspective. A repeated routine for writing (e.g., time is provided or a genre such as books or a journal is supported) also seemed to encourage a sense of control; children in classrooms without such allowances for writing were more likely to label classroom-sponsored writing of any sort as assigned. Finally, open materials such as lined or unlined paper were more likely to engender a sense of writing as self-sponsored. Story starters on dittos, on the other hand, no matter how free-wheeling in content, were often viewed as teacher-initiated.

As Clark and Florio (1982) suggest, ownership of curriculum-sponsored writing can be confusing, especially if the teacher intervenes in any way. Two examples illustrate that point. First, George regarded his extensive journal as self-initiated even though his teacher required journal writing; however, he expressed a sense of shared ownership when his teacher encouraged him to revise one piece for a class book. Although the teacher never offered (in writing) specific suggestions for improvement, George acknowledged her control over later drafts when he agreed to comply with her request to prepare the piece for classroom publication.

More dramatically, Jason in grade 2 changed the entire nature of his self-sponsored journal when the teacher interrupted and refocused his direction. In Figure 2a, Jason's highly individualistic and expressive style is enhanced with drawing. Two weeks later, in Figure 2b, his teacher gently suggested that he do less drawing and more writing. Like the children who changed their writing styles for diaries in Clark and Florio's study (1982), Jason proceeded to alter his writing until, in Figure 2c a month later, it resembles the cataloguing style Bloome (1984) discusses. At the same time, Jason continued to write books freely. During our meeting somewhat later, he saw both books and journals as self-initiated but claimed he wrote the journal because he "had to" and the books because he "wanted to."

In both cases, the teacher's awareness of her appropriate role at each level of control appears to be critical. Florio and Clark (1982) suggest that curriculum-sponsored writing "relies on the teacher . . . to free the children to design and control as much of the writing process as it will take to reach fruition" (Florio & Clark, 1982, p. 126). In other words, the curriculum *sponsors* or encourages that the writing be done, but beyond that, the writer is free to compose, control, and dispense with the product as he or she chooses. When such freedom is diminished or rescinded within curriculum-sponsored writing, as it is in curriculum-perceived or constrained writing, children sense the draining away of their control and revert to strategies (cataloguing, "fixing" what the teacher corrects,

Figure 2a. Curriculum-sponsored writing (a) becomes curriculum-distorted writing (b–c) from Jason, second grade.

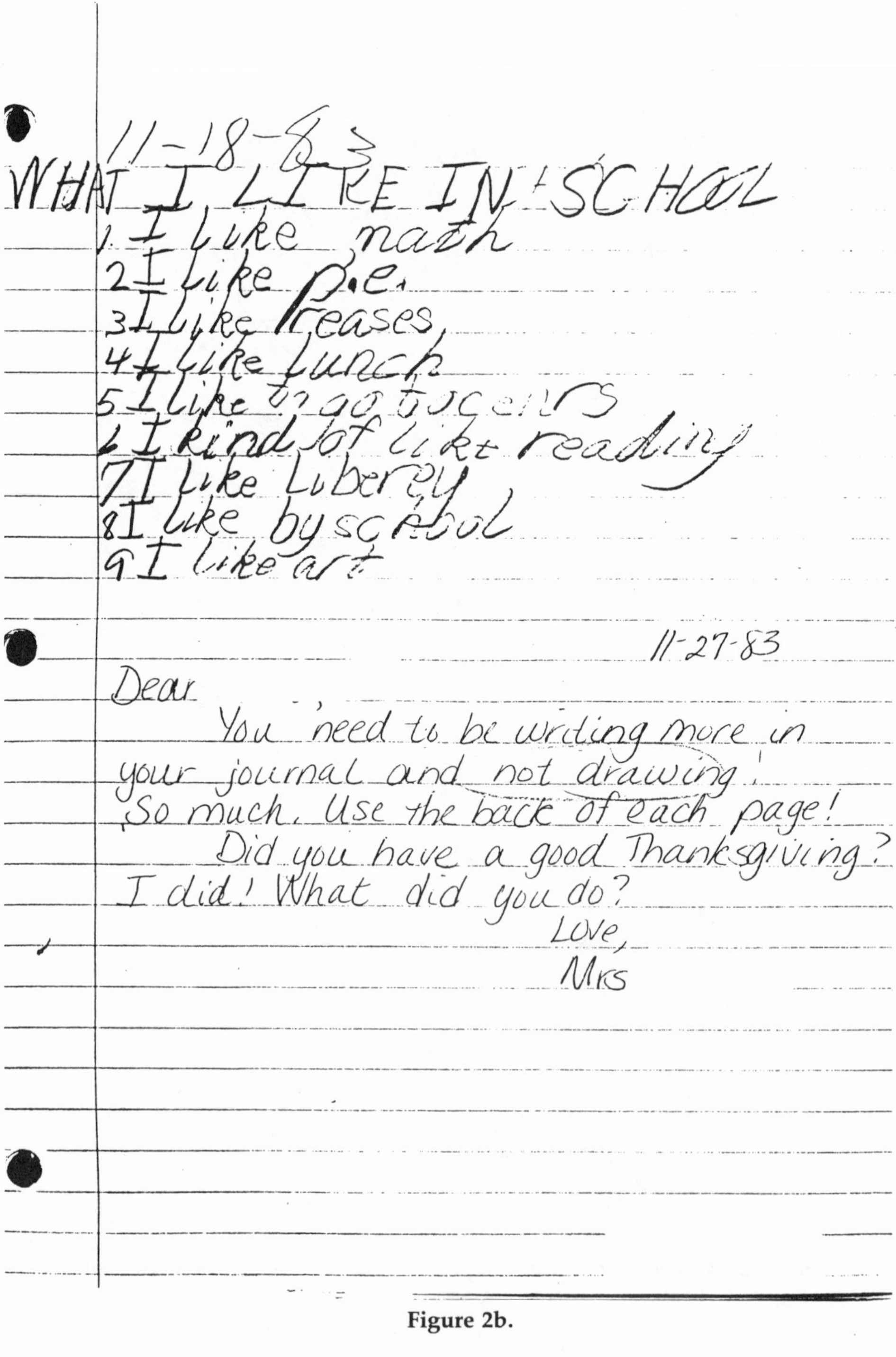

11-18-83

WHAT I LIKE IN SCHOOL
1. I Like math
2. I like p.e.
3. I like reases,
4. I like lunch
5. I like to go to gens
6. I kind of likt reading
7. I like Liberey
8. I like by school
9. I like art

11-27-83

Dear ,
        You need to be writing more in
your journal and not drawing!
So much. Use the back of each page!
        Did you have a good Thanksgiving?
I did! What did you do?
                        Love,
                        Mrs

Figure 2b.

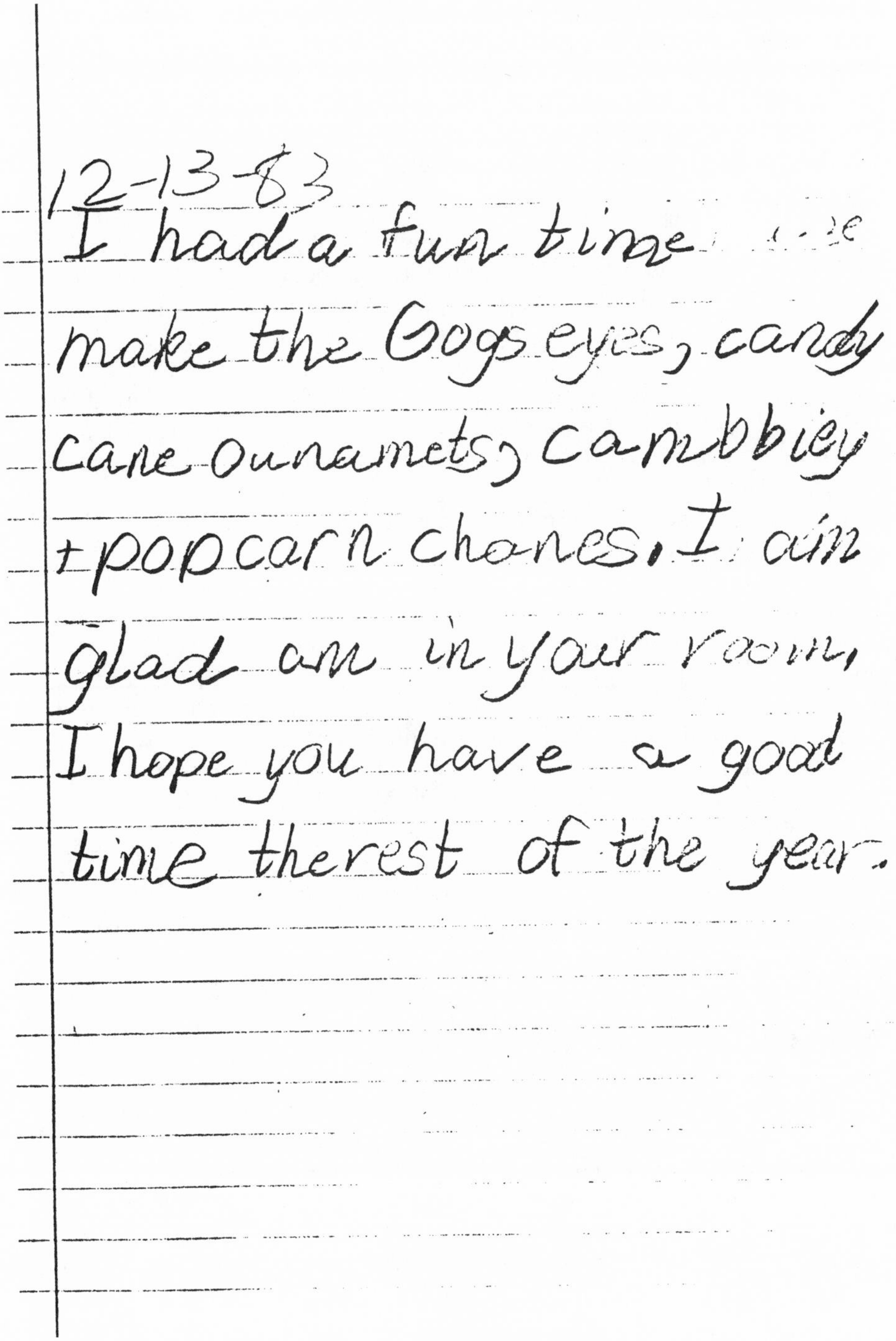

12-13-83
I had a fun time ...e
make the Gogs eyes, candy
cane ounamets, cambbiey
+ popcarn chones. I am
glad am in your room,
I hope you have a good
time the rest of the year.

Figure 2c.

etc.) that worked for them at levels where they had less control. As a result, children's senses of ownership may also disappear as products become as much the teacher's as their own.

Official Writing: Curriculum-surpassed

Occasionally in a child's eyes the curriculum may disappear when a piece of writing surpasses an assignment and becomes "my own." Brandt (1986) has theorized that context can impede *or* enable meaning making. If we visualize curriculum-sponsored writing as the cusp, or fulcrum, of classroom writing, we have seen how a teacher's intervention may impede expanded meaning and ownership, as in Jason's case above. On the other hand, such free production of writing supported by the curriculum may be essential if classrooms are to enable real growth in writing and children are ever to move beyond the curriculum to making writing their own.

Curriculum-surpassed writing appeared rarely among these 20 children, but often enough to reveal its potential. I considered writing curriculum-surpassed if it was originally given as, or based on, an assignment. In these pieces, however, writers found some reason to claim ownership to such an extent that they forgot, or were willing to reject, any concern for academic purposes. Nancy Martin (1983) describes a perfect example of this writing: "He had accepted the teacher's request to write about a monster and had made the task his own. From then on, its purpose lay in the satisfaction of making it, and in his assumption that the teacher would share his satisfaction" (p. 99). For children in the present study, such writing often emerged when they found a meaningful, adult-like audience, purpose, and genre for a piece of writing; in some way, an assignment not only became their own, but also surpassed the "had to" demands of the curriculum.

Cathryn's New Year's resolutions provide an example. In Figure 3a, second-grader Cathryn wrote under her teacher's invitation an appropriate piece to share with "some of the class." She claimed to do it to "impress the teacher," to feel little involvement in it, and to find no recognizable genre into which it could fall ("just writing for subjects"). On the same day, she followed up independently on this assignment by accessing a teacher–student written dialogue pattern which the teacher had established earlier (Figure 3b). The reader feels like an intruder sharing this intimate piece addressed only to the teacher and senses the enthusiasm that consumed Cathryn as she wrote her "letter."

More than any single factor, what sets this piece apart as curriculum-

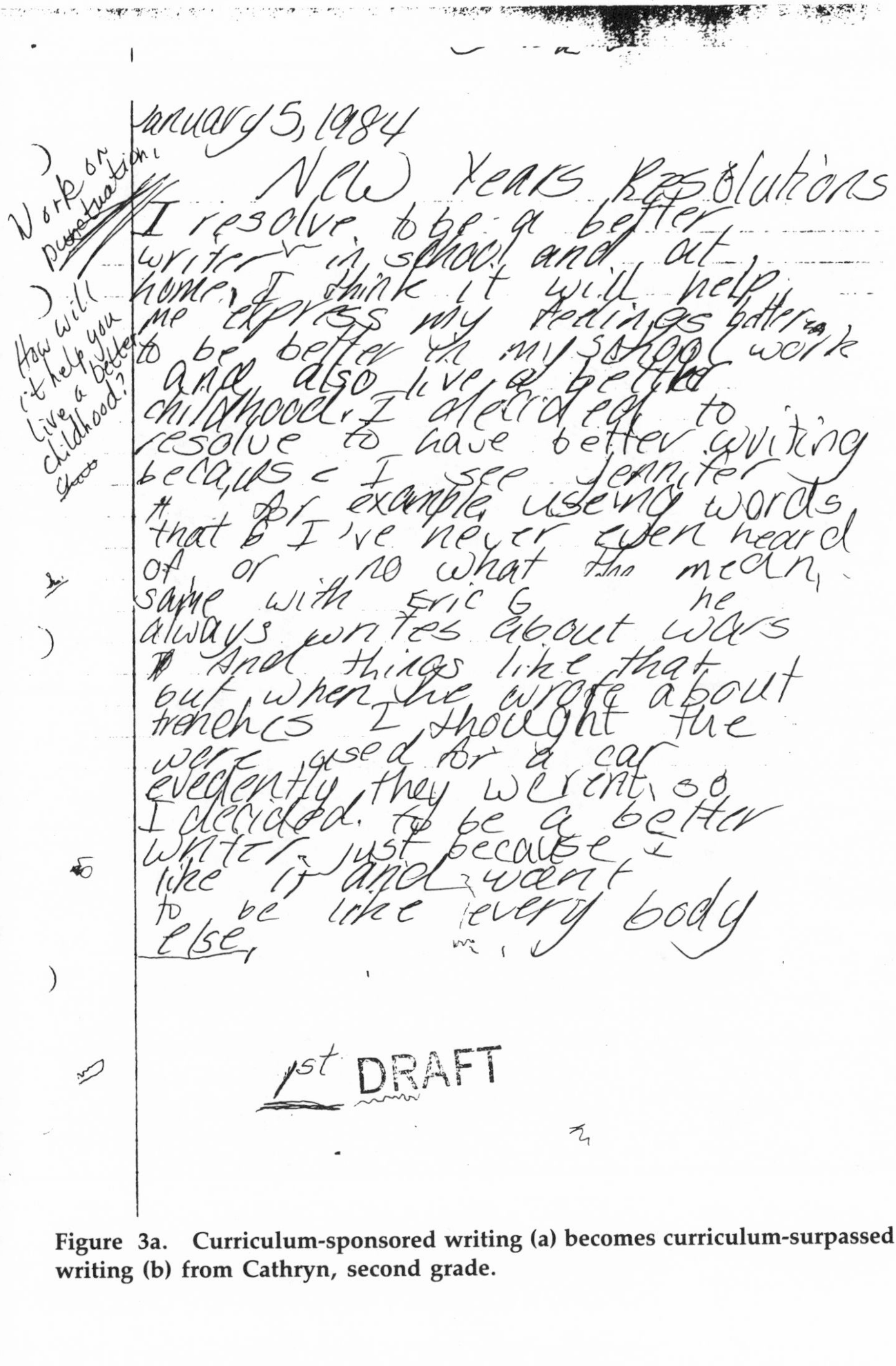

January 5, 1984

New Years Resolutions

I resolve to be a better writer in school and out home. I think it will help me express my feelings better to be better in my school work and also live a better childhood. I decided to resolve to have better writing because I see Jennifer for example useing words that I've never even heard of or no what they mean, same with Eric G. he always writes about wars and things like that but when he wrote about trenches I thought the were used for a car evedently they weren't so I decided to be a better writer just because I like it and want to be like everybody else.

Work on punctuation.

How will it help you live a better childhood?

1st DRAFT

Figure 3a. Curriculum-sponsored writing (a) becomes curriculum-surpassed writing (b) from Cathryn, second grade.

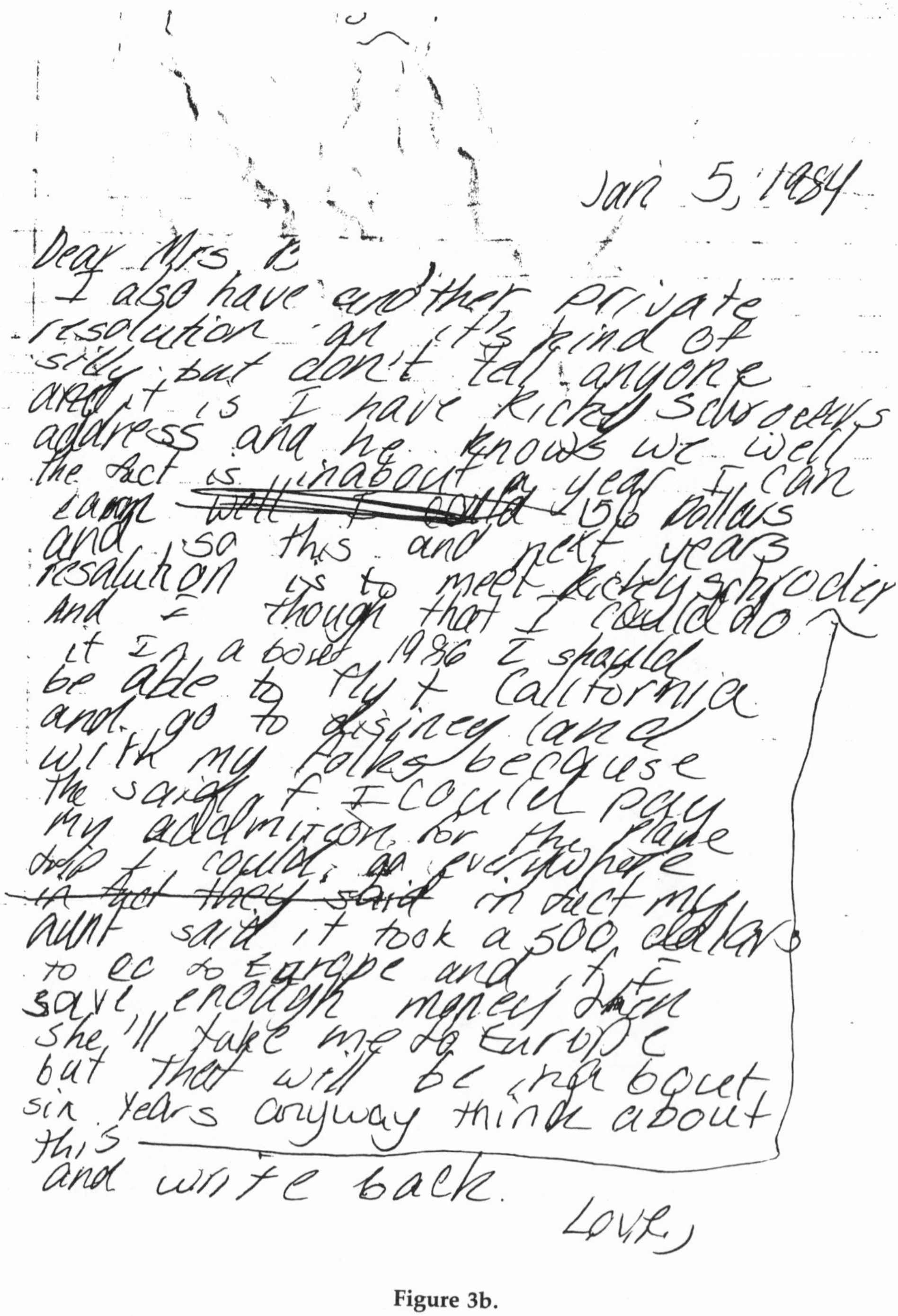

Jan 5, 1984

Dear Mrs. B
I also have another private
resolution an it's kind of
silly but don't tell anyone
are it is I have Ricky Schroeder's
address and he knows we well
the fact is in about a year I can
earn ~~well I coulda~~ 150 dollars
and so this and next years
resolution is to meet Ricky Schroder
and I though that I could do
it In a bout 1986 I should
be able to fly t California
and go to disney land
with my folks because
the said if I could pay
my admicon for the ride
orld I could in everywhere
~~in fact they said~~ in fact my
aunt said it took a 500, dollars
to ec do Europe and if I
save enough money then
she'll take me to Europe
but that will be in about
six years anyway think about
this
and write back.

Love,

Figure 3b.

surpassing is that in many ways Cathryn discovered a more real and focused context the second time she wrote. Similarly, she and other children at times found equally transactional, other-oriented needs to be filled by assignments: Cathryn's extended, often-revised (with peer input) play for a media festival, Zac's story with which he hoped to win a contest, Lee's informative book on parakeets to let his grandmother "know about them cause she's got one and needs to know this stuff." A writer's sincere need to communicate meaning to an audience marks these products as distinctive (see Fontaine, this volume; Staton & Shuy, this volume).

Others such as George and Daniel, both in third grade, became equally engaged in journal stories or accounts of true-life experiences intended, as yet, for no one but themselves; they assumed, as Martin (1983) recognized in successful writing episodes she observed, a spectator's stance. In these instances of curriculum-surpassing writing, children wrote only for the pleasure of creation. Others, such as Darin, continued collecting data for a science report after it was due "just to know more and cause it was fun."

Rather than composing these pieces because they "had to," these children wrote because they "wanted to" or experienced some adult-like need to write. They often identified broad audiences beyond the classroom or specific persons, including just themselves, for whom this writing was done. In most cases, they clearly identified recognizable adult genres and expressed a high level of involvement for curriculum-surpassed pieces.

Ownership within curriculum-surpassed writing. Curriculum-surpassed writing occurred at all grade levels, a significant point considering the fact that children in grades 4 and 5 rarely considered curriculum-sponsored writing to be self-initiated. When they *did* accept ownership of a curriculum-sponsored activity, their implementation tended to go beyond the requirements of the original assignment. More willing to view curriculum-sponsored writing as their own, children in grades 1 through 3 were also more likely to take off on their own to create *if* opportunities for such writing, including time and specified and supported genres, were available in the classroom.

Unofficial Writing for Self and Others

Unofficial writing might at first appear to be the most desirable alternative for helping students experience ownership of writing in school. Because it is completely free of curricular constraints, initiated and composed totally by children, and evaluated or used only by them, a total sense of control seems likely. Previous researchers (e.g., Clark & Florio,

1982; Dyson, 1984a, 1984b, 1985, this volume; Fiering, 1981; Hudson, 1984, 1986) have explored unofficial writing and discovered its vivacity, its freedom from adult restrictions. However, unofficial writing is generally not supported or even recognized by the school *nor* by children as "real" writing. Unlike previous researchers, I would like to propose that this may be for good reason.

Children at all grade levels in the present study were actively engaged in unofficial writing. Its wide range of variation revealed its experimental nature. Children cited many genres for their unofficial writing at school. In the first grade, Lisa wrote "I hate boys" in the spaces among pictures on a reading ditto and kept a "friends list" in her desk that was often revised. She and others scribbled, drew, copied random poems, filled in adult forms available in the classroom, and wrote notes to the teacher to express their love. By the second grade, pencil games with peers, and notes to rock stars appeared as well. By the third and fourth grades, notebook covers, poetry, "playing school," and decoratively handwritten names arose. And in the fourth and fifth grades, friendship notes, such as that displayed in Figure 4 among Richard and two friends, were common among both boys and girls.

Perhaps because time was not set aside, extended pieces such as that in Figure 4 were rare. Unlike Dyson (1984b) and Clark and Florio (1982), I found few children engaged in extended composition at this level. Notable exceptions included poems or stories which some of these children, recognized as good writers by their peers, were invited to write for boyfriends or girlfriends of others; in another case, MaryAnne, a fifth grader and an extensive self-sponsored writer at home, spent her spare time developing ongoing projects from home, rarely considering "schoolwork" as writing at all and only infrequently engaging in unofficial writing with peers. Instead, however, more like the children in Fiering's (1981) study, children here constructed brief, immediately useful, and largely unplanned writing.

Limitations of unofficial writing. As in earlier studies (Clark & Florio, 1982; Dyson, 1984b; Fiering, 1981), the unofficial writing of these children involved a wider and different range of genres, audiences, and purposes than official, school writing. However, the nature of these contextual features must be considered. The genres that appear here— but not in official school writing—are limited to those enjoyed only by children or indifferently by adults: games, brief communications such as notes, doodling including decorated names, and drawing. The audience, limited to one peer or sometimes a teacher, is usually present and requires written communication over oral *only* because silence is enforced; frequently, audience is irrelevant as the child writes merely to fill time quietly.

For these children, unofficial writing was done just in passing. Most often, they claimed to write these products simply out of boredom and only occasionally in order to remember something (a movie star's address, a phone number) or to communicate, often in the "intimate, transactional" ways which Clark and Florio (1982) described. Perhaps the most revealing point that children made about their unofficial writing was that they rarely felt it was highly involving. Some stories and notes were "fun," but quite often unofficial writing was just "OK," no more exciting than some of the more curriculum-bound assignments. After it was "used," it was discarded, often crumpled in balls and stuffed in the backs of desks.

In general, children would not have "counted" these unofficial products as "real" writing unless the definition given for this study had emphasized that any mark on paper was to be included. At the beginning of the study, they were surprised when I considered unofficial writing as equal to other types; however, as the study continued, they happily discussed more and more of these products. They gleefully claimed ownership and enjoyed the unofficial, underground nature of such writing (giggling that "she'd be mad if she caught us").

Their hesitation to recognize unofficial writing as "real," then, may stem from their tendency to equate "real" writing to that done officially in school and sanctioned by the teacher. However, I believe that their initial distinction may be more valid when the genres, audiences, and purposes of unofficial writing are compared with those for curriculum-sponsored or curriculum-surpassing writing. At all three levels, children identified useful, adult-like contexts: recognizable genres, real audiences, expressive and transactional purposes. However, unofficial writing may be less "real" when it is compared with more extensive motivation, effort, and sense of achievement associated with curriculum-sponsored or curriculum-surpassing writing. Although experimentation may be productive, lack of support (or need) for unofficial products to reach full transactional or literary potential may reduce their value as experienced by children themselves.

SUMMARY AND CONCLUSIONS

The 20 children who shared their insights for this study reveal, as a group, that children can in fact help us see the school curriculum in new ways. The following conclusions are suggested as a result of this analysis.

1. *A child's sense of ownership of classroom writing more closely parallels an adult's definition of composer rather than that of the initiator of an activity.*

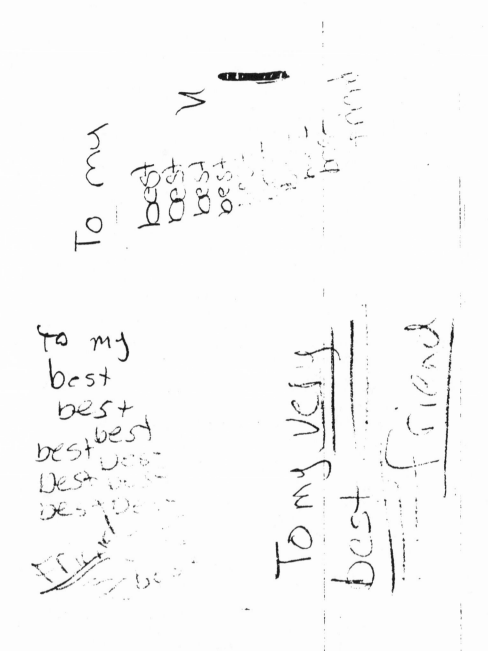

Figure 4a. Unofficial writing, front and back, from Richard, fourth grade.

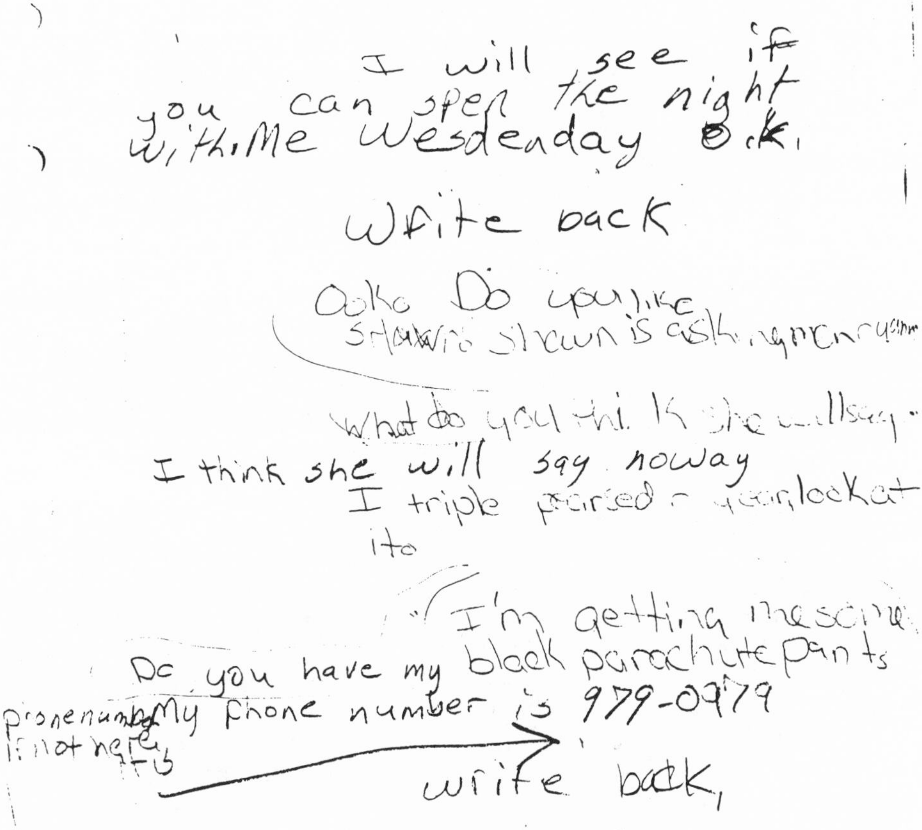

I will see if you can spen the night with me Wesdenday o.k.

Write back

O.K. Do you like
s(kawie shown is asking men yann

what do you thi 1k she willsay.
I think she will say noway
I triple paried - yearlocket
ito

I'm getting mescine
Do you have my black parachute pants
prsnenumbMy phone number is 979-0979
is not here's
write back,

Figure 4b.

Classroom writing can be seen within a continuum of control, a balance of ownership that sometimes tips toward the writer but often tips toward control by the curriculum. Although teachers assign or initiate the vast majority of official school writing, children assume control of some writing in school—both official and unofficial. As children gain more control in the amount, content, and format of writing, they are more likely to perceive it as their own even if a teacher has made the assignment. In other words, the more they compose, the more likely they are to assume ownership of a particular product.

2. *As children are permitted to compose more of a product, they are also more likely to be confused as to how to handle an assignment.* Children correctly perceive that a delicate balance is at play in school writing between the freedom to compose and the demands of the curriculum or expectations of the teacher. As a result, they construct representations of the requirements of the contexts within which they work, at times more successfully than at other times. In order to deal with confusion about expectations, children may fall back on strategies which worked for more curriculum-constrained writing; they may create their own means and goals for accomplishing the task (which may distort the teacher's means and goals for learning); they may properly interpret the approved boundaries and goals before, but often after, teacher intervention; or at times, they may become so involved in a particular product that the curricular demands become irrelevant.

When children recognize that their own representations were misguided or unacceptable, they may accede control or become confused. In short, freedom to compose may be essential if children are to sense ownership, but it is also more likely than completely constrained writing to mislead and confuse them.

3. *When children do assume control of writing, they have usually found their own meanings, purposes, audiences, and genres to work within.* Curriculum-surpassing writing which is self-sponsored, purposeful, alive, rich in meaning for both writer and audience would seem to be the goal, but rarely the outcome, of curriculum. Florio and Clark (1982) believe that curriculum-sponsored writing is "highly promising as a place to begin to construct that part of the school curriculum concerned with acquisition of both writing skills and values about literacy and its power" (p. 127), and the findings of the present study would support this assumption (see also Daiute & Dalton, this volume).

Yet, two problems hinder the ultimate and complete success of most curriculum-sponsored writing tasks. First, no matter how much freedom is encouraged, explicit or implicit boundaries usually exist. Children's representations of contextual demands may be abrogated at any time in the writing process leaving most children unwilling—after several attempts to define and act on their own representations—to experiment beyond accepted interpretations. In contradiction, however, most curriculum-sponsored writing tasks remain context-less, without clear genres, purposes, or audiences (Applebee, 1984; Britton et al., 1975; Hudson, 1984, 1986). Thus children are stuck in the double-bind of being forced to construct their own contexts for official writing while being repeatedly discouraged from doing so.

When children continue to act upon their own representations of an assignment, they tend to claim ownership and control of official writing.

If their representation of an assignment includes a clearly understood sense of a real need and context for writing—e.g., an audience, purpose, and genre—their writing is more likely to surpass the demands and constraints of the curriculum.

4. *Official writing can, and perhaps must, occur to enable real growth in writing.* Several researchers have shown that unofficial writing encourages wide experimentation and complete freedom for children to devise purposes, messages, and forms for writing. However, that may not be enough. In general, children's unofficial writing appears to be shorter and to involve less time, commitment, and energy than some official writing, especially when extended composing is permitted.

Rubin (1984) has suggested that development in writing may be seen at least in part as a matter of acquiring two things: "a wide repertoire of discourse functions and acuity in discerning the contexts of written communication" (p. 215). While unofficial writing among children may engender a sense of ownership and encourage a wide range of genres and purposes for writing, it is doubtful whether unguided, unofficial writing alone would help children acquire concepts of writing at a functional, adult level. For example, audience demands are far less important when the audience is immediately available to request clarification. Similarly, brief genres common to unofficial writing are unlikely to encourage a sense of mature reasoning or expressive detail.

Instead, it may be incumbent upon adults to provide situations, models, and insights which reveal adult needs and possibilities to children as they develop into writers able to deal with the varied contextual demands of adult written discourse. In short, official writing may be necessary to socialize children into the writing community of adults.

REFERENCES

Applebee, A. N. (1984). *Contexts for learning to write: Studies of secondary school instruction.* Norwood, NJ: Ablex.

Bissex, G. (1980). *GNYS at work: A child learns to read and write.* Cambridge, MA: Harvard University Press.

Bloome, D. (1984, October). *Gaining access to and control of reading and writing resources: K–8. Final report.* (ERIC Document Reproduction Service No. ED 251 830)

Boomer, G. (1985). *Fair dinkum teaching and learning: Reflections on literacy and power.* Montclair, NJ: Boynton/Cook.

Brandt, D. (1986). Toward an understanding of context in composition. *Written Communication, 3,* 139–157.

Britton, J., Burgess, T., Martin, N., McLeod, A., Rosen, R. (1975). *The development of writing abilities* (11–18). London: Macmillan Education.

Clark, C. M., & Florio, S. (1982). *Understanding writing in school: A descriptive study of writing and its instruction in two classrooms*. Final Report to the National Institute of Education (Grant No. 90840). East Lansing: Michigan State University, Institute for Research on Teaching.

Dyson, A. H. (1984a). Learning to write/Learning to do school: Emergent writers' interpretations of school literacy tasks. *Research in the Teaching of English, 18*, 233–264.

Dyson, A. H. (1984b). *Understanding the how's and why's of writing: The development of children's concepts of writing in primary classrooms. Vol. 2: The second grade data*. (ERIC Document Reproduction Service No. ED 249 535)

Dyson, A. H. (1985). Second graders sharing writing: The multiple social realities of a literacy event. *Written Communication, 2*, 189–215.

Emig, J. (1971). *The composing processes of twelfth graders*. (Research Report No. 13). Urbana, IL: National Council of Teachers of English.

Fiering, S. (1981). Commodore School: Unofficial writing. In D. H. Hymes (Ed.), *Ethnographic monitoring of children's acquisition of reading/language arts skills in and out of the classroom: Vol. 3*. Final report to the National Institute of Education. (ERIC Document Reproduction Service No. ED 208 096)

Florio, S., & Clark, C. M. (1982). The functions of writing in an elementary classroom. *Research in the Teaching of English, 16*, 115–130.

Glaser, B. G., & Strauss, A. L. (1967). *The discovery of grounded theory: Strategies for qualitative research*. New York: Aldine.

Goetz, J. P. & LeCompte, M. (1984). *Ethnography and qualitative design in educational research*. Orlando, FL: Academic.

Gundlach, R. A., Litowitz, B. E., & Moses, R. A. (1979). The ontogenesis of the writer's sense of audience: Rhetorical theory and children's written discourse. In R. L. Brown, Jr., & M. Steinmann, Jr. (Eds.), *Rhetoric 78: Proceedings of theory of rhetoric: An interdisciplinary conference* (pp. 117–129). Minneapolis: University of Minnesota Center for Advanced Studies in Language, Style, and Literary Theory.

Hansen, J., & Graves, D. H. (1986). Do you know what backstrung means? *Reading Teacher, 39*, 807–812.

Hudson, S. A. (1984). Contextual factors and children's writing. (Doctoral dissertation, University of Georgia). *Dissertation Abstracts International, 45*, 1669A.

Hudson, S. A. (1986). Context and children's writing. *Research in the Teaching of English, 20*, 294–316.

Langer, J. A. (1985). Children's sense of genre: A study of performance on parallel reading and writing tasks. *Written Communication, 2*, 157–187.

Martin, N. (1983). What are they up to? Some functions of writing. In N. Martin (Ed.), *Mostly About Writing* (pp. 63–99). Montclair, NJ: Boynton/Cook. Reprinted from A. Jones & A. Mulford, (Eds.). (1971). *Children Using Language*. Oxford: Oxford University Press.

Moffett, J. (1985). Hidden impediments to improving English teaching. *Phi Delta Kappan, 67*, 50–56.

Perl, S., et al. (1983). How teachers teach the writing process: Overview of an ethnographic research project. *Elementary School Journal, 84,* 19–24.

Rubin, D. L. (1984). The effects of communicative context on style in writing. In A. Pellegrini & T. Yawkey (Eds.), *The development of oral and written language: Readings in applied and developmental psycholinguistics* (pp. 213–231). Norwood, NJ: Ablex.

Whale, K. B., & Robinson, S. (1978). Modes of students' writings: A descriptive study. *Research in the Teaching of English, 12,* 349–355.

Chapter 3

Communicative Tasks and Communicative Practices: The Development of Audience-Centered Message Production

Barbara J. O'Keefe and Jesse G. Delia
University of Illinois, Urbana–Champaign

Many verbal communication skills are uniformly distributed in human communities: the overwhelming majority of people can manage an orderly sequence of turn taking in conversation; produce and recognize grammatical sentences; understand, remember, and retell a story; and so on. Even so, there is enormous individual variation in the success with which many communication tasks are managed. Individual differences in performance have been observed across a range of communicative tasks, involving such diverse processes as reference and description, persuasion and behavioral regulation, comforting and interpersonal problem solving, and conflict management and negotiation (for reviews, see O'Keefe & Delia, 1982, 1985; Burleson, in press); skill variations have been noted by researchers working with communication in both oral and written media (Gould, 1978, 1980; Kroll, 1983). Some differences in performance are attributable to general maturation and task-specific experience (Hidi & Hildyard, 1983; Higgins, 1976; Kroll & Lempers, 1981; Langer, 1985; Piché, Rubin, & Michlin, 1978; Prater & Padia, 1983). But the existence of a pattern of individual differences across communicative tasks, media, and educational levels (e.g., Applegate, 1980a, 1980b; Burleson, 1984; Kline & Ceropski, 1984; O'Keefe & Delia, 1979) suggests that at least some individual variation in message production and comprehension originates in the ways individuals learn to use communication, regardless of the specific form that communication might take.

In this chapter we present a systematic analysis of such a pattern of individual differences in communication competence. Our analysis is based on our program of research on individual differences in social cognition and message production. Until recently, our work has been similar to much of the research on written communication development that conceptualizes developmental and individual differences in competence as deriving from differences in audience awareness, audience adaptation, and cognitive egocentrism (Ede & Lunsford, 1984; Kroll, 1978; Nystrand, 1982; Rubin & Piché, 1979; Smith & Swan, 1978). We have explored the development and correlates of differences in the ability to produce messages that reflect sensitivity to audience needs and concerns in a wide range of tasks, involving both spoken and written communication (see Delia, O'Keefe, & O'Keefe, 1982; O'Keefe & Delia, 1982, 1985).

As our work has progressed, we have refined our understanding of differences in communicative performance. In particular, we have come to reject a traditional developmental analysis based on the concepts of social perspective-taking and audience adaptation, in preference to a view of message production as a process of practical reasoning used to derive messages that will serve goals (for an explicit discussion of this kind of rational, goal-based model of messages, see Brown & Levinson, 1978). In this chapter we summarize the major findings of our research program, discuss our shift away from the analysis of global message adaptations to a focus on goal integration, present an alternative analysis of individual/developmental differences in message production as reflecting differences in goals and differences in reasoning about how to achieve them, and discuss some implications of this alternative approach for research on social cognition and the development of communication across oral and written media.

INDIVIDUAL AND DEVELOPMENTAL DIFFERENCES IN AUDIENCE-CENTERED MESSAGE PRODUCTION

The idea that audience analysis and adaptation is the basis for effective and successful communication is very ancient, appearing in the oldest treatises on the art of rhetoric (Nystrand, 1982). This idea and its correlate, that message inadequacy may be attributed to a failure in audience adaptation, have been foundational to many theoretical analyses of communicative development. This concept has also played a major role in recent analyses of the composing process (Berkenkotter, 1981; Flower & Hayes, 1980).

The predominant model of audience adaptation employed in developmental and composition research locates audience-based message design in the process of role taking (e.g., Barritt & Kroll, 1978; Bereiter, 1980; Flavell, Botkin, Fry, Wright, & Jarvis, 1968; Kelley, Osborne, &

Hendrick, 1975; Swanson & Delia, 1976). Role taking, also called perspective taking, is a covert inference process in which the viewpoint of one's receiver is imaginatively constructed (see Selman, 1980; Shantz, 1975). This conception of role taking arose through the fusion of Mead's (1934) analysis of the social basis of thought and meaning with Piaget's (1955) analysis of development as proceeding from a state of egocentrism toward increasing perspectivism.

Simple models of role taking and its role in communication have been criticized on several counts. Most important, role taking does not operate uniformly across differing inference domains (Hudson, 1978; Kurdek & Rodgon, 1975; Rubin, 1978), and role taking does not appear to be a single logical operation, but rather an amalgamation of conceptually and empirically distinguishable mental operations (Delia & O'Keefe, 1979; Flavell, 1974; Shantz, 1975; Turiel, 1977). Moreover, efforts to show developmental relationships between role taking and communication performance have generally met with failure (Burleson, 1984; Dickson, 1981; Shantz, 1981; Shatz, 1978). Most researchers have concluded that in general the basis for successful message design is a set of skills that is tied closely to the message task, and not some generalized ability to decenter or imagine another's viewpoint (Ammon, 1981; Asher, 1979; Glucksberg, Krauss, & Higgins, 1975; Shantz, 1981; Shatz, 1978).

Even though our research program was influenced by both the general rhetorical image of message design as audience adaptation and by the widely shared developmental model of audience adaptation as role taking, it differed in several important ways from most research on the development of functional communication skills. First, we directed our research efforts at developing an analysis of communicative development, and of the role of sensitivity to audience, within realistic and potentially complex situations. We have been concerned with the kinds of communication tasks that Britton, Burgess, Martin, McLeod, and Rosen (1975) termed "transactional," tasks in which language is used instrumentally to have specific effects on other people. In such intrinsically person-centered situations (e.g., where persons want to teach or persuade; where the communication focuses on the feelings and interpersonal needs or problems of interactants; where the regulation of an individual's behavior is at issue), communicative choices (e.g., which of several types of persuasive appeals to use; whether to take a hard line in correcting a subordinate) will be guided by psychological representations of the audience (Applegate & Delia, 1980).

Second, our research has been distinctive in its reliance on a general method of qualitative message analysis that can be employed in evaluating messages produced in differing genres and within different media. Our procedures for message evaluation begin with identification of the

principal types or categories of messages produced when people address a specific task (e.g., making a request); the message types are then
hierarchically ordered in terms of their success at meeting task requirements, where task requirements are understood in terms of effects on
message recipients that must be produced to achieve success. Whereas
the categories or types of messages that have been identified vary as a
function of the specific message genre being investigated (e.g., comforting or regulating conduct), the model of functional adaptation against
which message types have been evaluated is applicable to any person-
centered task. This model (elaborated in the concept of "person-centered" message design) was first employed in research by Clark and
Delia (1976) on the development of persuasive communication strategies
and Applegate and Delia (1980) in their research on the development of
skill at regulating conduct and comforting. Subsequent work has refined
the basic model (e.g., Burleson, 1982; Delia, Kline, & Burleson, 1979),
applied it to the analysis of new message genres (e.g., instructional communication and parental communication; see Applegate, 1980b; Applegate, Burke, Burleson, Delia, & Kline, 1985), and extended it to the analysis of message rationales as well as message strategies (e.g., O'Keefe &
Delia, 1979). The development of a set of hierarchical message analysis
systems that can be used in evaluating messages (and rationales given
for them) produced for diverse tasks in terms of a common, underlying
model of transactional communication competence has enabled us to de-
tect patterns of individual and developmental difference that assert
themselves independently of task and medium.

A third distinctive feature of our research program is its analysis of
social cognition and its role in message production. In conceptualizing
the influence of social cognition on message production we shifted away
from a focus on social role taking toward concern with general processes
of interpersonal interpretation. Building upon a theoretical foundation
provided by Kelly's (1955) theory of personal constructs and Werner's
(1957) organismic-developmental theory, we viewed interpersonal impressions as the primary basis for person-centered message choices. The
cognitive systems employed in interpreting behavior and forming impressions change in regular ways over the course of development, and
changes in these attributes are associated with developments in communication skill. Among the most important aspects of interpersonal construct systems are those characteristics that reflect developmental
changes toward increasing complexity: With development interpersonal
construct systems become more differentiated, abstract, integrated, and
articulated.

We derived measures of these aspects of the interpersonal construct
system from the content and structural analysis of our subjects' free-

response descriptions of their friends and acquaintances. For example, construct differentiation was assessed by counting the number of attributes mentioned in free descriptions of peers. Construct abstractness was assessed through computing the number or proportion of constructs mentioned in impressions that designate psychological, motivational, or related abstract attributes (e.g., "honest," "insecure," "strong moral character"), as opposed to concrete behaviors or physical attributes (e.g., "has red hair," "walks like a duck"). Level of impression organization was determined by analyzing the pattern of structural relationships used in representing and reconciling inconsistency and variability in descriptions of others (highly organized impressions contain themes that connect specific attributes, e.g., "John is sometimes overly aggressive and bitingly sarcastic because he is socially insecure and feels awkward around people he doesn't know well"; relatively disorganized impressions mention attributes with no explicit connections or themes used to unify the impression, e.g., "John is aggressive, witty, and finds it hard to get to know people"). (For discussion of our approach to interpersonal cognition see Crockett, 1965; Delia, 1976; O'Keefe, 1984; Scarlett, Press, & Crockett, 1971. Research relating to the validity and reliability of our measurements is presented in Burleson & Waltman, in press, and O'Keefe & Sypher, 1981.)

In addition to de-emphasizing role taking and exploring the importance of other kinds of social cognitive developments that would be important to person-centered message production, we also reconceptualized the role of social cognition in guiding message production. Whereas many prior theorists (e.g., Flavell et al., 1968) conceived of social cognition as influencing message production through providing information about the specific message recipient that could be used in making message choices in a specific situation, we came to conceive of construct system development as playing several different roles in influencing communicative competence. In particular, we realized that interpersonal construct system development might influence message production through advancing the message producer's knowledge of *messages* rather than the message producer's knowledge of message *recipients*.

People rely on interpersonal construct systems to represent communication-relevant differences among message recipients; identifying a difference between differing recipients is a basis for audience adaptation. But in addition, the kinds of adaptive strategies that are constructed must be related to the kind of difference identified in recipients, since the nature of the construct used to discriminate among recipients also points to the alternative lines along which communicative adaptation can be made. For example, a message producer who classifies message recipients only in terms of relatively transitory and superficial attributes such as mood (e.g., "happy" versus "grumpy") can be expected to make different kinds of adaptations on the basis of that perceived difference than, say, a message producer who classifies recipients in terms of highly developed psychodynamic syndromes (e.g., "liberal, free thinking, and tolerant" versus "dogmatic and ego-involved in the issue").

We also recognized that even though the interpersonal construct system provides the basis for acquiring a repertoire of message strategies, constructs alone cannot produce strategies. Strategies for message design were seen to be acquired through processes of behavioral experimentation (trying alternative courses of action and shaping techniques in light of their success), observation of the message strategies of others, and direct influence by socializing agents such as parents and teachers (Applegate & Delia, 1980; Applegate et al., 1985; Delia & Clark, 1977).

Hence, development of the interpersonal construct system, by providing not only more constructs to use in representing message recipients and but also increasingly abstract, psychologically centered conceptions of message recipients, was thought to influence (a) the addition of strategies to one's repertoire (as differences among receivers are recognized, the need for additional strategies is created); (b) the quality of available communication strategies (as representations of receivers become increasingly abstract and psychological, so does the conception of a type of task, and hence the kinds of strategies that are included in the repertoire of strategies available for that task type); and (c) the use of available communication strategies (since recognizing the communication-relevant attributes of receivers governs the selection and implementation of strategies from the repertoire on any particular occasion).

These expectations have been supported in a host of studies carried out over the past 10 years. Since summaries of this work are available elsewhere (e.g., Burleson, in press; O'Keefe & Sypher, 1981), we need only highlight the major relevant findings here.

1. The relationship of construct differentiation and abstractness to the person-centeredness of message strategies and rationales for message choices has been demonstrated in cross-sectional designs to hold across the span of development from early childhood to adulthood for persuasive and regulative communication tasks (Burke & Clark, 1982; Clark & Delia, 1977; Delia & Clark, 1977) and for comforting tasks (Burleson, 1983, 1984). These relationships have also been found in a childhood developmental study using a longitudinal design (Delia, Kline, & Burleson, 1979).

2. The same pattern of correlations between construct system characteristics and the quality of message strategies obtains within age-
   homogeneous groups of children and adults (Applegate, 1980a;
   Applegate & Delia, 1980; Burke, 1979; Burleson, 1984; Kline, 1984;
   Kline & Ceropski, 1984; O'Keefe & Delia, 1979; Samter & Burleson,
   1984).

3. This general pattern of relationships holds across a wide range of
   transactional communication tasks. Many of the investigations we
   have discussed employed a common research paradigm: Subjects
   are presented with a hypothetical situation that specifies a communicative goal which the subject is asked to pursue by formulating a
   message. This method permits us to establish generality by having
   subjects respond to several situations of the type being studied in a
   given investigation. Moreover, this method permits the investigation of a diverse set of communicative objectives (such as situations
   requiring persuasion, comforting, gaining compliance with a behavioral directive, or protecting another's feelings). This method also
   has the advantage of permitting the elicitation of rationales for
   message choices, and we developed systems for assessing the au-
   dience-centeredness of rationales. The relationship between construct system characteristics and person-centeredness has been of
   a similar magnitude (correlations in the range from .40 to .80)
   across contexts and communicative objectives (e.g., Applegate,
   1982a, 1982b; Burleson, 1983; Clark & Delia, 1977; Delia, Kline &
   Burleson, 1979; O'Keefe & Delia, 1979; Samter & Burleson, 1984).

4. Similar relationships between construct system features and person-centeredness are found when subjects are asked to produce
   messages in role-played hypothetical situations and in actual interpersonal interaction contexts (e.g., Applegate, 1980b, 1982b). In
   most investigations with adult subjects, we have asked subjects to
   write what they would say if confronted with a given communication situation; in most investigations with child subjects, we have
   asked for oral responses. However, in some investigations, we
   have used written tasks in prototypical writing contexts. O'Keefe
   and Delia (1979), for example, asked subjects to persuade a target
   person by writing him or her a letter; they found the expected relationship between construct system properties and the number and
   quality of persuasive strategies. In short, comparable results are
   obtained for oral and written communication when subjects are
   asked to respond to a hypothetical communication situation; and
   the results produced through use of a hypothetical situation
   method are consistent with those obtained when subjects produce
   messages in actual social situations (see Applegate, 1980b, for a
   general discussion of relevant methodological issues).

SOURCES OF AUDIENCE-ADAPTATION IN MESSAGE DESIGN

As can be seen from the preceding summary, the focus of much of this research has been on assessing the generality and dependability of the developmental relationship between message production and social cognition. However, our recent research has attempted to specify the mechanism or process through which interpersonal construct system characteristics influence message production. In addressing this issue, O'Keefe and Delia (1982) argued that to understand exactly why interpersonal construct system development and impression formation processes are related to message production, clearer and more specific conceptions of the message features that covary with differences in impressions are needed. They criticized the use of relatively global dimensions, such as "person-centeredness" or "audience-adaptation," in constructing message analysis systems, pointing out that there are a great many different message characteristics which could be seen as embodying "person-centeredness" or "audience adaptation." They argued that one feature—the degree to which messages address multiple aims and objectives—had been most central to the model of person-centered message competence used in analyzing and evaluating messages.

Their reconstruction of the model of person-centered message competence led O'Keefe and Delia to hypothesize that construct systems play a role in eliciting the goals that drive message production in addition to (and perhaps instead of) a role in strategy acquisition, selection, or implementation. They proposed that construct differentiation and abstractness influence message production through influencing the kind and number of goals that a communicator construes as relevant in a situation, since people who represent social situations in a more multidimensional fashion are led to design messages addressing more situational goals simultaneously. Indirect evidence for their hypothesis was provided by Husband (1981), who found that managers' construct differentiation was related to success at attaining multiple managerial goals, and Kline (1984), who demonstrated that construct differentiation is associated with the propensity to pursue goals of showing respect and consideration to others while pursuing a regulative goal.

O'Keefe and Shepherd (in press) have provided direct evidence that messages vary systematically in multiple goal integration and have confirmed the hypothesis that goal integration is related to the differentiation of the interpersonal construct system. They undertook an investigation of strategies for goal integration that communicators used in face-to-face argumentative interactions, and developed a system for analyzing messages in terms of the goals being pursued and the manner in which competing and contradictory goals were managed. The act of disagreement, as analyzed by O'Keefe and Shepherd, involves an intrinsic risk of showing disrespect or inconsiderateness (i.e., of threatening "face"; see Brown & Levinson, 1978) and is potentially disruptive to coherent and sustained interaction. They analyzed argumentative messages in terms of the degree to which message producers employed strategies that integrated the goals of advancing the argument, supporting face, and sustaining interaction.

O'Keefe and Shepherd (in press) observed that persuaders used three different ways of managing the conflict among these goals: Some persuaders simply forged ahead with no effort to deal with more than one goal; some persuaders would pursue the main goal (persuasion) and handle the problem of showing respect and consideration by appending conventionally defined politeness forms, such as hedges, compliments, apologies, and accounts (for more detailed descriptions and examples, see Brown & Levinson, 1978) to their messages; and some persuaders included explicit contextualizing phrases and statements that redefined the situation as one in which there was no conflict among goals or wants. Subjects who were relatively low in construct differentiation were particularly unlikely to use either conventional politeness forms or situation redefinition. Subjects who were relatively high in construct differentiation used both conventional politeness and situation redefinition to support face and maintain interaction, but they were especially prone to employ situation-redefining strategies.

O'Keefe and Shepherd (in press) interpreted these three modes of goal management simply as three strategies for dealing with goal integration in an argumentative situation. However, O'Keefe (in press) has recently argued that these three different "strategies" result from individual differences in more fundamental processes guiding message construction and interpretation. She argued that differences in the adaptation of messages to meet task requirements cannot be reduced to differences in goals being pursued: For example, one can adapt messages to provide face-support either by incorporating conventional politeness forms or by redefining the situation. These two strategies function differently (O'Keefe and Shepherd, in press, found that they differed in their effects as well as their form), but the two kinds of strategies are designed to serve the same goals. This observation led O'Keefe to argue that an analysis such as that offered by O'Keefe and Delia (1982) or O'Keefe and Shepherd (in press) is necessarily incomplete, and to offer an extended model of the process of person-centered message production. Generalizing the findings of O'Keefe and Shepherd (in press), she hypothesized that simple expression, reliance on conventionalized forms of discourse action, and situation redefinition through linguistic manipulation reflect three different ways of generating messages to serve goals.

THE LOGIC OF MESSAGE DESIGN

O'Keefe (in press) offered a formal analysis of message variations due to differences in goals and differences in reasoning about how to achieve them. She argued that a two-dimensional analysis (minimally) is required to understand functional variation in messages: People differ in their motivations or goals, and people differ in the beliefs about communication ("message design logics") they employ in reasoning from goals to communicative means.

3 Communication-constituting Premises

An individual can employ any of three different fundamental premises in reasoning about communication (O'Keefe, in press). Each of these three premises is associated with a constellation of related beliefs and operations: a communication-constituting concept, a conception of the functional possibilities of communication, unit formation procedures, and principles of coherence. She called these systems of belief and practice "message design logics"; the three message design logics which she identified are called expressive, conventional, and rhetorical. The properties of the three message design logics are displayed in Table 1.

An *expressive* message design logic reflects the view that communication is a process of expressing and receiving encoded thoughts and feel-

Table 1. Characteristic Content and Function of the 3-Message Design Logics*

Characteristic	Expressive	Message Design Logic Conventional	Rhetorical
Fundamental premise	language is a medium for expressing thoughts and feelings	communication is a game played cooperatively by social rules	communication is the creation and negotiation of social selves and situations
Key message function	self-expression	secure desired response	negotiate social consensus
Temporal organization of messages	reaction to prior event	response specified by present context	initiate movement toward desired context
Message/content relation	little attention to context	action and meaning context-determined	communication process creates context
Internal message coherence	subjective and associative	intesubjective and rule-focused	intersubjective and style-centered
Method of managing face goals	editing	politeness forms	context redefinition

*This table was adapted from Fig. 1 in O'Keefe (in press).

ings. Characteristically, those using an expressive logic fail to distinguish between thought and expression; in producing messages, they
"dump" their current mental state, and they assume that others produce messages the same way. Expressive communicators do not generally alter expression systematically in the service of achieving effects,
nor do they ordinarily find anything other than "literal and direct"
meaning in incoming messages.

A *conventional* message design logic is based on the view that communication is a game played cooperatively, according to social conventions
and procedures. Within conventional logic, thought and expression are
related in a less isomorphic way by subordinating expression to achievement of effects. Language is treated as a means of expressing propositions, but the expressed propositions are specified by the social effect
one wants to achieve (utterance content is specified in the sense that uttering a given set of propositions under certain conditions counts as performing an action that is associated in sociocultural practice with the effect the message producer wants to achieve; for example, uttering a
certain kind of proposition under the right conditions counts as performing a request, and performing a request is a way to get certain
wants satisfied simply by exploiting conventional obligations among
persons; see Searle, 1969). Conventional communicators treat communicative contexts (the roles, rights, and relations that situations contain) as
having fixed parameters (that is, they take social structure—roles and
norms—to be both manifest to all and relatively inflexible) and design
messages by selecting what they take to be the contextually appropriate
actions.

A *rhetorical* message design logic reflects a view of communication as
the creation and negotiation of social selves and situations. The rhetorical view subsumes knowledge of conventional means to achieve goals
within the view that social structure is flexible and created through communication. Rather than seeing selves and situations as fixed by convention and rather than seeing meaning as fixed in form and context, self,
situation, and meaning are bound together in dramaturgical enactment
and social negotiation. For the rhetorical communicator, social reality is
created by what and how something is said or written, and so messages
are designed to portray a scene that is consistent with one's wants; the
discourse of others is closely interpreted to determine the nature of the
drama and the perspective they are enacting (for examples of rhetorical
message strategies and modes of interpretation, see Goffman, 1969).

O'Keefe (in press) offered a detailed analysis of the kinds of message
features that are diagnostic of each of these three message design logics
and designed a technique for classifying messages according to the
message design logic from which they derived. In an initial investiga-

tion, she found that level of message design logic (the three logics are developmentally ordered from expressive to conventional to rhetorical; see below) was strongly and positively related to the message producer's sex and level of interpersonal construct differentiation.

Message Design Logic and Methods of Goal Integration

Generalizing the findings of O'Keefe and Shepherd (in press), O'Keefe (in press) argued that competing and contradictory goals are managed differently by persons employing different message design logics. She illustrated this point by showing how the competing goals of regulating conduct and satisfying face wants can be handled. She pointed out that the expressive communicator does have a way of expressing his or her wants while also attending to face wants, and that is through editing the message or being less than frank or distorting the truth a bit. Likewise, there are conventional solutions to face-threatening situations derivable from a conventional message design logic. These essentially involve off-the-record communication and the incorporation of conventional politeness forms (e.g., apologies, compliments, hedges, excuses) in messages. Finally, a rhetorical logic of message design makes it possible to deal with face-threatening situations by redefining the situation, transforming one's social self or identity.

Based on this analysis of goal management strategies, O'Keefe also developed a system for classifying regulative messages as to the kind of goal set that (theoretically) motivated their design. Messages in which no goal was clearly served were classed as minimal; messages which clearly served only a single goal (either the regulative task or satisfying face wants but not both) were classed as unifunctional; messages which contained elements designed to serve both the task and face goals were classed as multifunctional. Consistent with O'Keefe and Delia's (1982) hypothesis, with findings by Kline (1984), and with the directly relevant work of O'Keefe and Shepherd (in press), she found that message goal structure was also positively related to the message producer's interpersonal construct differentiation: High-differentiation message producers were less likely to produce unifunctional messages; low-differentiation message producers were less likely to produce multifunctional messages.

IMPLICATIONS OF RATIONAL GOALS ANALYSIS

O'Keefe's analysis of the premises that individuals characteristically employ when making inferences about communication has a number of implications for the analysis of developing skills in spoken and written communication.

Explaining Styles in Message Production

This formulation offers a better interpretation of a suite of characteristics that tend to co-occur in messages. There are a number of message features which have been observed to covary and which seem to have some importance for the way messages work.

One of these characteristics is *a subjective as opposed to an objective sense of relevance*. Some messages manifest a subjective, personal, and idiosyncratic sense of relevance, as opposed to one that is objective, impersonal, and universal. In order to understand the connections among message elements one must know or guess the details of the message producer's unique experience and personal biography. To see what we mean by a subjective versus objective sense of relevance, consider the game "Password." In this game a target word is given to a message sender, who helps a message receiver guess the target word by providing one-word clues. Finding good clues (e.g., synonyms, antonyms, or words that co-occur with the target word in well-known expressions or phrases) requires not simply that an individual know common associations among words and ideas in the community, but also have the ability to distinguish common knowledge from idiosyncratic and personal associations (Asher, 1981). The practice of distinguishing between purely personal and public knowledge (especially in organizing messages) is what we mean by an *objective* sense of relevance.

We used "Password" as an experimental task in a pilot study (never published) we conducted some years ago, and what we mean by a *subjective* sense of relevance is well exemplified by the performance of one of our subjects. This fellow was given the word "bundle" as a target word, and the first clue he gave was the word "baby." Not surprisingly, the receiver was unable to guess the target word, even after better clues were subsequently provided. When the sender was asked why he used the clue "baby," he replied that he had once seen a movie called "The Baby Bundle" and so he naturally associated these two words. This message sender failed to distinguish between incidental associations that are a product of unique personal history, and associations that are current in the communicative practices of his social group.

A second feature of messages is *unfocused versus planful organization*. Many messages exhibit a "stream-of-consciousness" form of organization. The message seems to follow a flow of thought from association to association, with no goal guiding the production of message elements or their connection to each other. By contrast, some messages show a high degree of organization. Some overall goal (or set of goals) is being pursued through use of the message; this goal is actualized in a plan involving subgoals, with message elements clearly designed to serve the attainment of the subgoals that will actualize the plan and attain the primary goal. The following two messages exemplify this contrast; the subjects who provided them were asked to play the role of a group leader dealing with a procrastinating group member.

1. You stupid jerk. Why did you wait so long to tell us you were getting behind on your part. You screwed up all of our grades. You're gone. I'm getting you out of this group. Everybody else feels the same way. I hope you have fun when you take the class next semester.
2. Ron, you have to get it done. We can't finish the project until your part of it is done. How much is left to do? What have you gotten done? Have you outlined or have you any idea of the format or info for the part that isn't done? Well, do that tonight before the meeting and we'll finish it that way. Make sure the outline is clear so the others won't have to do more work than necessary.

The individual sentences in example (1) could be put in any order; they do not relate to each other as parts of a plan for dealing with the immediate problem (they do, of course, share a common theme). But the sentences in example (2) are directly related to an underlying plan for solving the problem, and are correspondingly arranged in a particular order.

Third, some messages employ *self-directed as opposed to audience-centered forms of expression*. In some messages, speakers use referential terms that are, from the audience's viewpoint, insufficiently explicit. The expression used would be adequately descriptive, informative, or referential only for someone who already knew most of what the speaker knows about the topic of discussion. Examples (3) and (4), both found in Britton et al. (1975), illustrate this contrast. Each example is a story written by a young child.

3. I was scared for I wasnt used to it and as well as that things wornte as nice as they are because my Mur Mun came But even from that day to never this I have never stayed to dinner (Britton et al., 1975, p. 42)
4. One day the Iron Man was in his scrap-metal yard when the little boy Hogarth came by.
   Hello Iron Man he said. I have come to ask your help. I will help if I can sais the Iron Man and his voice rumbaled like a thunder storm

only much louder. Well said Hogarth the sky is falling and it was
so low when we sent a space rocket up to the moon it only went
100 miles till it got there.
Well said the Iron Man if I help I will have to have a rocket made
me but I dont think we will be abel to make one.
Of cors we will said Hogarth (Britton et al., 1975, p. 43).

As Britton et al. point out, the forms of expression employed in example
(3) are insufficiently explicit for a reader; only a reader who already
knew what the writer was describing would understand the text. On the
other hand, example (4) is perfectly intelligible.

A number of observers have noted that these characteristics (and the
global effects that they produce, such as the apparent "autonomy" of
the discourse) covary in messages. The covariation in these properties
served as the basis for our own classifications of messages in terms of
listener adaptation and person-centeredness. This package of message
features has also been interpreted as reflecting egocentrism versus perspectivism in the Piagetian tradition; as the operation of a restricted versus an elaborated code (Bernstein, 1971); as development away from an
oral style and toward a textual style of language use (Olson, 1977; Olson
& Torrance, 1981).

Each of these earlier interpretations has confronted some major difficulty. As we pointed out earlier, the idea that communicative development reflects some general movement away from egocentrism has faced
severe criticism. Bernstein's distinction between an "elaborated" and a
"restricted" code confounds stylistic variations in speech (e.g., formal
versus informal style) with functional variations in messages; moreover,
it distinguishes only two modes of functioning in communication, and
even these do not appear to be clearly distinguishable using Bernstein's
formulation. The idea that these features are associated with oral versus
written media is contradicted by the fact that both oral and written
messages vary along this set of dimensions. And simply to label the
package of dimensions, as we have done in conceptualizing messages as
varying in "person-centeredness," is inadequate from the standpoint of
explaining how and why this set of features appears in messages.

The Dimensions of Developmental Change in Communication

The development of message design logic.   In O'Keefe's reanalysis of
individual and developmental differences in transactional communication performance, the progressive abstraction and integration of concepts of communication is the primary axis of growth in communication
skill. The three alternative message design logics form a natural devel-

opmental progression, and the mechanism of development is a straightforward consequence of the process of acquiring information about communication. At the most basic level, verbal means of communication are organized around the expression of ideas in linguistic units. Until and unless an individual acquires the principle of expression (the notion that there is or can be a direct correspondence between semantic intentions and verbal expressions) he or she cannot possibly crack the linguistic code. The use of linguistic expressions to perform actions involves the integration of an expressive system within a system of conventional rights and obligations (including distinctively communicative rights and obligations such as Grice's [1975] Cooperative Principle); spontaneous expression is supplanted by the expression required for the performance of conventionally defined actions. And the ability to reorder social situations through language requires that one come to have an abstract sense of communication as a process in which ways of speaking and acting are not merely responses to the situation but constitutive of the situation; conventionalized action is reorganized within an elaborated conception of communicative effects. So there is a natural order to these three message design logics; the expressive premise is a logical prerequisite to conventional functioning, and the conventional premise is a logical prerequisite to rhetorical functioning.

Message design logic and the development of communication competence. This way of conceiving of development in communication explains many of the observed characteristics of young children's speech and of unskilled writing: These characteristics reflect the operation of an expressive message design logic. Beginning writers and young children frequently give the appearance of inattention from the perspective of the audience; this appearance is arguably manifested in the sorts of message features identified above (a subjective sense of relevance, unfocused organization, self-directed forms of expression). But what produces these message features?

The common explanatory mechanism—a supposed lack of perspective-taking ability—provides a less satisfactory explanation than does O'Keefe's rational goals analysis. It is clear that perspective-taking ability is not a sufficient condition for effective message design. Persons operating with an expressive design logic will produce expressive messages regardless of how well they might understand the other person. Similarly, persons with a conventional design logic will produce messages that operate within established situation parameters regardless of their knowledge of the message recipient. In short, no matter what information an individual has that might be relevant to a communicative situation, message structure and content are constrained by the message producer's assumptions about what communication is and how it works; message design logic directs the message producer to the elements of his or her representations (of the situation, recipient, or world in general, no matter how developed or acquired) that are relevant to the process of message design, so that even if information is available, the message producer may not appreciate the relevance of the information for message construction.

In short, the concept of perspective taking cannot provide, by itself, a complete account of message production; something like the concept of message design logic is required to account for the organization and production of discourse. But once communicative development is understood as a process of constructing progressively more sophisticated message design logics, the concept of perspective taking is no longer required to explain developments in communication skills.

In order to move from an expressive to a conventional message design logic, an individual needs to develop only a model of social structure (knowledge of roles, rights, obligations, rules, norms, etc.) and recognize that utterances can be generated by contextual requirements rather than the stream of consciousness. And since conventional functioning rests on taking manifest social structures as given rather than negotiable, the concept of perspective taking is unnecessary to explain the acquisition of a sense of social structure (except in its most trivial and adevelopmental sense; see Cicourel, 1974).

To move from a conventional to a rhetorical message design logic an individual needs to develop a general theory of character and its expression in communicative action and achieve the recognition that modes of action create situations—context can be altered by messages, texts can create selves. Decisions about what sort of actions to undertake are governed by the requirements of the task being undertaken, and not by an individual model of the message recipient. For example, a message producer does not need to know anything particular about the audience to see that enacting a posture of tolerance and rational disinterest in an argument (as opposed to a posture that conveys high personal involvement and commitment) will make conflict resolution easier to achieve, but knowledge of how to enact these postures and knowledge of argument are both clearly required. In short, neither the sorts of information that are putatively acquired through perspective taking nor message adaptation based on the idea of individuating the message for the audience is required for highly adaptive "person-centered" message production.

Since it is possible for a person to have "perspectival" information (from perspective taking) and yet not produce adequate messages (because they have an expressive message design logic), and since it is also possible for a person to lack "perspectival" information and yet manage to produce adequate messages (because they have a suitable message design logic), one should expect that indices of perspective taking skill and communicative performance will not be strongly positively associated—and of course this is precisely what the empirical evidence indicates.

But there is a systematic, developmental relationship between dispositional characteristics attributed to potential message recipients and message adaptation. Delia and Clark (1977) investigated the relationship between attributed psychological characteristics (e.g., personality traits, motivations) and audience adaptation across the age span from early childhood into early adolescence. Young children were able to infer dispositional qualities from behaviors and attribute them to potential message recipients but did not recognize the relevance of these inferences to communication. Older children came to see the relevance of the attributed qualities to communication, but only as a basis for predicting communicative failure or making a nonfunctional expressive reaction. In late childhood and early adolescence children made use of inferred knowledge of the receivers—first in cross-situationally applied conventional message forms and then in recipient-specific message designs. In addition, while older children spontaneously produce audience-adapted persuasive messages, O'Keefe, Murphy, Myers, and Babrow (in press) found that young children do not produce such strategies even if the receiver's perspective is made highly salient through experimental cueing. And further, construct differentiation is related to skill in message adaptation even when no individuating information about the message target is available (Delia, O'Keefe, & Paulson, 1985). Realizing that both the relevance of knowledge to message design and the construction of messages that respond to task demands are governed by message design logic, and not by perspective taking, provides a ready account for these otherwise puzzling results.

Message design logic and the development of skill in writing. O'Keefe's account of communicative development is consistent with prior work on the development of written communication. In their classic study of the development of writing Britton et al. (1975) observed that the early stages of writing are characterized by a lack of planning and coherence and a failure to attend to the requirements of task and audience. As in O'Keefe's formulation, they call this primitive mode of message design "expressive." However, in Britton's formulation the term "expressive" is used in at least two ways, which are not clearly distinguished. The sense in which early stages of communication are expressive is the sense in which O'Keefe uses the term, in reference to a principle of message design.

But Britton et al. use the term expressive in a second sense to refer to the function a message is designed to serve. This gives rise to their curious view that young children's communication is characterized by the dominant function of expression and children come to pursue other functions, such as the transactional function, only later. This idea stands in sharp contradiction to the facts about early communicative behavior which, as Halliday (1973) has observed, is predominantly instrumental in function. The contradiction can be resolved by recognizing the distinction to be drawn between the goals or functions that a message is designed to serve and the message design principles that are used in deriving its form.

Bereiter (1980) has also offered a very similar characterization of the development of writing skills. He characterizes the early stages of writing development as "associative."

> The simplest system capable of producing intelligible writing is that which combines the two skill systems of fluency in written language and ideational fluency. The resulting skill of associative writing consists essentially of writing down whatever comes to mind, in the order in which it comes to mind. . . . (p. 83)

As Bereiter notes, this method of "associative writing" has also been observed by Flower (1979) in unskilled college student writers. She calls their products "writer-based" prose, and points out that in such prose ideas are characteristically presented in the order they were acquired by the writer rather than in an order suited to the reader. Bereiter reports that less talented high-school writers he has interviewed even describe their writing as a process of putting down thoughts as they come to mind.

Just as O'Keefe has argued that use of an expressive message design logic is succeeded by use of a conventional message design logic, so Bereiter observed that associative writing develops into "performative writing," in which the conventions of the medium are mastered. And, parallel to O'Keefe's analysis of the rhetorical message design logic, Bereiter observed that performative writing is followed by "communicative writing," a development that results from the integration of social cognition with knowledge of writing conventions.

Bereiter's interpretation of this developmental progression, however, differs in several important respects from O'Keefe's. Bereiter, like Olson (1977), mistakenly interprets this developmental progression as unique to writing, and reflecting movement away from an oral style of message design. As we emphasized earlier, one of the most important facts about this progression in the functional organization of messages is that it appears across media: Message producers develop toward a rhetorical style in the production of conversational messages just as in producing written messages.

Bereiter also fails to distinguish between the development of general structures for reasoning about message design and the application of message design to particular ends. So, for example, he argues that there are two more advanced stages in the development of writing, beyond the "communicative" (what O'Keefe calls "rhetorical") stage. In contrast to the first three stages, which all involve advances in the ability to generate and organize message content, the two additional stages represent specialized ways of using writing ("unified," which is described as "poetic," and "epistemic").

In Bereiter's model, the development of writing proceeds in a unitary series of stages: no provision is made for the possibility that development proceeds differently or at different rates for different types of writing. By contrast, O'Keefe's analysis is based on an analysis of the skills to be acquired and integrated in the mastery of a particular class of communicative tasks (transactional) and leaves open the possibility that for other classes of tasks the nature of development may differ.

Finally, Bereiter conceives of social cognition and its role in communication in traditional "role-taking" terms, thereby failing to recognize the other ways in which social inference processes can be modeled (e.g., in terms of psychological interpretation) and other ways in which advances in social cognition can be related to communication (e.g., through influencing the kind and number of goals pursued).

Thus, the progression in modes of message design that O'Keefe has observed has parallels in independent descriptions of the development of communication skills by Britton et al. (1975) and Bereiter (1980). The analysis of transactional communicative development as involving the progressive acquisition and integration of knowledge about communication and as being reflected in the successive use of expressive, conventional, and rhetorical principles of message design provides a foundation for understanding both oral and written communicative development and a superior alternative to the traditional conception that the qualities of unskilled communication derive from egocentrism and skillfulness from perspective taking.

The Relationship of Social Cognition to Communication

In O'Keefe's (in press) analysis the relationship between social-cognitive skills and communication skills is reconceptualized. In most existing formulations, social cognition is treated as a skill or set of skills independent of an individual's system for producing and interpreting messages. However, O'Keefe has argued that the relationship between social-cognitive skills and communicative performance is created when processes of social-psychological inference become integrated with other communication skills, forming one new integrated system. In short, the implication is that for rhetorical communicators, psychological inference, and attribution are functions not of some separate social-cognitive system that exists apart from and feeds information into communication, but of the communication system itself.

This immediately suggests an alternative explanation for the observed relationship between developments in impression formation processes and developments in communication. In contrast to the traditional view that developments in social cognition precede and cause developments in communication, this analysis suggests that the integration of functions in message production and message interpretation creates distinctive modes of understanding other people (increasingly abstract and psychological modes) and distinctive modes of organizing messages (increasingly directed at influencing covert psychological states). Attitudes, values, needs, and particularly character (e.g., personality traits, moral values) come to be systematically controlled as kinds of meaning within communication processes. So, for example, as persons achieve a rhetorical mode of functioning, they become much more predisposed to process incoming messages not simply for their relevance to the explicit goals of the situation, but also as expressions of character and relationship. This accounts for the finding that "high differentiation" perceivers (who predominantly display a rhetorical message design logic) are much more likely than "low differentiation" perceivers to pursue face protection spontaneously as a goal (Kline, 1984). It also accounts nicely for the fact that "high differentiation" perceivers do not show uniformly higher differentiation across all categories of content in their representations of others, but instead show selectively elaborated representations of relationally and characterologically (e.g., impressions of personality, interpersonal style, and social and moral attitudes) relevant aspects of others (O'Keefe, 1984; O'Keefe & Shepherd, 1986).

The integration of psychological interpretation into the message production system thus transforms the social world for rhetorical communicators. The messages they design and the messages they receive are richer in meaning, since the situation is seen to have many issues progressing simultaneously. The systematization of character that is created through this integration extends the message producer's control of the communication process. Once character is codified, understood as regularly expressed in particular kinds of ways, it can be strategically enacted to alter the relationships or requirements of a situation. Character (psychological traits, moral values, political attitude, interpersonal style, etc.) becomes a communication process, a matter of behavior design, and no longer equivalent to personality.

CONCLUSIONS

In this chapter we summarized research on the development of audience-centered ("person-centered") modes of interpretation and message design. We have argued that one primary development—the construction of increasingly complex, abstract, and integrated conceptions of communication—leads to many different functional developments: depth processing of information about character, targeting psychological and relational objectives in constructing messages, recognizing distinctions between subjective and objective information, and so on. In reconceptualizing the developmental relationship between social cognition and message production, we have rejected the simplistic view that information about the audience and situation constrain message production in favor of the view that audience, situation, and message are interrelated in the process of communication.

Hence, while we see many different aspects of message design as reflecting implicit concepts of audience, we nonetheless reject a view of message production as audience adaptation. This view (which Kroll [1984], calls "rhetorical" and which Ede & Lunsford [1984], identify with analysis of "audience addressed") treats the audience as playing a constraining or limiting role on what a communicator may say. The audience is seen as holding all the power in a communicative transaction; the message producer must take the position or adopt the persona that the audience will understand and accept. As Long (1980) has complained, such a view encourages superficial analysis of audience characteristics and preconceptions as a basis for selecting or editing message contents, and underemphasizes the importance of processes of invention directed at bringing a community of opinion into being.

In contrast to the view of audience as a limiting factor in message production, we have put forward a view of audience as participating in many aspects of message design processes. Rather than seeing the audience as independent of the process of communication, an obstacle to which the message producer must accommodate, we have come to view concepts of audience as implicit in, and intrinsic to, the most fundamental processes on which individuals rely in designing messages—in particular, derivation of goals from representations of situations and reasoning employed in generating messages to serve goals. As Ede and Lunsford (1984) and Rubin (1984) have emphasized, communication is complex and audience-based information and reasoning can play different roles in different aspects of the message production process. Our research has demonstrated that coming to view people (i.e., audiences) in certain kinds of terms confers on message producers a different kind of agenda in most transactional communication situations, an agenda that incorporates face goals as important priorities to be met. Moreover, our research has shown that as message producers come to reason in increasingly abstract and integrated ways about communication, they come to appreciate that the audience may be invoked and not simply addressed. Ong (1975) has argued that the writer's audience is always a fiction; his argument reflects the discovery of the power of language to create new symbolic orders. The discovery and exploitation of this resource in language is characteristic of rhetorical message design logic; this is the source from which the inventive superiority of rhetorical functioning derives.

Just as we have rejected a view of audience as a limiting factor in message design, so we have rejected a view of goal, genre, or situation as a limiting factor. For example, we argued earlier that Britton et al. (1975) were mistaken in their efforts to attribute functionally significant message variations simply to variations in goals. Similarly, we reject Kinneavy's (1971) view that aims are the ultimate determinants of message form and function (for a detailed critique on this point, see Fulkerson, 1984). We have argued that message genres (e.g., transactional messages) may be defined on the basis of the tasks that situations present and the kinds of competencies that are relevant to their accomplishment. But as our work has shown, individual message producers can vary in the specific aims and goals they set themselves within a given situation. So, for example, two teachers facing a similar situation—a student who has made an error—might operate from different sets of aims, with one teacher simply setting the goal of correcting the mistake while the other adopts a complex set of goals, including correcting the mistake, teaching a general principle that the correct answer exemplifies, and giving support and encouragement to the student. And further, as our work has shown, even people with the same aims can produce different messages because they reason differently about the way to achieve their goals with language. Situations do not specify goals; goals reflect the interaction between an individual message producer and the exigency to be addressed. And goals do not generate messages; they motivate and direct message production but do not dictate message forms.

If there is a limiting factor in message production, it is message design logic. Message design logic determines the way in which discourse can be adapted to serve a particular kind of aim as well as the relevance of information about audience to the process of message design. Development in message design logic opens up the possibility of invoking an audience or a situation to bring a new symbolic order into being. In short, the primary constraint on message production is neither audience nor task, but rather the quality of the message producer's reasoning about communication.

REFERENCES

Ammon, P. (1981). Communication skills and communicative competence: A neo-Piagetian process-structural view. In W. P. Dickson (Ed.), *Children's oral communication skills* (pp. 13–34). New York: Academic Press.

Applegate, J. L. (1980a). Adaptive communication in educational contexts: A study of teachers' communicative strategies. *Communication Education, 29,* 158–170.

Applegate, J. L. (1980b). Person- and position-centered teacher communication in a day care center. In N. K. Denzin (Ed.), *Studies in symbolic interaction,* (Vol. 3, pp. 59–96). Greenwich, CT: JAI Press.

Applegate, J. L. (1982a, February). *Construct system development and identity-management skills in persuasive contexts.* Paper presented at the Western Speech Communication Association convention, Denver.

Applegate, J. L. (1982b). The impact of construct system development on communication and impression formation in persuasive contexts. *Communication Monographs, 49,* 277–289.

Applegate, J. L., Burke, J. A., Burleson, B. R., Delia, J. G., & Kline, S. L. (1985). Reflection-enhancing parental communication. In I. E. Sigel (Ed.), *Parental belief systems: The psychological consequences for children* (pp. 107–142). Hillsdale, NJ: Erlbaum.

Applegate, J. L., & Delia, J. G. (1980). Person-centered speech, psychological development, and the contexts of language usage. In R. St. Clair & H. Giles (Eds.), *The social and psychological contexts of language* (pp. 245–282). Hillsdale, NJ: Erlbaum.

Asher, S. R. (1979). Referential communication. In G. J. Whitehurst & B. Z. Zimmerman (Eds.), *The functions of language and cognition.* New York: Academic Press.

Asher, S. R. (1981). Training referential communication skills. In W. P. Dickson (Ed.), *Children's oral communication skills* (pp. 105–126). New York: Academic.

Barritt, L. S., & Kroll, B. M. (1978). Some implications of cognitive-developmental psychology for research in composing. In C. R. Cooper & L. Odell (Eds.), *Research on composing: Points of departure* (pp. 49–58). Urbana, IL: NCTE.

Bereiter, C. (1980). Development in writing. In L. W. Gregg & E. R. Steinberg (Eds.), *Cognitive processes in writing* (pp. 73–93). Hillsdale, NJ: Erlbaum.

Berkenkotter, C. (1981). Understanding a writer's awareness of audience. *College Composition and Communication, 32,* 388–399.

Bernstein, B. (1971). *Class, codes, and control.* London: Routledge, Kegan Paul.

Britton, J., Burgess, T., Martin, N., McLeod, A., & Rosen, H. (1975). *The development of writing abilities* (pp. 11–18). London: Macmillan.

Brown, P., & Levinson, S. (1978). Universals in language usage: Politeness phenomena. In E. Goody (Ed.), *Questions and politeness* (pp. 56–323). Cambridge, England: Cambridge University Press.

Burke, J. A. (1979). *The relationship of interpersonal cognitive development to the adaptation of persuasive strategies in adults.* Paper presented at the Central States Speech Association Convention, St. Louis.

Burke, J. A., & Clark, R. A. (1982). An assessment of methodological options for investigating the development of persuasive skills across childhood. *Central States Speech Journal, 33,* 437–445.

Burleson, B. R. (1982). The development of comfort-intending communication skills in childhood and adolescence. *Child Development, 53,* 1578–1588.

Burleson, B. R. (1983). Effects of social cognition and empathic motivation on adults' comforting strategies. *Human Communication Research, 10,* 295–304.

Burleson, B. R. (1984). Comforting communication. In H. E. Sypher & J. L. Applegate (Eds.), *Communication by children and adults: Social cognitive and strategic processes* (pp. 63–104). Beverly Hills, CA: Sage.

Burleson, B. R. (in press). Cognitive complexity and person-centeredness communication: A review of methods, findings, and explanations. In J. C. McCroskey & J. A. Daly (Eds.), *Personality and interpersonal communication.* Beverly Hills, CA: Sage.

Burleson, B. R., & Waltman, M. (in press). The role category questionnaire measure of cognitive complexity. In C. H. Tardy (Ed.), *Instrumentation in communication research.* Norwood, NJ: Ablex.

Cicourel, A. (1974). *Cognitive sociology.* New York: Free Press.

Clark, R. A., & Delia, J. G. (1976). The development of functional persuasive skills in childhood and early adolescence. *Child Development, 47,* 1008–1014.

Clark, R. A., & Delia, J. G. (1977). Cognitive complexity, social perspective-taking, and functional persuasive skills in second- to ninth-grade children. *Human Communication Research, 3,* 128–134.

Crockett, W. H. (1965). Cognitive complexity and impression formation. In B. A. Maher (Ed.), *Progress in experimental personality research* (Vol. 2, pp. 47–90). New York: Academic Press.

Delia, J. G. (1976). A constructivist analysis of the concept of credibility. *Quarterly Journal of Speech, 62,* 361–375.

Delia, J. G., & Clark, R. A. (1977). Cognitive complexity, social perception, and the development of listener-adapted communication in six-, eight-, ten-, and twelve-year-old boys. *Communication Monographs, 44,* 326–345.

Delia, J. G., Kline, S. L., & Burleson, B. R. (1979). The development of persuasive communication strategies in kindergartners through twelfth-graders. *Communication Monographs, 46,* 241–256.

Delia, J. G., & O'Keefe, B. J. (1979). Constructivism: The development of communication in children. In E. Wartella (Ed.), *Children communicating* (pp. 157–186). Beverly Hills, CA: Sage.

Delia, J. G., O'Keefe, B. J., & O'Keefe, D. J. (1982). The constructivist approach to communication. In F. E. X. Dance (Ed.), *Human communication theory* (pp. 147–191). New York: Harper & Row.

Delia, J. G., O'Keefe, B. J., & Paulson, L. (1985). *Construct differentiation, situational complexity, and the analysis of individual differences in alternative modes of communicative action.* Paper presented at the annual meeting of the Speech Communication Association, Denver.

Dickson, W. P. (1981). Referential communication activities in research and in the curriculum: A metaanalysis. In W. P. Dickson (Ed.), *Children's oral communication skills* (pp. 189–204). New York: Academic.

Ede, L., & Lunsford, A. (1984). Audience addressed/audience invoked: The role of audience in composition theory and pedagogy. *College Composition and Communication, 35,* 155–171.

Flavell, J. H. (1974). The development of inferences about others. In T. Mischel (Ed.), *Understanding other persons* (pp. 66–118). Totowa, NJ: Littlefield.

Flavell, J. H., Botkin, P. T., Fry, C. L., Wright, J. W., & Jarvis, P. E. (1968). *The development of role-taking and communication skills in children.* New York: Wiley.

Flower, L. (1979). Writer-based prose: A cognitive basis for problems in writing. *College English, 41,* 19–37.

Flower, L., & Hayes, J. R. (1980). The dynamics of composing: Making plans and juggling constraints. In L. W. Gregg and E. R. Steinberg (Eds.), *Cognitive processes in writing* (pp. 31–50). Hillsdale, NJ: Erlbaum.

Fulkerson, R. P. (1984). Kinneavy on referential and persuasive discourse: A critique. *College Composition and Communication, 35,* 43–56.

Glucksberg, S., Krauss, R., & Higgins, E. T. (1975). The development of referential communication skills. In F. Horowitz (Ed.), *Review of child development research* (Vol. 4). Chicago: University of Chicago Press.

Goffman, E. (1969). *Strategic interaction.* Philadelphia: University of Pennsylvania Press.

Gould, J. D. (1978). How experts dictate. *Journal of Experimental Psychology: Human Perception and Performance, 4,* 648–661.

Gould, J. D. (1980). Experiments on composing letters: Some facts, some myths, and some observations. In L. W. Gregg & E. R. Steinberg (Eds.), *Cognitive processes in writing* (pp. 97–127). Hillsdale, NJ: Erlbaum.

Grice, H. P. (1975). Logic and conversation. In P. Cole & J. L. Morgan (Eds.), *Syntax and semantics, Vol. 3: Speech acts* (pp. 41–58). New York: Academic Press.

Halliday, M. A. K. (1973). *Explorations in the functions of language.* New York: Elsevier.

Hidi, S., & Hildyard, A. (1983). The comparison of oral and written productions in two discourse modes. *Discourse Processes, 6,* 91–105.

Higgins, E. T. (1976). Social class differences in verbal communicative accuracy: A question of "which question?" *Psychological Bulletin, 83,* 695–714.

Hudson, L. M. (1978). On the coherence of role-taking abilities: An alternative to correlational analysis. *Child Development, 49,* 223–27.

Husband, R. L. (1981). *Leadership phenomenology: A case study and social cognitive correlates.* Unpublished doctoral dissertation, University of Illinois, Urbana–Champaign.

Kelley, R. L., Osborne, W. J., & Hendrick, C. (1975). Role-taking and role-playing in human communication. *Human Communication Research, 1,* 62–74.

Kelly, G. A. (1955). *A theory of personality.* New York: W. W. Norton.

Kinneavy, J. L. (1971). *A theory of discourse.* New York: W. W. Norton.

Kline, S. L. (1984). *Social cognitive determinants of face support in persuasive messages.* Unpublished doctoral dissertation, University of Illinois at Urbana–Champaign.

Kline, S. L., & Ceropski, J. M. (1984). Person-centered communication in a medical practice. In J. T. Wood & G. M. Phillips (Eds.), *Human decision-making.* Carbondale, IL: Southern Illinois University Press.

Kroll, B. M. (1978). Cognitive egocentrism and the problem of audience awareness in written discourse. *Research in the Teaching of English, 12,* 269–81.

Kroll, B. M. (1983). Antecedents of individual differences in children's writing attainment. In B. M. Kroll & G. Wells (Eds.), *Explorations in the development of writing* (pp. 95–118). New York: Wiley.

Kroll, B. M. (1984). Writing for readers: Three perspectives on audience. *College Composition and Communication, 35,* 172–185.

Kroll, B. M., & Lempers, J. D. (1981). Effect of mode of communication on the informational adequacy of children's explanations. *Journal of Genetic Psychology, 138,* 27–35.

Kurdek, L. A., & Rodgon, M. M. (1975). Perceptual, cognitive, and affective perspective taking in kindergarten through sixth-grade children. *Developmental Psychology, 11,* 643–650.

Langer, J. A. (1985). Children's sense of genre: A study of performance on parallel reading and writing tasks. *Written Communication, 2,* 157–188.

Long, R. C. (1980). Writer–audience relationships: Analysis or invention? *College Composition and Communication, 31,* 221–226.

Mead, G. H. (1934). *Mind, self, and society.* Chicago: University of Chicago Press.

Nystrand, M. (1982). Rhetoric's "audience" and linguistics' "speech community": Implications for understanding writing, reading, and text. In M. Nystrand (Ed.), *What writers know: The language, process, and structure of written discourse* (pp. 1–30). New York: Academic.

O'Keefe, B. J. (1984). The evolution of impressions in small working groups: Effects of construct differentiation. In H. L. Sypher & J. L. Applegate (Eds.), *Communication by children and adults: social cognitive and strategic processes* (pp. 262–291). Beverly Hills, CA: Sage.

O'Keefe, B. J. (in press). The logic of message design: Individual differences in reasoning about communication. *Communication Monographs.*

O'Keefe, B. J., & Delia, J. G. (1979). Construct comprehensiveness and cognitive complexity as predictors of the number and level of strategic adaptation of arguments and appeals in a persuasive message. *Communication Monographs, 46,* 321–340.

O'Keefe, B. J., & Delia, J. G. (1982). Impression formation and message production. In M. E. Roloff & C. E. Berger (Eds.), *Social cognition and communication* (pp. 33–72). Beverly Hills, CA: Sage.

O'Keefe, B. J., & Delia, J. G. (1985). Psychological and interactional dimensions of communicative development. In H. Giles & R. N. St. Clair (Eds.), *Recent advances in language, communication, and social psychology* (pp. 41–85). Hillsdale, NJ: Erlbaum.

O'Keefe, B. J., Murphy, M. A., Myers, R. A., & Babrow, A. S. (in press). The development of persuasive communication skills: The influence of developments in interpersonal constructs on the ability to generate communication-relevant beliefs and on level of persuasive strategy. *Central States Speech Journal.*

O'Keefe, B. J., & Shepherd, G. J. (1986). *Content and structure of impressions formed during face-to-face persuasive interactions.* Unpublished paper, University of Illinois, Urbana–Champaign.

O'Keefe, B. J., & Shepherd, G. J. (in press). The pursuit of multiple objectives in face-to-face persuasive interactions: Effects of construct differentiation on message production. *Communication Monographs.*

O'Keefe, D. J., & Sypher, H. E. (1981). Cognitive complexity measures and the relationship of cognitive complexity to communication. *Human Communication Research, 8,* 72–92.

Olson, D. (1977). From utterance to text: The bias of language in speech and writing. *Harvard Educational Review, 47,* 257–81.

Olson, D. R., & Torrance, N. (1981). Learning to meet the requirements of written text: Language development in the school years. In C. H. Fredericksen & J. F. Dominic (Eds.), *Writing: The nature, development, and teaching of written communication: Vol. 2, Writing: Process, development, and communication* (pp. 235–255). Hillsdale, NJ: Erlbaum.

Ong, W. J. (1975). The writer's audience is always a fiction. *Publications of the Modern Language Association, 90,* 9–21.

Piaget, J. (1955). *The language and thought of the child* (M. Gabain, Trans.). New York: World Publishing. (Originally published 1926)

Piché, G. L., Rubin, D. L., & Michlin, M. L. (1978). Age and social class in children's use of persuasive communicative appeals. *Child Development, 49,* 773–780.

Prater, G. L., & Padia, W. (1983). Effects of modes of discourse on writing performance in grades four and six. *Research in the Teaching of English, 17,* 127–134.

Rubin, D. L. (1984). Social cognition and written communication. *Written Communication, 1,* 211–246.

Rubin, D. L., & Piché, G. L. (1979). Development in syntactic and strategic aspects of audience adaptation skills in written persuasive communication. *Research in the Teaching of English, 13,* 293–316.

Rubin, K. H. (1978). Role taking in childhood: Some methodological considerations. *Child Development, 49,* 428–33.

Samter, W., & Burleson, B. R. (1984). Cognitive and motivational influences on spontaneous comforting behavior. *Human Communication Research, 11,* 231–260.

Scarlett, H. H., Press, A. N., & Crockett, W. H. (1971). Children's descriptions of peers: A Wernerian developmental analysis. *Child Development, 44,* 439–453.

Searle, J. R. (1969). *Speech acts.* Cambridge, England: Cambridge University Press.

Selman, R. L. (1980). *The growth of interpersonal understanding: Developmental and clinical analyses.* New York: Academic Press.

Shantz, C. U. (1975). The development of social cognition. In E. M. Hetherington (Ed.), *Review of child development research* (Vol. 5). Chicago: University of Chicago Press.

Shantz, C. U. (1981). The role of role-taking in children's referential communication. In W. P. Dickson (Ed.), *Children's oral communication skills* (pp. 85–104). New York: Academic.

Shatz, M. (1978). The relationship between cognitive processes and the development of communication skills. In B. Keasey (Ed.), *Nebraska symposium on motivation, 1977* (1–42). Lincoln: University of Nebraska Press.

Smith, W. L., & Swan, M. B. (1978). Adjusting syntactic structures to varied levels of audience. *Journal of Experimental Education, 46,* 29–34.

Swanson, D. L., & Delia, J. G. (1976). *The nature of human communication.* Chicago: Science Research Associates.

Turiel, E. (1977). Distinct conceptual and developmental domains: Social convention and morality. In C. B. Keasey (Ed.), *Nebraska symposium on motivation, 1977* (pp. 77–116). Lincoln: University of Nebraska Press.

Werner, H. (1957). The concept of development from a comparative and organismic point of view. In D. E. Harris (Ed.), *The concept of development* (pp. 125–148). Minneapolis: University of Minnesota Press.

Chapter 4

Using What They Know: 9-, 13-, and 18-Year-Olds Writing for Different Audiences*

Sheryl I. Fontaine
Claremont McKenna College

INTRODUCTION

The psychological concepts of egocentric and decentered thought often supply the theoretical framework for research on how individuals adjust their writing to the needs, interests, or knowledge of an audience. First investigated by Piaget (1926/1955), these concepts refer to the individual's ability to take account of others' viewpoints. According to Piaget, until children reach the stage of decentered thinking, they are unable to consider perspectives other than their own. Conversely, children who can take into account others' perspectives have decentered, are no longer rstricted by the solipsistic perspective of egocentrism. Piaget believed that some children retain their egocentric perspective for as long as 12 years. However, current research suggests that Piaget's belief may have been inaccurate; young children may be no more egocentric than adults (Borke, 1983; Butterworth, 1980; Cox, 1980; Donaldson, 1978; Light & Simmons, 1983; Ochs, 1979; Robinson & Robinson, 1982, 1983). According to this new analysis, Piaget's experimental tasks use words and situations that are unfamiliar to the children being tested. When the tasks are framed in situations familiar to children, in words they understand, evidence of egocentrism virtually disappears.

We might assume, from Piaget's original formulation and from this revised understanding of children's egocentricity, that children who

* This study was funded in part by a dissertation fellowship and a humanities grant from the University of California, and an NCTE Research Grant. The author would like to thank friends and colleagues at the State University of New York at Stony Brook and at the University of California, San Diego, for responding to drafts of this essay.

99

recognize alternate perspectives are then well equipped to *write* with regard to these perspectives. We might expect these individuals to translate into their texts syntactical or semantic adjustments appropriate to their own perspective and to that of the audience. But, contrary to these expectations, researchers have found that young writers are often much less able than older ones to adapt their writing to an audience (Bracewell, Scardamalia, & Bereiter, 1978; Crowhurst & Piché, 1979; Kroll, 1978; Rubin & Piché, 1979; Scardamalia, Bereiter, & McDonald, 1977; Smith & Swan, 1978). If youngsters are indeed less egocentric than had been presumed, then why does their sense of others' perspectives not regularly appear as audience adaptations in their writing?

It would seem that being able to decenter is a necessary but not sufficient attribute for individuals to adjust their writing for an audience. The writing task itself, for example, can either hinder or aid writers' attention to audience needs. Kroll (1984) found that there was no "blatant disregard for the reader's needs" (p. 424) when 9-year-old writers were given an appealing occasion and a plausible context for writing. But even after carefully designing a task, some researchers in speech (Alvy, 1973; Delia & Clark, 1977; Flavell, Botkin, Fry, Wright, & Jarvis, 1968; see also O'Keefe & Delia, this volume) and in writing (Atlas, 1979) have identified instances where subjects recognize the audience's perspectives, but do not translate these perspectives into adjustments in their speech or writing.

The research study described in this chapter was initially designed to explore several questions about writers' awareness of their audience. In this report I will focus on a single question: As writers get older, does the relationship change between what they know about the audience and the way they use this knowledge in their writing? Underlying this question are several related ones. Do writers construct their audiences? How do writers fill in incomplete descriptions of the audience? What do writers believe about how these audiences see the world? What do they assume each audience knows or does not know about them or about the topic of their writing? And once we see how writers have constructed the audiences, can we then see them using this information in their writing?

METHODS

Subjects and Data Collection

In a case study of 12 students from the San Diego, Calif., school system (Fontaine, 1984a), I asked four 9-year-olds, four 13-year-olds, and four 18-year-olds to write two letters about different memorable places that they had visited, the first one in response to an imagined letter from a good friend, the second one in response to an imagined letter from a great-aunt from France whom they had never met. The subjects were recommended by their teachers as being writers of average to good ability who were willing to take part in my project. This writing task and audience combination was, in part, chosen on the basis of several pilot studies that had tested a variety of topics and audiences with subjects at all three age levels.

These two audiences were also selected because I wanted to have somewhat realistic audiences—it is not uncommon for children to write letters to friends or to older relatives—and because I wanted two audiences whose differences were complex. A friend and an unknown aunt from France could be different from each other and from the writers in several ways: age, sex, interests, nationality, familiarity with the writer, and familiarity with the place the writer visited. I was not interested in whether my subjects would make adjustments for audience characteristics that I had previously identified. Rather, I wanted to give them room to explore the possible differences, letting them reveal which audience characteristics seemed important to them.

The writing tasks were separated by one week and were preceded by a training task which introduced writers to the procedures of the study (Fontaine, 1984b). These procedures included a composing-aloud protocol of the writing tasks and a stimulated recall discussion following each. After the two tasks were completed, writers responded to a series of oral interview questions focusing on the differences between writing to a good friend and writing to an unknown aunt from France. The interviews were intended to elicit any remaining information about the subjects' perception of the audience: the relationship between the audience and the content or style of the letters, the relative difficulty of writing to each audience, and the particular adjustments made for each audience. Six questions were asked. Numbers 1, 2, and 4 were asked twice—once in reference to each audience:

1. What will the friend/great-aunt find most impressive about this place?
2. How do you think the place in your essay might compare with what your friend/great-aunt saw?
3. Who was it easier to write for—a friend or a great-aunt? Why?
4. Did you believe your friend/great-aunt was already familiar with the place you wrote about? Did this make any difference in your letter?
5. Why did you write about these two places?
6. How did writing for a friend or great-aunt make a difference to your letters?

By collecting several kinds of information—writing protocols, stimulated recalls, interviews, and the written product—I could analyze various moments during and after composing, to see what the writers said about the audience's perspective and what specific textual or stylistic decisions writers made based on the two audiences.

Analysis of Data

Once the data were collected, they were transcribed for analysis. The thinking-aloud-writing protocol transcripts were first divided into the three major activities which take place during composing aloud: writing, reading from the evolving text or the research task, and thinking aloud. Because I wanted to analyze the thinking aloud portions of the transcripts, these sections were then broken into units of analysis called "thinking-aloud statements," instances of the writer thinking-aloud about a single topic. A thinking-aloud statement can be an incomplete phrase ("Oh, so my audience is. . ."); a sentence ("I don't think I spelled that right."); or a series of sentences ("There were so many people there, but it was still beautiful. I mean, it was still real pretty. It was like something I'd never seen before."). Those statements which made reference to or about the intended audiences were then identified and sorted into five categories (adapted from Berkenkotter, 1981):

1. *Analyzing the audience's knowledge or constructing the audience's characteristics.* ("In this letter I'm going to pretend that my friend knows that I left, but he didn't know where I went.")
2. *Setting goals and naming plans in relation to the audience.* ("Well, since I've never met her before, maybe I should tell her something about myself.")
3. *Evaluating the letter's content or style in relation to the audience.* ("I don't know if [the great-aunt from France] would know where [the Grand Canyon] is.")
4. *Reviewing, editing, or revising written text in relation to the audience.* ("This is a letter, right? I *am* writing a letter to my friend? That's good. That's cool.")
5. *Evaluating content and style or setting goals with relation to the secondary audience—the investigator.* ("I wonder if I—if [investigator's name] wants me to write like—It's a letter. Maybe I should include a part about—like 'I hope you're fine'.")

After being trained, a reader was asked to divide into statements the thinking-aloud portion of protocol transcripts from each grade level and then to identify and code the audience-related references made in those comments. In the first part of this reliability check, dividing the transcripts into discrete statements, the reader and I reached a level of 95%, 87%, and 95% exact agreement for the 9-year-old, 13-year-old, and 18-year-old writers respectively. In the second part of the reliability check, coding for audience-related statements, there was 100%, 80%, and 83% exact agreement. The older subjects made more indirect references to the audience than the younger ones, and the trained reader tended to be more generous than I had been in her interpretation of subjects' comments.

The stimulated–recall transcripts were coded for instances of unsolicited references subjects made about the audience or the effects of the audience. There were two kinds of audience-related references. (1) Subjects explained comments that they had made in their thinking-aloud protocols: [In reference to a comment in the protocol about getting "off track."] "If it's someone that you write to often, they usually know your personality well enough that you don't really need to explain what you're saying a whole lot." (2) Subjects explained decisions that they had not verbalized in their thinking-aloud protocols: "I don't like to try to convince someone because if she wrote to me then she would be happy that she had been there and then that place would be special to her, so I wouldn't challenge her."

Because I used the information from the stimulated recalls anecdotally, to illustrate what subjects said about the audience rather than to make quantitative comparisons, my reliability check was informal. I asked several readers to identify audience-related comments in the stimulated–recall protocols and found that they noted the same instances as I had.

The interview questions were designed to elicit straightforward responses about perceptions of the audience; they were used anecdotally and needed no reliability check.

RESULTS

In order to explore the relationship between what writers know about the audience and how they use this knowledge in their writing, results of the analysis will be presented in two ways. First, I will describe the quantitative results of the protocol analysis to give a general feeling for the attention that writers paid to audience during their writing process. Second, taking advantage of the detailed perspective provided by a case study, I will outline from the verbal data what the different-age writers know about the audience and then turn to both the verbal data and the writing tasks for evidence of how writers use this knowledge. In reporting my results, the 13- and 18-year-olds will be referred to as a single group of "older" writers. This is not to suggest that the two groups are identical. Rather, in terms of what these writers say about audience and how they use this information, there are more similarities between the two groups than there are differences. And, as I will point out, those differences that do appear are differences of degree, not of kind.

Quantitative Results of the Writing Protocol Analysis

The figures in Table 1 indicate that when writing to their great aunt from France, writers at all three ages made relatively more audience-related thinking-aloud statements than they did when writing to their good friend. The audience that would conceivably know less about the writers, the great-aunt, elicited from writers more audience analysis, and more statements about the audience in relation to goal setting and reviewing unwritten and written text. The only category where this was not true was goal setting and reviewing with respect to the investigator. In this category writers made more statements when writing to their good friend.

Table 1. Relative Frequency of Statements in Each Category of Audience-Related Protocol Statements

| | Categories of Audience-related Protocol Statements | | | | | |
| | 1 | 2 | 3 | 4 | 5 | |
Age	Analyzing or Representing the Audience	Setting Goals	Reviewing Unwritten Text	Reviewing Written Text	Goal Setting and Reviewing with Respect to the Investigator	Total
18-year-olds						
Task 1[a]	1.27	3.18	.94	.51	2.41	8.39
Task 2[b]	1.59	7.06	1.77	.46	1.14	12.75
13-year-olds						
Task 1	4.00	7.43	.57	.57	2.28	14.86
Task 2	6.65	9.84	1.64	0	.81	18.85
9-year-olds						
Task 1	0	6.80	.97	0	0	7.77
Task 2	5.17	6.90	0	0	0	12.06
Total						
Task 1	1.60	4.23	.94	.47	2.16	9.39
Task 2	2.91	7.59	2.10	.32	.97	13.89

Note: The values represent the number of audience-related statements per 100 total statements in the thinking-aloud protocols.
[a]Task 1 is the letter to the good friend.
[b]Task 2 is the letter to the great-aunt.

By adding the numbers in the last column of Table 1 we find that the 9-year-olds made only 19.83 audience-related statements per 100 statements in their writing protocols. The 18- and 13-year-old subjects made 21.41 and 33.71 audience-related statements respectively.

That the 13-year-olds made the largest number of audience-related statements is somewhat misleading. If we look from the table to the actual protocols, we see that while the 18-year-olds may have fewer statements, they tended to make longer, more complex statements than the 13-year-olds. For example, here are protocol statements from a 13-year-old and an 18-year-old. Each writer is setting goals for what to say to the great aunt, but the older writer, Sharon, also thinks about why she is setting these goals:

> OK, tell her about the lakes, then I could tell her about the house that my cousins live at (Eddie 1A).

> Since I don't know her then I'd probably want to thank her for the letter, and I wouldn't go into what I'm going to explain as rapidly as I would with someone else because they, they know me and they know what I've been doing, and they would know why I went somewhere (Sharon 1B).

The differences among the three age groups is more interesting when we consider that many of the 9-year-olds' "statements" appear in the form of unanswered questions which make reference to the audience, such as, "What do I tell him next?" When questions like this appear in the older writers' protocols, they are always followed immediately by an answer. If these unanswered questions are discounted, then the 9-year-olds' total is reduced to 16.17 statements per 100. While the sample is too small to calculate statistical significance, it is clear that the 9-year-old writers made fewer audience-related statements than did the 13- and 18-year-old writers.

Another consideration in the quantitative analysis is how the audience-related statements are distributed among the five categories. The statements of the 13- and 18-year-olds are distributed among all five categories. The 9-year-olds' statements appear in only three of the five categories—analyzing or representing the audience, setting goals, and reviewing unwritten text—and in no more than two categories in a single writing task.

9-Year-Old Writers

What writers know about the audience.   I will detail the results from three 9-year-old subjects: Beth, Jim, and Tracy. (Subjects' real names have all been changed.) The fourth 9-year-old writer interpreted the task in such a way that her data are anomalous for this report. (Rather than writing *to* her great-aunt, this subject wrote a letter *about* her great-aunt.)

The 9-year-old writers made several comments during their stimulated recall discussions and interviews in which they referred to the audiences' interests, location, knowledge of the place being described, and experience. Some writers explained, for example, how the places they wrote about would interest their audience. Beth told me:

> I chose [Disneyland] because I felt that [my friend] would like—because I thought it was a kid, so he'd like a place more like play. And I thought this aunt [the intended audience] would like to know about my other aunt [the topic of the letter] (Interview).

Tracy explained that she had been imagining her friend Linda when she wrote about going to the Pacific Ocean. According to Tracy, Linda enjoys the beach:

> When we go to the beach she always brings her bogie board, and she always goes and plays with it. I just remembered, you know, I took this friend out, and she liked it [the Pacific Ocean] a lot, so I thought I'd write about it (Stimulated recall 1A).

Jim wrote to his friend about camping in the Sierras and to his aunt about going to Cabrillo Monument (a national monument and whale-watching site in San Diego). He defended his choices of topic in terms of what would have impressed his audiences. Jim believed that his friend would be impressed by the bears he had seen on the camping trip. His great-aunt from France, "if she knows about Cabrillo monument," would be impressed by the fact that he had gone to Cabrillo Monument and *not* seen any whales.

Jim also made a connection between the location of his audience and economic conventions when he explained to me why his letter to a friend was so much longer (five pages) than his letter to his great-aunt from France (six lines):

> [The letter to my great aunt] is more like what most people would write for a letter because it's not very much. And it—for most people it'd cost a lot for them to send even just a little letter to a place that far away. And they wouldn't write too much either if they were writing to that place (Stimulated recall 1B).

Because I thought there might be a relationship between the writers' audience and the way writers presented their topics, I did not specify a discourse type for the original task. Rather than telling writers how to present the information in their letters, I described several ways that it could be done: tell a story about something that happened when visiting the important place; describe the important place; or try to convince the reader that the place is more memorable than anything he or she could have seen.

In a last example, Beth talks about the relationship between her knowledge of the audience and the way she presented her information to that audience. During our stimulated recall discussion of the letter to a friend, Beth explained that because she lacked certain information about her friend's point of view, she chose not to convince her friend that the place she saw was more memorable: "It's just that I was supposed to [reads from task] 'try to convince your friend' that we went somewhere better like. And I didn't know where he went."

How writers use their knowledge of audience.   The above description suggests that the 9-year-olds filled in for themselves details about their audiences' perspective, about their interests, experience, location, and familiarity with them. However, in other portions of their verbal reports, these young writers sometimes supplied contradictory accounts of their audiences. There was also little evidence of these other perspectives in the children's letters. While the 9-year-olds appear to be able to construct an audience and see parts of the world in relation to the audience, they often sustain neither a consistent view nor a consistent use of the audience throughout the research task—from writing protocol, to letter, to stimulated recall, to interview.

Recall Jim's explanation for why one of his letters was so much shorter than the other—that it would have cost too much to send a long letter all the way to France. Jim later contradicts himself, revealing a different explanation. When writing the long letter to his friend, Jim said he was "busy wanting to get out of math class" (Stimulated recall 1A). In contrast, Jim explained to me after completing his six-line letter to his great-aunt that he had been in a hurry to finish and return to science class (Extemporaneous conversation).

Tracy also contradicted herself. During our stimulated recall discussion, Tracy had explained that she wrote to her friend Linda about the Pacific Ocean because Linda enjoyed going to the beach. However, in her interview, when I asked whether her friend was familiar with the Pacific Ocean, Tracy apparently forgot her earlier description of Linda's perspective: "No, [she's not familiar with the ocean, but] I think she might have at least seen it in a book or a poster or something" (Interview).

The letters themselves gave little evidence that the 9-year-olds incorporated what they knew about the audience into their writing. Once I had removed any obvious clues (salutations, closing, direct references to the audience), I asked outside readers to decide who the intended audience was for each letter in the pair and to justify their choices. The readers could correctly name the audiences for only Beth's pair of letters.

The outside readers explained that they had determined the intended audiences of Beth's letters based on the "voice" she had used. The letter to her friend is "energetic" and "breathless," as if she were excitedly telling a friend about a fun day. The letter to her great aunt was "a simple catalog of events" that "revealed little about the writer," a voice which readers found appropriately distant and uninvolved for an adult audience. These qualities are apparent in the two letters (original spelling and punctuation in all examples):

> Dear friend,
>   I am going to tell you about the time I went to Disneyland. It was so exiting. There is this neat ride. I forget the name of the ride but I remember it goes down this waterfall. It was very scary. I almost fell out. I was so scared I hid under the dash board. When I stood up to sit down on the floor. I fell! It was close but I grabed on to my seat climbed back in and I did not sit on the floor I sat in my seat and held on. For lunch I had this delisious hamberger, fries and a large coke. We went home at 2:00 in the morning.

> Dear Aunt,
>   Last week I went to my other Aunts house. We went up to the Mountains. We also went to see a Man from Snowy River. We got some toys there too they have a two story house. They have romates too. Me and my sister slept on the floor it was uncomfortable when we woke up our back hurt. We had breakfast played dominoes and then we met my mom and dad at the deli. Then me and my sister went home.

Neither Tracy's nor Jim's letters give any hint that they had been written for different audiences. Consider Tracy's letters. Beyond the salutations, there appear to be no clues as to why the letters would be more appropriate for one or the other audience. Letter 1 was addressed to the great-aunt, letter 2 to a good friend:

> LETTER 1:
>   I read your letter and it was marvoles my most exciting place I have ever been to was Disneyland. I like Disneyland because it has fun rides and you have so much to do. When our family went to Disneyland I was never bored the first thing I did when I got there I planed what rides I was going on first. It took me a long time because all the rides were so exciting but I finlly figured it out. After I planed the rides I planed where I was going to meet my parents and where I was going to eat when I was hun-

gry. I went on many rides then I got hungry so my frined Tanya and I went and got a bite to eat then we went in a candy store and bought a bag of lickrish and we walked arond and saw different things. We ate our candy That night we slept in the Disneyland Hotel The next morning we ate breafast and went out to go on the rides That afternoon my family and I went home and unpacked. Someday we are going to Disneyland agin next time we go our family would like you to come. I hope you can make it.

LETTER 2:
   I read the letter you sent me and my most exciting place I have been in is the Pacific Ocean. It is exciting to me because it has many creacters like starfish and plan fish. It had many big animals like whales and dolifans and shark My family and I have been whale watching befour on or boat. We see lots of whales and dolfins. Sometimes we see schools of seals, and sea lions swimming around or boat. One day I would like to invite you to see many different animals we see in the ocean. Sometimes when we go to the ocean the waves are very big thats why we have to ware life jackets so we don't fall overbord and will not trande [drowned]. One of the times when you come on the boat with us I'm sure you will ware a life jacet to.

13- and 18-year-old Writers

What writers know about the audience.   The thinking-aloud-writing protocols indicate that both the 13- and 18-year-old writers made decisions based on their audience's interest, nationality, and age. Sharon had in mind her audience's interests when selecting the places she would write about in her letters. Here are two comments she made in her writing protocols. The first is in reference to the letter to her friend; the second is in reference to the letter to her great-aunt:

> A friend might not think [the Louvre] is very interesting if they're not—if they don't see the value in the art that I saw—which is what made it interesting to me.

> I'd like to write about somewhere that I went that would be very exciting to [my great-aunt] because she's used to Europe. So I should probably write about a place that maybe she hasn't had a chance to see.

   Writing-protocol comments suggest that several of the older subjects made content decisions based on the fact that their great-aunt lived so far away, in France. (The task instructions only mention France; Paris is not named.):

> I guess I'll pretty much want to explain the country more than anything else because she's never been here (Eddie 1A).

I'll say maybe [New York] is not as extravagant as Paris is, but it, they have lots of things in big department stores there (Carrie 1B).

I'd like a nice analogy here [subject writes] "thicker than." What's the rainiest part of France? [subject reads] "thicker than" [subject writes] "a Paris cloudburst"—I mean she does live in France (Kent 1B).

A third way that the older subjects thought about the audience was in terms of age:

If that was my great aunt that lived in France I probably wouldn't go into too much detail. I'd probably confuse her—especially since she's probably going to be pretty old (Janet 1B).

How writers use their knowledge of audience. Unlike the 9-year-olds, the older writers made comments in their interviews and stimulated recalls that were consistent with those they made during their writing protocols. The retrospective comments either corroborated earlier remarks about audience attributes or added new, but consistent, information.

Two outside readers correctly identified in every case the intended audiences for the writers' letters. To illustrate how easy it was to identify the intended audiences for whom the older subjects wrote, here are the opening paragraphs from two pairs of letters. The first letter in each pair was written to a good friend; the second was written to a great-aunt from France.

18-YEAR-OLD WRITER
Dear Tony,
    How's it going? Glad you had a good time at Franconia Notch. Your description reminded me of a place in the Adirondacks (which I might already have told you about) called Lake Tear of the Clouds. It's about half a mile south of Mt. Marcey, the highest peak in New York, in the saddle between Gray Peak and Mt. Skylight. It's the highest source of the Hudson River, 4300 feet above sea level.

Dear Grandma Ditmer,
    I wish we could have gotten to the Alps when we were in Europe. It seems we missed a lot. There are a lot of beautiful places in America also. Yellowstone National Park, in northeastern Wyoming, is a fantastic place. Most of the people who go there see the big geysers (like Old Faithful) and the Grand Canyon of the Yellowstone. But even without these big attractions, there are several gorgeous spots in the park. One of my favorite places in the park, and even in the world, is the Gibbon Meadows near the Norris Geyser Basin campground.

13-YEAR-OLD WRITER
Dear John,
    You think you've got me beat! But I have been to a better place than you could ever imagine, which I wouldn't think of ever forgetting. Do you remember last Christmas when we went away? We went to Kenya, you know, in Africa. Well, there's no comparison!

Dear Madame Schmidt,
    How are you, and when will you come visit us? I went to a neet place last summer too. Can you guess where? I went to Minnisota, and I went there to go to a french camp. There are many many trees and I'm sure that there were just as many lakes.

In the letters written to Tony and Grandma Ditmer (both of whom are real people), the writer begins the letter to his friend more casually than the letter to his great-aunt. Although both letters begin by making reference to places that his correspondents visited, the writer uses colloquial language with Tony, dropping the subject of the second sentence. The same kind of reference to Grandma Ditmer is polite and "correct." While the letter to Tony makes reference to their past conversations, it is clear from the first paragraph that he writes to Grandma Ditmer, that he imagines her as someone who is not familiar with United States geography, who may not know where Yellowstone Park or Wyoming are.

    The strongest distinction between the letters to John (a real person) and Madame Schmidt (a fictitious name) is in the tone that the writer uses. The letter to John sets up a competitive situation; the writer nearly dares John to have visited a more interesting place than Africa. In the letter to Madame Schmidt, the writer uses a polite tone; the opening lines are formulistic.

DISCUSSION

Because my sample is small and my study descriptive, I do not generalize about the audience awareness of all writers based on this research. However, I can reflect on the patterns illustrated by my subjects.

    The audience of the great-aunt from France elicited more writing-protocol statements from subjects than did the good friend. When writing to the audience with whom they were less familiar and with whom they would have less in common, writers spent more time thinking about the audience—analyzing it, deciding what would be appropriate to say, reflecting on how a great-aunt might react to parts of the letter.

Although the experimental task designated two audiences, certainly the subjects were aware that the investigator was also a very real audience. The 13- and 18-year-old writers made more references to the investigator when writing to their friend than when writing to their great-aunt. (The 9-year-olds made none at all.) This may be because there is a greater difference between the designated audience, good friend, and the investigator, than there is between the designated audience, great-aunt, and the investigator. In fact, several of the writers were heard resolving the difference between what they would say to a good friend and what the investigator, an unfamiliar, teacherly type, would expect in a letter.

Given the audience of "good friend" and "great-aunt from France," writers at all three ages filled in these general descriptions with appropriate details about age, nationality, and interest. The older writers made more references to the audience in their writing protocols and supplied more detail than the younger ones—making references to the city in which the great-aunt lived in France or a particular kind of food their good friend may have eaten at Disneyland. But what most differentiates the older writers from the younger ones is not *what* they know about their audience, but *when* and *how* they call forth and use this knowledge. The 13- and 18-year-old writers talked about the audiences' perspectives during their writing protocols as well as in their retrospective interview and stimulated recall accounts. Unlike most of the 9-year-olds, these writers apparently thought about the audience as they wrote. Quite possibly as a result of this, the intended audiences were easily distinguished in the older writers' letters.

Not all of the 9-year-olds used what they knew about the audience in a consistent or adaptive way. They had little sense that the audience about whom they spoke and for whom they retrospectively justified writing decisions could have been a present, generative construct in their writing. If we were to envision Flower and Hayes's (1981) cognitive model of the composing process for these 9-year-olds, the arrows connecting the structural units in the model would not be solid. That is, although the audience features exist in the writer's long-term memory and task environment, they do not feed into the writing process. They seem to circle around the process, their existence acknowledged by these novice writers but their significance not yet understood.

CONCLUSIONS AND IMPLICATIONS

If the subjects in my study are able to consider and construct viewpoints other than their own, why then do all of them not use this knowledge in their writing? As I have suggested, lack of egocentrism is apparently a necessary but not sufficient cognitive attribute for composing essays that take the audience into consideration.

To understand why not all writers use what they know about audience, we might consider two ways that spoken and written language can function: socially—to create, express, or sustain human relationships; and conceptually—to express or describe experience, ideas, or interpretations.

The social function of speech is almost immediately evident to children. Their speech is met by an interactive response and commonly accompanies actions to which the meaning of words is clearly relevant (Donaldson, 1984). Whether this response is verbal or physical, it is clearly stimulated by the child's language and continues the communicative situation initiated by the child. Written language is not responded to in the same way. Children's scribbling is not done with either the intent or the result of communication (Teberosky, 1982). The scribbles change into early attempts at letters and words. But because of the way we learn to write—mastering a shifting hierarchy of letters, words, phrases, sentences—the social function of writing is often postponed when we enter school (see Staton & Shuy, this volume). In the early years of schooling children worry about perception and motor control (Ferreiro & Teberosky, 1982); the social function of writing is characteristically discouraged in exchange for a concern with scribal correctness: correct letter shapes, correct spelling, correct punctuation, correctly writing on the line, correctly erasing without ripping the paper (see Dyson, this volume). When the rules of correctness are sufficiently mastered, the child begins to write stories. Once again, the social function of writing is set aside—this time it is displaced by the conceptual function of expressing ideas, and relating experiences. An additional problem for young children is their tendency to keep the functions of language separate (Halliday, 1977, p. 31). Even if writing functions socially at home—notes from Mom and Dad on the kitchen table—this function may be left behind when the child gets on the school bus.

Returning to the 9-year-old writers in my study, we can now see that those who did not incorporate into their letters their awareness of the audience's perspective may not yet acknowledge the social function of writing. It is not surprising, then, that Tracy addressed her letter to "Dear Friend," rather than use her friend's name because, "I just thought she was, you know, [the task] meant a friend, but not [to use] the name" (Stimulated recall 1A). In fact, whereas the eight older writers used real or imagined names in their salutations, all four 9-year-old writers used generic salutations of "Dear Friend," or "Dear Great-Aunt." For the most part these young writers used their letters to express ideas and to relate their experiences. They did not acknowledge the social function of their writing.

Older writers are much more likely than younger ones to shift back and forth, using both the social function and the conceptual function of writing. Both functions appear in the thinking-aloud-writing protocols of the 13- and 18-year-old subjects.

Writing researchers who interpreted their findings with regard to Piaget's claim that young children are egocentric have attributed lack of audience awareness to what they believed was writers' age-related inability to take others' perspectives (Kroll, 1978; Rubin & Piché, 1979). However, these interpretations are highly suspect in light of the recent re-evaluation of tasks which tested children's egocentricity. Many now believe that these tasks were improperly suited for the children and that we may have underestimated children's ability to consider perspectives other than their own. This leaves us to find other explanations for the research that has found essays of younger writers less appropriately audience-adapted than those of older writers. To find these explanations we have had to look behind and beyond the essays toward what writers may know about the audience but may not be using in their writing.

One possible explanation is that children can identify and discuss appropriate audience adjustments, but because their available rhetorical strategies are limited in relation to their age, they are unable to instantiate these adjustments in their writing (Alvy, 1973; Delia & Clark, 1977).

My work suggests an additional, but not contradictory explanation. Lack of audience awareness may be an indication that writers do not acknowledge the way writing functions socially. While some writers may be aware of others' perspectives, and may even have appropriate rhetorical strategies, they do not necessarily integrate others' perspectives into the writing process, a process which for them is essentially conceptual not social in nature. This suggests that audience awareness has as much to do with the way we learn to use writing as it does with writers' age-related abilities and explains why even older writers do not always adapt their writing for different audiences.

Additional research on audience awareness could begin by broadening our data base. Because we have had to search beyond the essay to answer questions about audience awareness, our research methods have come to include the case study, a method which allows us a detailed look at the writer but often limits the number of subjects that can be manageably sampled. Consequently, we need to replicate such studies, moving toward making reliable generalizations about writers. My research points to a strong relationship between instruction and the awareness of writing's social function (see Daiute & Dalton, this volume;

Rafoth, this volume). Further research might explore the difference between what writers do in controlled or "schooled" writing and in their own personally controlled "real" writing (see Hudson, this volume). Discussions should also continue about how to integrate the social function of writing into our classrooms, not at the expense of the conceptual function, but to its advantage.

REFERENCES

Alvy, K. T. (1973). The development of listener-adapted communication in grade-school children from different social class backgrounds. *Genetic Psychological Monographs, 87*, 33–104.

Atlas, M. A. (1979). *Addressing as audience: A study of expert-novice differences in writing.* (Tech. Rep. No. 3). Pittsburgh: Carnegie Mellon.

Berkenkotter, C. (1981). Understanding a writer's awareness of audience. *College Composition and Communication, 32*, 385–399.

Borke, H. (1983). Piaget's mountains revisited: Changes in the egocentric landscape. In M. Donaldson, R. Grieve, & C. Pratt, (Eds.), *Early childhood development and education: Readings in psychology* (pp. 254–259). New York: Guilford Press.

Bracewell, R. J., Scardamalia, M., & Bereiter, C. (1978). *The development of audience awareness in writing.* (ERIC Document Reproduction Service No. ED 154 4333).

Butterworth, G. E. (1980). The origins of auditory-visual perception and visual perception in human development. In H. Pick & R. Walk (Eds.), *Perception and experience* (Vol. 2). New York: Plenum Press.

Cox, M. V. (Ed.). (1980). *Are young children egocentric?* New York: St. Martin's.

Crowhurst, M., & Piché, G. L. (1979). Audience and mode of discourse effects on syntactic complexity in writing at two grade levels. *Research in the Teaching of English, 13*, 101–110.

Delia, J. G., & Clark, R. A. (1977). Cognitive complexity, social perception and the development of listener-adapted communication in 6, 8, 10, and 12 year-old boys. *Communication Monographs, 44*, 326–345.

Donaldson, M. (1978). *Children's minds.* New York: W. W. Norton.

Donaldson, M. (1984). Speaking and writing and modes of language. In H. Goelman, A. A. Oberg, & F. Smith (Eds.), *Awakening to literacy.* Exeter, NH: Heinemann.

Ferreiro, E., & Teberosky, A. (1982). *Literacy before schooling.* (K. G. Kastro, Trans.). Exeter, NH: Heinemann.

Flavell, J. H., Botkin, P. T., Fry, E. L., Jr., Wright, J. W., & Jarvis, P. E. (1968). *The development of role-taking and communication skills in children.* New York: Wiley.

Flower, L., & Hayes, J. R. (1981). A cognitive process theory of writing. *College Composition and Communication, 32*, 365–387.

Fontaine, S. I. (1984a). *Writing for an audience: How writers at three age levels demon-*

strate an awareness of the audience and respond to two contrasting audiences. Unpublished doctoral dissertation, University of California, San Diego.

Fontaine, S. I. (1984b). *We have ways to make you talk: Gathering thinking-aloud writing protocols from children.* Unpublished manuscript, English Department, State University of New York at Stony Brook.

Halliday, M. A. K. (1977). *Language as a social semiotic.* Baltimore: University Park Press.

Kroll, B. M. (1978). Cognitive egocentrism and the problem of audience awareness in written discourse. *Research in the Teaching of English, 12,* 269–281.

Kroll, B. M. (1984). Audience adaptation in children's persuasive letters. *Written Communication, 1*(4), 407–427.

Light, P., & Simmons, B. (1983). The effects of a communication task upon the representation of relationships in children's drawings. *Journal of Experimental Child Psychology, 38,* 81–92.

Ochs, E. (1979). Planned and unplanned discourse. In T. Givon (Ed.), *Syntax and semantics* (Vol. 12, pp. 51–80). New York: Academic Press.

Piaget, J. (1955). *The language and thought of the child.* (M. Gabain, Trans.). New York: New American Library. (Original work published 1926)

Robinson, E. J., & Robinson, W. P. (1982). The advancement of children's verbal referential communication skills: The role of metacognitive guidance. *International Journal of Behavioral Development, 5,* 329–355.

Robinson, E. J., & Robinson, W. P. (1983). Children's uncertainty about the interpretation of ambiguous messages. *Journal of Experimental Child Psychology, 36,* 81–96.

Rubin, D. L., & Piché, G. L. (1979). Development in syntactic and strategic aspects of audience adaptation skills in written persuasive communication. *Research in the Teaching of English, 13,* 293–316.

Scardamalia, M., Bereiter, C., & McDonald, J. D. S. (1977). *Role-taking in written communication investigated by manipulating anticipatory knowledge.* (ERIC Document Reproduction Service No. ED 151 792).

Smith, W. L., & Swan, M. B. (1978). Adjusting syntactic structures to varied levels of audience. *Journal of Experimental Education, 46,* 29–34.

Teberosky, A. (1982). Construcción de escrituras a través de la interacción grupa. In E. Ferreiro & M. Gomez Palacio (Eds.), *Nuevas Perspectivas Sobre los Procesos de Lectura y Escritura* (Siglo 21). Mexico City.

Part Two

Creating Social Contexts Through Writing

Chapter 5

From Accounting to Written Language: The Role of Abstract Counting in the Invention of Writing*

Denise Schmandt–Besserat

Center for Middle Eastern Studies, University of Texas at Austin

The invention of writing in Sumer was the final outcome of a series of four stages in the development of data processing which took place in the ancient Middle East over the course of several thousand years, roughly between 8000 and 3000 B.C. Interestingly, the date of 8000 B.C. also marks the beginning of farming in the Fertile Crescent, and 3000 B.C. the rise of cities and the emergence of state bureaucracy in Sumer. The fact that major steps in the evolution of data processing occurred in the context of economic and social firsts is no coincidence. The development of counters and writing made possible the accurate accounting of goods. The invention of tokens and writing, therefore, are closely tied to the evolution of the economy based on food redistribution practiced in the ancient Middle East.

In this chapter, I suggest that the evolution from concrete to abstract counting was crucial to the advent of written language. To understand this process, it is necessary first to review key stages in the token system, and then to show how writing was tied to the invention of abstract numbers.

---

* I want to express my appreciation to William W. Hallo, who is currently engaged in a full study of the tablets of Godin Tepe, for his permission to use two tablets, (Gd.73.290 and 295). I thank Marjorie Irwin for editing the manuscript.

THE TOKEN SYSTEM

Sumerian writing evolved from a system of accounting with tokens in four main stages: (1) tokens, (2) impressed markings on envelopes, (3) impressed markings on tablets, (4) pictography (Schmandt–Besserat, 1986). With each stage the symbols become further removed from the concrete entity they represent.

Tokens

In the first stage, which lasted from about 8000 to 3200 B.C., tokens were used for counting and accounting. These counters, measuring about 1 to 3 cm across, were modeled in clay into multiple shapes. The artifacts are known from excavations all over the Middle East and, in particular, in Iraq, Iran, Syria, Turkey, and Israel, where they have been recovered in sizable numbers in all major prehistoric sites of the 8th–4th millennia B.C.

During the first four millennia of their existence, the tokens most frequently used were cones, spheres, disks, cylinders, and tetrahedrons as depicted in Figure 1. These objects are referred to as "plain tokens" because they usually have a plain surface, devoid of any markings. "Complex tokens" began occurring about 3350 B.C. They are characterized by a greater variety of types, including further geometrical forms, such as ovoids, biconoids, triangles and paraboloids, but also miniature replicas of items of everyday life, such as jars or animal heads. Complex tokens, as shown in Figure 2, also often bear markings such as sets of incised lines and punctations.

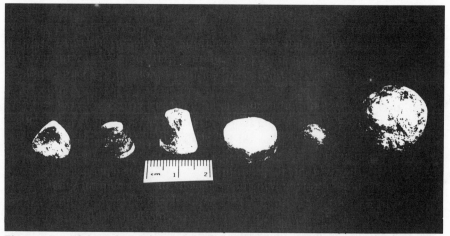

Figure 1. Plain tokens from Seh Gabi, Iran, ca. 4000 B.C. Courtesy Royal Ontario Museum, Toronto, Canada.

Figure 2. Complex tokens from Uruk, Iraq, ca. 3300 B.C. Courtesy Vorderasia-tisches Museum, Staatliche Museen zu Berlin, DDR.

Impressed Markings on Envelopes

The second stage in the evolution of data processing came about 3200 B.C. when tokens began to be stored in clay cases (Schmandt–Besserat, 1980). These cases were spherical, hollow clay balls of which about 200 have been recovered, most still intact, in half a dozen archaeological sites in Iraq, Syria, and Iran. When opened, the clay envelopes are found to yield a small number of counters, 3 cylinders and 3 disks, for example (see Figure 3).

On the outside, the cases displayed the imprints of administrative seals. But more importantly for the study of the development of writing, some envelopes also bore markings. These signs consisted of the negative imprint of each counter held inside. In other words, each token enclosed within the envelope had been pressed in the soft clay surface prior to being included. For example, an envelope yielding three disks and three cylinders displayed on the outside three circular and three long markings (see Figure 3). The markings served, obviously, to indicate the content of each case. The envelopes and the imprints of tokens they bore represent the turning point between tokens and writing. They illustrate how, at this stage, the three dimensional tokens were supplemented by graphic signs.

Impressed Markings on Tablets

In the third stage, ca. 3100 B.C., written tablets replaced the envelopes filled with tokens (Schmandt–Besserat, 1981). The tablets were simpler since they consisted of solid clay balls bearing impressed markings in the shape of tokens. For example, spheres like those depicted in Figure 4 were rendered by deep circular markings and cones by wedges. The use of impressed tablets resulted, therefore, in substituting signs for tokens.

Pictographs

Pictographs traced with a stylus in the soft clay of tablets mark the fourth and last stage. The incised signs, like those in Figure 5, were an-

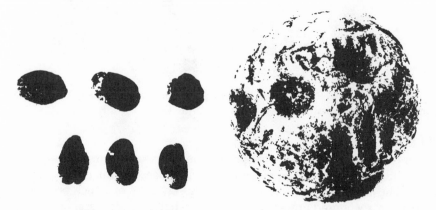

Figure 3.   Envelope and its token content from Susa, Iran, ca. 3200 B.C. Courtesy Departement des Antiquités Orientales, Musée du Louvre, Paris.

Figure 4.   Impressed tablet from Godin Tepe, Iran, ca. 3000 B.C. Courtesy T. Cuyler Young, Jr., Royal Ontario Museum, Toronto, Canada.

Figure 5.   Pictographic tablet from Godin Tepe, Iran, ca. 3000 B.C. Courtesy T. Cuyler Young, Jr., Royal Ontario Museum, Toronto, Canada.

other improvement since they reproduced more accurately the outline of tokens and the markings they bore. More importantly, once the idea was born that tokens could be represented by pictograph, it became evident that other items could be expressed by graphic signs. A boar, for example, could be shown by a small sketch of a boar's head. Pictography marks, therefore, the first true takeoff of writing, when the script finally broke away from its token antecedent.

The idea of storing tokens in envelopes and impressing their shape onto the surface started a domino effect in the manipulation of symbols. The token shapes were perpetuated by impressed signs on envelopes and tablets. The impressed signs on tablets were soon complemented by pictographs traced with a stylus, which in turn developed into the Sumerian cuneiform script used in the Middle East from about 2900 B.C. to the Christian Era. The origin of Sumerian writing, therefore, was the transmutation of three-dimensional clay symbols into two dimensional graphic signs.

THE FUNCTION OF TOKENS

The direct link between counters, impressed signs, pictographs, and Sumerian cuneiform writing constitutes the key to decoding the meaning of certain tokens. Some cuneiform signs can be traced backward, through the stages of their evolution as pictographic or impressed signs and finally to the original token prototypes. The sign for "oil," for example, can be followed from a cuneiform sign to a pictograph, further to an impressed sign on an envelope, and finally to the original token (see Figure 2, top left).

Unfortunately, there are only a few instances where a clear correlation can be made between a token and a later cuneiform sign. Whenever such linkages can be traced, however, the tokens are found to represent units of goods. For example, the main types of plain tokens stood for products of the farm. Cones and spheres, in particular, were the symbols for measures of grain, probably roughly equivalent, respectively, to our liter and bushel of cereal, whereas cylinders represented animals. Complex tokens, such as ovoids and disks bearing incised markings, stood for such finished products as jars of oil and units of textiles and garments. Thus the token system, precursor of Sumerian writing, appears to have been used specifically and exclusively, for keeping track of goods.

The evolution of the token system also supports the idea that the counters had an economic function. The appearance of the plain tokens ca. 8000 B.C. coincides with the beginning of farming, suggesting that the need for counting was brought about by agriculture (Schmandt–

Besserat, 1982). The earliest assemblages of tokens, which consisted mainly of cones, spheres, disks, and cylinders, suggest that the goods first accounted for were cereals and animals.

Complex tokens, on the other hand, can be correlated with the rise of cities. The multiplication of counters corresponds to the beginning of production of manufactured goods in urban workshops. This explains why complex tokens stood for finished merchandise such as oil, bread, textiles, garments, and metal, whereas plain tokens were symbols for staple foods.

The decline of the token system and the advent of impressed and pictographic writing, ca. 3100 B.C., in turn, corresponds to the creation of the state. Even at that time, tablets continued to be used by the Sumerian bureaucracy for the sole purpose of keeping track of goods in exactly the same way as tokens were. There were no literary, no religious, no historical texts written during the first 300 years of writing. Except for a small number of lexical texts, or lists of signs, meant for the training of scribes, there were only economic texts between 3100 and 2900 B.C. (Nissen, 1986). The impressed and pictographic texts featured accounts involving products already familiar from the token system, such as animals, grain, oil, bread, textiles, garments, or metal. It is important to note that these items were entered in the form of mere lists involving only the name of the product and the number of units, for example, "33 jars of oil" (see Figure 5). There were yet no signs for verbs, prepositions, or determiners, which would have allowed the expression of sentences of spoken language (Feldbush, 1985). Pictography was still used as a mere accounting device to keep track of the entries and expenditures of storehouses in the Sumerian temples. Some of these accounts were, probably, receipts of offerings to the temple.

USE OF THE TOKEN SYSTEM

The token system was an archaic device for collecting, manipulating, organizing, storing, and retrieving data concerning economic products. It can be viewed, therefore, as functioning as an extension of the brain with the advantage of being more predictable and reliable than human memory.

One of the major advantages of the token system was to allow the collection of information on multiple items without burdening the mind. It is proposed, for example, that tokens had probably been invented for the preparation of festivals which necessitated the pooling of large amounts of various foods over long periods of time (Schmandt–Besserat, 1982).

Because the tokens were easy to handle, they enhanced data manipulation. The counters could be ordered and reordered according to any possible criteria. For example, they could be sorted, alternatively, according to types of goods, contributors, or entries, and expenditures. Furthermore, the tokens could be presented in particular visual patterns, such as the sets of dots on our dominoes, helping the user to grasp and identify the information instantly.

The tokens served as a reliable data bank. They could be stored, saving data indefinitely. The information they yielded remained available for retrieval at all times since the data encoded could be, at will, translated into speech by any individual initiated in the system.

The system also had the potential of serving as a communication device between distant parties, since they were light and small and could be easily transported.

The most important role of the tokens was probably, however, to serve as durable and tangible proofs of transactions. They constituted, perhaps, official receipts of dues or served as binding documents of oral agreements. In this role, the token system must be considered as a powerful means of control.

WRITING AND ACCOUNTING

Tokens encoded two kinds of information: (1) the nature of the items counted, (2) the number of units involved. The peculiarity of the token system was to fuse these two kinds of data with no possibility of dissociating them. On the one hand, the type of merchandise was indicated by the shape of the token; for example, an ovoid was a jar of oil, whereas a sphere was a bushel of grain. On the other hand, the quantity of units was designated by the number of tokens in one-to-one correspondence. For instance, four ovoids represented four jars of oil, and five ovoids stood for five jars of oil. It was not possible with tokens, therefore, to express "5" as an abstract entity, because each token stood always for one unit of a particular good. Five ovoids, for example, represented, literally "one jar of oil, one jar of oil, one jar of oil, one jar of oil, one jar of oil."

Because of the two main characteristics of the token system, namely (1) the use of different counters to count different types of goods, and (2) the representation of number in one-to-one correspondence, it has been proposed that the token system lacked counters to express abstract numbers (Schmandt–Besserat, 1984). Abstract numbers are understood to be numbers such as 1, 2, 3, 4, which can be applied to count any and every item, for example, 1, 2, 3, 4 bushels of grain and 1, 2, 3, 4 jars of oil. Accordingly, it is postulated that the token system illustrated a stage of counting that preceded the invention of abstract numbers.

The phase of counting defined by the absence of abstract numbers is known as "concrete counting." Instead of abstract numbers, such as 1, 2, 3, 4, which can be applied to count any and every item, concrete counting used different number words to count different things. A parallel can be seen in the Tsimchians of British Columbia, who practiced concrete counting. They counted 1, 2, 3 canoes with the following sequence of number words—*k'amaet, g'alpeeltk, galtskantk*, whereas *k'al, t'epqadal, gugal* were the number words to count 1, 2, 3 men (Boas, 1889). Accordingly, I propose that the many token shapes corresponded to the different numerations used to count different types of good, prior to the invention of abstract numbers in the ancient Middle East.

When tokens were replaced by their imprint on clay envelopes and on tablets, there was no semantic change between the tokens and their impressions. At these third and fourth stages quantity was still indicated, therefore, by repeating the marking as many times as the number of items counted. Also, each type of good was still accounted for with a particular sign, showing the continued use of concrete counting.

When pictographic writing came about, however, the pictographs were no longer repeated in one-to-one correspondence. Instead, they were preceded by abstract numerals or signs like our digits 1, 2, 3, 4, expressing abstract numbers. These numerals consisted of impressed cones and spheres, which formerly stood for measures of grain, but from then on also meant, respectively, "1" and "10." Thirty-three jars of oil were shown by three circular signs derived from spheres and three wedges derived from cones (see Figure 5).

Starting about 3100 B.C., and for centuries to come, the Sumerians expressed abstract numbers and measures of grain with the same signs. This appears confusing to us but does not seem to have affected the Sumerian accountants who, according to the context, could easily identify the correct information.

Why the grain signs were selected for abstract numerals can only be guessed. Three reasons come to mind. First, they were the signs most commonly used, since grain was the major staple in the ancient Middle East. Second, they offered a sequence of measures which could be translated into ascending numerical units. For example, the wedge standing for the basic unit became 1, whereas the sphere, which represented the next larger unit, became 10. Third, and lastly, impressed numeral indicators were immediately recognizable, since they differed from the incised pictographs identifying the items counted.

Pictographic writing was, therefore, the first system of written language to provide two kinds of signs: the first being used exclusively to indicate abstract numbers and the second open to the expression of any other tangible items of human endeavor.

INCREASING ABSTRACTION FROM TOKENS TO WRITING

The study of the immediate forerunners of the Sumerian script demonstrates that each stage of evolution from tokens to writing corresponds to a new step in dealing with economic data in increasingly abstract terms, and culminating with the invention of abstract numerals.

Tokens

The use of tokens meant abstracting data in several ways. First, actual goods were replaced by symbols. Second, tokens abstracted the common property of a class of goods. Third, they removed the data from their actual physical context. And fourth, they separated data from linguistic discourse.

The tokens were abstract symbols standing for units of real goods. One can argue that some tokens in geometrical shapes, such as the cylinder, which represented one animal, were more abstract than those representing miniature jars and tools. In all cases, however, the choice of shape to represent a particular commodity was arbitrary.

Tokens abstracted the common properties of a class of items. The sphere represented, for instance, any possible bushel of grain, regardless of its accidental and unique particularities of size, color, quality, and so forth. The sphere, in other words, represented an ideal, abstract bushel of grain standing for any unit of that class.

Dealing with tokens meant abstracting commodities from their usual context. For instance, the cylinders representing numbers of sheep allowed an administrator to deal with the animals as abstract entities, without concern for their actual whereabouts and needs. The small clay spheres used to manipulate data concerning grain eliminated the weight and bulk that make the handling of cereal difficult. As a consequence, the data, removed from any daily life contingency, could be considered with greater objectivity.

Lastly, data are usually conceived and communicated in a linguistic context, while tokens presented information bare, removed from any discourse.

The tokens remained, however, deeply rooted in the world of objects. The fact that they were three-dimensional artifacts that could be grasped in the hand, touched and manipulated lent to the counters a particular concrete quality. What seems most significant is the concrete way tokens were used to express plurality. For example, a set of three jars of oil is, in reality: one jar of oil + one jar of oil + one jar of oil. And this is the way it was shown by tokens. "Three" does not exist in the physical world—it is an abstract construct of our mind. The token system did not represent such abstractions, but instead dealt only with concrete entities.

Impressed Signs

The reduction from three-dimensional tactile tokens to two-dimensional signs which could no longer be grasped in the hand removed the symbols one step further from the actual goods they represented. The loss of volume and tactility constituted, therefore, a further step in abstraction which cannot be overemphasized. On the other hand, there was no semantic change between tokens and their corresponding impressed signs. For instance, a sphere token and an impressed circular sign stood alike for a bushel of grain. In particular, the impressed markings went on fusing together the notion of the nature and quantity of a product. They also continued to translate plurality in one-to-one correspondence. For example, three circular markings were used to express three bushels of grain. The impressed signs, therefore, still were capable of representing only concrete entities.

Pictography

The leap in abstraction at the fourth stage of evolution was to dissociate the notion of number of units from that of the good counted. The recognition that two jars of oil, two bushels of grain, and two animals were all instances of "two-ness" allowed merchandise to be dealt with in further abstract terms. This resulted in the creation of two distinct systems of symbols: impressed numerals and incised pictographs. Numerals represent the first signs expressing an abstract idea.

CONCLUSION

The abstraction of number/nature of the item counted was a technological advance that facilitated the more complex accounting practices of a state bureaucracy. More than this, however, it was an intellectual breakthrough. Writing and abstract counting which derived from the archaic token system were unparalleled achievements of the Sumerians, for both served as instruments of order and control which are the base of civilization.

REFERENCES

Boas, F. (1889). Fifth report on the northwestern tribes of Canada. *Proceedings of the British Association for the Advancement of Science*, 881.
Feldbush, E. (1985). *Geschriebene Sprache*, 153.
Nissen, H. J. (1986). The archaic texts from Uruk. *World Archaeology*, 17(3), 317–334.

Schmandt–Besserat, D. (1980). The envelopes that bear the first writing. *Technology and Culture, 21*, 357–385.

Schmandt–Besserat, D. (1981). From tokens to tablets: A re-evaluation of the so-called "numerical tablets." *Visible Language, 15*(4), 321–344.

Schmandt–Besserat, D. (1982). The emergence of recording. *American Anthropologist, 84*(4), 871–878.

Schmandt–Besserat, D. (1984). Before numerals. *Visible Language, 18*(1), 48–60.

Schmandt–Besserat, D. (1986). The origins of writing. *Written Communication, 3*(1), 31–45.

Chapter 6

Discourse Community: Where Writers, Readers, and Texts Come Together

Bennett A. Rafoth
Indiana University of Pennsylvania

INTRODUCTION

Research in rhetoric and composition has yielded many different perspectives on audience, or what may be called the reader–writer relationship. For centuries, Aristotle's discussion of persuasion and the demographic characteristics of a given listening audience guided most approaches to audience. With the New Rhetoric of the 20th century, however, views about the nature of persuasion *vis-à-vis* those who would be persuaded began to change, and classical notions about audience grew more complex as the study of rhetoric began to draw heavily upon social and psychological research (see Fontaine, this volume). When attention turned to writing as distinct from speech, some theorists argued that the writer's audience was, after all, "a fiction." Now in recent years, the notion of audience seems to grow even more diffuse as researchers from various disciplines probe the interdependence of writers, readers, and texts.

In composition research, the goal of most perspectives on audience is to show how a particular view of audience helps to describe and explain a variety of composing process phenomena and a variety of features in written products. If there is anything that these perspectives share, it is that they address, to one degree or another, some aspect of writers/speakers, readers/listeners, and the discourse between them by means of the term "audience." It would thus seem that audience has a conceptual status more or less independent of the various perspectives that inform it. Capturing the essence of this conceptual status has proven difficult, however. Whether audience is given a concrete or abstract representation, identifying the center of gravity around which its various perspectives might revolve has been troublesome.

Recently, for example, Ede and Lunsford (1984) have suggested a kind of dual approach to audience that enables focus on the reader, on one hand, and focus on the writer, on the other. And Kroll (1984), in a synthesis of current perspectives on audience, offers a conceptual framework based on three different perspectives: rhetorical, informational, and social. Both of these articles help to show the viability of competing perspectives; they also illustrate the way in which notions of audience tend to be split from the outset—in two directions by Ede and Lunsford and in three by Kroll. The point *from* which such splits occur is hard to pinpoint. Yet until we can identify a pivotal center from which different perspectives of audience emanate, audience will remain an ambiguous concept. This ambiguity is problematic because it indicates there may be a more fundamental concept for capturing the range of linguistic and rhetorical phenomena for which we typically invoke the notion of *audience*.

In this chapter, I will suggest that *discourse community* may be conceptually more useful than audience for capturing the language phenomena that relate writers, readers, and texts. Whereas the audience metaphor tends naturally to represent readers or listeners as primary, and to admit writers and texts only as derivatives, discourse community admits writers, readers, and texts all together. Instead of forcing the question "Who is the audience for this writer or this text?" (Park, 1982, 1986), discourse community directs attention to the contexts that give rise to a text, including the range of conventions that govern different kinds of writing (see Irvine & Elsasser, this volume; Zellermayer, this volume). To explore the advantages of discourse community over audience, it is helpful to look at a few fields which have already begun to use a similar concept to help overcome problems like those posed by audience in composition studies. I will proceed, therefore, by first turning to the fields of rhetoric, literary criticism, and linguistics in order to show how these fields have attempted to achieve, via notions of *field* or *community*, some degree of explanatory control over a variety of context-sensitive language phenomena. I will then return to composition theory to suggest why a notion such as *discourse community* is a better alternative to *audience*.

Argument Field, Interpretive Community, Speech Community

In such fields as rhetoric, literary criticism, and linguistics, writing theorists can find theoretical problems that impinge on their own, especially questions of how to explain a seemingly endless variety of language phenomena with reference to a few basic concepts. In contemporary rhetoric, argument theorist David Zarefsky (1982) investigates how we can best explain how arguments originate, how they compare and contrast, and how they can be judged valid. In literary criticism, critic Stanley Fish (1980) inquires about the proper role of literary criticism in the face of two seemingly opposing facts: (1) Readers can and do interpret texts in very different ways, and (2) Texts are stable. And in linguistics a number of scholars, beginning with ethnographer Dell Hymes (1972), question how language variations reflect social categories, and how these social categories define and constrain interpersonal interaction in communicative situations (Romaine, 1982; Saville–Troike, 1982). In all three cases, and in composition studies as well, theorists pursue the same general goal: to understand the relationships between writers/ speakers, readers/listeners, and the discourse between them.

Argument field. How do arguments originate? How may they be compared? What standard may be used to judge their validity? Answers to fundamental questions about the origin, comparison, and validity of arguments have proved difficult to ascertain because of the many sociocontextual variables that influence argument. The doctrine of "separate but equal," for example, was in its time founded on arguments that would be dismissed in most present-day U. S. courts (but likely accepted in a different arena, such as South Africa). Most arguments are not simply a matter of logic, but neither are they ruled by chaos. What counts as a good argument is always determined in light of some cultural context. Public debate on a national issue such as abortion is affected by individual beliefs, which are in turn shaped by media coverage and opinion polls. As one theorist notes, "Deliberative rhetoric is a form of argumentation through which citizens test and create social knowledge in order to uncover, assess, and resolve shared problems" (Goodnight, 1982, p. 214). To understand fully any particular argument about shared problems, it is necessary to look beyond claims and warrants; the student of argumentation must instead look to who is involved in the argument, what standards of deliberation these participants adhere to, and what values they hold dear. Thus there are differences in the standards for arguments among friends versus those for academic arguments versus those for legal debate, for example (Goodnight, 1982; Willard, 1981; 1983).

In searching for underlying principles of argument, rhetorical theorists in recent years have found it useful to speak of *argument fields* as a way of marking the frame of reference for examining arguments. By identifying the field in which a particular argument takes place, one may better understand how that argument came about, how it differs from related arguments, and how it may be evaluated. For example, in the legal profession lawyers often develop arguments based on judicial precedent and then compare the case at hand with previous judgments; judges then evaluate these precedent arguments to arrive at a decision. Lawyers and judges function together in the courtroom by presuming certain norms for arguing. Similarly, in addressing juries or explaining the proceedings and outcomes of adjudication to the press, lawyers and judges work hard at getting relative outsiders socialized into the field. A critic's understanding of this kind of deliberation must begin with the legal profession and its standards for argument (Zarefsky, 1982). Similarly, one who wishes to engage lawyers in debate on a legal point must also be familiar with these standards when following or criticizing them. In short, effective discourse in law depends largely on one's familiarity with the argument field of law.

Shared standards and community norms are thus essential to what makes up a field of argument. According to Willard (1981), fields are social comparison processes in which individuals "check their thinking against the views of others. As we study [fields], we are studying how [people] build order as a social enterprise" (p. 28). With the notion of argument field, theorists have tried to look beyond logic, which can be psychologically impotent when opposed by tradition, popular authorities, or short-term interests. Theorists have also tried to look beyond audience, recognizing that audiences can sometimes have little importance to the origin, differences, and evaluation of arguments. In terms of evaluation, for example, a good argument is not necessarily one an audience will accept; the Surgeon General offers excellent arguments for quitting smoking, but many smokers reject them.

Interestingly, Zarefsky's questions about the origin, comparison, and validity of arguments reflect broad concerns in composition research: Where do writers' ideas come from? How does one essay compare with another? How can essays be properly evaluated? Each of these questions has been addressed through some notion or other of audience. Thus some researchers have investigated the origin of writers' ideas and found that talking with readers is a productive source (Daiute, this volume; Flower, 1981; Murray, 1979; Rubin, 1983; Staton & Shuy, this volume). Other studies have compared written products and found that essays may be sorted according to their intended audience (Britton et al., 1975; Faigley & Hansen, 1985; Grobe, 1981; Rafoth, 1984, 1985; Rubin & Piché, 1979; see also Fontaine, this volume). And finally, there are studies that have evaluated essays according to how well they meet the needs of an audience (Lloyd–Jones, 1977; Odell, 1981).

Interpretive community. Literary texts are permanent and often remote in time and space from their readers. This, according to Fish (1980), has made it relatively easy for critics to cast themselves as model readers, lending an authority to their interpretations that is not always deserved. It is a trap that Fish says he fell into as a critical theorist. He explains that he was struck by the problem that the concept of audience poses for literary interpretation: Divergent interpretations of a text result from the fact that there are as many audiences as there are readers, and audiences are continually created anew. As a way out of this critical quagmire, Fish at first suggested two levels of critical interpretation: one, the shared reading, based on the linguistic competence or shared system of rules that holds between readers; and two, the emotional reaction to the first level. This second level was considered subjective and idiosyncratic, unlike the primary, objective level. Accordingly, the proper role of literary criticism was to suppress the subjective in favor of the objective. This meant that it was necessary to posit an ideal reader who was consummately well informed and with whom only deficient readers would disagree: "Agreement was secured by making disagreement aberrant" (pp. 14–15).

Ideal readers, however, are no more plausible than homogeneous, ideal speakers. In later rejecting his original formulation, Fish (1980) proposed the notion of *interpretive community*, which he explained in such a way as to preserve both subjectivity and objectivity:

> An interpretive community is not objective because as a bundle of interests, of particular purposes and goals, its perspective is interested rather than neutral; but by the same reasoning, the meanings and texts produced by an interpretive community are not subjective because they do not proceed from an isolated individual but from a public and conventional point of view. (p. 14)

Fish went on to conclude that what is seen as real and normative is a function of a particular interpretive community, and that there is no such thing as a natural or correct reading, only "ways of reading that are extensions of community perspectives" (pp. 15–16). The business of criticism was therefore to determine how readings proceed from a number of possible perspectives:

> This determination will not be made once and for all by a neutral mechanism of adjudication, but will be made and remade again whenever the interests and tacitly understood goals of one interpretive community replace or dislodge the interests and goals of another. The business of criticism, in other words, was not to decide between interpretations by subjecting them to the test of disinterested evidence but to establish by political and persuasive means . . . the set of interpretive assumptions from the vantage of which the evidence (and the facts and the intentions and everything else) will hereafter by specifiable. (p. 16)

With the concept of interpretive community, Fish thus attempted to offer literary criticism a means for grounding in social context the variety and similarity of interpretations. In so doing, he tried to overcome the problem of granting absolute authority to certain ways of reading, while at the same time avoiding a non-theory in which anything goes. Like the idea of a discourse community, Fish's interpretive community is based on prevailing norms about how any given writers, readers, and texts should be related.

The significance of interpretive community may be seen in a recent analysis of how students learn to write in the social sciences. Faigley and Hansen (1985) followed one student through two courses, one on writing in the social sciences taught by an English professor, and one on crime taught by a sociology professor. On the very same essay, the student received a B− from the English professor and an A from the sociology professor. In contrasting the two instructors' comments, Faigley and Hansen observed the English professor's almost exclusive attention to matters of style, expression, and sentence structure, as opposed to the sociology professor's concern for the breadth and depth of information. The two researchers also noted the apparent difficulty that the English professor had in following his own grading criteria: " 'I will ask questions such as, "Would a professional in your field consider this worthwhile reading?" ' "

Speech community. The concept of speech community in linguistics may be traced back as early as 1933, when Leonard Bloomfield sought to show that similarities in speech patterns among particular groups were due to the frequency of interaction among their members (and not due to environmental factors such as climate and topography, as conventional wisdom in the 19th century held). Since then, the speaker's definition of the situation, particularly how that speaker identifies with others, has been shown to provide a more satisfactory explanation of language subgroups than frequency of contact. Today definitions of speech community tend to emphasize the role of speakers' shared rules and norms, following Hymes (1972): "A speech community is defined as a community sharing rules for the conduct and interpretation of speech, and rules for the interpretation of at least one linguistic variety" (p. 54). Since Bloomfield, however, the notion of speech community has served the same fundamental purpose: to relate social interaction to linguistic variation and change (Hymes, 1972). Thus Labov (1970) argued that pronunciation variation on Martha's Vineyard has social significance because speakers who use the centralized variants of two diphthongs mark solidarity with their community, thereby strongly identifying themselves with the local people and life on the island.

Sociolinguists and ethnographers have used speech community as a theoretical construct to describe and explain the persistence of both widespread variety and (relative) uniformity in language use among different groups of people: Why many native Southerners in the United States continue to speak "Southern," why many Black American speakers frequently alternate between Black dialect and Standard American English, and so on. The idea of speech community helps researchers identify boundaries that reflect certain sociolinguistic parameters which speakers themselves recognize. Researchers then use these speech community boundaries in explaining how language differences relate to social separation, unity, and stratification. Within some Armenian communities in the United States, for example, Armenian is the language of choice between Armenians. Because they also live and function in the larger American community, they also use English to participate in the Standard American English speech community, while Armenian continues to serve as a means of maintaining a separate identity in that community (Saville–Troike, 1982).

Nystrand (1982) notes that writers, like speakers, are also influenced by the "speech" community of their readers. He points out that the writer's audience is different from the writer's speech community because writers can affect their audience on a particular occasion through particular texts. The writer's speech community, by contrast, is a much more stable entity and is rarely so affected by particular occasions and texts; instead, the community affects the writer by tacitly imposing conformity to its ways of writing (see also Zellermayer, this volume).

COMMUNITY VS. AUDIENCE IN WRITING

Taken together, the concepts of argument field in rhetoric, interpretive community in criticism, and speech community in linguistics offer important insights for composition theory generally and for the problem of audience specifically. First, all three concepts attempt to derive their descriptive and predictive power from a pluralistic view of what is normal and expected. Different communities of arguers, readers, or speakers will have different yet valid expectations for carrying on arguments, formulating correct readings of a text, or speaking appropriately. In a similar vein, various groups of writers and readers have different, yet valid, expectations for what written discourse should be like.

Second, all three concepts show the need for interweaving communicators, messages, and pertinent contexts into a single fabric: Argument theory, long dominated by formal approaches focusing on the logical structure of messages, has found it necessary to give wider acceptance to the roles of participants and particular topical domains. Literary criticism has recognized the limitations of granting interpretive authority to certain privileged readers and so acknowledges the various perspectives of different readership communities. And linguistics, with deep roots in the acontextual study of phonology, morphology, and syntax of "ideal speakers," has nonetheless asserted a position for sociolinguistics and contextual studies of language in use. In other words, whereas argument theory may be said to have been once largely concerned with idealized messages or texts, literary criticism with ideal readers, and linguistics with ideal speakers, all three fields have more recently found reason to subordinate these initial formulations to the larger framework of community.

Focus on discourse community differs from approaches to audience in composition, where perspectives that emphasize either writers, texts, or readers emerge not from a single, underlying framework but stand more or less independent of, and sometimes in opposition to, each other. The result is a diversity of perspectives that have only a vague and ill-defined notion of audience as their point in common.

Kroll's (1984) framework illustrates this diversity by showing three current perspectives on audience which, despite their relative strengths, are each limited in the particular aspect of audience they address. This same diversity reveals itself more subtly (and less acutely) in Ede and Lunsford's (1984) notion of dual emphases, toward audience-addressed and audience-invoked. Ede and Lunsford recognize implicitly, however, that the underlying ecology of their two alternatives is "the complex series of obligations, resources, needs, and constraints embodied in the writer's concept of audience" (p. 165). They also note that a sense of audience is guided by a sense of purpose and "by the peculiarities of a specific rhetorical situation. . . " (p. 166). Here we see a theory of audience which, though still split, begins to face head-on the conceptual problem of the *nature* of audience. The dual emphasis on audience-addressed and audience-invoked reflects, like other perspectives, a concern for two important ways one's sense of audience can be manifested, while the recognition of "obligations, resources, needs, and constraints" hints at the more fundamental questions that audience theory must address.

How then can the notion of community help define and unify audience in composition studies? Before addressing this question directly, it is necessary to bring into better focus some of the more important issues that have been addressed under the banner of audience. This will then lead to why audience per se is a conceptually inadequate term for addressing these problems, and how a better concept can emerge from the notion of community.

The Writer as Agent and Object of Influence

Good writers are often said to possess a keen sense of audience. Exactly what constitutes a sense of audience has been difficult to pinpoint, however. In various notions of audience, composition theorists have seen the universe of discourse as shaping different kinds of relationships between participants. On the one hand, audience has been used to suggest that the writer is an *agent* of influence on readers. By this account, writers are the primary actors in discursive events. This may be seen in what Ede and Lunsford call the "audience-addressed" view or in what Kroll (1984) calls the "rhetorical" perspective, where the writer is viewed as adopting communication strategies that will most effectively take advantage of the audience's predispositions, and hence be most convincing (see Fontaine, this volume). In addition, the writer as agent of influence also coincides with Ong's (1975) notion of "fictionalized" audience, or what Ede and Lunsford label "audience-invoked." This view points to the absence of any known, specific body of readers in many writing situations and emphasizes the great freedom writers have in conceptualizing their own audience—to invoke, create, or fictionalize a potential audience. Despite the contrasts that have been drawn between "audience-addressed" and "audience-invoked" (Ede & Lunsford, 1984; see also Long, 1980), both show the power the writer has in effecting change in readers, whether it be a tangible audience the writer knows and exploits or a remote audience who "play[s] the role in which the author has cast him. . ." (Ong, 1975, p. 12).

On the other hand, audience suggests that the writer is at the same time an *object* of outside influences. This account emphasizes the constraints an audience exerts on the writer. It may be seen in what Nystrand (1982) calls the "linguistics of writing," which is the "examination of the effects of readers, as speech community of the writer, upon writers and the texts they compose" (p. 2). It may also be seen in what Kroll (1984) labels the "informational perspective" of audience, which draws upon cognitive processing theories about readers' short- and long-term memory limitations and emphasizes how best to "get information into the reader's head" (p. 176). The linguistic and rhetorical devices that enable readers' "uptake" of information therefore become norms constraining writers' encoding of information. The notion of writer as object is likewise present in the rhetorical perspective, because in adapting to an audience, the author accepts certain constraints, as in the 1960s when white Americans dropped "Negro" from their vocabularies and replaced it with "Black."

To one degree or another these views reflect the familiar struggle between individual and society in which every person is both separate from the group and capable of individual action and at the same time a part of the group and subject to group influences (see Dyson, this volume). It is an opposition which seems to be rooted in the very nature of language and to permeate all types of communication. Thus Edward Sapir (1933) wrote that language is perhaps the greatest force of socialization that exists, and then later in the same essay, "In spite of the fact that language acts as a socializing and uniformizing force, it is at the same time the most potent single known factor for the growth of individuality" (p. 19). Many ordinary acts of politeness, for example, are a means for dealing with this opposition between individual and society by making one's needs or opinions known without appearing to impose on others (Brown & Levinson, 1978). Writers are both agents of influence when effecting change in their readers, and at the same time the object of influence when conforming to established constraints.

An adequate theory of audience thus needs to balance several concerns: writers, who influence and are influenced by, readers; readers, who influence and are influenced by, writers; and texts, which can over time come to embody the norms for writers writing and readers reading. Most theories of audience, however, have found it difficult to balance simultaneously these concerns (but see Bruffee, 1984; Walzer, 1985). The notion *audience* has itself been an obstacle to achieving this balance, denoting as it does the literal interpretation of *audience as readers* and thereby evoking a static Aristotelian notion of writers acting to influence identifiable yet passive readers (Rubin, 1984).

In seeking an alternative to audience we therefore look to a concept that would represent writers, readers, and texts as dynamically interactive, and thus help to (1) describe the interrelationships between discoursers and their texts, and (2) explain the constraints under which these relationships function. Such a concept may lie in the notion of *discourse community*.

Norms in a Discourse Community

The writer who can successfully engage readers is also one who knows and can manipulate the norms for written discourse, norms that are held consensually between readers and writers and embodied in texts. As both agent and object of influence, the writer functions together with readers in a community of particular norms. These reflect standard assumptions about how readers, writers, and texts can be related to each other, and as such help to impose order on the limitless variety of alternatives in the universe of discourse. Community norms and expectations are embodied not only in writers who address and invoke audiences, nor only in the audiences themselves, but in the particular *community* of writers and readers who engage themselves through the medium of text, all together (writers, readers, texts) making up a discourse community. Thus texts, which are often the only visible manifestation of a community (such as readers of Nancy Drew mysteries, for example, or subscribers to *The New Yorker* magazine), also embody community norms. Community norms are like the guidelines readers and writers use to navigate a text, much as roadways are the means by which motorists get from here to there.

Indulge, for a moment, an extension of this analogy. A road is normative in the sense that it is the commonly accepted means for getting from one point to another. Some roads are more normative than others: highways are efficient, but backroads can lead to the same destination. Roadways are not absolute norms but changing ones: New roads are created and old ones abandoned or widened as needs change. Some travelers stray, by accident or design, from the road entirely and find themselves quite alone. The point is obvious: Writers and readers use the norms of their discourse community to construct and construe a text, usually taking the familiar route over the offbeat, and often capable of effecting gradual change on accepted ways.

What are the norms for writers, readers, and texts? Essentially, they are the familiar and expected ways of reading and writing discourse, as embodied in the way most writers write, most readers read, and most texts appear in any given discourse community. Norms are thus probabilistic rather than absolute, and always linked to a particular community, such as evolutionary biologists or computer hackers. These ways of reading and writing discourse are not merely mechanisms for facilitating information processing, like indenting paragraphs or maintaining cohesive ties. Rather, they are ways of reading and writing that influence content as well as form (see Rubin, 1984), reflecting the unique ways a community creates and organizes its knowledge (Bizzell, 1986). For example, in scientific discourse certain topics, such as ESP or divination, are not to be taken seriously by members of the scientific community or those who read scientific writing. In the discourse of tabloids found at the checkout lanes of supermarkets, on the other hand, such topics are stock in trade. Similarly, in the discourse of high-school theme papers, summary conclusions are often considered desirable, while in the discourse of college students' essays, conclusions that merely summarize are considered naive.

Norms and expectations that obtain in different kinds of reader–writer–text relationships pertain to five general areas, resembling several of Dell Hymes's (1972) categories for the description of communicative events: *Purpose, Participants, Genre, Setting,* and *Code.* Each of these may be associated with a set of norms. A persuasive *purpose* is attended by such norms as frequent use of "should," for example, and claims supported by facts, the restatement of key arguments, and documentation—all features which tend to distinguish deliberately persuasive aims from expressive ones, for instance. *Participants* include those writers and readers who share a text, such as reporter, editor, and newspaper reader. Norms for particular *genres* are the conventions which by and large constitute the genre, such as length (for short stories and sonnets), opening lines ("Once upon a time" for bedtime stories), and formats (hypothesis, procedure, results for lab reports). *Setting* includes the norms that come into play by virtue of physical and institutional circumstances surrounding writer, reader, and text: whether a text is composed in class or out of class, whether it is a first or final draft, whether the reader has read it once or more than once, and whether it appears alone or with related texts. And *code* refers to norms concerning the writer's native language(s), grammatical and stylistic conventions (including the "right" of a writer to violate conventions as well as the reader's tolerance for such violations), structuring of given-new information, and whether the text is in Braille or visual print. By determining the operative norms in these areas for writers, readers, and texts, one may begin to form the outline of a particular discourse community.

CONCLUSION

If we can subsume the notion of audience within something like *discourse community*, considerable leverage is gained over the many phenomena for which "audience" is only marginally helpful. This is because the conceptual metaphor of audience inevitably orients our thinking toward readers and questions about their possible responses to texts, stereotypes about their likely attitudes and beliefs, and musings about whether they really exist at all—all important questions, but only features of some larger picture which concepts of audience never quite seem to capture. The notion of discourse community at least holds within its literal level the idea of writers and readers (community) and text (discourse). The notion of community, from Latin *communitae* ("held in common"), includes the dimension of shared knowledge and norms, which describe what writers and readers bring to a text and carry from it. The notion of discourse, from Late Latin *discursus* ("conversation") and Latin ("a running back and forth"), refers to the dynamic nature of negotiated meaning.

Theories of audience have often been criticized for privileging the role of readers while failing to appreciate the writer's powers of imagination and reflection. As Elbow (1987) has stated, "What most readers value in really excellent writing is not prose that is right for readers but prose that is right for thinking, right for language, or right for the subject being written about" (p. 54). In other words, claims Elbow, writers are sometimes at their best when ignoring audience. The concept of discourse community is not incompatible with this argument because individual interests do not necessarily conflict with community interests; the two are often complementary. Whole communities have been redefined or redirected by the private initiatives of individuals such as William Shakespeare, Charles Darwin, or Noam Chomsky. Creativity in thought and expression is highly regarded (normative, in a sense) in many communities. Writing teachers, in fact, have a responsibility to establish creativity and reflective thought as characteristic of the community of writers.

The concept of discourse community does have limitations, which it shares with argument field, interpretive community, and speech community. Some proponents of argument fields have been criticized for excessive relativism in virtually ignoring the propositional content of arguments (Wenzel, 1982) or for failing to emphasize the role of purpose in argument (Rowland, 1982). The notion of interpretive community has been called "elusive" and leading to "an explosion of communities with no important gain" in the ability to predict a community's stands on specific issues (Beaugrande, 1984, p. 551; see also Goodheart, 1983; Stiebel, 1984). And the notion of speech community, at least as employed by Labov (1966, 1972), has been challenged for its failure to accommodate the linguistic change that occurs when members of a community do not share identical constraints on how a variable rule gets applied (Romaine, 1982).

To one degree or another, the many criticisms of the three concepts point to the problem of relativism: Fields and communities have fuzzy boundaries that allow for a good deal of overlap, making the application of such concepts difficult. The same may certainly be said of discourse communities. Human beings, such as they are, have multiple allegiances that overlap and conflict, and human discourse reflects this overlap and conflict all too well. For all these problems, and they are significant, I believe the notion of community is better suited to exploring the relationship between writers, readers, and texts than is audience. Indeed, in argument theory, literary criticism, and linguistics, we see it is not sufficient to understand spoken and written discourse as a straightforward matter of senders and receivers. Rather, the communities in which writers/speakers and readers/listeners align themselves, together with the discourse norms by which these communities have been symbolized, give a theoretically more powerful concept by which we can describe and explain the forces that bind and separate writers, readers, and texts.

REFERENCES

Beaugrande, R., de. (1984). Writer, reader, critic: Comparing critical theories as discourse. *College English, 46,* 533–559.

Bizzell, P. (1986). What happens when basic writers come to college? *College Composition and Communication, 37,* 294–301.

Bloomfield, L. (1933). *Language.* New York: Holt, Rinehart, & Winston.

Britton, J. L., Burgess, T., Martin, N., McLeod, A., & Rosen, H. (1975). *The development of writing abilities (11-18).* London: Macmillan Education.

Brown, P., & Levinson, S. (1978). Universals in language usage. In E. N. Goody (Ed.), *Questions and politeness: Strategies in social interaction* (pp. 56–289). Cambridge, England: Cambridge University Press.

Bruffee, K. A. (1984). Collaborative learning and the "conversation of mankind." *College English, 46,* 635–652.

Ede, L., & Lunsford, A. (1984). Audience addressed/audience invoked: The role of audience in composition theory and pedagogy. *College Composition and Communication, 35,* 115–171.

Elbow, P. (1987). Closing my eyes as I speak: An argument for ignoring audience. *College English, 49,* 50–69.

Faigley, L., & Hansen, K. (1985). Learning to write in the social sciences. *College Composition and Communication, 36,* 140–149.

Fish, S. (1980). *Is there a text in this class? The authority of interpretive communities.* Cambridge, MA: Harvard University Press.

Flower, L. (1981). *Problem-solving strategies for writers.* New York: Harcourt Brace Jovanovich.

Goodheart, E. (1983). The text and the interpretive community. *Daedalus, 112,* 215–31.

Goodnight, G. T. (1982). The personal, technical, and public spheres of argument: A speculative inquiry into the art of public deliberation. *Journal of the American Forensic Association, 18,* 215–227.

Grobe, C. (1981). Syntactic maturity, mechanics, and vocabulary as predictors of quality ratings. *Research in the Teaching of English, 15,* 75–85.

Hymes, D. (1972). Models of the interaction of language and social life. In J. J. Gumperz & D. Hymes (Eds.), *Directions in sociolinguistics* (pp. 35–71). New York: Holt, Rinehart, & Winston.

Kroll, B. M. (1984). Writing for readers: Three perspectives on audience. *College Composition and Communication, 35,* 172–185.

Labov, W. (1966). *The social stratification of English in New York City.* Washington, DC: Center for Applied Linguistics.

Labov, W. (1970). The study of language in its social context. *Studium Generale, 23,* 66–84.

Labov, W. (1972). *Sociolinguistic patterns.* Philadelphia: University of Pennsylvania Press.

Lloyd-Jones, R. (1977). Primary trait scoring of writing. In C. R. Cooper & L. Odell (Eds.), *Evaluating writing: Describing, measuring, judging.* Urbana, IL: National Council of Teachers of English.

Long, R. C. (1980). Writer–audience relationships: Analysis or invention? *College Composition and Communication, 31,* 221–226.

Murray, D. (1979). The listening eye: Reflections on the writing conference. *College English, 41,* 13–18.

Nystrand, M. (1982). Rhetoric's "audience" and linguistics' "speech community": Implications for understanding writing, reading, and text. In M. Nystrand (Ed.), *What writers know* (pp. 1–28). New York: Academic Press.

Odell, L. (1981). Defining and assessing competence in writing. In C. R. Cooper (Ed.), *The nature and measurement of competency in English* (pp. 95–138). Urbana, IL: National Council of Teachers of English.

Ong, W. J. (1975). The writer's audience is always a fiction. *Publications of the Modern Language Association, 90,* 9–21.

Park, D. (1982). The meanings of "audience." *College English, 44,* 247–257.

Park, D. (1986). Analyzing audiences. *College Composition and Communication, 37,* 478–488.

Rafoth, B. A. (1984). Audience awareness and adaptation in the persuasive writing of proficient and nonproficient college freshmen. (Doctoral dissertation, The University of Georgia, 1984). *Dissertation Abstracts International, 45,* 2788–A.

Rafoth, B. A. (1985). Audience adaptation in the essays of proficient and nonproficient freshman writers. *Research in the Teaching of English, 19,* 237–253.

Romaine, S. (1982). What is a speech community? In S. Romaine (Ed.), *Sociolinguistic variation in speech communities* (pp. 13–24). London: Edward Arnold.

Rowland, R. C. (1982). The influence of purpose on fields of argument. *Journal of the American Forensic Association, 18,* 229–245.

Rubin, D. L. (1983). *Oral communication instruction to improve writing skills among four populations of basic writers.* Athens, GA: University of Georgia, Department of Language Education.

Rubin, D. L. (1984). Social cognition and written communication. *Written Communication, 1,* 211–245.

Rubin, D. L., & Piché, G. (1979). Development in syntactic and strategic aspects of audience adaptation skills in written persuasive communication. *Research in the Teaching of English, 13,* 293–316.

Sapir, E. (1933/1949). Language. In D. G. Mandelbaum (Ed.), *Edward Sapir: Culture, language and personality* (pp. 1–44). Berkeley, CA: University of California Press. (Originally published 1933, in E. R. A. Seligman & A. Johnson [Eds.], *Encyclopedia of the social sciences,* [Vol. 9, 155–168]. New York: Macmillan).

Saville–Troike, M. (1982). *The ethnography of communication.* Oxford: Basil Blackwell.

Stiebel, A. (1984). But is it life? Some thoughts on modern critical theory. *Modern Language Studies, 14,* 3–12.

Walzer, A. E. (1985). Articles from the "California Divorce Project": A case study of the concept of audience. *College Composition and Communication, 36,* 150–159.

Wenzel, J. W. (1982). On fields of argument as propositional systems. *Journal of the American Forensic Association, 18*, 205–213.

Willard, C. A. (1981). Field theory: A Cartesian meditation. In G. Ziegelmueller & J. Rhodes (Eds.), *Dimensions of argument: Proceedings of the second summer conference on argumentation* (p. 21–42a). Annandale, VA: Speech Communication Association.

Willard, C. A. (1983). *Argumentation and the social grounds of knowledge*. University, AL: University of Alabama Press.

Zarefsky, D. (1982). Persistent questions in the theory of argument fields. *Journal of the American Forensic Association, 18*, 192–203.

Chapter 7

Writing Apprehension in the Classroom Context

John A. Daly
University of Texas at Austin

Anita Vangelisti
University of Texas at Austin

Stephen P. Witte
Stanford University

Considerable research indicates that people differ in their attitudes toward the act of writing. Some people enjoy, even savor, the experience of putting pen to paper; others find writing a troublesome, uncomfortable, and even fearful experience (for a review of related research, see chapters by Rose, Daly, Self, and Boice in Rose, 1985). The bulk of the research on this individual difference in attitudes toward writing falls under the rubric of *Writing Apprehension*. Briefly, writing apprehension is a construct that refers to a person's predisposition to undertake or to avoid writing tasks. From a theoretical perspective, writing apprehension exists along a continuum, ranging from complete absence to debilitating presence. Since 1975, when Daly and Miller (1975a, 1975b) introduced the construct and demonstrated that it could be reliably and validly measured, a large number of studies have focused on how writing apprehension influences and relates to a range of human behaviors and attitudes, particularly among persons for whom school-sponsored and teacher-directed writing figures importantly (see Daly, 1985).

This chapter takes a direction different from that of most previous research on the writing apprehension construct. Here, we explore the role of writing apprehension in the context of the classroom; we do so primarily by focusing on the relationship between teachers' writing apprehension and some of their instructional practices. This focus is important for a number of reasons. Previous research has shown that writing apprehension is related to students' writing performance, as measured both indirectly (i.e., standardized tests) and directly (Daly, 1978; Faigley, Daly, & Witte, 1981; Selfe, 1985; Witte & Faigley, 1981). Other research has shown that writing apprehension correlates with such features of written texts as number of words, number of t-units, and language intensity (Daly, 1978; Daly & Miller, 1975c; Garcia, 1978). Assuming that writing apprehension is in part an acquired trait, such studies raise interesting questions of whether and how teachers might contribute to the development of writing apprehension in individuals.

The classroom is not only where most children learn to write, but it is also where their feelings or attitudes about the act of writing develop (Barnes, 1976; Dyson, 1984; Edwards, 1981; Mehan, 1978; Smith, 1982). This environment, largely set up and controlled by teachers, helps to determine students' views of the act of writing, to define pupils' notions about the roles that writing plays in their lives, and to shape the manner in which students regard writing and written texts. The present chapter is more specifically motivated by a relatively small number of previous studies that focus upon three related questions: (1) What is the relationship between students' writing apprehension, their course choices, and their satisfaction with curricula? (2) How do students' levels of writing apprehension relate to teachers' perceptions of students? and (3) How does teachers' writing apprehension relate to their classroom practices? Collectively, these three questions call attention to the potential relationships between the psychological and social dimensions of writing in classroom contexts.

The first question, addressing the relationship between students' writing apprehension, their choice of courses and their satisfaction with courses, has been examined in some of Daly and Miller's (1975b) research. Daly and Miller asked undergraduate students to complete the writing apprehension measure and a questionnaire probing their attitudes about, and expectations of, courses that required writing. Daly and Miller reported that students scoring high on the writing apprehension measure had significantly lower expectations of success in such courses than did students scoring low on the measure. Not surprisingly, when contrasted with low-apprehensives, high-apprehensives expressed less willingness to enroll in writing-oriented courses. In addition, and perhaps providing a partial explanation for these findings, high-apprehensive students evaluated their own performances in courses that required writing more negatively than did low-apprehensive students. Moreover, high-apprehensive students were less satisfied with writing-oriented courses than were their low-apprehensive counterparts.

Other research supports the relationship between students' writing apprehension and their satisfaction with courses. Using young adolescents as respondents and their own Attitude Toward Writing measure, Jeroski and Conry (1981) report that writing attitudes correlated significantly with students' satisfaction with curricula, their perceptions of their improvement in writing, and their interest in writing activities. In each case, the reported relationships were in the direction expected: the more positive students' attitudes about writing were, the greater were student-reported levels of satisfaction, interest, and perceived improvement. In a similar vein, Selfe (1985), basing her findings on interviews with a very small sample of high- and low-apprehensive writers, reports that high-apprehensives tended to dislike composing, had little confidence in their writing ability, and feared evaluation of their written products.

Findings such as these appear to generalize to students' choices and preferences for curricula. For example, Daly and Miller (1975b) report that the average writing apprehension score of students enrolled in advanced composition classes was significantly lower than that of the general student population. In another study, Daly and Shamo (1978) reported that writing apprehension interacted with the perceived writing requirements of academic majors and thereby affected the desirability of those majors. The high-apprehensive individuals in that study tended to prefer majors that they perceived to require comparatively little writing. In contrast, the low-apprehensives preferred majors that, in their eyes, required more writing.

The second important research focus, one tied more directly to the major thrust of this chapter, is the exploration of how teachers respond to students who vary in levels of writing apprehension. Daly (1979), for example, had elementary and secondary school teachers read descriptions of four hypothetical students. These students were described identically except for two characteristics, which were manipulated experimentally. The first manipulation was students' level of writing apprehension. Two students were described as prototypical high-apprehensives; two other students, as prototypical low-apprehensives. The second manipulation was the hypothetical students' sex. Teachers, after reading one of the four resulting descriptions, made a series of predictive judgments about the students. Daly reports that analyses of the teachers' responses yielded a large and statistically significant main effect for writing apprehension. That is to say, the teachers had significantly higher and more positive expectancies for low-apprehensive students than they had for high-apprehensive ones. However, as Daly notes, this main effect must be viewed within the context of a significant interaction between sex and writing apprehension: The responding teachers in Daly's study regarded high-apprehensive female students and low-apprehensive male students least positively and regarded high-apprehensive males and low-apprehensive females most positively. The interaction effect suggests a general sex bias on the part of the responding teachers: Females who like to write and males who don't like to write seemed to conform to teachers' expectations. Violations of these expectations in either direction (i.e., males who like to write, or females who don't) tended to result in negative judgments by the teachers.

The third research focus, directly related to the present chapter, is the relationship between teachers' writing apprehension and attitudes toward writing and their teaching practices. This small body of research suggests that teachers vary in their levels of writing apprehension and that this variability relates to the type of instructional materials teachers consider important, what they judge relevant to instruction, and how they teach different materials. The findings of two studies are particularly relevant to the investigations we report here.

In one of these studies, Gere, Schuessler, and Abbott (1984) report on the results of their administration of a four-dimension measure of teachers' attitudes toward writing instruction. The four dimensions included in the measure were (1) the importance of Standard English, (2) the importance of defining and evaluating written tasks, (3) the importance of student self-expression in writing, and (4) the importance of linguistic maturity in writing. The authors correlated teachers' attitudes toward these four dimensions of writing instruction with scores on the Daly–Miller writing apprehension measure.

For both male and female teachers, Gere et al. report a significant and inverse correlation between writing apprehension and attitudes toward the importance of linguistic maturity. The linguistic maturity score emphasized certain positive behaviors on the part of both students and teacher (e.g., "The experience of composing can and should nurture the pupils' quest for self-realization and their need to relate constructively to their peers" and "The teacher–pupil conference can and should aid the learners in finding their strengths and encourage them in correcting some of their weaknesses") as well as a number of process notions associated with expert or mature writers. Gere et al.'s finding indicates that the high-apprehensive teachers were less willing to endorse or foster "linguistically mature" beliefs than were the low-apprehensive teachers.

For the female teachers in their sample, Gere et al. also report significant positive correlations between writing apprehension and attitudes toward both the importance of Standard English and the importance of defining and evaluating writing. The Standard English dimension was exemplified by statements such as "Students should not be allowed to begin sentences with *and, or, few* or *but*" and "Students should be required to prepare written outlines before they begin writing expository papers." A high score on this dimension appears to represent rigid and traditional beliefs and rules about writing. The dimension that emphasized defining and evaluating writing included statements such as "Grades are the most effective way of evaluating compositions" and "Every error on a student's composition should be indicated." The primary focus of this latter attitudinal dimension seems to be on the importance of thorough, rigorous marking ("evaluating") of student papers. Gere et al.'s findings for these two dimensions suggest that the more apprehensive female teachers are, the more likely they are to have a set of rigid beliefs about writing evaluation and instruction. For male teachers, Gere et al. found no significant relationship between writing apprehension and attitudes toward Standard English, and they report only a small, but statistically significant, inverse relationship between writing apprehension and attitudes toward evaluating and defining writing.

In brief, these findings suggest that high-apprehensive female teachers are more likely to be concerned with issues of form and usage and—perhaps as a way of reducing their own writing anxiety—are more likely to approach writing instruction in a dogmatic fashion. For female teachers, Gere et al. also report that writing apprehension is inversely and significantly related to attitudes toward the importance of self-expression in student writing. According to the authors, higher writing apprehension is also associated with greater rigidity of rules and with less liberalism about style, self-expression, and nontraditional (but perhaps very important) process behaviors. Lastly, although there was an interesting tendency for writing apprehension to be higher among teachers in elementary and secondary schools than in community colleges and universities, Gere et al.'s data reveal no significant difference in level of writing apprehension as a function of teaching experience, sex, or grade level taught.

Unlike the Gere et al. (1984) study, Claypool's (1980) research focuses directly on the relationship between teachers' writing apprehension and the frequency with which they assign writing tasks. Claypool's data consist of responses from 192 secondary school teachers to a questionnaire assessing how often they made classroom assignments that required writing on the part of their students. Claypool reports a significant difference between high- and low-apprehensive teachers in the number of writing assignments made. High-apprehensives, on average, reported making seven writing assignments yearly; but the low-apprehensives reported making, on average, 19.9 writing assignments each year. Claypool also divided the 192 teachers into four groups based on subjects taught: language arts, social studies, math and science, and applied arts and sciences. She found that language arts teachers had the lowest apprehension level and that math and science teachers had the highest apprehension.

Taken together, this body of prior research suggests that writing apprehension is related, in a number of important ways, to the classroom context for school-sponsored or teacher-directed writing. In particular, writing apprehension appears to manifest itself in students' choices of classes and majors, in students' writing performances, in teachers' perceptions of students, in teachers' attitudes toward dimensions of writing instruction, and in the frequency of teacher-assigned writing tasks. The three studies that we report below explore some additional connections between writing apprehension and the classroom. Our first two studies examine the impact of teachers' writing apprehension on the classroom environment. Broadly speaking, we ask: Is there a relationship between the apprehension that teachers have about writing and the ways in which they use and evaluate writing in the classroom? Study 1 focuses on the relationship between teachers' writing apprehension and the writing that students complete in classrooms, and Study 2 focuses on the relationship between teachers' writing apprehension and the nature of the criteria they use to evaluate writing assignments. Unlike Study 1 and Study 2, Study 3 is a *post hoc* analysis of a large data base from a national assessment of writing. In Study 3, we investigate whether variables such as frequency of school-based writing assignments are related to students' levels of writing apprehension and to their performances as writers.

Study 1: Teaching and Teachers' Writing Apprehension

Study 1 explores the possible relationship between writing apprehension, teachers' classroom behaviors, and their emphasis on writing activities. Cognizant of the findings of previous research, we formulated three hypotheses to test in Study 1. Given a relationship between writing apprehension and occupational choice (Daly & Shamo, 1976), we hypothesized that teachers high in writing apprehension would teach subject matters that require little writing and that teachers low in writing apprehension would select subject matters that require substantially more writing. More specifically, we hypothesized *an inverse relationship between teachers' writing apprehension and the relevance those teachers report for writing in their chosen subject areas*. Second, we hypothesized that even when teachers teach the same subject matter, writing apprehension would influence the degree to which they emphasize writing activities. That is to say, we hypothesized *an inverse relationship between teachers' writing apprehension and their reported classroom emphasis on writing*. Third, we hypothesized that teachers would differ in the amount and types of writing they themselves engaged in as a function of their apprehension. More specifically, we hypothesized *an inverse relationship between teachers' writing apprehension and their self-reported writing activities.*

Design of study 1. For Study 1, 185 elementary and secondary school teachers enrolled in graduate courses in a four-state area participated as part of a class project. The median number of years of teaching experience for the group was 5.3. During a designated class period, each of the 185 teachers received and completed five, randomly ordered measures:

> *Writing Apprehension.* Teachers completed the 20-item version of the writing apprehension measure (Daly & Miller, 1975a). The instrument's reliability (alpha) in this study was .95.
>
> *Writing Emphasis.* Responses to the statement, "I emphasize writing more than most teachers in my subject and grade level," were elicited on a 7-point scale bounded by the words "strongly disagree" and "strongly agree."
>
> *Writing Relevance.* Using a 7-point scale bounded by the words "very irrelevant" and "very relevant," teachers responded to the question, "How relevant is writing to your subject area?"
>
> *Learning Activities.* A list of seven activities that require some sort of student writing was presented to the teachers, who were asked to indicate the likelihood of their assigning each activity. Each activity was matched with a response scale bounded by the words "very unlikely" and "very likely." The activities listed were (a) essay exams, (b) homework requiring writing, (c) classroom composition work, (d) journal writing, (e) letter writing exercises, (f) written book reports, and (g) diary writing. For the main analyses these seven activities were formed into a composite. The internal consistency estimate (alpha) for the seven taken together was .83.
>
> *Writing Behaviors.* Teachers responded to seven statements about how often they themselves engaged in different types of writing activities (writing personal letters, writing business letters, writing memos, writing notes to students' parents, writing newsletters, doing creative writing, and writing in diaries). To each statement, the teachers responded on a 5-point scale bounded by the words "very seldom" and "very often." The seven activities formed a composite with an alpha reliability of .63.

Results of study 1: Hypothesis 1. Our first hypothesis posited a significant and inverse relationship between the teachers' writing apprehension and the reported relevance of writing in the subject area taught by teachers. The hypothesis was confirmed ($r = -.25$, $p < .001$).

Hypothesis 2. Our second hypothesis proposed an inverse and significant relationship between the teachers' writing apprehension and reported emphasis on writing in the classroom. We tested our second hypothesis in two ways. First, we analyzed teachers' reports of their general emphasis on writing. Based on this dependent measure, the second hypothesis was also confirmed ($r = -.26$, $p < .001$). Because there was a significant correlation between the relevance measure and the emphasis measure ($r = .40$, $p < .001$), we computed a partial correlation, which controlled for relevance, between emphasis and writing apprehension. That correlation, while smaller, was also statistically significant ($r = -.18$, $p < .008$).

Another way we tested the second hypothesis was to relate writing apprehension to the measure of writing-based learning activities. The correlation, as expected, was significant and negative ($r = -.17$, $p <.008$). Again, in an attempt to control for the potential confound of different writing requirements across subject areas, we calculated a partial correlation, which controlled for relevance within subject area, between apprehension and the learning activities measure. The partial correlation was nonsignificant ($r = -.09$, ns). Thus, when the writing requirements of a given subject area are controlled, the relationship between teachers' writing apprehension and their selection of writing-based activities is not significant.

Hypothesis 3. Our third hypothesis stated that writing apprehension would be inversely and significantly related to the specific writing behaviors of the teachers. This hypothesis, through the use of a zero-order correlation, was also confirmed ($r = -.37$, $p < .001$). When we partialed out the measure of writing relevance, the correlation, though smaller, was still statistically reliable ($r = -.34$, $p < .001$).

Secondary analysis of study 1 data. A secondary analysis of the Study 1 data tested our three hypotheses within grade level. The question this analysis sought to answer was whether the pattern of associations independent of grade level would be consistent across grade levels. This analysis was suggested to us by some of the responding teachers, who proposed that there were substantive differences in the relevance of writing at different grade levels, and by the finding of a significant and inverse ($r = -.17$, $p < .01$) correlation between writing apprehension and teacher grade level.

For this secondary analysis, we divided the teachers into four groups according to grade level taught. The groups were as follows: (1) kindergarten through second grade ($n = 39$), (2) third grade through fifth grade ($n = 51$), (3) sixth grade through eighth grade ($n = 42$), and (4) ninth grade through 12th (n = 40). Zero-order correlations and partial correlations controlling for writing relevance were computed and are presented in Table 1. As Table 1 indicates, a number of the zero-order and partial correlations within grade level taught are statistically significant. The pattern of results reported in Table 1 suggests that writing apprehension does differentially influence the decisions and emphases of teachers at different grade levels. The first-order partial coefficients suggest that writing apprehension has its most powerful effects on teachers' classroom behaviors in the third through fifth grades. In those grades, all four of the measures are inversely and significantly correlated with the teachers' writing apprehension. For this same group of teachers, controlling for the relevance of writing to the teachers' subject matter areas only slightly reduces the magnitude of the three remaining correlations. With the exception of the first-order partial correlation between teachers' writing apprehension and the writing-based learning activities they assign, the same observations hold for the teachers of students in grades 9 through 12.

The results of Study 1 suggest that teachers' writing apprehension is related to teachers' writing-related behaviors and to teachers' emphasis on writing within the classroom. The general pattern is for high-apprehensive teachers, when compared with their low-apprehensive counterparts, to teach subject matters for which writing is perceived as less relevant and to use fewer exercises and activities that demand writing from students. When the perceived relevance of writing to the subject matter is controlled, these relationships while smaller in magnitude, remain statistically significant. The secondary analysis, which used the grade levels taught as a classificatory variable, supported and extended our initial findings, especially for teachers of grades 3–5 and grades 9–12.

Table 1.   Zero-Order and Partial Correlations Between Teachers' Writing Apprehension and 4 Writing-Related Measures

Grade Level	Activities	Behavior	Emphasis	Relevance
K–2	−.23*	−.25*	−.11	−.24*
	−.17	−.27*	.23	
3–5	−.37*	−.45*	−.35*	−.14
	−.35*	−.42*	−.33*	
6–8	−.03	−.25*	−.37*	−.43*
	−.16	−.14	−.18	
9–12	−.25*	−.50*	−.36*	−.40*
	−.09	−.47*	−.30*	

Note: The upper line of correlations are the zero-order coefficients. The lower line presents the first-order partial correlations controlling for relevance in subject area. (*p < .05)

Study 2: Teachers' Writing Apprehension and Their Writing Assignments

Study 1 found a significant inverse relationship between the writing apprehension of teachers and the choices they make about writing assignments. The results of Study 1 suggest that high-apprehensive teachers are less likely than their low-apprehensive counterparts to use learning activities that require their students to write. Yet, regardless of the apprehension of the teachers studied, virtually every teacher indicated that, at some times, he or she chooses to use writing-based instructional activities. This finding raises an important question: When teachers do use learning activities that require students to write, are teachers' evaluative standards at least partly a function of their writing apprehension? That is to say, do high-apprehensive teachers, when using a writing assignment as a part of the instructional process, differ from low-apprehensive teachers in what they expect? To answer this and related questions, we conducted Study 2.

Design of study 2.   For Study 2, we administered a short form of the Daly–Miller writing apprehension measure (*alpha* = .94) to a group of 145 in-service elementary and secondary schoolteachers enrolled in graduate courses in communication. The entire sample of teachers also answered two questions about the amount of writing required of students at their grade level ("In your subject area and grade level, how much writing is typically required of children?" and "In your class, how much writing do you require your students to do?"). Responses to the two questions were highly correlated ($r = .82$, $p < .001$). Writing apprehension was also correlated with the teachers' responses to both questions (typical: $r = -.12$, $p < .08$; your class: $r = -.22$, $p < .004$). A partial correlation, which controlled for the amount of writing typically required within the teachers' grade levels and subject areas, was then computed between teachers' writing apprehension and the amount of writing teachers required in their own classes. The partial correlation was statistically significant ($r = -.23$, $p < .003$), suggesting that teachers' writing apprehension is inversely related to the degree to which writing is emphasized in a classroom even after the "average," or typical, writing requirements of a grade and subject matter area are controlled. This is a straightforward replication of the finding in the first investigation.

After computing the mean score on the 20-item, writing apprehension measure ($M = 57.74$, sd = 13.97, $n = 145$), we identified teachers whose scores were one standard deviation above or below the mean. Twenty-five high-apprehensive ($M = 79.08$, sd = 7.87) and 25 low-apprehensive teachers ($M = 38.40$, sd = 6.83) were identified on the basis of having, respectively, the highest and lowest scores on the apprehension measure. These 50 teachers responded to an extensive questionnaire about their writing attitudes and classroom practices. The teachers who fell within one standard deviation of the mean did not complete the larger questionnaire. That questionnaire included the following items:

> *Good Writing*: "What does good writing mean to you in terms of your students? What makes their writing good?"
>
> *Bad Writing*: "What does poor writing mean to you in terms of your students? What makes their writing poor?"
>
> *Advice*: "If you were to advise people about what it takes to be a good teacher of writing at your grade level, what would be your advice?"
>
> *Best Writing Assignment*: "If you wanted to create the best writing assignment possible for your students, what would it be? We'd like you to write that assignment down, as completely as possible, on the lines below. Don't leave any part of your instructions out."
>
> *Last Assignments*: Teachers were asked to write down up to 10 of the last writing assignments they used in their classes.

The 50 teachers' responses to each item or question were content analyzed. For the content analyses, we created categories that effectively summarized the teachers' responses, which for the first three measures consisted of descriptors of students' writing. The teachers' responses were coded by two raters. In no case was coding agreement for a category less than 85%.

Results of study 2:   *Question 1.* To code the teachers' responses to the "good writing" question, we created four categories of descriptors:

> *Category 1* ("mechanics"): Included in Category 1 were responses emphasizing such things as spelling, grammar, punctuation, and neatness (e.g., "being able to put their ideas down correctly—e.g., subject–verb agreement, complete sentences, punctuation used correctly").
>
> *Category 2* ("expression"): Category 2 included responses that named such qualities such as creativity, good word choice, and good ideas (e.g., "their writing is 'good' as long as they are expressing their feelings"; "expression is primary . . . "; "Being able to use imagination and creativity are important").
>
> *Category 3* ("structure"): Included in this category were responses that focused on such features as organization, development of ideas, good outlines, and so forth (e.g., "good sentence structure"; "logical organization"; "supporting details").

Category 4 ("process"): Included in Category 4 were comments about planning, revising, using first drafts, etc. (e.g., "write and rewrite are the tools of a good writer"; "good writers plan what they write").

Each of the 50 teachers' responses were coded into one or more of the four categories. Our analyses of these data indicated that a significantly higher proportion ($z = 3.12$, $p < .001$) of low-apprehensive teachers (95% compared with 54%) included Category 2 ("expression") descriptors in their descriptions of good writing than did high-apprehensive teachers. There were no statistically significant differences in the proportions of low- and high-apprehensive teachers who used descriptors included in Category 1 ("mechanics"; high: 64%, low: 50%), Category 3 ("structure"; high: 44%, low: 54%), or Category 4 ("process"; high: 0%; low: 4%). Another way of analyzing teacher responses would be to use proportions that adjusted for the differing number of comments each teacher provided. When proportions were calculated we found two significant differences due to writing apprehension. First, high- ($M = .43$, sd $= .39$) and low-apprehensive ($M = .21$, sd $= .23$) teachers differed in their emphasis on mechanics ($t = 2.29$, $p < .02$). Second, they differed in the proportionate mention of expression: Low apprehensive teachers ($M = .49$, sd $= .22$) included mentions of expression significantly more ($t = 1.81$, $p < .05$) than high-apprehensive teachers ($M = .33$, sd $= .38$). In reviewing the teachers' responses we also noted that 32% of the low-apprehensive teachers actually wrote disclaimers about a focus on mechanics, emphasizing that their major concern was instead with content and ideas (e.g., "I am not as concerned with grammar and spelling as I am with the development and expression of ideas."). Interestingly, not a single high-apprehensive made such a disclaimer. In addition, a close inspection of the teachers' responses suggested that high-apprehensive teachers focused more on "rules" about writing than did their low-apprehensive counterparts, who seemed far more tentative about "musts" in student writing.

Question 2. For our analyses of the teachers' responses to our second question, which focused on poor writing, we used the same categories of descriptors used in analyzing responses to the first question. Two changes were necessary. First, the process category did not appear relevant for responses to the question. Teachers simply didn't bring process notions up when describing poor writing. Second, the teachers' responses mandated the use of a fifth and sixth category of descriptors:

Category 5 ("effort"): Included in Category 5 were statements about the involvement of the writer, the amount of effort put into writing, and so forth. (e.g., "When a student has not put effort into it . . . "; "They don't try, and write as little as they can get by with").

Category 6 ("copying"): In this category were included comments about students' copying from published sources, from other students' work, etc. (e.g., "They sometimes copy ideas from other students"; "When students copy an article out of a book or another students' paper and hand it in as their own original paper . . . ").

Analyses of the 50 teachers' responses to the second question revealed two significant differences between the high- and low-apprehensive teachers. First, a significantly smaller ($z = 1.87$, $p < .05$) proportion of high-apprehensive teachers (9% compared with 32%) used Category 5 ("effort") descriptors than did low-apprehensive teachers. Second, proportionately more ($z = 2.79$, $p < .01$) low-apprehensive teachers (59% compared with 18%) used Category 2 ("expression") descriptors than did the high-apprehensive teachers. There were no significant differences between two groups of teachers in their use of descriptors included in Category 1 ("mechanics"; high: 55%, low: 36%), 3 ("structure"; high: 64%, low: 55%), or 6 ("copying"; high: 9%, low: 5%). A second way of analyzing the data would be to use proportions that adjusted for the relative frequency of idea units offered by each teacher. When these analyses were completed, statistically significant differences appeared for two of the variables: mechanics ($t(42) = 1.88$, $p < .03$; high: $M = .36$, sd $= .41$; low: $M = .17$, sd $= .27$) and expression ($t(42) = 3.01$, $p < .004$; high: $M = .07$, sd $= .16$; low: $M = .27$, sd $= .28$). Marginally significant differences emerged for effort ($t = 1.59$, $p < .06$; high: $M = .07$, sd $= .23$; low: $M = .21$, sd $= .36$) and structure ($t = 1.54$, $p < .07$; high: $M = .43$, sd $= .39$; low: $M = .27$, sd $= .29$). The pattern suggests that highly apprehensive teachers emphasize more mechanics and structure while less apprehensive teachers emphasize expression and effort.

Question 3. The third question we posed in Study 2 sought teachers' advice on what is involved in being a good teacher of writing at their grade levels. The teachers' responses were again grouped in categories. With two exceptions, the categories used to code the responses to our third question were similar to those used to code the responses to the first two questions. Those four categories accommodated responses that emphasized (1) mechanics, (2) expression, (3) structure, and 4) process (see above). The two additional categories were ones that accommodated responses emphasizing practice and feedback in writing instruction:

(5) *Practice*: In this category were included statements about the value of practicing writing (e.g., "They need to practice it a lot"; "The students should write everyday").

(6) *Feedback*: Responses included in this category emphasized the importance of teachers' responding positively to students' writing (e.g., "Never cut down but encourage and show another maybe better way"; "Offer encouragement"; "Concentrate on the positive points of the paper"; "Tell those with too many negatives something *good* about their paper").

Our analyses of the teachers' responses revealed two significant differences between the two groups of teachers. There was a significant difference in the proportion of high- and low-apprehensive teachers who remarked that good teachers of writing emphasize teaching students how to "express" themselves ($z = 2.28$, $p < .05$), and there was a significant difference in the proportion of teachers in each group who wrote that good teachers teach students how to "structure" or organize their writing ($z = 2.07$, $p < .05$). Significantly more low-apprehensive teachers emphasized teaching "expression" (66% versus 29%) while significantly more high-apprehensive teachers emphasized teaching "structure" (29% versus 5%).

Question 4. Our fourth question asked teachers for their best writing assignments. Analyzing the teachers' responses to the fourth question was initially difficult because most teachers' assignments were developed for their particular subject areas. That is to say, high school science teachers wrote assignments that had something to do with science, language arts teachers wrote assignments that focused on stories or poems, and so on. To analyze the responses to question four, we thus had to develop a content-free group of categories, categories that were not tied to subject matter. The coding system we developed included six categories. Descriptions of those categories appear below:

Creativity: Each essay assignment was coded for its originality or creativity on a three-step scale (low, moderate, high). For instance, one teacher's assignment that was rated as highly creative asked students to write stories about an "adventure they might have if they were suddenly transported to another time— past or future." An example of an assignment coded as having low creativity was "Pick a sport which interests you. Write the origin, basic rules, and explain briefly how to play the sport."

Process Emphasis: Assignments were also rated on a three-step scale for the degree to which the task specifications emphasized behaviors that typically fall under the rubric of writing process.

Such behaviors included revising or rewriting and prewriting activities, such as "thinking about what you will write before actually writing."

Rules: The number of specific rules about writing given in each assignment was counted. Rules governed such things as the
length of the essay and the placement of one's name on the
page.

Emphasis on Mechanics: Using a three-step scale, we coded each assignment for the degree to which it emphasized spelling, punctuation, grammar, and use of conventions. The scale was de-
vised so that a low score indicated an emphasis on mechanics.

Specificity: Each assignment was rated on a three-step scale for how
specific it was in terms of instructions. For instance, a highly
specific assignment was "We have just finished reading our
story. I want you to retell the story in writing. We talked about
how the story had a beginning, a middle and an end. You will
write three paragraphs, the 1st paragraph will tell us about the
beginning of the story. (Review: a paragraph has a topic sentence, a few detail sentences)—Repeat for 2nd paragraph middle, and 3rd paragraph the end." An example of a very nonspe-
cific assignment is "Compose a short story."

Topic Control: A three-step scale was used to code each assignment
in terms of who chooses the topic the student is supposed to
write about. At one extreme were cases where the teacher alone
determined the topic students were to write about (e.g., "I
would like you to write a paper on what you like about music
class, and what you don't like about music class. Please write
neatly and use complete sentences. If you write, 'I don't like
singing' or some other similar statement, please explain why
you don't like it, or why you do like it"). At the other extreme,
students had a great deal of latitude in choosing topics (e.g.,
"Write a paper about something that interests you"). A middle
score implied the teacher gave students some choice in writing
topics (e.g., "Pick one of the following three topics. . . ").

Using the six different categories as dependent variables, we conducted a series of *t*-tests to compare the writing assignments of the high-
and low-apprehensive teachers. Significant differences were identified
for all categories of responses except specificity. Compared with the assignments offered by the high-apprehensive teachers, low-apprehensive teachers' assignments displayed more creativity ($t(30) = 2.01$, $p
< .03$; high: $M = 1.61$, sd $= .77$; low: $M = 2.21$, sd $= .86$), invoked
fewer rules ($t(30) = 1.79$, $p < .05$; high: $M = 1.77$, sd $= 1.64$; low: $M =$

.79, sd = 1.43), placed less emphasis on mechanics ($t(30)$ = 2.15, $p <$ .02; high: M = 2.38, sd = .65; low: M = 2.79, sd = .42), and offered students more choice in writing topic selection ($t(30)$ = 1.78, $p < .05$; high: M = 1.61, sd = .77; low: M = 2.16, sd = .90). In addition, 26% of the low-apprehensive teachers included in their assignments some statement that fit within the process category, but none of the high-apprehensive teachers made any such statements in their assignments.

Question 5. The fifth and final question to which the teachers in Study 2 responded focused on their in-class assignments that required students to produce writing. The 50 teachers were asked to list up to 10 such assignments that they had recently used. Our initial analysis of these data sought to determine whether the number of assignments listed by high- and low-apprehensive teachers differed significantly. Using a *t*-test, we compared the two groups and found no statistically significant difference ($t(33)$ = .64, ns) in the average number of assignments described by low- (M = 5.71, sd = 2.47) and high- (M = 5.05, sd = 3.45) apprehensive teachers.

We then coded the teachers' assignments in two ways. The first focused on the purposes for writing that the teachers specified in their writing assignments. We identified four major purposes and then used those four purposes as the basis for coding each assignment. The writing purposes we identified are the following:

1. *Disciplinary*: Writing serves to punish students for something they did or did not do.
2. *Informational*: Writing serves either as a way for students to demonstrate their knowledge or as a means for them to acquire knowledge.
3. *Expressive*: Writing serves as a way for students to play, to develop their understanding of themselves, or to create fictional worlds.
4. *Functional*: Writing serves as a means to request something or to respond to someone or something.

The second way we coded the teachers' assignments focused on the audiences. We identified five categories of audience and used them to code each assignment. The five audience categories were (1) the self, (2) an imagined (often unspecified) audience, (3) the teacher, (4) a significant other, and (5) a general (often unspecified) audience.

Two important trends emerged from the coding of the assignments in terms of purpose and audience. First, high-apprehensive teachers' assignments focused far less often on the expressive purpose (z = 1.62, $p < .10$) than the assignments made by low-apprehensive teachers. Second, the assignments by teachers who were low-apprehensive fell into significantly more ($t(35)$ = 2.14, p < .02) audience and purpose categories (M = 3.53, sd = 1.18) than the assignments by high-apprehensives (M = 2.55, sd = 1.54). In essence, low-apprehensive teachers' assignments were marked by greater variability in purpose and audience than were the assignments of high-apprehensive teachers.

Collectively, the results of Study 2 indicate that high-apprehensive teachers have different perceptions of classroom writing tasks and texts than low-apprehensive teachers. These differences suggest that apprehension affects the expectations teachers have for their students' writing. Highly apprehensive teachers assign and anticipate writing with different characteristics than low-apprehensive teachers. Low-apprehensive teachers seem less bound by rigid rules, emphasize creative expression and effort more, and worry less about mechanical structure than their counterparts high in apprehension.

Study 3: Contextual Influences on Students' Writing Apprehension and Performance

Taken together, Study 1 and Study 2 showed that the writing apprehension of teachers can affect the amount and types of writing that teachers assign and students do in the classroom, as well as the criteria that teachers have for evaluating student writing. In short, Study 1 and Study 2 demonstrated that teachers' writing apprehension affects writing instruction in a number of ways. These findings suggested the need for a third study, one that would look at the relationship between students' attitudes about writing and the classroom context. We believed that such a study should address a question like the following: Since teachers' writing apprehension affects the ways in which classrooms are structured, do teacher-controlled classroom variables related to writing apprehension affect students' feelings about writing and their writing performances? Stated somewhat differently, the question we sought to answer in Study 3 is whether such things as the number of writing assignments students complete in classes affect students' apprehension about writing and, in turn, their competence as writers. The importance of posing such a question is, of course, obvious: If we find that classroom variables related to writing have little effect on either students' attitudes about writing or on their performance on writing tasks, then the findings reported for Study 1 and Study 2 are, in essence, less than meaningful. If, on the other hand, classroom variables do affect students' writing-related attitudes and behaviors, then the findings regarding teachers previously described are potentially quite important.

Design of study 3. To explore the question we have posed, we conducted Study 3. For Study 3, we used an intact data set that was collected as part of the 1978 National Assessment of Educational Progress assessment of the writing skills of 13-year-olds. The sample used for Study 3 was composed of 2,776 thirteen-year-olds drawn, by means of a systematic sampling procedure, from a variety of schools and regions of the United States.[1] For the 1978 NAEP writing assessment, each student completed an essay that was reliably evaluated using a primary-trait scoring system (cf. Lloyd–Jones, 1977). For the purposes of Study 3, the score a student received on this essay served as his or her performance measure. As part of its 1978 writing assessment, NAEP also collected data on eight other indexes, which we also used in Study 3. The indexes are:

> *Writing Apprehension* (WAT): A shortened version of the writing apprehension measure, which consisted of 11 items (e.g., "I like to write down my ideas"; "I am no good at writing"; "Expressing ideas through writing seems to be a waste of time") was completed by each student. The *alpha* reliability for this measure was .83.
>
> *Writing Frequency in School* (FREQ): Students indicated how many reports and essays they had written during the preceding 6 weeks as part of any school assignment.
>
> *Writing Instruction* (INSTRUCT): Students answered seven questions about the instruction they had received in writing. The items were the following: (a) In the general English, literature, or grammar classes you have taken during the past 2 years, about what part of the class time was spent on instruction in how to write reports and essays? (b) Are you encouraged to jot down ideas and make notes about the topic of your paper before you write it? (c) Are you encouraged to make outlines of your papers before you write them? (d) Do you write a paper more than once before you turn it in to your teacher? (e) When your papers are returned, do they have written suggestions on how to improve your writing? (f) When your papers are returned, do your teachers discuss them with you? (g) After your papers are returned, do you work on the paper again to improve it? Students' responses to these questions were first standardized and then formed into a composite index.

---

[1] Because of the nature of the sampling techniques used by the National Assessment of Education Progress (stratification and clustering), the data we used fail to meet standard assumptions used in normal regression methods. Because of the representative sampling procedure used by NAEP, each student has a weight assigned to him or her and it is necessary to utilize a design effect of two (meaning the sample, for analyses, is essentially one-half of the total) in the regression analyses.

Home Environment (HOME): Students completed four items that when formed into a composite index assessed, to some degree, how conducive their home environments were to literacy (and implicity, writing). The four items were the following: (a) Does your family get a newspaper regularly? (b) Does your family get any magazines regularly? (c) Are there more than 25 books in your home? (d) Is there an encyclopedia in your home?

Socioeconomic Status (SES): In line with prior work with the National Assessment (e.g., Haertel, Walberg, Junker, & Pascarella, 1981), parents' education level served as an indirect measure of students' socioeconomic status. Mothers' and fathers' education correlated .54 ($p < .00001$).

School Support of Writing (SCHOOL): Principals of the schools from which the student data were collected completed a questionnaire that included items about the school's support for writing instruction. These questions (which were formed into a composite variable) focused on whether (a) individual writing instruction was available to students, (b) training for writing teacher was given, (c) assistance was available to writing teachers, and (d) writing teachers taught fewer classes.

Student Sex (SEX) *and Race* (RACE): During the administration of the tests, the administrator of the test recorded each student's sex and race (scored here as minority or nonminority).

Results of study 3. The primary purpose of Study 3 was to develop a model of the relationships among the variables described above. The model that was tested is presented in Figure 1. The final outcome variable for the model was students' performance on the essay developed, administered, and scored by NAEP. The exogenous variables were the students' sex, race, SES, and home environment. Between the exogenous variables and the final performance measure were four intervening variables: writing apprehension (WAT), writing instruction (INSTRUCT), writing frequency (FREQ), and school support for writing (SCHOOL). Because the NAEP sample we examined for Study 3 was composed of 13-year-olds who seldom, if ever, choose which classes to take, apprehension was posited to follow the other three intervening variables. That is to say, we tested the hypothesis that writing instruction (INSTRUCT), frequency of writing (FREQ), and school support (SCHOOL) affect students' writing apprehension. On the other hand, we implicitly assumed that for the NAEP sample used in Study 3, writing apprehension should not significantly affect the three other variables. Were this a sample of college students, or even senior high school pupils, this model and its underlying assumptions might be inappropriate because students' writing apprehension might impact their choices of courses which, in turn, might affect their responses to the indices that measure of writing frequency and school writing.

Our analysis of the data suggested that the entire model had a statistically significant multiple correlation of .33 ($p < .00001$) with the students' performance on the essay. The individual beta weights that were statistically reliable are displayed in Figure 1. Our analysis resulted in several significant findings. First, the analysis showed a significant link between sex and writing apprehension. This outcome replicates earlier findings that females tend to be less apprehensive about writing than males (e.g., Daly & Miller, 1975b; Dickson, 1978). Second, the analysis revealed a significant relationship between minority status and writing apprehension. Minority pupils reported more positive attitudes about writing than white children. This finding is identical to one observed by Haertel et al. (1981) for science attitudes. Third, an inverse relationship between SES (as measured by parents' education) and writing apprehension was found. Fourth, the analysis detected an inverse association between writing apprehension and home environment. Fifth, an inverse relationship between writing apprehension and writing performance was revealed, again replicating earlier research (for a summary, see Daly, 1985).

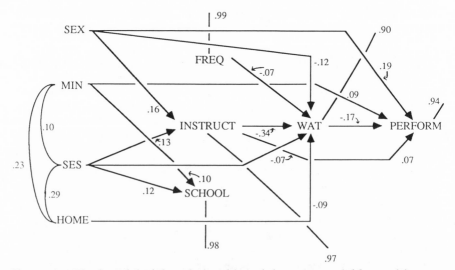

Figure 1. Final model of the relationships of classroom variables, writing apprehension, and writing performance. (Key: SEX = male/female; MIN = minority status; SES = socioeconomic status; HOME = conduciveness of home to literacy; FREQ = frequency of school writing; INSTRUCT = amount and quality of writing instruction in class; SCHOOL = school support for writing; WAT = writing apprehension; PERFORM = performance on NAEP writing assessment essay.)

Most interesting was the finding that while two of the three school writing variables (writing frequency and writing instruction) were significantly associated with writing apprehension, only writing instruction was related to writing performance, and this association was only marginally significant ($p < .07$). Given the data that we analyzed, it appears that writing activities in the school are only marginally related to the writing performances of 13-year-olds in the 1978 NAEP writing assessment. The impact of writing activities appears to be largely mediated through students' writing apprehension. Indeed, when the effects are decomposed, the analyses support this interpretation. The major way in which school writing affects the writing performance of 13-year-olds is indirectly through students' writing apprehension. Students' writing apprehension is, in turn, affected by teacher-controlled variables, such as the frequency of assigned writing and the amount and types of writing used in instruction.

This finding is especially important given the results we reported for Study 1 and Study 2 above. Recall that we reported that teachers' writing apprehension affects both the amount and types of classroom writing tasks assigned to students. Teachers high in writing apprehension are far less likely to have students participate in frequent writing (FREQ) or to engage in the many types of tasks that the writing instruction variable (INSTRUCT) in Study 3 taps. Seen in the context of the findings reported for Study 3 (viz., that school writing and frequency of writing affect students' writing apprehension which, in turn, affects students' writing performance), the importance of teacher writing apprehension becomes obvious: Teachers establish a context for writing that is partly dependent upon their own likes or dislikes of writing. To the degree that teachers are apprehensive of writing, they are likely to encourage fewer writing-related activities and to focus more on rigid criteria which may, in turn (and we must be cautious about the inferential leaps being made here), deleteriously affect students' attitudes about writing as well as their writing performance.

In addition to providing links to Study 1 and Study 2, Study 3 also generated some new, and quite interesting, insights into the writing apprehension construct. Perhaps the most intriguing findings are those associated with the different exogenous variables. Previous research on writing apprehension has not probed the demographic correlates of the writing apprehension construct. For instance, the finding that white students report less positive feelings about writing than their nonwhite counterparts, if not an artifact of social desirability, offers evidence for potential changes in certain educational assumptions. The findings that individuals from higher SES homes and from homes that emphasize literacy tend to have lower apprehension is also important. Such findings initiate a bevy of questions about why variables such as these are related to writing apprehension. Moreover, this study represents one of the few uses of the data collected by the National Assessment of Educational Progress on writing. It is surprising to us that so few scholars interested in writing have made use of the NAEP data.

Some Concluding Remarks

The three studies we conducted were primarily designed to explore some relationships between teachers' writing apprehension and their classroom practices. In concert with the findings of previous research, our exploration of those relationships suggests a causal chain of circumstances and events that may be having a major impact on the development and maintenance of writing-related skills and attitudes among students. Our findings, which we regard as tentative, suggest that teachers' writing apprehension affects their views of their own subject matter areas, their views of students, the frequency and types of assignments they give, and the way they value and evaluate student writing. These teacher-controlled variables appear, in turn, to influence the development of writing apprehension among students. Once students become apprehensive about writing, their ability to perform well on measures of writing competence appears to decline.

Clearly, there are limitations to the investigations described in this paper. In all three studies, self-reports provide the primary sources of data. While in some cases, self-reports represent the optimal procedure (e.g., in the case of measuring writing apprehension as a general disposition), in other cases different methods might have yielded more conclusive findings. Consider the first two studies where we used teachers' self-reports of classroom practices rather than systematic observations of what actually occurred in their classrooms. Yet, at the same time, it might be argued that in self-reports teachers will typically avoid presenting a negative image of themselves or their teaching. To the extent that this is true, if observational data were used, relationships and differences observed in these studies might, indeed, be even stronger.

If our tentative findings and inferences prove correct, then educators will need to develop ways of reducing writing apprehension among students, of reducing writing apprehension among teachers, or of preventing high-apprehensive teachers from influencing the development of writing apprehension among their students. Moreover, if our tentative findings and inferences prove correct, educators may want to examine the nature and wisdom of certain educational practices now in vogue. One of these takes the form of writing across the curriculum programs that require teachers in disciplines, such as mathematics, the sciences, and engineering, to teach writing. Our research, as well as previous research, suggests that teachers in such disciplines are typically highly apprehensive about writing. The data we examined for the present chapter suggest, further, that these teachers are likely to give writing assignments and to invoke evaluative criteria that differ in important ways from the assignments and criteria of teachers who are not apprehensive about writing. The question, of course, is whether these differences promote the development of writing apprehension among students. The results of our research lead us to suspect that they do.

Perhaps the most important conclusion that we can draw from the three studies reported in this chapter is that school-sponsored or teacher-directed writing is closely related to attitudes about writing, both the teachers' attitudes and the students' attitudes. This conclusion has far-reaching implications. For instance, future work, probably ethnographic in nature, will need to carefully observe teachers to determine just how they transmit their feelings about writing to their students. While in some cases it may be direct (e.g., "I hate to write") it is probably far more often much less direct and less obvious. In the studies reported in this chapter we suggest it may be communicated by the sorts of assignments students receive and the evaluative criteria teachers use in judging students' writing. But in what other ways do teacher behaviors contribute to students' apprehension? It may be that teachers unwittingly influence students' attitudes simply by the way they talk about assignments or the ways they distribute materials for writing. However it occurs, though, students' attitudes about writing are formed, at least in part, by teachers. Consider one example that one of the authors (Daly) found in interviews with children about their beliefs about writing. A 4-year-old child approached Daly and told him that he was "going to write a book." Daly asked him whether he was a good writer and the child responded affirmatively. Daly asked him how he knew he was a good writer and the child answered ". . . cause I draw good pictures." For a child of 4, books are mostly composed of pictures. A year and a half later Daly again asked the child about writing and what it meant to be a good writer. At that point the child responded that he was a good writer ". . . because my letters are neat." A year or so later, the child was again probed. "Why are you a good writer?" asked Daly. The answer he received was ". . . because the teacher likes my writing." Clearly, over time the child was coming to judge writing in terms of the values established by his teachers. It may be that certain exercises, teaching techniques, and even instructional strategies affect children's feelings about composing. It will be the challenge of subsequent research efforts—both qualitative and quantitative—to continue to chart the genesis and transmission of those values about writing, to explore how values derive from the social context whether that context be defined in terms of home, community, school, or workplace.

REFERENCES

Barnes, D. (1976). *From communication to curriculum*. Harmondsworth, England: Penguin Books.

Claypool, S. H. (1980). *Teacher writing apprehension: Does it affect writing assignments across curriculum*. Washington D.C.: ERIC Document Reproduction Service (ED 216 387).

Daly, J. A. (1978). Writing apprehension and writing competency. *Journal of Educational Research, 72*, 10–14.

Daly, J. A. (1979). Writing apprehension in the classroom: Teacher role expectancies of the apprehensive writer. *Research in the Teaching of Writing, 13*, 37–44.

Daly, J. A. (1985). Writing apprehension. In M. Rose (Ed.), *When a writer can't write: Studies in writer's block and other composing process problems* (pp. 43–82). NY: Guilford.

Daly, J. A., Bell, R., & Korinek, J. (in press). Interrelationships among attitudes toward academic subjects. *Contemporary Educational Psychology*.

Daly, J. A., & Miller, M. D. (1975a). The empirical development of an instrument to measure writing apprehension. *Research in the Teaching of English, 9*, 242–249.

Daly, J. A., & Miller, M. D. (1975b). Further studies in writing apprehension: SAT scores, success expectations, willingness to take advanced courses and sex differences. *Research in the Teaching of English, 9*, 250–256.

Daly, J. A., & Miller, M. D. (1975c). Apprehension of writing as a predictor of message intensity. *Journal of Psychology, 89*, 175–177.

Daly, J. A., & Shamo, W. (1976). Writing apprehension and occupational choice. *Journal of Occupational Psychology, 49*, 55–56.

Daly, J. A., & Shamo, W. (1978). Academic decisions as a function of writing apprehension. *Research in the Teaching of English, 12*, 119–126.

Daly, J. A., & Wilson, D. (1983). Writing apprehension, self-esteem, and personality. *Research in the Teaching of English, 17*, 327–342.

Dickson, F. (1978). *Writing apprehension and test anxiety as predictors of ACT scores*. Unpublished M.A. Thesis, West Virginia University.

Dyson, A. H. (1984). Emerging alphabetic literacy in school contexts: Toward defining the gap between school curriculum and child mind. *Written Communication, 1*, 5–55.

Edwards, A. D. (1981). Analyzing classroom talk. In P. French & M. MacClure (Eds.), *Adult–child conversation*. New York: St. Martin's.

Faigley, L. L., Daly, J. A., & Witte, S. P. (1981). The role of writing apprehension in writing performance and competence. *Journal of Educational Research, 75*, 16–21.

Garcia, R. J. (1978). An investigation of relationships: Writing apprehension, syntactic performance, and writing quality (Doctoral dissertation, Arizona State University). *Dissertation Abstracts International, 77*, 4211.

Gere, A. R., Schuessler, B. R., & Abbott, R. D. (1984). Measuring teachers' attitudes toward writing instruction. In R. Beach & L. Bridwell (Eds.), *New directions in composition research* (pp. 348–361). New York: Guilford.

Haertel, G. D., Walberg, H. J., Junker, L., & Pascarella, E. T. (1981). Early adolescent sex differences in science learning: Evidence from the National Assessment of Educational Progress. *American Educational Research Journal*, *18*, 329–342.

Jeroski, S. F., & Conry, R. F. (1981). *Development and field application of the Attitude towards Writing scale*. Paper presented at the annual conference of the American Educational Research Association, Los Angeles.

Lloyd–Jones, R. (1977). Primary trait scoring. In C. R. Cooper & L. Odell (Eds.), *Evaluating writing: Describing, measuring, judging* (pp. 33–66). Urbana, IL: National Council of Teachers of English.

Mehan, H. (1978). Structuring school structure. *Harvard Educational Review, 48*, 32–64.

Rose, M. (Ed.). (1985). *When a writer can't write: Studies in writer's block and other composing process problems*. New York: Guilford.

Selfe, C. (1985). An apprehensive writer composes. In M. Rose (Ed.), *When a writer can't write: Studies in writer's block and other composing process problems* (pp. 83–95). NY: Guilford.

Smith, F. (1982). *Writing and the writer*. New York: Holt, Rinehart, & Winston.

Witte, S. P., & Faigley, L. L. (1981). *A comparative evaluation of analytic and synthetic approaches to the teaching of writing*. Austin: University of Texas. (ERIC Document 209 607).

Part Three

Creating Texts Collectively

Chapter 8

Children's Use of Narrative Language in Peer Interaction

Lee Galda and A. D. Pellegrini
The University of Georgia

The purpose of this chapter is to examine the way in which children convey meaning through narrative language. Narrative language, which is a subset of narrative thinking (Bruner, 1986; Hymes & Cazden, 1980), is used to convey meaning through personal, story-like language. Narrative language and thought are typically contrasted to thinking and talking in the paradigmatic mode (Bruner, 1986). Paradigmatic language is typified by impersonal, objective language, if such a thing is possible. Developmentalists (e.g., Olson, 1977; Pellegrini, 1985a) have suggested that preschoolers' use of the explicit oral language characteristic of paradigmatic thought is a precursor to literacy.

In this chapter we will be making a different argument, at the risk of contradicting our earlier thoughts on the topic. We will examine the narrative mode of language and thought, which is prevalent during the preschool period, describing the ways children use this mode in peer discourse and the functions it seems to serve. Descriptive work in this area is necessary, we feel, for a number of reasons. First, narrative thought and language are dominant in the preschool period (Bruner, 1986). In order to understand that period, we must understand the narrative mode. Second, to describe only preschoolers' use of the paradigmatic mode, a typically adult mode, is equivalent to gauging children's status against an adult standard. Our aim is to describe the modal form of thought and language during the preschool period. Third, following our developmental orientation, we would like to examine, in the future, the extent to which these narrative forms become transformed into literate behavior. Fourth, narratives are important in the literate culture of school. Children learn to read by reading stories and in many cases learn to write by beginning with personal narratives.

Essentially, our argument is that the narrative mode is not better or worse than the paradigmatic mode, but complementary in that it, too, serves specific and essential functions. It is not only the dominant mode in the oral culture of childhood; it is one way in which children move toward literacy, through stories told, heard, and read about themselves and others (Scollon & Scollon, 1981). Narrative is not one fixed form but comes in a variety of forms (Heath, 1983; Michaels, 1986) which are culturally shaped. Children learn to use narratives to function in the oral culture in which they are raised. Their use of oral narrative is deliberate, systematic, and context sensitive. As such, children's narratives reflect linguistic skills which have been serving them well in their own oral culture. When school begins, the transition into literacy requires that children expand their understandings about how language works as they leave behind the oral culture in which they have been successful to take on a different set of demands inherent in the literate culture of the school. The transition can best be facilitated by "experiences in school that favor the learning of written culture through the *medium of the oral culture*, thus building on the interpretive skills and linguistic understandings that children bring to the school experience, as a basis for further learnings" (Cook–Gumperz & Gumperz, 1981 p. 107). Understanding what children already know about how to use language enables us to help them to apply and revise these understandings as they encounter the new culture of school literacy as embodied by the tasks of reading and writing.

Bruner (1984, 1986) has recently suggested that the uses of narrative and paradigmatic modes could be described along two axes: vertical and horizontal (following Jakobson, 1960). Bruner (1986) suggests that the vertical axis is concerned with word selection and the horizontal with word combinations. More specifically, the vertical axis allows choice of specific lexical items. The paradigmatic end of the axis is characterized by objective reference, or the use of linguistic devices (e.g., cohesion, elaborated noun phrases, and third person pronouns) to create a context-free description. To use Bruner's (1984) example: New York is the biggest city in North America. In this example, explicit denotative reference is the goal of specific lexical choice.

The narrative end of the vertical axis, however, is more concerned with connotation than with denotation (Bruner, 1984). That is, narrative word choice is determined by personal experiences and interpretations. As such, the narrative mode is often typified by personal factivity, affective verbs, and deontic modals.

The horizontal axis is concerned with the combinative, or generative, aspect of language; words can be combined in terms of topic/comment and noun/verb relations. Different combinations reflect different ways of conveying meaning. The noun/verb structure of narratives tends to reflect agent/action and agent/process relations, to use Chafe's (1970) terms, because narratives are concerned with human actions and intentions. Further, when state verbs (e.g., *is*, *are*) are used in narrative language they tend to reflect personal factivity: feelings, motives, and duties. Because narratives reflect people acting in real time and space, noun/verb phrases tend to be conjoined with temporal and additive conjunctions (e.g., *then*, *and*).

The paradigmatic mode, as noted above, is relatively free of human factivity and context-bound information. In this mode the noun/verb structures often reflect formal descriptions (e.g. patient/state, *The wood is dry*.) and logical argument (e.g., patient/process, *The wood dried*.). These structures, in turn, are often conjoined with causal and adversative conjunctions (e.g., *but*).

To summarize thus far, we have characterized two modes of thought and language. In the narrative mode personal actions and factivity are typically described with context-dependent discourse. The paradigmatic mode, on the other hand, aspires to context-free logical propositions. Subjunctivization dominates the narrative mode (Bruner, 1986); objective, causal argumentation the paradigmatic.

Comparisons of these two modes usually result in implicit or explicit value judgments of each (Hymes & Cazden, 1980). Generally, the paradigmatic mode has been considered a higher, more developed form than the narrative. It may be, as Hymes and Cazden (1980) cogently point out, that whenever two forms of a language exist, high/low assignments are made. In the present case, the high/low dichotomy is thought to reflect cognitive sophistication. That is, paradigmatic language, because it is thought to be context free (if such a language variant exists) and causally motivated, is said to be more abstract than its context-bound sibling, narrative language. The high/low comparisons in paradigmatic/narrative thought and language have been applied to: different periods of historical development, where earlier, "less developed" societies used context-bound language (e.g., Goody & Watt, 1968; Olson, 1977); different contemporary societies, where syntagmatic thought is "more primitive" than paradigmatic thought (e.g., Luria, 1976); different social classes, where context-free, elaborated codes are more sophisticated than context-bound restricted codes (Bernstein, 1971); different periods of human development, where context-bound thought develops into context-free abstract thought (Pellegrini, Galda, & Rubin, 1984); and different forms of scientific inquiry where narrative forms of data are viewed as unscientific (Stone, 1979).

The position we take is that the two modes are *different*, with no high/low distinction; in most cases they are complementary (Bruner, 1986; Hymes & Cazden, 1980). This assumption is based on three premises. First, both modes of thought are equally valid for providing answers to scientific questions. As has been noted by scholars in a number of fields, narrative and personal accounts of events provide valuable scientific information (e.g., Stone, 1979). It has been noted that physics, the "quintessential science," is 99% personal conceptualization and 1% observation (Quine, 1978, quoted in Bruner, 1986). The value of narrative, or personal, accounts of phenomena, *vis-à-vis* paradigmatic accounts, is further supported by constructivist philosophy (e.g., Goodman, 1984; Kant, 1965) and psychology (Bruner, 1986), which argues that reality and cause–effect claims are constructed by perceivers; they do not exist in an objective world.

The second premise is that the use of either one of the two modes, like the use of any other variety of language, is context-dependent. Just as children use more "context-free" language with naïve listeners than with informed listeners (Pellegrini, 1984), so, too, contextual variables affect the use of narrative and paradigmatic language. For example, in experiments utilizing the classical impression formation paradigm (Asch, 1946), adults and children were given trait terms (e.g., sensitive, good-natured) about a hypothetical person and asked to describe what that person was like (Asch & Zukier, 1984). Subjects generated stories when given incongruent terms (e.g., sensitive/greedy), but descriptions when they were given congruent terms (e.g., sensitive/philanthropic).

These results suggest that when subjects were put into an ambiguous situation they constructed stories to reduce the ambiguity. It may be that narratives serve as "scaffolds" (Bruner, 1983) in ambiguous situations. That is, when speakers are put into ambiguous, or otherwise demanding, situations, they assimilate the ambiguity by constructing a narrative in which the ambiguity can be resolved. Thus, we would expect speakers to use more narrative strategies in ambiguous situations than in more clearly defined situations.

The third premise for our assumption of the complementary nature of narrative and paradigmatic language is closely related to our specific interest in young children. A significant portion of preschool children's peer interaction can be characterized by their use of narrative language. When preschoolers play together they often construct, at both the lexical (e.g., Pellegrini, 1986) and the discourse structure levels (Pellegrini, 1985b), make-believe themes by using language forms that resemble narratives. It seems reasonable that in order to examine children's thought, *from their perspective*, we should observe them in their dominant mode, the narrative mode.

In this chapter we will examine children's use of narrative language while they are playing with a peer in two contexts, a functionally ambiguous context and a functionally explicit context. We are interested in when narrative strategies are introduced and the ways in which they are introduced and sustained. We hypothesize that children will use narrative strategies as scaffolds in ambiguous situations. That is, children may use familiar, personal narratives as a way of introducing and sustaining discourse in ambiguous, demanding contexts. This hypothesis is based partly on the previous work by Asch and Zukier (1984) and Crowhurst and Piché (1979), who found that students use narratives when confronted with conflicting or demanding information.

DATA COLLECTION AND ANALYSES

We asked individual children to tell stories about both functionally ambiguous (e.g., blocks) and functionally explicit (doctor kits) props and then to play with these props with a peer. We then determined the extent to which their personal narratives were incorporated into their playful discourse with a peer.

The cases presented here are part of a larger, ongoing, study of children's play in different contexts. The total sample which we examined was composed of 43 boys and 43 girls ranging in age from 26 to 68 months. These children were observed in two sets of tasks. They were asked individually by an experimenter to tell a story about each of two sets of props: functionally ambiguous props (small and large blocks made of wood and plastic, pipe cleaners, and assorted styrofoam shapes) and functionally explicit props (doctors' kits, dolls, smocks, blankets, and pill bottles). Children's responses were audiotaped and transcribed. The stories generated in these situations were their "personal narratives."

The children were also observed playing with a same-age, opposite-sex peer with these same props. Each dyad was observed in an experimental playroom playing with the ambiguous props for two separate 20-minute sessions and with the explicit props for two separate 20-minute sessions.

Each play session was audiovisually recorded through a one-way mirror. Utterances and corresponding contextual cues were transcribed from the tapes. The order in which children were observed in the different contexts was counterbalanced.

The cases analyzed in this chapter are representative, we think, of the ways in which our whole sample used narrative strategies. First, there were cases of well-formed narratives being constructed by both participants. Second, there were cases where one child used a collective monologue strategy to tell a story while playing. Third, there were several cases in which neither child constructed narratives during their play.

The decision as to whether a personal narrative was incorporated into peer discourse was based on lexical ties in the two speech events (i.e., peer discourse and personal narrative). More specifically, Halliday and Hasan's (1976) categories for lexical cohesion were used to determine if the two texts were related. The categories include: same item (e.g., cow, cow), synonym (e.g., cow, Mama cow), superordinate (e.g., cow, farm animal), general item (e.g., cow, bovine), collocation (e.g., cow, bull).

Once a tie was established between a personal narrative item and peer discourse, the interrelation of subsequent utterances to the introductory personal narrative theme utterance was judged, again, according to lexical relations in adjacency pairs.

RESULTS/DISCUSSION

We begin with a description of the general occurrence of personal narratives in children's play episodes. Of the 172 play observations (i.e., 43 dyads observed in 4 play contexts), personal narratives were present in 31 (18%) observations. Of these 31, 23 were observed in the ambiguous context and 8 in the explicit context ($p < .05$, Sign test). Thus, our prediction that the ambiguous context would elicit more personal narratives was supported. These results suggest that when children encounter ambiguity, or other cognitive demands, they resort to narrative language.

These results are similar to the previously cited work of Asch and Zukier (1984) and Crowhurst and Piché (1979), who concluded that the cognitive demands of the tasks forced subjects to construct a personal story about the stimuli with which they were presented. These personal experiences, as expressed through narrative, enabled them to function in a situation that was very demanding.

Children's use of narrative strategies in the ambiguous play contexts may have helped to introduce and sustain discourse with their peers. As shown repeatedly (e.g., Garvey, 1984; Pellegrini, 1982), children go through great pains to introduce and sustain play-related discourse. It seems, however, that children's use of personal narratives is not a very successful strategy for sustaining discourse. Of the 65 story-based narratives introduced in the 31 play observations, 42 were not sustained for more than two turns ($p < .05$, Sign test). Only 19 of 65 ($p < .01$, Sign test) were sustained for six turns or more. In the ambiguous context and in the explicit context, 27 of 49 and 14 of 16, respectively, of the introduced personal narratives were not sustained more than two turns ($p < .01$, Sign test). These data suggest that personal narratives were not bases for sustained discourse.

Case Study 1

We will now examine more closely a select number of cases to illustrate the ways in which children used personal narratives in their play. In the first case we will discuss Andy and Jane, two 3½-year-olds, playing with blocks. Andy introduced a personal narrative immediately after Jane disagreed with him about the location of a play prop. In response to this conflict, Andy introduced the new personal narrative: "A ship running/" This ambiguous theme introduction was not taken up by Jane. She continued with the play theme she was enacting before Andy's attempt to introduce his personal narrative.

This case is illustrative in at least two ways. First, a personal narrative was introduced after a verbal conflict between speakers: After Jane disagreed with Andy, he immediately introduced a personal narrative. As noted above, speakers often resort to such strategies when presented with demanding or conflicting information. Second, this example illustrates the importance of linguistically explicit theme introduction for sustaining discourse. In this example, the introduction was too vague for Jane to respond.

Case Study 2

In the second play episode with blocks, Andy also attempted to introduce a personal narrative as a basis for a play theme. This theme was introduced to counter the play theme introduced by Jane. In this episode, however, Andy explicitly introduced his theme: "I got a spaceship/'tend I'm in the water making more magic for men/". Note that in this introduction Andy, using explicit object and situation transformations, set the stage for a new theme (i.e., transforming a block and the floor into a spaceship and water, respectively). Further, the explicit stance marker (Bruner, 1986; Feldman, 1974) of " 'tend" informed Jane that they were about to engage in make-believe play.

This explicit theme was taken up by Jane using an additive conjunction: "And nobody wasn't there/". Andy, in turn, accepted Jane's contribution: "Okay/" and went on to define the play context further: " 'tend this was the door/" with Jane adding: "What'll be the dog house/". This theme was sustained for 12 turns, probably because of the explicit introduction provided by Andy and his stance markers " 'pposed" and " 'tend," which notified Jane of the fantasy mode. "Pretend" was being used to set the stage for the upcoming enactments, and "supposed" was used to direct Jane into the appropriate role behavior for the play theme.

The importance of such planning utterances for sustaining of social dramatic play has been discussed by Sachs and her colleagues (Sachs, Goldman & Chaillé, 1984). They noted that a large portion of the utterances in fantasy play serves a planning function.

This last example is illustrative of how a personal narrative can serve as the basis for sustained discourse. Compared with the first example, this case illustrates the importance of speakers' using explicit introductions in getting interlocutors to respond. After initial uptake, planning and management utterances are needed to sustain the discourse. In this second block episode, Andy took on the role of "stage manager." He told Jane what she was " 'pposed to do" and how the props were to be transformed, e.g., "and 'tend it was umm . . . the that/". Jane, too, redefined props but did so all within the theme suggested and managed by Andy. In short, both Jane and Andy participated in Andy's play theme, each contributing six turns. This play theme formally ended with a property dispute: Andy would not share a play prop with Jane.

The case of Andy and Jane illustrates the way in which a personal narrative can be used a basis for a discourse topic by two interlocutors. This case also illustrates the way in which a topic introducer might manage the discourse. Though Jane did make contributions to the development of the topic, Andy made explicit suggestions as to what was expected.

Case Study 3

The next case to be presented also has a jointly constructed play theme, but both players seem to share more equally in developing the theme. Gene and Nell are two 4-year-olds playing with the dramatic props. Early in the episode a prop conflict develops over the ownership of one of the tools. At this point, Nell introduced a personal narrative: "OK/ We're going to the hospital/ If you're ready?/ That OK?" Notice that when this new theme was being introduced, Nell was trying to assure up-take by Gene by making provision for Gene's contribution by posing a question. The question ("If you're ready?) ensured that Gene would respond to the introductory utterance (Pellegrini, 1981).

Gene did indeed respond by telling Nell to "Put (the doll) you down to sleep/". Nell agreed, "OK"/, then went on to name the baby as "Jenny Harla." Gene agreed, repeating the name and adding, "Her baby is sick/".

This particular episode lasted for 14 turns. The difference between this episode and the Andy and Jane episode is clear. Gene and Nell jointly constructed the discourse topic by first accepting each other's contribution and then by each contributing to the topic themselves. Individual contributions to the theme were often encouraged by each. Contributions were made in response to specific questions, posed in the preceding turn, e.g., "That OK/". Thus, both speakers used their knowledge of pragmatic conventions (i.e., Grice's, 1975, Quantity Maxim) to elicit individual contributions to the discourse.

Case Study 4

In the next case to be presented, a personal narrative was used as a successful discourse topic because both children had the same personal narrative for the props. That is, both children in the story condition told similar personal narratives about the props; both told stories about the blocks that involved a river. In this case, Nick and Sara, two 5½-year-olds, were playing in the block context. Nick introduced his personal narrative, "It's gonna be the river, OK/" after a conflict. Note that he used an explicit introduction and ended his turn with a question. Sara agreed, "OK/", then added to the theme by introducing an element of her personal narrative: "That can be the bridge/ And here can be the river/ It's gonna ooch your head/ What is this/".

Again the last utterance is a question, thus assuring a response. Nick responded by answering the question. This episode continued for 37 turns. This theme was sustained, we think, because the children shared a common behavioral script for the props and because they both used discourse strategies which help sustain discourse (e.g., explicit reference and posing questions). The difference between the case of Gene and Nell and the successful case of Nick and Sara was that Nick and Sara both shared knowledge about the props. As a result of this, and their discourse strategies, they were able to maintain thematically consistent discourse for 37 turns.

These three cases illustrate a number of things about children's use of personal narratives in discourse. First, children tend to introduce personal narratives into discourse immediately after a conflict with their peers. They may be using the personal narratives as a way of trying to get the play and discourse back on track. They were using their personalized scripts for the objects as a basis for subsequent discourse. Second, the cases also illustrate that this strategy is most successful when children use specific discourse strategies, e.g., explicit introductions, open conversational slots for interlocutors to fill, and planning utterances. Both interlocutors must work at constructing the theme by using these strategies if the discourse is to be sustained.

Case Study 5

In the last case to be presented, we have Michael and Mary, two 5½-year-olds, playing with the blocks. This case is different from the previously discussed cases to the extent that we have one child, Michael, repeatedly introducing a personal narrative, about "fire demons," and the other child not responding to the topic. The first time Michael introduced his topic was after Mary tried to introduce a topic of her own. She defined a round piece of styrofoam as "a wheeler." Michael acknowledged her topic by noting, "I thought those were lights on the top." He then introduced his own topic, "You know what I'm making?/ Fire demons . . . / It's a good fire demon." This rather unclear introduction was not taken up by Mary so the theme ended.

However, when Mary tried to introduce another topic of her own, Michael reintroduced the fire demon theme: "I'm making fire/" Nancy responded to the theme unenthusiastically with "I don't think I'll make fire/" Michael tried to involve her further in the theme by posing a question "You don't like fire?" Mary responded, "No," and Michael monologued for 42 utterances about fire and fire demons. Mary, feeling left out, asked, "Will you play with me?" Whereupon Michael willingly pointed out: Na . . . Um/ This can be the whole part of the fire demon part/ And that's the wall where he can't get out/ This side/ And we gotta make some walls/ . . . Back here/". Mary, by now eager to play, went along with the theme: "We need to make some round walls/".

This theme was sustained for 18 turns with Michael doing the bulk of the talking. Mary's role was merely to comment upon Michael's ideas. The episode ended when Mary disagreed with Michael and suggested an alternate role for a character. This case, like the first, has one child directing the play theme.

Assimilative and Accommodative Narratives

The case studies presented above suggest that children tend to introduce personalized narratives into discourse when they conflict with their peers. Conflicts, as we have seen, can result from a disagreement over prop or role transformations or a general unwillingness or inability to consider another person's point of view. In order to more thoroughly examine the discourse contexts which elicited children's use of personal narratives, we examined the utterances which directly preceded the 65 instances of personal narratives. These results are presented below in Table 1.

Instances of the first category, *Preceded by conflict*, were introductions of personal narratives immediately after verbal conflict or disagreement. The category *First utterances* refers to language that children generated at the beginning of an observation; they were literally the first utterances recorded for an observation. In the third category, *No previously sustained discourse*, personal narratives were introduced into a nonsustained discourse context. That is, children's previous themes had not been sustained for more than two turns. When children integrated their personal narratives into ongoing, coherent discourse, this was classified as *Embedded in ongoing theme*. In these instances, children's personal narratives were accommodated to already present themes.

The first three discourse contexts in which personal narratives appear seem to be related to the extent that they indicate the presence of uncertainty and ambiguity, reflecting situations in which children are unsure of what is expected of them. Children may have introduced personal narratives into these uncertain or ambiguous situations in an attempt to provide order. In Piagetian terms, these uncertain situations resulted in states of conceptual disequilibration to the extent that children were not sure about what to do next. In order to minimize the conflict they assimilated the uncertainty to their own perspectives. That is, they introduced a highly personalized topic to reduce the uncertainty.

The highly personalized nature of these narratives is evidenced by the general lack of up-take of these topics by play partners. Children's use of such assimilatory personal narratives accounted for 60% of all narratives used.

Children also used personal narratives to serve an accommodative function (20% of the time) by introducing them into ongoing, coherent discourse. That is, they adapted their personal narratives to the ongoing, mutually negotiated discourse topic.

Table 1. Discourse Contexts of Personal Narratives

Discourse Context	Frequency	%
1. Preceded by conflict	36	37.8
2. First utterances of observation	5	7
3. No previous thematically sustained discourse	10	15
4. Embedded in ongoing theme	12	18

Assimilative and Accommodative Personal Narratives

Based on the assimilative and accommodative functions served by each strategy, one would expect each to have different effects on subsequent discourse. That is, assimilative personal narratives, being more idiosyncratic and personal, should be less likely than the accommodative strategies to elicit a related response. Accommodative personal narratives indicate children's willingness and ability to take interlocutors' points of view. In short, the accommodative personal narratives may be an indicator of children's sociocentricity.

As of way of testing this proposition, we calculated the probability of each type of personal narrative eliciting a relevant response. We then compared the probabilities associated with assimilative and accommodative narratives. Such a comparison is admittedly problematical, because each type of narrative is embedded in a different discourse context. The accommodative personal narrative is embedded in an already coherent discourse theme. As such, interlocutors are more likely to see utterances as relevant in this context (Grice, 1975). Assimilative personal narratives, on the other hand, tended to occur when new discourse was beginning or had broken down. It would seem more difficult to elicit a relevant response in this context.

To mitigate the problem of differing contexts, we examined the probability of each type of personal narrative eliciting a coherent theme lasting at least four turns. This is obviously a more conservative criterion level than the elicitation of just a single relevant response. This more conservative level should help compensate for interlocutors' assumptions of topic relevence in response to the accommodative personal narratives. Thus, we examined sequences of utterances that followed both assimilative and accommodative personal narratives. In presenting these findings, we first describe interlocutors' utterances following each type of personal narrative. Second, we describe the transitional probabilities (lags) (Gottman & Bakeman, 1979) of utterances following each of the introduced personal narratives (to four turns). This procedure is explicated below.

In this first, descriptive phase, we will illustrate the types of utterances which children generated after the introduction of assimilative or accommodative strategies. We identified five types of discourse response strategies following each personal narrative and their occurrence after each. The response strategies include: Expands information, No up-take, Disagrees, Agrees, and Repetition. We observed a total of 39 assimilative personal narratives and 26 accommodative personal narratives. In order to determine the probability with which the five discourse response strategies followed each introduction, we used the transitional probabilities procedure (lag) outlined by Gottman and Bakeman (1979). This procedure allows us to determine the probability of each strategy's place in the sequence of four turns.

Nonsustained Topics

We will first discuss the occurrence of those personal narratives which resulted in no up-take, or were not responded to, by interlocutors. There were 28 cases in which a strategy was not taken up by an interlocutor. There was no significant difference between the success of the assimilative (16 instances) and the accommodative (12 instances) strategies. The unexpectedly high rate for the accommodative strategy was due primarily to one dyad, who contributed six cases of no up-take. When children introduced accommodative strategies (after one or two lexical items) it was typically embedded in a clause that was related to the ongoing discourse theme. Children tended to ignore this new, and often peripheral, information, instead preferring utterances tied to the existent themes.

Since "no-up-take" necessarily means that the discourse topic was not sustained across conversational turns, it was dropped from the subsequent sequential analysis. The probabilities are calculated, following Gottman and Bakeman (1979) by, first, listing the frequency with which a particular strategy occupies a certain sequential slot. For example, Strategy 2, expands information, followed Assimilative Narrative Introduction (Strategy 1) 15 times. The transitional probability is calculated by dividing 15 by the total number of times Strategy 1 was observed: 23, or .65.

Figures 1 and 2 illustrate the transitional probabilities following the introduction of accommodative and assimilative personal narratives respectively. By way of illustration, in Figure 1 the probability of Strategy 2 (Expands information) following itself is .96, the probability of Strategy 4 (Agrees) following Strategy 1 is .04.

Strategies Following Assimilative Narratives

In Figure 1 the strategies following the introductions of assimilative personal narratives are displayed. The Expands information strategy (Strategy 2) had the highest likelihood (.65) of following the introduction of an assimilative personal narrative. The following strategies also followed assimilative personal narratives: disagree (.17), repeats (.13), and agrees (.04). In most cases interlocutors added new information to the narrative line. The extent to which assimilative personal narratives were extended

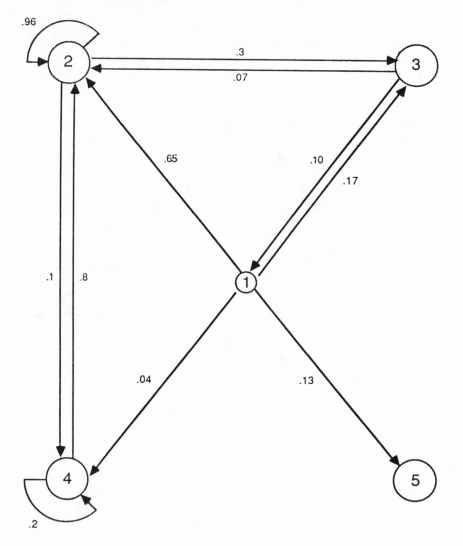

*The zero probabilities are not shown.

1. Assimilative narrative introduction
2. Expands information
3. Disagrees
4. Agrees
5. Repetition

Figure 1. State transition diagram for a five-state system following assimilative strategies.

was surprising, since such narratives were by definition highly idiosyncratic. One would have expected, especially in light of previous work on peer discourse (e.g., Keenan & Klein, 1975; Pellegrini, 1982), that interlocutors would have repeated previous utterances as a way to disambiguate them.

Our data indicate that the probability of a repetition following an assimilative personal narrative was .13. Where assimilative personal narratives led directly to an initial disagreement (.17), the disagreements tended to escalate. That is, they were responded to with another disagreement (.69). Where assimilative personal narratives elicited a repetition, the discourse tended to end there. Repetitions seem to be indicators that cooperative discourse will probably not occur. The occurrence of repetition and the subsequently short-lived discourse may be the result of narratives which were even more ambiguous than other assimilative narratives. This requires further research.

Disagreements, on the other hand, sometimes resulted in the interlocutors' expanding on the discourse theme. There was a probability of .3 of disagreement leading to expanded information. That disagreement is adaptive, in a communicative sense, is supported by Piagetian theory, which suggests that conceptual conflict with peers results in children's increased sociocentricity (Pellegrini, 1985a; Pellegrini & Perlmutter, 1988).

Strategies Following Accommodative Narratives

Figure 2 displays the probabilities of different discourse strategies following the introduction of accommodative personal narratives. Like the data for the assimilative personal narratives, expansions typically followed the introduction (.38) and expansions, in turn, elicited further expansions (.75).

Conflicts, on the other hand, often resulted in the accommodative personal narratives being discontinued. This is probably the result of the accommodative personal narrative not really fitting into the ongoing discourse. The interlocutors had sustained discourse before the introduction of the accommodative personal narrative. The disagreement may have indicated that one of the children thought that they should continue with the topic that was already working. In the assimilative context, in contrast, there was ambiguity and uncertainty. Interlocutors may have been more willing to resolve conflicts in the interest of sustaining discourse. Likewise, in the accommodative contexts, children were motivated to sustain discourse. In these instances when they disagreed with the introduced accommodative personal narrative, the disagreement may, in fact, have been in the interest of maintaining the original coherent theme.

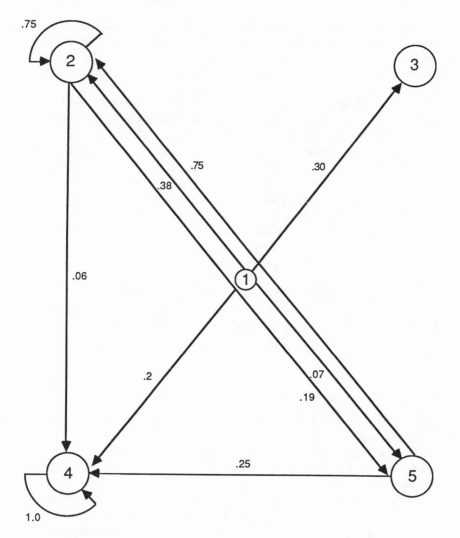

*The zero probabilities are not shown.

1. Assimilative narrative introduction
2. Expands information
3. Disagrees
4. Agrees
5. Repetition

Figure 2. State transition diagram for a five-state system following accommodative strategies.

Accommodative personal narratives led to agreements with .2 probability. These agreements led always (1.0) to further agreement. The accommodative theme did not continue beyond the second agreement. The data in Figure 2 suggest that when accommodative personal narratives can be integrated into the discourse (by expanding information), there is a high likelihood of the discourse being continued. Where interlocutors do not expand on the information, the discourse ends. This may be the result of interlocutors' having been content with the topic of the conversation before the introduction of the accommodative personal narrative.

To conclude this section, we have shown that assimilative and accommodative narratives served different discourse functions. Interlocutors, in turn, responded differently to each of these two narrative strategies. Generally, assimilative narratives were more ambiguous and, as a result, interlocutors experienced difficulty extending the assimilative narrative line. Accommodative narratives, on the other hand, often resulted in extended discourse.

CONCLUSIONS

In this chapter we attempted to describe the ways in which children used narrative language in peer discourse. As we have noted, narrative language is very common during the preschool period. In order to identify the developmental precursors of literacy, generally, and written language, specifically, it is necessary to document modal behaviors of the preschool period. Specific aspects of narrative language, such as the use of assimilative personal narratives, may predict later literacy.

The course of action followed in this study, as noted above, is very different from traditional examinations of the development of literacy. For example, researchers have examined children's engagement in symbolic play to predict literacy (e.g., Pellegrini, 1985a). Such studies have been guided by Piagetian and Vygotskian theories, which point to the "semiotic function" developed in early childhood as the basis for subsequent language development and literacy. However, the results of empirical studies testing this theory are not encouraging (See Fein, 1979, for a review). Given these results, or lack of results, it seems that we may have been asking the wrong kinds of questions about the development of literacy. This led us to try to redefine the variables of interest in early childhood. Again, our choice of the narrative mode was based on its dominant role during this period and our belief that some of the narrative strategies used by children may have important developmental implications. To our knowledge, no one has examined systematically the development of the narrative mode of thought.

Our next concern is also a criticism of the extant structural theories that have been applied to examinations of the development of literacy. These theories posit developmental synchrony within periods and, as a result, are not concerned with individual differences. It may be that there is "more than one road to literacy" (Wolf, personal communication).

The work of Wolf and her colleagues (in press) suggests that there are many "different intelligences" and that children use them in different ways to accomplish a number of different tasks, including literacy. Further, Cook–Gumperz and Gumperz (1981) have argued forcefully for the importance of recognizing the influence of the oral cultures which children bring to the formal literate culture of school. Knowing how children use oral language in their own cultural contexts, in this case oral narratives, is essential for understanding the kinds of transitions they must make as they encounter reading and writing.

In short, we hope this chapter will stimulate some rethinking of notions of development and literacy. Structural theories of development (see Malkus, Feldman, & Gardner, 1988, for a critique) and unidimensional definitions of literacy (see Wolf, et al., 1988, for a critique) may be restricting our vision.

REFERENCES

Asch, S. (1946). Forming impressions of personality. *Journal of Abnormal Social Psychology, 41,* 258–290.

Asch, S., & Zukier, H. (1984). Thinking about persons. *Journal of Personality and Social Psychology, 46,* 1230–1240.

Bernstein, B. (1971). *Class, codes, and control, Vol. 1: Theoretical studies towards a sociology of language.* London: Routledge & Kegan Paul.

Bruner, J. (1983). *Child's talk.* New York: Norton.

Bruner, J. (1984). *Narrative and paradigmatic modes of thought.* Invited address to Division 1 of the American Psychological Association, Toronto.

Bruner, J. (1986). *Actual minds, possible worlds.* Cambridge, MA: Harvard.

Chafe, W. (1970). *Meaning and the structure of language.* Chicago: University of Chicago Press.

Cook–Gumperz, J., & Gumperz, J. (1981). From oral to written culture: The transition to literacy. In M. Farr (Ed.), *Variation in writing: Functional and linguistic-cultural differences. Vol. 1, of writing: The nature, development, and teaching of written communication.* Hillsdale, NJ: Erlbaum.

Crowhurst, M., & Piché, G. (1979). Audience and mode of discourse effects on syntactic complexity in writing at two grade levels. *Research in the Teaching of English, 13,* 101–109.

Fein, G. (1979). Echoes from the nursery: Piaget, Vygotsky and the relationships between language and play. In E. Winner & H. Gardner (Eds.), *Fact, fiction, and fantasy in childhood* (pp. 1–14). San Francisco: Jossey–Bass.

Feldman, C. (1974). Pragmatic features of natural language. In M. LaGaly, R. Fox, & A. Bruck (Eds.), *Paper from the 10th regional meeting of the Chicago Linguistics Society* (pp. 151–160). Chicago: Chicago Linguistics Society.

Garvey, C. (1984). *Children's talk*. Cambridge, MA: Harvard.

Goodman, N. (1984). *Of minds and other matters*. Cambridge, MA: Harvard.

Goody, J., & Watt, I. (1968). The consequences of literacy. In J. Goody (Ed.), *Literacy in traditional societies* (pp. 27–68). Cambridge, England: Cambridge University Press.

Gootman, J., & Bakeman, R. (1979). The sequential analysis of observational data. In M. Lamb, S. Suomi, & G. Stephenson (Eds.), *Social interaction analysis* (pp. 185–206). Madison: University of Wisconsin Press.

Grice, G. (1975). Logic and conversation. In P. Cole & J. Morgan (Eds.), *Syntax and semantics* (Vol. 3, pp. 41–58). New York: Academic.

Halliday, M., & Hasan, R. (1976). *Cohesion in English*. London: Longman.

Heath, S. B. (1983). *Ways with words*. Cambridge, England: Cambridge University Press.

Hymes, D., & Cazden, C. (1980). Narrative thinking and storytelling rights: A folklorist's clue to a critique of education. In D. Hymes (Ed.), *Language in education: Ethnolinguistic essays* (pp. 126–138). Washington, DC: Center for Applied Linguistics.

Jakobson, R. (1960). Linguistics and poetics. In T. Sebeok (Ed.), *Style and Language*. Cambridge, MA: MIT.

Kant, I. (1965). *The critique of pure reason*. New York: St. Martin's.

Keenan, E., & Klein, E. (1975). Coherence in children's discourse. *Journal of Psycholinguistic Research, 4*, 365–380.

Luria, A. (1976). *Cognitive development*. Cambridge, MA: Harvard.

Malkus, U., Feldman, D., & Gardner, H. (1988). Dimensions of mind in early childhood. In A. Pellegrini (Ed.), *Psychological bases of early education* (pp. 25–38). Chichester, England: Wiley.

Michaels, S. (1986). Narrative presentations: An oral preparation for literacy with first graders. In J. Cook–Gumperz (Ed.), *The social construction of literacy*. Cambridge, England: Cambridge University Press.

Olson, D. (1977). From utterance to text. *Harvard Educational Review, 47*, 257–281.

Pellegrini, A. (1981). One aspect of the development of preschoolers' communicative competence: Specific answers to specific questions. *Psychological Reports, 49*, 581–582.

Pellegrini, A. (1982). Explorations in preschoolers' construction of cohesive text in two play contexts. *Discourse Processes, 5*, 101–108.

Pellegrini, A. (1984). The effect of dramatic play on children's generation of cohesive text. *Discourse Processes, 7*, 57–67.

Pellegrini, A. (1985a). Relations between preschool children's symbolic play and literate behavior. In L. Galda & A. Pellegrini (Eds.), *Play, language and story: The development of children's literate behavior* (pp. 79–97). Norwood, NJ: Ablex.

Pellegrini, A. (1985b). The narrative organization of children's play. *Educational Psychology, 5*, 17–25.

Pellegrini, A. (1986). Play centers and the production of imaginative language. *Discourse Processes, 9*, 115–125.

Pellegrini, A., Galda, L., & Rubin, D. (1984). Context in text: The development of oral and written language in two genres. *Child Development, 55,* 1549–1555.

Pellegrini, A., & Perlmutter, J. (1988). The role of verbal conflict in preschool children's social-cognitive development. In A. Pellegrini (Ed.), *Psychological bases of early education* (pp. 229–244). Chichester, England: Wiley.

Quine, W. (1978). Other worldly. *New York Review of Books.* Nov. 23.

Sachs, J., Goldman, J., & Chaillé, L. (1984). Planning in pretend play. In A. Pellegrini & T. Yawkey (Eds.), *The development of oral and written language in social context* (pp. 119–128). Norwood, NJ: Ablex.

Scollon, R., & Scollon, S. (1981). The literate two-year-old: The fictionalization of self. In *Narrative, literacy and face in interethnic communication.* Norwood, NJ: Ablex.

Stone, L. (1979). The revival of narrative: Reflections on a new old history. *Past & Present, 25,* 3–24.

Wolf, D., Davidson, L., Davis, M., Waters, J., Hodges, M., & Scripp, L. (1988). Beyond A, B, and C: A broader and deeper view of literacy. In A. Pellegrini (Ed.), *Psychological bases of early education* (pp. 123–152). Chichester, England: Wiley.

Chapter 9

Talking Our Way into Writing and Reading: Dialogue Journal Practice

Jana Staton
Center for Applied Linguistics

Roger W. Shuy
Georgetown University

One of the first things we all had to learn as children was a sense of direction: how to find our homes, where we keep our sox, where to put our toys. This linearity and directionality was a "given"—an indisputed fact of our young lives. Our parents fully participated in this learning, and their instruction was accurate and indisputable.

Once we got to school age, however, the role of our caretakers in matters of directionality became ambiguous. We were told where to keep our books and hang our jackets, but when it came to the directionality of our learning, things became confused. To this point in our lives, we had accomplished a number of important life skills, some physical, some cognitive. Perhaps the most crucial of the cognitive abilities was how to speak and understand our native language. We learned it without formal drills in sound–letter contrasts and without any specific teaching. We knew that we had things to tell people and things to hear and understand. In short our focus was on making meaning in the world in order to get things done.

What was deepest in our lives was meaning. It had to get outside of us in ways that others could understand; so we listened to older people for a while, then began to use some of their strategies to make our meaning clear. The significant thing about this was the direction of our learning. We learned from deep to surface, from meaning to words and sounds.

Even more significant is the fact that, equipped as we were with such a directionality of learning, we had to do an about face once we started school. From this point on, teaching reversed this direction, asking us to learn from surface to deep. Reading instruction focused on letter–sound correspondences, saving comprehension for later. Writing instruction was also deferred, on the flimsy assumption that children could not write until they had learned to read and that initial writing consisted of learning to make the letters of the alphabet. In short, directionality was reversed.

This constitutes one of the most counterproductive asymmetries in traditional education: Schools have taught children in a direction which opposes the way they learn things in nonschool settings. Native language learning is not the only example of this. Examine almost any nonschool learning, such as learning to ride a bicycle, learning to eat, or learning to whistle, and we can observe that the surface refinements come much later than our deep structure intentions and meaning.

It is our contention that even though conventional teaching goes in the opposite direction of most childhood learning, there are instances in which the child's natural communicative competence can be built into reading/writing activities, so that the same bottom–up direction of learning is maintained. The practical, classroom-based instance we have studied most intensely is the use of dialogue journals, in which student and teacher carry on a written conversation each day throughout the school year. The example of a handwritten dialogue journal (Figure 1) from Leslee Reed's sixth-grade classroom in Los Angeles illustrates the conversational, functional nature of this unusual kind of writing and reading. Student and teacher are writing back and forth without formal salutations, and are using the rich variety of language functions available from oral conversation: "I forgot what it was," "Thank you," "didn't you get it?"

This chapter describes the rationale for instructional practices, such as dialogue journals, which use the natural social conditions inherent in oral language to provide the basis for mastering written communication. We are assuming that reading and writing can be from the very beginning functional, useful modes of communication, like speech, even when the marks on paper are not intelligible to us (cf. Harste, Woodward, & Burke, 1984), even when the child's "reading" does not yet involve decoding specific words (Teale & Sulzby, 1986).

Our argument is that written communication can be mastered most easily if the learners' first uses of reading and writing occur in the same sociolinguistic and interpersonal conditions that exist for speaking and hearing. Note that we are not arguing that written language is "the same" as spoken communication, and therefore that the forms of spoken language provide the basis for written competency. We do not believe that writing is simply "speech written down." It is much more like

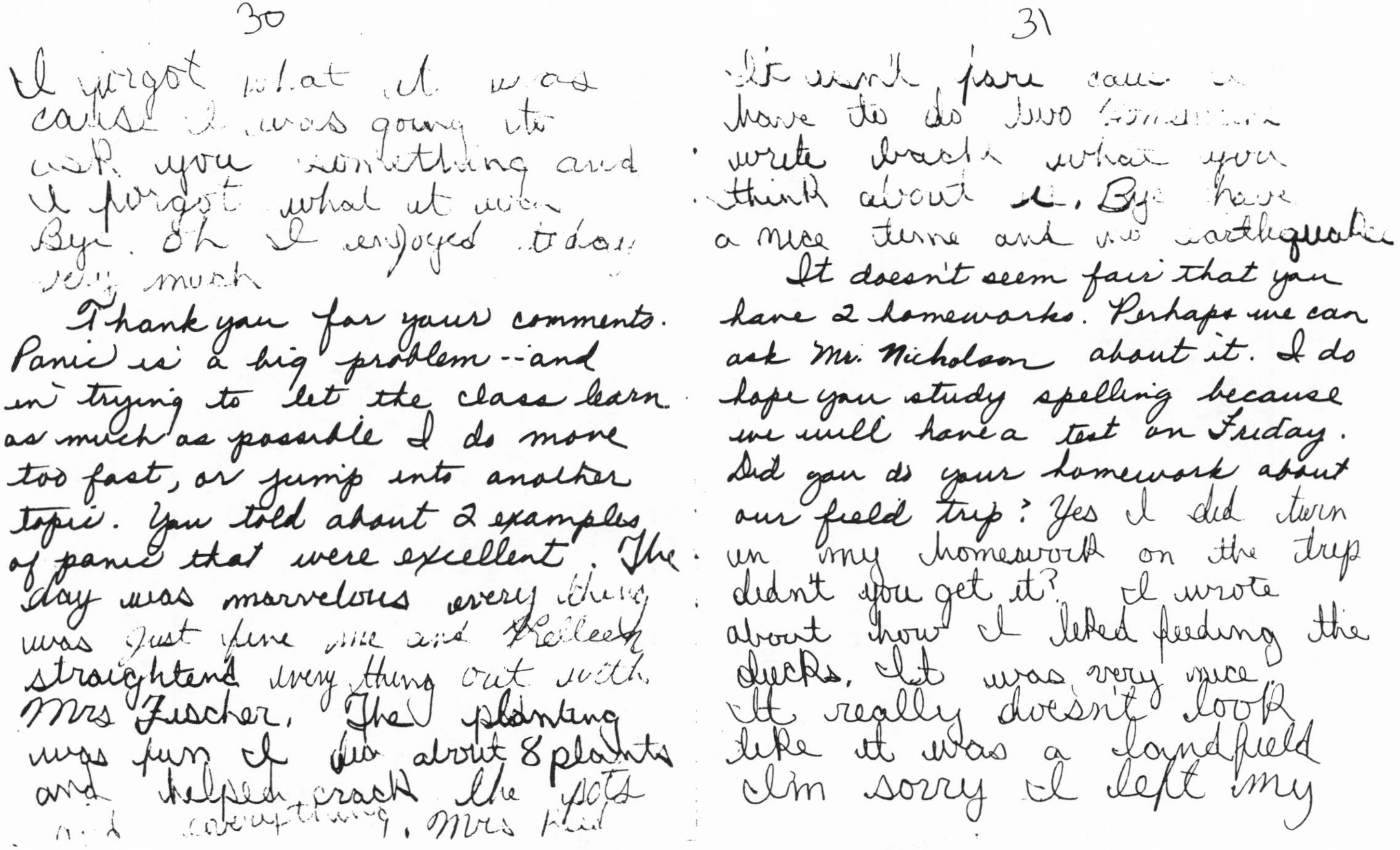

Figure 1. Handwritten pages from sixth-grade dialogue journal.

"thoughts" written down. But we do argue that communicative competence in written language requires the same functional conditions as oral competence, and that such practices can and do exist for children in classrooms and at home. (In fact, we believe that the continued advantage of the child from a middle-class background comes from experiencing literacy under more functional conditions at home, prior to and throughout schooling, so that such children are seemingly always one step ahead of the school curriculum.)

In the particular integrated literacy event of dialogue journal use, which we have been studying since 1979, writing and reading proceed in the same direction that the child has already established by school age.

THE CONDITIONS OF SPOKEN LANGUAGE USE
WHICH LEAD TO COMPETENCY

By studying how children so successfully acquire their native language outside of schools, we can begin to get clues and insights into how we might best structure their school experiences in learning to read and write. We believe that this communicative competence in an oral language is a natural and generalizable human ability, but that it develops so effectively in all children only because all cultures have developed certain conditions for its occurrence which lead to and ensure continued competency. These conditions are:

- The meaning of the learner's utterance is supported by the context—setting, participants, prior events, topic frames are present or at least known to the participants.
- A real audience in the use of language exists, known to the speaker and in need of hearing what the speaker has to say.
- Meaning is interactively negotiated between speakers over time, with ample opportunities for feedback, clarification, and elaboration of points.
- There is ample access to experienced speakers so that the learner can acquire models for how to understand and represent events and how to get things done using language in this particular language and culture.
- The communication is generally functional or purposeful for the speaker, and can often change or make a difference in the world because it occurs.

- The topics are generally chosen by the speaker, or else chosen by another about real concerns of the speaker-learner.
- The focus of communication is on meaning and message, not on language forms. Only when variations in form interfere with comprehension is clarification requested.

Not too surprisingly, much of real-life written communication also occurs under these conditions. When we write a letter to a friend, a memo to a supervisor, or even an academic paper, these conditions are likely to be present. When we read newspapers or seek out information in our work, we do so within topic frames that we have selected. Only when we get to the school setting, to the classrooms where reading and writing are taught, are these conditions not present in full force, or at all.

What happens when children come to school and learn to read and write? Traditionally, we eliminate all the conditions which have made our use of spoken *or* written language successful in the real world. Traditionally, school writing eliminates real, functional audiences, the writer's own needs and purposes, the struggle for an interactive negotiation of meaning in a self-generated topic. Then, external evaluation of the written form of the writing is added, focusing on the most surface features, and interrupting the writing process to make corrections.

Our data, particularly from young students, show that by beginning reading and writing under conditions very similar to those in which children learned to speak, we can help a greater number of students begin with competence in reading and writing, and maintain that competence as the content and purpose become increasingly complex in later years (cf. Kreeft, Shuy, Staton, Reed, & Morroy, 1984; Staton, 1985; Staton, Shuy, Kreeft, & Reed, 1988).

DIALOGUE JOURNALS: A WRITTEN CONNECTION TO SPOKEN COMPETENCE

The first and obvious task, if we are to begin with existing settings and practices which take advantage of the child's already developed directionality of learning to read and write, is to attempt to locate such practices. Classroom note passing, refrigerator door bulletin boards, and advertisements suggest themselves, but such practices and settings are difficult to control. And, in fact, even if it were possible to make good use of such literacy events, we are still faced with the asymmetry of school values, which tend to focus on correcting spelling and grammar forms, ignoring the deep structure meanings that the writers might intend. Nor has the conventional Language Experience Approach captured exactly what we mean, since such activities are often whole class procedures, with the teacher's part of the literacy reduced to little more than writing down what the children say. Observation of the Language Experience Approach in many classrooms reveals, in fact, that the teacher regularly corrects the child's grammar and vocabulary during this procedure. That is, there is no dialogue here; therefore, there is no communication in the sense we mean.

In 1979, Staton discovered a practice in the Los Angeles sixth-grade classroom of Leslee Reed in which each student wrote a brief message every day to the teacher, who took the journals home each night and wrote back, creating a written conversation, which was readily adapted to each child's reading and writing ability. Examination of these journals revealed exactly the type of setting and practice we were looking for—real conversation in writing which met the criteria noted above (Staton et al., 1988).

A dialogue journal contains a genuine conversation, written rather than spoken. The simple written format provides a means by which individual students at any age, but particularly in elementary school, can carry on a private discussion with their teacher. The interactive format of equal "turns" on the same topic is quite different from students' traditional personal journals, in which a teacher may occasionally make a marginal comment on a student's entry, but only days or weeks after the student wrote it. The distinguishing characteristics of dialogue journals are their *interactive, functional* nature, and the creation of mutually interesting, *self-generated* topics. Such dialogues can occur on a daily (or other) basis throughout the school year, extending the conversation across time for purposes of communication, self-understanding, negotiation of classroom tasks and relationships, and problem solving. In the elementary school classroom, this simple, teacher-developed practice unites meaningful, functional reading and writing as a single whole, just as speaking and listening are a seamless whole in oral discourse.

An example from a young, just-beginning reader/writer (Figure 2) illustrates how the written interaction partakes of the discourse forms of oral speech such as asking direct questions, turn taking, and sharing important personal information, yet produces the "complete thoughts" and more elaborated, meaningful written code which writing demands.

This second-grade student, Kwarteng, began the school year highly resistant to any kind of literacy. But a dialogue with his Chapter 1 resource teacher proved irresistible, and he began to move into this quite literate discussion of reading very quickly. Even though the dialogue journal does not focus on forms, Kwarteng uses the teacher's writing as a model for spelling new and difficult words ("siseata" in turn 4 im-

Day 1

Kwarteng: *I like t writ in the Journal.*
And I lik SULA [Step Up Language Arts]
Teacher: *I am glad you like SULA. It is nice to have you. You are very helpful in here. What do you like to do?*

Day 2

Kwarteng: *My best thin is writ.*
Teacher: *I am glad that you like to write. What do you like to write about? Do you like to read? I love to read.*

Day 3

Kwarteng: *Do you lik read to us. we lik listing to sistares.*
Teacher: *I love to read to you, especially when the story is a good one, like* Ramona the Pest. *I am glad that you like listening to stories. Do you read at home?*

Day 4

Kwarteng: *Yes I lik to read to my litti siseata about Juak and the bansitk She love it wnah I am reading to her.*
Teacher: *Your sister is lucky that you read* Jack and the Beanstalk *to her! How old is she? What is her name? There are lots of wonderful books that you can read to her.*

Day 5

Kwarteng: *My sistres name is Maria   she is one yers old   I love her.*
Teacher: *I have a sister, too, and I love her very much. She is older than I am and she used to read to me like you read to your sister. What else do you read to her?*

Day 6

Kwarteng: *I like to read abeout litte red*
raed word too. My Mom reads to me too.

Figure 2.   Kwarteng talks his way into reading and writing.

proves to "sistres" in turn 5). The major concern for many first- and second-grade teachers, "complete sentences," happens naturally when Kwarteng is expressing his own thoughts.

As a communicative event, dialogue journal communication is defined by a set of essential, distinguishing characteristics:

- Both writers are equally empowered to express their own purposes, and to communicate about real concerns and issues, bringing up their own topics and commenting on the other's topics.
- There is a focus on meaning and on mutual understanding rather than on correct form. Unclear statements elicit clarifying questions or restatements, rather than red marks.

- The communication is private and not subject to public scrutiny during the dialogue, nor afterward without consent (unless some life-threatening situation is brought up).
- The exchange takes place in some tangible form, such as a bound composition book, readily portable and equally accessible to both parties.

Dialogue journals use the natural supports of interactive conversation as the context and discourse structure for reading and writing. This provides maximum support for learners by activating all the child's existing competencies, in the service of a new mode of language. One of the first rules of learning is to vary only one aspect at a time. Eventually, of course, children will need to master more and more extended monologue forms of discourse with less responsive, or less present audiences. But at first, there is no need for either reading or writing to be an entirely unsupported, noninteractive event which the teacher enters into only as an outside evaluator.

Getting from Oral to Written Communication

The oral nature of the dialogues allow students to use their communicative competence in accomplishing written communication.

If we were to list the major strengths of oral communication, we might come up with the following: interactive, functional, participants are known, context is shared. If we were to make a similar list of strengths for written communication, we would make a quite different list, including reflectivity, lack of interruptions, permanence, privacy, and audience not present. Dialogue journal writing envelops the characteristics of both lists (Table 1). At the same time, the written dialogues share the crucial features which make writing so important as a tool for extending thought and gaining reflective self-awareness: the writing is private and reflective and each turn is as long, or as short, as is needed—no interruptions. The audience is not immediately present,

Table 1.   Integration of Oral and Written Characteristics in Dialogue Journals

Oral	Written
Interactive	Reflective
Functional	Lack of interruptions
Audience present	Audience not physically present
Shared context	Private from peers
Self-generated topics	Permanent record which can be modified

and the dialogue forms a permanent record so that one's ideas and thoughts are available for rereading and adding to or changing.

The following example (Figure 3) from a sixth-grade ESL student in one of Leslee Reed's classes demonstrates the integration of features customarily associated with oral language. These oral language features include direct address to an audience ("Isn't the right?"), reference to shared context (vacation), and free introduction of new topics ("Speaking of fire balls. . ."). The written language characteristics of this passage are manifest as reflective, elaborated discourse complete with some modifications, and revision or adding onto earlier ideas.

Note how this student, who has been in the United States only 2 years and is still working on the forms of English syntax and spelling, is able to use his communicative competence and familiarity with oral discourse to support and extend his thinking; the "hedges" and conditionals and requests for confirmation which are a natural part of negotiated discourse ("I think . . . but I'm not sure") allow his thoughts to flow in a natural way into written form.

THE DIALOGUE JOURNAL AS READING EVENT

Because the writing is so visible, it's easy to forget that dialogue journals are equally a *reading* event. Yet these interactive written conversations are one practical instance of reading and writing bound together in a single, functional experience. Through the dialogue, student and teacher construct a mutually interesting reading text about self-generated topics, with the teacher elaborating on some of the topics introduced by the student.

The dialogue journal gives the teacher continual evidence of what the student can comprehend in reading and a better means of diagnosing the child's appropriate reading level. Teacher responses naturally provide students with coherent, multisentence reading texts, because that is the way the human mind works. In recent studies, we have found that in these longer discourse structures, teachers automatically adjust their writing to the inherent reading level of each student, providing a reading text which is "just beyond" the grasp of the reader (Staton, 1985). Typically, these teacher-composed passages are more cognitively demanding than school-adopted basal readers (Staton, 1986). The success of the dialogue journals can be traced to the competence of each teacher's mind as a creative language user.

In addition, studies of the comprehension of deaf students (who typically have difficulty in mastering written communication) by Shuy have shown that comprehension and inferencing abilities in responding to

Feb. 17, 1981

Ben: *That five days vacations was fast! It seems like yesterday we had the first day off of the five days vacation. Its feels like a fire ball passing.*

Speaking of fireballs. Did you listened to the news about a meteor about Earth's size might colide with Earth? They might have figured out about the dinousaurs. They think that a meteor might have colided with Earth a long, long time ago during the dinosaurs time. They think that's going to happen again. But they already know what to do. There going to send a remote control rocket right into the meteor so it wouldn't colide with earth. I think there going to send the powerful rocket in the whole wide countries or world.

Mrs. Reed: *Yes! I heard about the meteor theory being a good way of explaining what happened to all of the dinosaurs.*

I'm not worried about getting hit with another meteor!

Feb. 18, 1981

Ben: *I know. There's nothing to worry about. They will think of using rocket. There's a lot of way to destroy those meteor that comes near and skid near Earth. I wonder how many planets did they explored besides Venus and that planet that has a ring Saturn. It was amazing when they discovered that Venus has a ring just like Saturn. Our Scientist today is getting better and better all the time. Pretty soon there going to be all famous and explore planets that nevere had been explored before in life.*

I saw this funny show last night. The title was . . .

Feb. 18

Mrs. R: *That show sounds fantastic! . . .*

Some of our scientists will become famous because they are learning more and more about space. Saturn has 52 rings—not just one. They've also discovered that some of the rings are braided like a chain!

Feb.19, 1981

Ben: *And it also has two moons traveling at the same time around Saturn. Isn't that right? But there's more than two moons that I know. It's really, really amazing how they discover things like that with modern machines and all. Another planet has a ring too! I forgot what was the name but I know there's one more planet that has ring. What was that name of the planet again, Mrs. Reed? I think the planet is Venus. But I'm not sure. Imagine that. All the time those rings has been around Venus for many, many thousands of years and no one noticed it yet until 1979 (I think).*

Figure 3.   Speaking of fireballs: Integration of oral and written language characteristics.

the teacher's comments are at a high level of competence, despite very low "tested" levels of reading ability (Shuy, 1984, 1986).

In a study of the reading comprehension of deaf students in a high school for the deaf, the Stanford Achievement Test for Hearing Impaired Students was the standard measure of comprehension (Shuy, 1984). One student scored at the 4.5 grade reading level, despite the fact that she was in the 11th grade. (Such low scores are common among deaf students.) If it is agreed that reading comprehension consists of determining the main idea or gist of a text, inferring indirect or unclear text and, to a lesser extent, recalling the subordinate factual details found in a text, this student actually did very well in her dialogue journal interactions. In stark contrast, very few of the Stanford questions tested for main idea, and fewer still tested for inferencing ability. This approach is endemic to reading comprehension measures, which apparently find it easiest to construct and score short-term memory of factual details (i.e., "What color was the girl's dress?").

Equally troublesome is the fact that such tests are not performance measures. On the contrary, they are events which operate outside the real contexts of life. This probably accounts for the deaf students' great difficulty in getting the correct answers to test questions in which the desired answer hinged on the students' ability to recognize and comprehend prepositions (such as to, at, with, etc.) effectively. A 25% error rate was found for these questions. For deaf students, inferencing takes place naturally. The fewer the clues, the more inferencing is necessary in order to comprehend. Deaf people become very proficient at inferring meaning, since they get so few clues from the hearing world.

Since these same deaf high school students kept dialogue journals with their teachers during the school year, the researchers had the unique opportunity to compare the students' comprehension in the interactive dialogue journals with their scores on the Stanford test. Interestingly, the same student who scored at the 4.5 reading level on the test showed evidence of 100% comprehension of her teacher's 35 propositions through her written responses to messages in which these propositions were embedded. She comprehended 91% of the 66 questions asked by her teacher, again as evidenced in her journal responses. She requested clarification at every instance in which the teacher's entry was ambiguous or too indirect. From this student's evidence of main idea comprehension in a natural, performance context, it is difficult to believe that she comprehends at only a fourth-grade level.

With a first-grade class, Ruth Sedei (one of the teachers working with our colleague, Joy Kreeft, on a new study of dialogue journal use in ESL classrooms) has been using dialogue journals as her first reading strategy with a group of children who are coming to school without much, if any, familiarity with English. Indeed, these children are without prior literacy or school experience in any language. Rather than beginning at the surface level with workbook drills, Sedei has turned the reading period into a reading/writing conversation through dialogue journals. Her children are still very confused about many school activities and are just beginning to learn English letters and words, but they are clear about one thing: they can "talk on paper" to their teacher each morning by writing/drawing a message, and each will get a turn to go up to the teacher's desk when reading time comes later the morning. Figure 4 illustrates how these children use a combination of invented spelling and drawing—anything that works toward the ultimate goal of communicating a meaningful message.

Sedei splits the class with her aide and calls each child up individually. She asks each child to read the message to her aloud and to discuss it, a necessity, since the combination of invented spelling and the child's limited English knowledge can make for some mystifying messages. This gives both student and teacher a chance to clarify orally anything that isn't clear. With those students who have little to say initially about their entries, or who cannot remember what they wrote, her questions and comments help them to remember, to extend their entries orally, and to understand that whatever they put down *is* informative and valuable. Sedei then writes back to the child immediately, reading it aloud as she writes while the child watches and listens. Then she and the student read her reply together and sometimes discuss the topic a bit more.

There is much rereading of this private written interchange at other spare times during the morning, and the next day the cycle of dialogue continues. With more literate children, or for those writing in their first language, such additional oral assistance in reading might not be necessary. But for these beginning readers and writers, this maximally supported approach is necessary during the first two months of school. Gradually, more independent readers and writers emerge. As the year progresses, all the students begin to write and read the teacher's replies without help, and they are able to move from this personal text to trade books and other reading material.

COMMUNICATING IN THE RIGHT REGISTER

To this point, we have noted that the special conditions of school communication traditionally dictate a type of oral language which is unlike the kind of oral language that children use everywhere else but in the classroom. Previous analyses of classroom oral language (Shuy, 1985; in

October 4, 1986

TOESSSMondAy

MondAyMSEQ

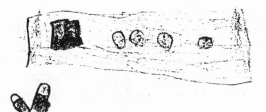

I love music. I like

pianos. What instrument

do you like best?

Figure 4. Dialogue journal used as a beginning reading text (from Peyton, 1987).

xylophone

October 5 1980

I LOVE

I LOVE XYlophone

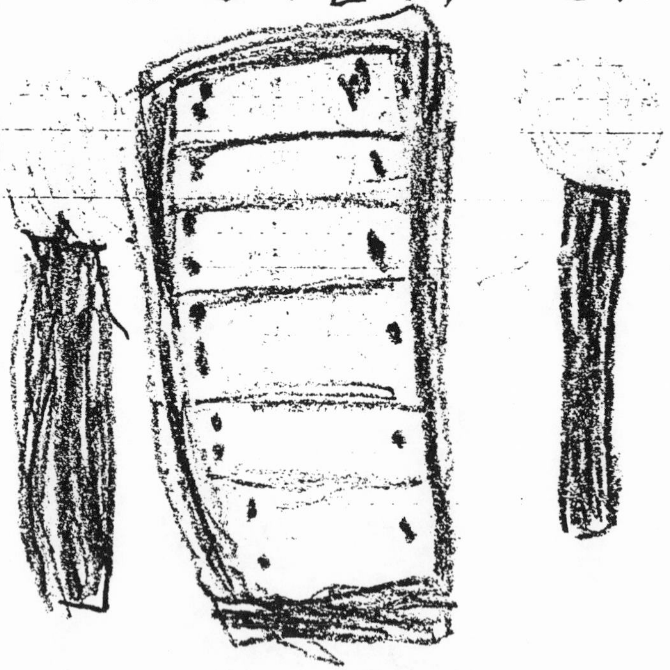

You made a beautiful picture
of the xylophone.
What songs do you like
to sing?

Figure 4. (continued)

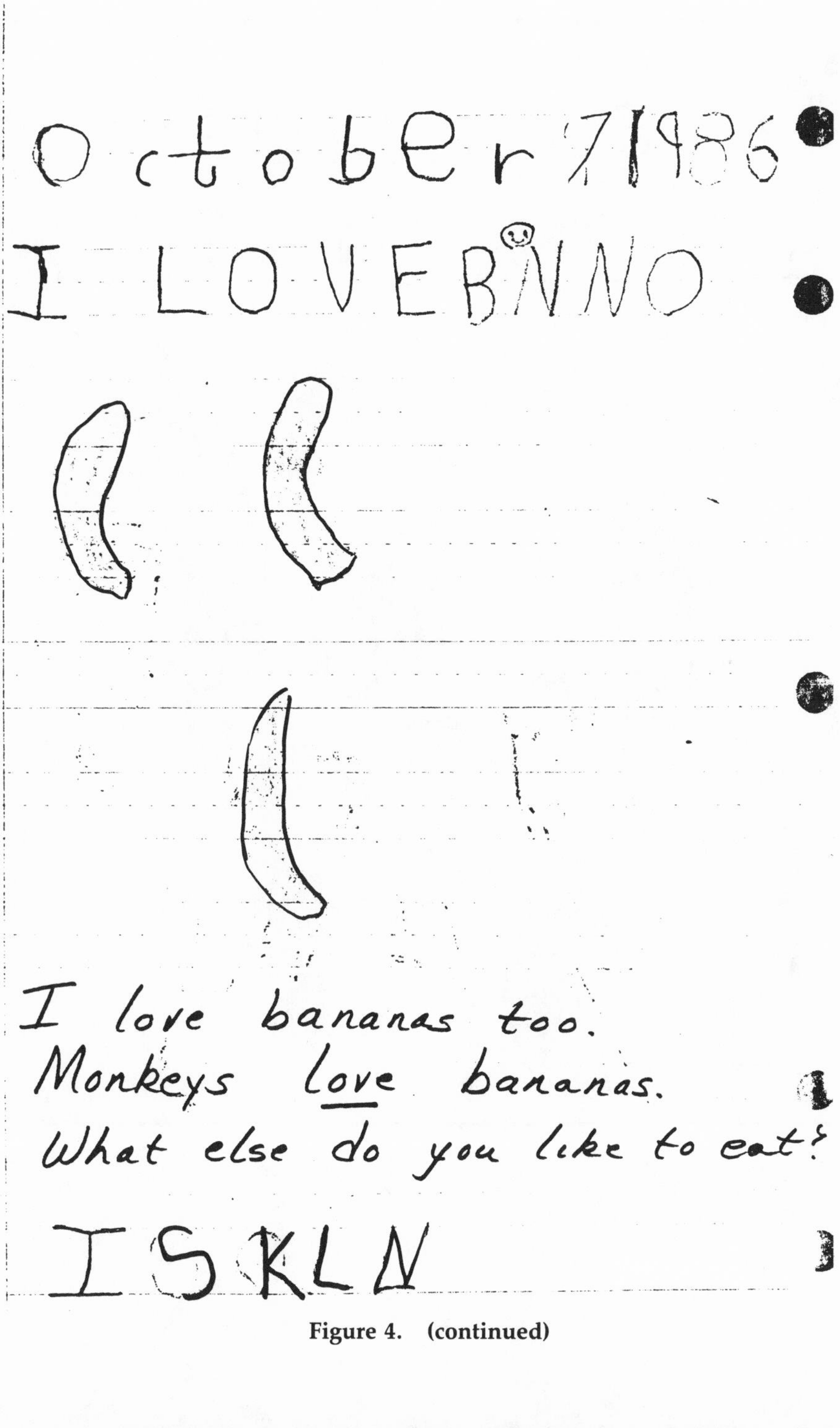

October 7 1986

I LOVEBNNO

I love bananas too.
Monkeys love bananas.
What else do you like to eat?

ISKLN

Figure 4.   (continued)

October 8 1986
I LOVEISKLN

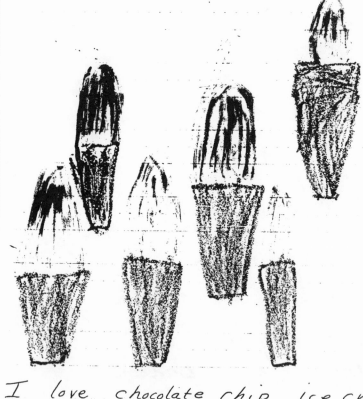

I love chocolate chip ice cream.
What kind do you like?

Figure 4. (continued)

press) in fact, show that teachers produce more than 95% of the utterances in classrooms, that only 3% of the students' utterances are questions (most of which are procedure questions) while about one-third of the teachers' utterances are questions (information or assessment questions). In addition, teachers spend about one-third of the time evaluating student responses and another third of their time giving directives and managing. There is nothing in the hundreds of dialogue journals analyzed to date which even comes close to such percentages. In dialogue journal writing, the quantity of communication is roughly equal between student and teacher and the major differences in type of utterances are as shown in Table 2.

The summary chart in Table 2 reveals that in their dialogue journal writing, students double the number of questions they ask their teachers in classroom oral language. Masked by percentages alone is the fact that dialogue journal questions are primarily requests for new information and not merely procedure questions such as "Should we use a pencil or a pen?" A more notable difference, however, is the contrast in reporting personal facts and opinions, where journal entries are five times higher than in classroom talk. In the area that might be considered closest to high-order thinking (predicting, evaluating, and complaining), the journal writing of students shows cognitive strength: 23% of their writing is in this category, as opposed to only 3% in classroom talk.

In terms of teachers' language, journal writing reduces question asking and warning/directive giving by more than half. What increases most significantly is the teachers' involvement in personal issues and opinions.

Table 2. Comparison of Classroom Talk to Dialogue Journal Writing

	Students' Classroom Talk	Dialogue Journals
Asking questions	3%	6%
Personal facts, opinions	10%	50%
General facts	80%	15%
Predicting	1%	9%
Evaluating	2%	10%
Complaining	0%	4%
Other	4%	5%

	Teachers' Classroom Talk	Dialogue Journals
Asking questions	35%	15%
Personal facts, opinions	1%	33%
General facts	20%	15%
Predicting	1%	6%
Evaluating	20%	13%
Warnings, directives	20%	10%
Other	3%	5%

Having shown that oral language in classrooms is not very conversational, we may ask why writing could be any more natural or conversational than speech. In most conventional classroom writing, it is *not*. The essayist tradition is greatly limited to certain types of speech acts, primarily to the reporting of general facts. There is little or no opportunity to practice the important life skills of producing well-formulated opinions, predicting (a high-order inferencing process), or asking information questions (intuitively, one would think that learners would ask information questions). At the very heart of the learning process, in fact, are issues of generalizing, seeing relationships, making comparisons, and inferring meaning from disparate sources. Conventional classroom writing simply does not permit this. The focus, instead, is on reporting facts gleaned from books and occasionally constructing a conclusion based on such facts. Nor does traditional classroom talk offer many opportunities for anything but factual responses to teachers' recitation questions (Schneider, Hyland, & Gallimore, 1985).

If it is wise practice for instruction to move from what is known to what is being learned, the relationship of oral language conversation (which children already have learned) to written language skill (which they are now beginning to learn) is crucial. Here the concept of language register plays an important part in the process. Register is defined as the verbal repertoires available to a person, ranging roughly from formal to informal. There has been little research on the acquisition of language registers, but common sense and logic can provide insights into how much acquisition takes place.

Children speak the dialect (grammar, vocabulary, pronunciation) of the language they hear and interact with, not surprisingly. In terms of styles and registers, they also learn to speak the registers they are expected to interact with. Martin Joos (1961) introduced the notion of registers as follows:

Frozen—fixed expressions, often archaic
Formal—monologues, speeches, sermons
Consultative—business dialogue
Casual—informal dialogue
Intimate—used by spouses, families, people very close to each other

It is not difficult to imagine that most of the language addressed to a preschool child will be in the intimate and casual styles. It is also clear that schooling takes place largely in the consultative style and that the formal style, if learned at all, is reserved for speech-making activities more regularly associated with high school and college. This leads us to hypothesize an acquisition sequence for styles or registers, as follows (Figure 5):

We have pointed out that Joos's pattern or register acquisition for oral language began with intimate and casual talk before consultative talk was learned. Now let us hypothesize that written language learning has some of the same characteristics as oral language learning. A long held, but seldom adhered to, principle of education is that we should start with children *where they are*. Just where are children who start school at 6? They have spoken a language for 5 or 6 years but they haven't yet written it. They have spoken in intimate and casual styles, but not consultative and formal styles yet. What type of style, therefore, comes closest to where these children are? Obviously, the casual style. But what kind of writing is done in the casual style? With the exception of note passing, there is not much casual writing, largely because writing is a school-learned subject. Sometimes letters to close friends or family approach casual style. But, on the whole, there is very little writing available that reads like casual conversation written down. We see glimpses of it in novels or short stories when dialogue is recorded, but not much else.

Now let us take Joos's chart and recast what it must look like for written language (Figure 6):

As this chart illustrates, traditionally formal writing is begun in the schools without concern for where the children are in their language learning, particularly with regard to register. Secondly, writing instruction begin with formal writing, expecting the child's development to take place without passing through the same stages of development that oral language learning has permitted, namely, first learning the intimate, then the casual, then the consultative and, finally, the formal registers.

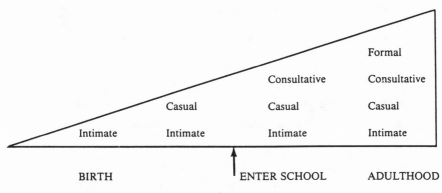

Figure 5.   Acquisition of spoken registers.

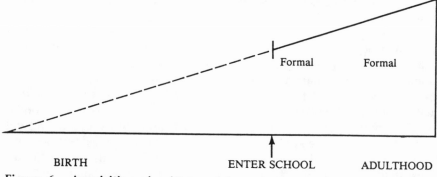

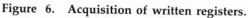

Figure 6. Acquisition of written registers.

Consider for the moment what it would feel like to have to speak in a register that one does not know. This problem is compounded, of course, for second-language learners who are busy learning to communicate at all, much less in the expected register. Now transfer this feeling to what it must feel like as children to be told to write in a style they have not often heard or seen, much less learned.

Research carried out on hundreds of journals in many types of settings and ages has made it clear that dialogue journal writing allows students to use the same register as their oral language. Therefore, dialogue journal writing comes closer to where children are in the language-learning process. They write the way they talk in dialogue journals, largely because the genre is dialogue. Dialogue journal teachers recognize that intercommunication is the most important aspect of such writing and they deliberately abstain from correcting the children's errors in form. These teachers respond to the children's ideas, they challenge, they ask questions, they give their own opinions, they urge, they even evaluate.

But are teachers who adopt these procedures really teaching? To answer this question, we have to be sure that we agree on what *teaching* means. If teaching means lecturing and correcting, they probably aren't "teaching." But this is an inadequate definition of teaching by any standard. We have already noted that the most cognitively rich learning experience in a child's life takes place before he or she even attends school. Was there teaching involved? Of course there was. The mother, the father, the caretaker, and the older siblings all taught. But they did not use drills, textbooks, or black-line masters for worksheets. Their major strategy was to *model* in a natural context. And this is exactly what dialogue journal teachers do. They model. But they also scaffold their students, moving them from the casual register into a more consultative style. This concept is not the focus of this chapter, and will only be illustrated here. Scaffolding occurs when the child wants to do something and the teacher helps. The teacher appropriates the student's goal to a higher-order task, as follows (Figure 7):

This conversation occurs in a more casual register, indicated by such phrases as "showing it," "clinched," and the use of dashes. But the content moves from a discussion of the event to an intense concern with its meaning, and with fairness. Both participants' writing becomes more consultative and precise in syntax and vocabulary: They get definite answers: "It would eliminate arguments and would also overcome human error." In this brief exchange, we see how a teacher uses the same language-acquisition processes that facilitate a young child's marvelously complex learning of a first language, to move into more adult levels of reasoning and language use.

In order to get to this kind of conversational learning through scaffolding, however, an important earlier task must be accomplished—the teacher and student must have arrived at a level of mutuality, trust, and cooperation that makes such scaffolding possible. The above example is also an example of such mutuality.

George: *It's football season again and Rams are certainly showing it. They clinched a playoff berth by beating the Falcons yesterday. I was so happy I almost threw a party. I am begginning to like football more and more.*

Mrs. Reed: *You have only a short time to enjoy football—the season ends with New Year's day, usually. My husband is watching the Oilers against the Steelers.*

George: *I watched that game, too. Houston (Oilers) won just barely one a disputed play.*

Mrs. Reed: *That disputed play may change football. I heard a commentator say he felt the time had come for the instant replay to step in and be a part of the referee's call. What do you think?*

George: *I think they should use the instant replay. The broadcasters use it, and they get definite answers.*

Mrs. Reed: *It would eliminate arguments and would also overcome human error. It will be interesting to see how this develops.*

George: *Today when I read the sports section they said that the N.F.L.'s president said that the disputed play went the opposite way that the referee called, very clearly. The president also said it was a hometown call because he lived in one of the towns playing. He's going to get fined.*

Mrs. Reed: *The referees should not be from the "home town," but I suppose it would be extremely difficult for anyone involved in the game to avoid having a personal bias.*

Figure 7.   Written conversation as a mode of interactional scaffolding.

Once mutuality is established (and it may take weeks of interaction to get to such a place), the parent–child relationship can be achieved and learning by modeling and scaffolding is facilitated. But all of this takes place primarily because the development of a natural, interactive, functional, and self-generated context has made such mutuality and trust possible.

CONCLUSION

In this century Vygotsky (translated in 1978) was one of the first researchers to point out that literacy must be as functional for the learner as is oral speech, or the living written language becomes an artificial exercise:

> Teaching should be organized in such a way that reading and writing are necessary for something. If they are used only to write official greetings to the staff or whatever the teacher thinks up (and clearly suggests to them), then the exercise will be purely mechanical and may soon bore the child. . . . Reading and writing must be something the child needs. . . .
>
>   Writing must be . . . meaningful for children, an intrinsic need should be aroused in them, and that writing should be incorporated into a task that is necessary and relevant for life. Only then can we be certain that it will develop not as a matter of hand and finger habits but as a really new and complex form of speech. (pp. 117–118)

Dialogue journals stand as just one instance of all the kinds of functional reading and writing in which children could be engaged if we established opportunities for them to do so in the classroom. In this chapter, we have indicated some of the theories which help explain the effectiveness and benefits of ongoing written conversations, but the practice itself did not spring from theory or research, and it was validated in classrooms well before we became aware of it (cf. Atwell, 1987), for a direct application to secondary settings). The practice thus stands as a practical, concrete instance, validating the theories.

Essentially, practice and direct instruction in literacy skills are only *half* of learning to read and write. The other half, which must also be part of each school day, is the functional use of reading and writing for one's own purposes, with the response in kind from an interested audience able to stretch and enlarge the learner's mind continually.

REFERENCES

Atwell, N. (1987). *In the middle: Writing, reading and learning with adolescents.* Upper Montclair, NJ: Boynton/Cook.

Harste, J., Woodward, V. A., & Burke, C. L. (1984). *Language stories and literacy lessons*. Portsmouth, NH: Heinemann.

Joos, M. (1961). *The five clocks*. New York: Harcourt.

Kreeft, J., Shuy, R. W., Staton, J., Reed, L., & Morroy, R. (1984). *Dialogue writing: Analysis of student–teacher interactive writing in the learning of English as a second language*. Final Report to the National Institute of Education, NIE–G–83–0030. Washington, DC: Center for Applied Linguistics. (ERIC DRS No. ED 252–097).

Peyton, J. K. (1987). *Getting started with writing: Interactive writing with first grade ESL students*. Paper presented at the annual TESOL meeting, April 21–25, Miami Beach, FL.

Schneider, P., Hyland, J., & Gallimore, R. (1985). The zone of proximal development in eighth grade social studies. *Quarterly Newsletter of the Laboratory of Comparative Human Cognition, 7*, 113–119.

Shuy, R. W. (1984). Method for dynamic assessment of reading comprehension in dialogue journals. Report No. 5 of the Dialogue Journal Project, Gallaudet College, Washington, D.C.

Shuy, R. W. (1985). A comparison of oral and written language functions. In K. Jankowski (Ed.), *Scientific and humanistic dimensions of language* (pp. 471–480). Philadelphia: John Benjamins.

Shuy, R. (1986). Dialogue journals and reading comprehension. *Dialogue, 3*(1), 1–2. Washington, DC: Center for Applied Linguistics.

Shuy, R. W. (1988). Identifying dimensions of classroom language. In J. Green & J. Harker, *Multiple perspective analysis of classroom discourse processes*. Norwood, NJ: Ablex.

Staton, J. (1985). Using dialogue journals for developing thinking, reading, and writing with hearing-impaired students. *Volta Review, 87*(5), 127–154.

Staton, J. (1986). The teacher's writing as text. *Greater Washington Reading Council Journal, 10*(1), 3–4.

Staton, J., Shuy, R. W., Kreeft, & Reed, L. (1987). *Dialogue journal communication: Classroom, linguistic, social and cognitive views*. Norwood, NJ: Ablex.

Teale, W. H., & Sulzby, E. (Eds.). (1986). *Emergent literacy: Writing and reading*. Norwood, NJ: Ablex.

Vygotsky, L. S. (1978). *Mind in society: The development of higher psychological processes*. In M. Cole, V. John–Steiner, S. Scribner, & E. Souberman, (Eds. and Trans.). Cambridge, MA: Harvard University Press.

Chapter 10

Unintentional Helping in the Primary Grades: Writing in the Children's World*

Anne Haas Dyson

University of California, Berkeley

After a pleasant year in kindergarten, Regina had assumed that she would return to kindergarten the next fall. Then she found that she was going to be in *first* grade:

> I got so sad. Cause I didn't know who was gonna be my friend. . . . I was spending all my time thinking Sunday, "What'em I gonna do? What 'em I gonna do? Tomorrow's school!" That's when I was turned into a first grade[r]. I say, "I want to go to my ol' [class]. I bet nobody's gonna be my friend."

As it happened, Regina did have friends in the first grade. In fact, most of the children from her kindergarten class were members of her new combined first/second-grade class. And was she happy in this new situation? "You better believe it."

The influence of peers on the schooling experience has been discussed primarily in the literature on older schoolchildren (Goodlad, 1983; Labov, 1982). But children in the early school years are intensely interested in each other. During these years, children's awareness of themselves and their peers increases notably, as they work to define

---

* Support for this work was provided in part by a seed grant from the Spencer Foundation, distributed by the School of Education, University of California–Berkeley, and by the Office of Educational Research and Improvement/Department of Education (OERI/ED), through the Center for the Study of Writing. However, the opinions expressed herein do not necessarily reflect the position or policy of the OERI/ED and no official endorsement by the OERI/ED should be inferred.

I thank Mary Gardner and Carol Heller, my research assistants. I thank also the children's teacher, who provides her children with ample opportunity and support for writing—and thus provides me with ample opportunity to learn about learning to write.

themselves as competent members of their social group—as "me too'ers"—and at the same time, as unique, special beings, special parts of that group (Gardner, 1982).

In this self- and group-creating work, which extends throughout the life span, symbolic tools—including drawing and writing—can play a particularly helpful role, for the use of any symbol system is both a communicative act using a social tool and an expression of individual uniqueness (Vygotsky, 1962).

In this chapter I argue that, in classrooms that allow writing to blossom within the children's world—as a part of their efforts to define themselves as socially competent but unique individuals—written language will help children meet these social challenges and, at the same time, these social concerns will help children develop as writers. That is, the academic and the social will be intertwined. This mutually supportive situation can be created even without explicit attempts by the teacher to have children help each other. Just by "being kids," children may unintentionally help each other become literate.

Conversely, classrooms may work to separate the academic and the social lives of children. Children's social lives may be played out primarily in opposition to—or, at least, around and under—official academic concerns. These classrooms, particularly those serving urban, nonmainstream children, may contribute to the opposition between social and academic success highlighted in studies of inner city adolescents (Labov, 1982; Ogbu, 1985). As Regina suggested, it may be better to fail and have friends than to be promoted and have none.

To illustrate these suggested connections between the social and academic dimensions of classroom life, I will look closely within Regina's classroom in "O Elementary," a magnet school in an urban area on the West Coast. In this room, the social and academic concerns of children were interwoven in the official classroom community because children had ample official opportunities to use language for their own purposes and to support and respond to each other.

In the first part of this chapter, I provide a backdrop for looking in this classroom. I examine literacy as an aspect of growing up and becoming a member of society. A major portion of that growing up happens at school; I thus highlight the social and academic divisiveness schooling may promote. To illustrate this divisiveness, I give a brief look at another, more traditional primary classroom.

The second and major part of this chapter centers on Regina's classroom. Finally, in the third section, I clarify and qualify the concept of unintentional helping. I balance this discussion of the power of children's social lives with a consideration of children's need for sensitive, guiding teachers.

GROWING UP WITH WRITTEN LANGUAGE: LITERACY
AND DAILY LIFE

The theoretical perspective undergirding this chapter is both sociolinguistic and developmental. I assume that written language is a social
tool that functions in varied ways in our society. As children grow up,
they learn about this tool—its purposes, its features, its processing
demands—as they encounter it in meaningful activities (see Staton &
Shuy, this volume; Daiute, this volume). Even in communities where
literacy assumes a relatively minor role, children are not isolated from
written language (Heath, 1983). The adults who live with children write
notes, jot down phone numbers and needed grocery items, fill out
forms and checks, and so children take to pen and paper too. Children
participate in literacy activities with more skilled others, explore and
play with print's functions and features, and use it as a means of self-expression (Dyson, 1981; Gundlach, McLane, Stott, & McNamee, 1985;
Tizard & Hughes, 1984). From the beginning, then, literacy is woven
into the familiar fabric of everyday life.

In observing young children using written language, though, I take a
developmental stance. That is, I assume that children do not simply attempt to imitate adult models. Children actively construct written language, as they do other sorts of symbol systems, in ways that are sensi-
ble from their own points of view (Clay, 1975; Ferreiro & Teberosky,
1982; Hudson, this volume; Piaget & Inhelder, 1969).

LITERACY AND SCHOOLING

In our culture, beginning formal schooling marks the beginning of special attention to the written language symbol system. Children from a
variety of backgrounds go to school and expect to learn to read and write
(Heath, 1983). Of course, many educators now recognize that children
read and write in their own ways well before formal schooling begins.
Nonetheless, I have observed that kindergartners in traditional classrooms often connect learning to read and write "like grown-ups" to
turning 6 and starting first grade—a belief consistent with that of the
dominant culture. As 5-year-old Courtney explained while drawing
Santa Claus, "I would spell Santa Claus if I was 6."

Although both adults and children may value literacy, it does not follow that adults and children share the same perspective on literacy and
how it is to be learned. As noted above, children interpret behaviors
modeled by adults in ways that make sense in their own lives (Cazden,
1986; Corsaro, 1985; Steinberg & Cazden, 1979).

Literacy and the Social Lives of Children

Children's lives in group settings center on their relationships with each other. In the child collective arising in a day care or elementary classroom, children find the comfort of being members of a group that is "in this together" and, at the same time, the opportunity to define their individual uniqueness further as they compare themselves with their peers (Rubin, 1980). As Dewey (1916) noted, schoolchildren are not preparing to become social participants—they are social participants. In fact, the whole of childhood socialization can be viewed as "children's participation in and production of a series of peer cultures in which childhood knowledge and practices are gradually transformed into knowledge and skills necessary to participate in the adult world" (Corsaro, 1985, pp. 74–75; see also in this volume; Daiute & Dalton; Fontaine; Hudson; Pellegrini & Galda; Rafoth).

The developmental literature portrays the years from 5 to 7 as a time when children's awareness of self and others is particularly visible, for these years are "a watershed" for trends that have been gradually taking shape over the preschool period (Gardner, 1982). Particularly, symbols (words, pictures, numbers, music) become a dominant force in children's behaviors (Flavell, 1985; Gardner, 1982; Nelson, 1985; Vygotsky, 1962, 1978). This fluency and control over symbols allows young children (a) to express themselves in delightful and unique ways, (b) to be increasingly effective communicators and collaborators with others (Cooper, Marquis, & Ayers–Lopez, 1982; Garvey, 1977, 1984; Korzenik, 1977), and (c) to explore a basic tool of our society, a tool used by adults and thus of interest to children (Schickedanz & Sullivan, 1984; Tizard & Hughes, 1984). That is, it allows them opportunities to participate in the social world and to explore their own mental worlds.

So young children, bearing the tools of words, pictures, and other symbols, enter formal schooling and continue there the work of creating the "I," the "you," and the "we." The thesis of this chapter is that the way in which writing is bound up with the creation of self and others in school will be affected by the way in which classrooms provide opportunities for the academic and the social lives of children to intertwine. Schools do not simply help children become literate; they present that literacy within activities and imbue it with values that may make it work in more or less productive ways within the child collective of particular classrooms (See Irvine & Elsasser, this volume; Staton & Shuy, this volume).

Child Response to School Literacy

Many observers have pointed out that aspects of traditional American schooling may make school literacy a negative unifying force in children's lives, particularly for urban minority children. That is, children may join together in their discomfort with or, more strongly, their rejection of academic demands. Among those aspects of school life most often cited as divisive are those that touch on children's relationships with each other—on the "I" and the "we": children having to work silently, to value adult more than self and peer approval, to compete with friends for that adult approval (Gilbert & Gay, 1985; Gillmore, 1983; Labov, 1982; Philips, 1972; Tharp et al., 1984).

The main concern in this chapter is with the social lives of a group of socially and ethnically diverse primary schoolchildren who share a particular experience—an urban public school classroom. In this situation, some children may be better able than others, for both personal and social reasons, to cope productively with the school's demands. Nonetheless, the stories of most children's school lives—in fact, of our own school memories—are threaded with the "I" and the "we"; that is, regardless of cultural background, they are stories of children finding themselves among their friends.

Literacy may be bound up with children's social concerns in positive or negative ways. In a previous study in an ethnically and socially diverse second-grade classroom, I found that school literacy was, to some extent, a unifying force among the children in that it provided them with a common problem: a force to grapple with (Dyson, 1984, 1985a, 1985b). Since I have discussed that classroom elsewhere, it will receive only a brief examination here. The room deserves a peek, though, as it illustrates well how children's social and academic lives can be alienated, one from the other, and thus provides a contrast to the tight intertwining of children's social and academic concerns in School 0.

In this room, located in "School A" in a small Southeastern city, children's daily work consisted primarily of completing the "seatwork" that filled the chalkboards each morning. There were misspelled words and unpunctuated sentences to be righted, suffixes and prefixes to be added to bare roots, words in need of sentences, sentences in need of missing words.

Each morning, as the children made their way down the rows to their desks, they compared the amount of boardwork each reading group received; children with the least amount of written work occasionally rejoiced; children with a great deal of written work more often complained among themselves about the unfairness of it all.

In doing their morning work, the children were to proceed quietly, carefully, and quickly. While the children did not talk about being quiet or careful during that work, they did remark about quickness. Whispers of "Which one are you on? I'm on 10, are you?" linked closely seated children together as they sat in their separate desks doing their "own" work.

Accuracy became important only when the teacher checked their work. At that point, the whispers changed: "I got that one right." "I did too." "So?" In the whispers, success was put on display; failure was kept quiet or shrugged off.

Thus, in the work that took the majority of the language arts period, the children joined together as kids who had to do the assigned work. As a group, they rejoiced in having less work, bragged about spending the least amount of time on that work, and, depending on their evaluated performance, they defined success as meeting the teacher's standards.

This assigned work, however, was not the only writing that the children did. The clandestine communication noted above suggested the existence of the children's social world, which operated around and underneath the official academic world. And, in the children's world, there was much use of the social tool of writing. In effect, there was an "underground writing curriculum" (Dyson, 1985b).

This curriculum was child-controlled and revealed itself primarily when the children's boardwork was completed. At that time, the children were relatively free to do as they pleased, as long as they were quiet and stayed in their desks or at a small table in the back of the room. This underground curriculum, however, also revealed itself during whole class *Weekly Reader* lessons, when pencils and paper could easily be hidden behind a propped-up newspaper, and, less often, during the morning boardwork period when a child apparently elected to take a break.

Within the underground curriculum, the children used writing to link themselves in what seem more positive ways than those of the official curriculum. Literacy connected the children quite literally as they passed notes or phone numbers across the rows. More typically, though, literacy connected the children as they monitored each other's behavior and joined in on similar activities. They were particularly attentive to the practical and playful uses that others made of print—desk placards that stood on their desks announcing their names, phone numbers, and, in some cases, their positions (e.g., police chief), trash bins taped to the sides of their desks, containers for pencils and crayons, "Keep Out" signs, and telephone number books.

The children also produced more extended written language. On days when boardwork was light, two or three children might be seen at the table in the back of the room, writing stories, copying stories from books (a surprisingly popular activity), drawing pictures with captions, and, on one occasion, writing letters to boyfriends!

In the underground curriculum, the children admired quantity. More was better than less. More stories, more poems, more words—all could be bragged about. In addition, though, the children were interested in the content of other children's stories and poems; children who sat next to each other could be observed reading a peer's story or admiring an interesting constructed object.

The productivity and variability of the literacy produced by the second graders in the underground writing curriculum were impressive. Yet, that curriculum was controlled partly by the amount of "official" work the children were given, and in addition, most of the interactions among children were limited to children within whispering distance of each other. Further, children typically interacted only with others experiencing similar degrees of academic success, since the children sat according to reading group membership.

The possibility of bringing the liveliness of the unofficial curriculum into the official one was hinted at during one brief activity that occurred daily every other month—the 10-minute morning free-writing period (for an extensive description of this activity, see Dyson 1985a). During this period the children were free to write whatever they wanted, and then, if they chose, they could read their work to their peers.

As an audience, the children rewarded entries they perceived as humorous with audible laughter and, when the child writer had returned to his or her seat, with whispered requests such as "Can I see it?" They also adopted for their own use appealing topics of others.

Beyond these general responses that seemed to characterize the class, I noted that individual children appeared to use this activity to achieve certain social ends. For example, Ayrio and his close friends most often wrote about experiences they shared, such as Cub Scout meetings or YMCA soccer games, or objects of mutual interest, such as video games or recent movies. Free writing was an opportunity to proclaim their friendship. For Bonita, on the other hand, free writing seemed to provide an opportunity to present herself positively to her peers; she wrote and read pieces about things she was going to get to do—but often, in fact, never did. (For examples of the children's behaviors, see Dyson, 1985a.)

As a result of observing this class, the concept of "unintentional helping" began emerging. That is, it seemed that the children were helping each other learn about literacy—the range of purposes for which it can be used, the techniques used to capture an audience's interest, the power of print to help one achieve social status. But this help was not being intentionally offered. That is, there were no "peer tutoring" programs, no "peer writing conferences," no official "collaborative writing activities." Children made use of an available tool—writing—simply because of their interest in each other and their desire to be a part of the social scene in their room, that is, to be accepted and perhaps even admired by others. School provided them with paper, pencils, and some practice on conventions; the children provided each other with purpose and "sense."

This concept of "unintentional helping"—of the linking of children's social lives with literacy—blossomed for me in School 0. Here was a classroom where there were fewer fences between the social and the academic concerns of children.

THE LINKING OF CHILDREN'S ACADEMIC AND SOCIAL LIVES: INTRODUCTION TO THE OBSERVED CHILDREN OF SCHOOL 0

The classroom of interest here was a combined first/second grade. Like the room discussed above, its social and ethnic membership reflected the diversity of its community. There were 30 class members from Anglo, Asian, Black, Hispanic, Middle Eastern, and mixed ethnicities. Their teacher, Margaret, was an Anglo female in her sixties. ("Margaret" is a pseudonym, like most names used in this chapter.) Margaret was the children's language arts teacher; she had also been the language arts teacher for most of the children the previous year in kindergarten and first grade.

The children in this classroom were situated much differently than the children in School A. When the children arrived each morning, they sat in chairs arranged in a circle. During this opening meeting, Margaret talked with them about a particular language arts concept, such as punctuation, contractions, homonyms; she sometimes read them stories; and she "celebrated" the work of those who had completed a journal (a homemade construction paper book consisting of approximately 13 lined/blank paper pairs). "Celebrating" a journal involved letting the child pick three stories to read to the class, highlighting what was special about that child's work, and presenting the child with an "award"—a homemade certificate, signed by Margaret and her aide, Susan, telling the child to "write on."

After the opening meeting, preparation for journal writing began. Although each of the children had a personal journal, they each selected a pencil from a tin can and a packet of markers from a basket. Then they went to their tables, which seated six to eight, and began to draw, write—and talk.

Margaret, her aide, and on occasion parent volunteers, circulated among the children, talking to them about their topics, helping with spelling, and urging loud children to "be quiet and get to work." Talking among the children, while not specifically encouraged, was expected and not prohibited.

I observed in this room an average of two times a week from February through May 1986; two research assistants, Carol Heller and Mary Gardner, also observed twice a week. In total, our team observed the children an average of 6 hours per week. In our observations we focused on seven children: four first graders and three second graders. (A fourth observed second grader was a member of a different class; see Table 1.) I had earlier observed these same children an average of twice a week from January through May 1985.

Compared with the orderliness of School A, I initially found Margaret's room overwhelming. Entering the room in January 1985, I was immediately struck by all the talk. This talk was not just a quiet hum but was punctuated by laughter, loud bids for a peer's attention ("Hey Jake!"), and an occasional yell (from the children, not Margaret, who never yelled). Moreover, the spirit of the room was different, although I could not initially say why. Soon, though, I no longer noticed the talk—I just listened to it. And the spirit of the room was clear. It was the spirit of a room with a strong child collective.

In the following sections, I describe the nature of this child collective and highlight the connection of this collective to the children's writing. The information reported comes primarily from the data collected during 1986 in the form of audiotape transcripts supplemented with field notes gathered during 46 days of observation. (For a description of data collection and analysis techniques used in this project, see Dyson, 1986.)

To illustrate the linking of the academic and the social in this class-

Table 1.   Age, Gender, and Ethnicity of Focal Children

	Age[a]	Gender	Ethnicity
First graders			
Maggie	6.1	Female	Anglo
Regina	7.1	Female	Black
Jesse	6.7	Male	Anglo
Rueben	6.11	Male	Hispanic
Second graders			
Sonia	7.3	Female	Hispanic
Mitzi[b]	7.4	Female	Anglo
Jake	7.6	Male	Mixed (Black/Anglo)
Manuel	8.4	Male	Mixed (Hispanic/Anglo)

[a]Age as of Feb. 1, 1986 (given in years. months).
[b]During the observations from February through May 1986, Mitzi was not in the same classroom as the other seven children.

room—and, particularly, the concept of unintentional helping—I will begin by introducing the children as a collective, as a group. In examining the ways in which the children expressed themselves as a group, it will become clear that official school writing was woven throughout these social behaviors. Then, I will focus on the observed children's behaviors during the journal activity, examining social themes underlying the children's interactions; this section will illustrate most clearly the concept of "unintentional helping," as children will be seen responding socially and in coincidentally helpful ways to each other.

THE CHILD COLLECTIVE

The School 0 children displayed a sense of being "kids" in school together in varied ways. First, they frequently joined together *to engage in collective or joint action*, sometimes doing spontaneously group activities previously initiated by Margaret. For example, they spontaneously sang "Happy Birthday" when Margaret announced that it was her birthday, just as they regularly sang to the "birthday child." At the work tables, when one child began reciting a television commercial jingle or singing a pop song ("Born in the U.S.A." was especially popular), others joined in.

Sometimes the group was called to action by a spokesperson. One day Margaret announced that the reading teacher would be retiring soon. Jake immediately stood up and exclaimed:

Example 1
Many people don't want Rebecca to leave cause she's got all those puzzles and stuff. How many people don't want Rebecca to leave?

All of the children raised their hands, apparently wanting to have their say in the matter. Margaret assured them that the puzzles and games belonged to the school, not to the retiring teacher.

A second way of expressing their identity as "kids together" was *to activate a group memory*. Some memories were of activities or interests the children shared outside of school—television shows, popular singers, baseball and football teams. But many were shared school experiences: "Remember when" a child got in trouble, when they made "fruit" in art class, when they played in the sand on the playground during a rainstorm? Jake considered a vehicle he had "invented" (i.e., he had drawn in his journal) to be a significant event his peers should recall:

Example 2[1]
Jake: Who made up the bubble cars?
Rueben: My brother have a bubble car.
Jake   (louder) Who made up the bubble cars?
Sonia: Your dad for one thing.
Jake: I made up the bubble cars.
Sonia: Well, how in the world could Rueben have one?!
. . .   [omitted data.]
Jake: I was the creator of the bubble car.
Sonia: You're not a famous inventor.

On another day, Sonia acknowledged that Jake might indeed be famous for his invention by the time he was 10. As if to support this prediction, when Jake stood before the class to share a completed journal, several children shouted, "Bubble cars!"

As a third mechanism for expressing the collective, the children joined together *to react or respond to school procedures and activities.* Who was the substitute teacher? Was she mean? Would she know where the special game they were supposed to play was? And, like the children in School A—and like workers in any organization, for that matter—they wondered if they were being treated fairly:

Example 3
Sonia: Finally I get free time.
Jake: I should get free time. I should get extra credit [a term Margaret never used] because I finished two journals and I'm gonna finish my story. I should get some credit. She doesn't give me credit. [Margaret never talked about giving children "credit."]
Jesse: I know. She never gives you credit.
Jake: She doesn't give ME credit, that's for sure.
Jesse: She never gives me credit, for sure.

Example 3 illustrates two characteristics of the children's talk about school procedures: the use of "school jargon" and the emphasis on the teacher's authority. In addition to "credit," the children used the terms "flunk" and "pass" or "get promoted," although I never observed Margaret use these terms. They also discussed older children who had been "expelled" or "suspended."

In their own classroom, Margaret was a low-key authority figure, from my viewpoint as observer. She expected the children to follow the rules, but she quietly and respectfully pointed out these rules when there was a need. But to the children, Margaret seemed to be another "superhero," one with powers to be feared, depended upon, or defied:

---

[1] For transcript conventions, see Appendix.

Example 4
Jesse has used the scotch tape to shape a boat in his journal, an inappropriate use of scotch tape in this classroom.

Jake: You might have gotten busted by Margaret. You shouldn't have taken such a chance, because she will bust.

A fourth way in which the children expressed the child collective was *to identify and share their common problems* as "kids." Certainly their problems included concerns shared with adults, including AIDS, starvation in Africa, terrorists in airports, the Challenger space tragedy, and the possibility of a war between the United States and Russia. In fact, Sonia, Jesse, and Jake once discussed their desire to wait to grow up "til everybody dies . . . and there wouldn't be anybody but us." This was wise, explained Jake, as "there might be a Vietnam again":

Example 5
Jake: They're going to ship out machine guns and, everybody, even the kids. They'll give them to every single kid in the United States.
Jesse: Except for babies.
Jake: Kids would be wild. Kids would be the best.
Jesse: I know. They just die first, Man. I know why. Kids are small.
Jake: The kids are small. The kids are mean.
Jesse: I know.
Jake: I'm the slyest. I'm the—I'm sly.

Perhaps Jake saw himself as surviving such a horrible but—for a child captivated by war stories—exciting prospect.

Among the more frequently discussed and more modest problems were losing teeth (having "The Great Gap" in the front, as they called it), whether or not there was a Santa Claus, getting, keeping, and losing friends and pets, riding a bike without training wheels, just getting a bike, completing a journal, figuring out a spelling, and finding a black marker that actually wrote.

Jake considered writing itself to be a problem kids confronted:

Example 6
Jake has stopped writing and begun drawing. His journal entry does not seem finished to me, so I ask him if he is done writing. Jake answers philosophically:

Jake: I think so. When I was in kindergarten I learned, I liked to write. When you get older you don't like to write.
Dyson: Why?
Jake: That's just the way with kids, some kids.
Dyson: Oh. What happens to those kids?

Jake:	Um. They like to write and write and write. So they just write, because they love to write.
Dyson:	And then what happens to those kids?
Jake:	And then [large sigh], some kids just stop writing for a while.
Dyson:	Why?
Jake:	I don't know. That's happening to me. That's why I like to draw more than I like to work. [Note that work is writing, not drawing.]
Dyson:	Mmmmmmmmmm.

So Jake appears to admit indirectly that his story is not quite up to his usual standard. But he explains that what is happening to him is just the way some kids are—it's a common problem, just a stage. Not to worry.

SOCIAL CONCERNS DURING JOURNAL TIME: NETWORKING

The previous section presented ways in which the children proclaimed themselves to be a group—"kids"—facing common challenges, creating a collective memory, and capable, albeit in a modest sense, of taking collective action. In illustrating the child collective, I have not placed examples that pertain to writing in a separate section, because they did not occur in a "separate section" of classroom life—written language was interwoven with the child collective.

This section pushes further inside the collective itself, describing the social themes or intentions that seemed to underlie the children's interactions—their "networking"—within the group. That is, the focus will not be on the children's distinctive relationship to the adult world, but on their relationships with each other as reflected in their talk. That talk reflected a desire to be not only a competent part of the group—a competent kid—but also a special, distinctive part of that group, worthy of esteem.

Managing Resources

As previously noted, the children did not use their own pencils and marking pens, but selected these valued commodities each day from the common stores. One social concern or intention, then, was to manage these tools: "This is my eraser." "I need a blue." "Which is the darkest green?" "Who needs purple?" In addition, the children selected their own space, also a valued commodity: "Don't squish me." "Get your book off mine." "Don't bump me."

As with any valued commodity, materials and space could be used to establish positive or negative links with others. Rueben, for example, frequently offered his markers to other boys, "You wanta use mine? You can use mine." Jesse consistently turned down Rueben's offers as he wanted to use Jake's markers. Jake, on the other hand, had a colored pencil feud with Kenji that lasted the entire semester. Jake and Kenji "ripped each other off" by taking the "whole tin can" of colored pencils when the other was not looking, made "straight deals" about who would get to use the pencils on a particular day, and considered the possibility, if they weren't careful, of "getting busted" for failing to share.

Not only pencils and markers, but the products of those tools were also valued. In School A, *less* official writing was better, while in School 0, *more* was better. The children noted how many pages they had left before their current journal would be completed and how many journals they had already completed ("I'm on my third journal"). Speed and quantity were in fact valued in many activities. For example, Jake, Jesse, and Rueben valued these qualities in baseball, among other areas: a "helluva good baseball player" throws fast and makes many home runs. Sonia valued them in name writing; one day she even brought a watch with a second hand and timed all the kids at her table to see who was fastest. And, while just being a "little kid" could be a rationale for one's lack of ability in a particular area, all of the children participated in conversations in which more "years old" was clearly better. Seven-year-old Jake even bragged to 6-year-old Jesse, "You'll always be behind me."

Displaying and Monitoring Competence

Like most of us, the children expressed clear desires to be competent at the things people their age should be able to do. The appropriate age was sometimes disputed, though, and there were mediating circumstances, like opportunity for practice. Writing, particularly spelling, appeared to be an important "competency," just as was bike riding. To illustrate, compare the following discussions, the first about bicycling, the second about spelling:

Example 7
Jake has just remarked that he has gotten a new bike.

Jake:	I just rode my bike up and down my hill 3 times—2 or 3 times.
Sonia:	(impressed) I can't even ride it once up and down the hill!
Jake:	Why?
Sonia:	Cause (irritated). I don't know how to ride, yet (very softly).
Jake:	You still have training wheels? (politely)
Sonia:	I'm learning how to ride on a two-wheeler.
Regina:	(squeals)

Maggie: I still have training wheels.
Regina: ⌈My training wheels was took off when I was 6.
Jake: ⌊I saw a 7-year-old . . . I saw a 7-year-old with training wheels.
Sonia: I still have training wheels.
Regina: By the time you're 6, the training wheels should be off.
Marcos: I don't get to ride my bike that much. That's why I have to have training wheels.

Example 8
Regina, a first grader, has just heard Wesley, a second grader, ask for the word *candy*, which Regina can in fact spell.

Regina: That is a shame.
Sonia: I don't know how to spell *candy*.
Regina: It's easy.
Sonia: How?
Regina: It's easy.
Jake: C-A-N-D.
Regina: Uh huh.
Sonia: Maybe my mom didn't teach me or I don't need to.

Regina states again that "that's a shame" and claims also to be able to spell *Mississippi*. However, she cannot spell *Mississippi*—and Wesley spells it correctly! Regina just grins and gets back to her story. (Later this same day, Regina does not know that "the kitchen sink" is a kind of ice cream, and Sonia retaliates, "You should know that by the time you're 5 years old.")

As the above conversations indicate, some of the children were more tolerant of shortcomings than others, but all were interested in sharing their own and hearing about others' accomplishments.

Displaying competence: "Look what I'm doing!" As suggested above, the children at times announced their knowledge or skill—"I know" how to spell a particular word, my phone number, my address, a funny story; "I can" draw a jet, throw a fastball. Most of the time, however, the children called attention to their ongoing work. In the beginning of the study, these calls of "Look what I'm doing" generally had to do with how many pages or journals they had completed (as previously discussed) or with their ongoing drawing:

Example 9
Regina has just drawn a picture of a candy house, which she thinks is really quite nice:

Regina: (to Sonia) Sonia, do you like this picture [her previous picture of a dentist's office] or that one [the candy house]?

Sonia: That one [the candy house].
Regina: Me too, because it's gonna be looking real pretty. Better than the first picture.
Sonia: Can I see the first picture in your journal?
Regina: Sure. That was my first picture. . . . This one says: "I went to the dentist. I had to stay in the line for a three minutes because he was not here." I had to stay in there for an, for 3 or 4 minutes, and I thought that I would be there for my whole life.

In Example 9, Regina also spontaneously displayed her story for a peer. This sharing of written texts, rather than drawings, emerged only after the first 2 months of data collection. The children were generally willing, but not always enthusiastic, listeners:

Example 10
Sonia: (to Marcos) Want me to read this to you, Marcos?
Marcos: OK. From the starting? (worried)
Sonia: YES!

In the sharing of their feats, be they drawing or writing or a nonliterary accomplishment, the children were aware of their own progress. For example, Jake noted that "This is the longest story I ever wrote" and, on another day, commented on his new "fresh A"; "This is fresher than my other A." Regina noted, "Shoot I never made an Indian before." Manuel observed, while displaying his journal, "I used to ask for every word [i.e., now I don't ask for every word]."

Monitoring competence: "what are you doing?"   As evident in the above examples, the children were clearly interested in each other's work. Drawing was easier to monitor than writing because it was more clearly displayed (i.e., one did not have to lean over and decipher a code). However, when the children asked for spellings or reread their stories, the spellings and the stories were available and were commented on by others.

Beyond simply expressing curiosity in each other's activities, the children's responses implied both positive and negative evaluations of others' efforts. Imitation is the sincerest form of flattery, as the saying goes, and indeed the children did pick up on each other's behaviors. Those behaviors ranged from producing appealing rhymes and phrases to using particular visual and artistic devices.

For example, Jesse was particularly observant of Manuel and Jake. He attempted, as did several other children, to imitate the visual effects Manuel created with careful shadings and color mixings:

Example 11
Jesse: How do you make that with—Oh yeah. There's that orange. Is this the right color?

   . . .

Manuel: Over here it's a little lighter.
Jesse: Oh, we did like this. Right?
Manuel: No, I think I need something a little darker but not too strong.

   . . .

You need a long pencil to do this.

Jesse picked up not only Jake's "tough talk" ("getting busted" or "ripped off") but also Jake's concern with periods. During writing, Jake consistently asked adults if he "had any sentences yet" or if he needed any periods. Jesse began asking similar questions—even though he had less grasp of the sentence concept. For example, one day Jesse bragged to the group that he only needed "two dots" [periods] in his whole story, as though that were a real accomplishment.

Not all the children's responses to others' efforts were positive. Noting others' errors or need for help often gave children opportunities to display their own skill. This was particularly true for spelling.

In this classroom, the observed children often asked adults, rather than other children, for spellings, perhaps because adults—who are supposed to spell better than children—were available for such requests. However, hearing another child express a need for a spelling consistently gave rise to offers of help from peers. These offers were not always accepted graciously; Jake, for example, did not like to have a first grader offer him help. In the face of such offers, he would attempt the word himself. The children also engaged in spelling duels, in which they would try to trip each other up on spellings. The following excerpt illustrates these behaviors:

Example 12
Regina has just written *Home Sweet Home* in her drawing and is quite pleased with herself:

Regina: Joshua, do you know how to spell *sweet*?
Joshua: S-E--
Chris: Uh uh. S-W.
Regina: S-W-E-T. How do you spell *home*?

Joshua can in fact spell *home*. He does so; then he has a question for Regina:

Joshua: How do you spell *pig*?
Regina: Pig? P-I-G. Pig.

Joshua then asks Regina about *seat*. Regina tries S-E-E.

Joshua No.
Regina: Oh. I don't know.
Joshua: Give up?
Regina: I don't want to know.
Joshua: I want you to know.

Soon Jake and Jesse enter into the spelling duel, which continues off and on throughout the remainder of journal time. Regina tries to draw Maggie in, but she can't quite get into the spirit:

Regina (to Maggie) Do you know how to spell *sweet*?
Maggie: I don't care if I don't.
Regina: Just spell it.
Maggie: OK. S-W-E-T.
Regina: No, S-W-E-E-T.
Maggie: Well, I was close but no cigar.

Spelling duels were engaged in by all the children in a gamelike spirit. Gloating about one's spelling skill, as Regina did earlier, was not acceptable. For example, when Rueben persisted in asking Jesse how to spell words he did not know, Jesse retorted: "Hey, just tell me another word what I can spell!" Jake consistently reprimanded children who gloated (including Jesse, Rueben, and Regina): "You didn't know how to spell *house* in the first place, so you shouldn't be talking."

The children not only critiqued others' mechanics, they also critiqued the content of their pictures or stories. They questioned the logic of others' efforts by referring to the internal consistency of the story; Jesse, for example, asked Jake how the "fastest jet in the world" could get captured by the bad guys? The children also questioned the consistency of objects or characters in the story with the way the world worked; to illustrate, Jake told Regina, "Brownies do not wear pink," as he noted her pink-shirted girl wearing a Brownie cap. In addition, they critiqued the written language itself, its clarity or grammaticality; for example, Maggie asked Jake, who had written about *shooting them*, "Who's the *them*?"; Regina noted that Jake's *There is sharks* needed an *are*.

In this critiquing, the children were often forced to wrestle with the distinction between the real and the story world. They marked their own and others' stories as "real" or "not real." Mitzi even accused Jake of "lying in your story," which suggests a concern with how real "not real" has to be. Manuel came closest to stating the intellectual issue explicitly; during a dispute about whether or not one could make a volcano out of sand he noted, "Well, anyway, it's a pretend story. In real life, it may [not] be true." That is, the criteria for literary truth are different from those for "real-life" truth. The children's operational definitions of these criteria were suggested and opened to criticism as they moved between story and "real-life" worlds.

In critiquing the content of another's drawing or story, the children were not engaging in behavior specific just to the journal activity. They regularly critiqued any peer statement that did not square with their perceptions of the world, including comments about how rain and snow operate, how dogs age, how young mothers can be (during the course of a "My-mother-was-a-teen-age-mother" discussion), how and whether being "a little bit chubby" is essential to the body's functioning, how bad "junk food" is, how probable World War IV is ("Did they already have World War III?"), whether or not everyone was indeed "born in the U.S.A.," and on and on. Their mental wrestling seems captured by Tizard and Hughes's (1984, p. 114) term, "passages of intellectual search." Tizard and Hughes apply this concept to mothers and their preschoolers, but these early school-age children's eagerness to explore verbally—puzzle through—confusions and contradictions certainly merits the term (see Pellegrini and Galda, this volume).

To this point, then, we have looked at the children spontaneously displaying their own competence and monitoring others' displays. In these interactions, the children were not working toward any clearly specified educational objective nor were they playing out the rules of any specific language arts activity. They were simply being kids together in their own classroom. Next, we turn briefly to an interesting and contrasting situation: the weekly spelling quiz.

Gauging competence through grading: "What'd you get?"   Shortly after the beginning of the study, Margaret, the children's teacher, initiated weekly spelling tests. She would give the children 10 words on Monday, telling the second graders to learn all of them and the first graders to study five of them; quizzes were held on Fridays. Margaret graded the quizzes by putting the number right on the top of each paper. She did not mark papers as "passing" or "failing"; she commented directly to individual children, remarking that they had done well or should study harder.

Margaret's low-key approach to this language arts activity contrasts with that of the teacher discussed earlier in School A, whose children could "pass" or "fail" such tasks. Nonetheless, Margaret's children reacted to this task just as the School A children reacted to tasks judged "right" or "wrong" by their teacher. The children did not focus on the spelling words themselves, as they did at least partly in their own spontaneous spelling duels, but attended solely to the evaluation of their performance. And that evaluation was different from the flexible evaluation provided by peers.

For during the spelling duels, a child could always point out to a peer something else he or she knew, dismiss a particular word as unimportant, bide time until an easier word came up, or find a word an overly confident peer couldn't spell—gloating peers would usually receive their due. Performance in the spelling quiz, on the other hand, was inflexible and defined by the teacher's written score. One could not say, "Ask me another word what I can spell" to the teacher, nor could one dismiss the necessity of the chosen words ("Maybe I don't need to [know how to spell it].")

Faced with these fixed scores, the children had to find other ways of ameliorating the evaluations—and the institutionalized gloating inherent in the scores' existence (i.e., the numbers proclaimed some children better than others). For example, in one observed event, Jake first admired and then, egged on by Jesse, put down Sonia for her good performance on a quiz:

Example 13
Margaret passes back the children's spelling papers, as they sit working in their journals. The children immediately begin displaying their own evaluations (their "number right") and monitoring those of others:

Sonia:	I got 9 right. I got 'em all right.
Jake:	She got almost—she got 'em all right. (looks at his own paper) 5 right. (neutral tone)
Jesse:	(laughs at Jake but does not reveal his own score)
Manuel:	7. I only got one wrong.
Sonia:	Uh uh.
Jesse:	(to Jake) Cross that out and put um 8 right.
Jake:	No. (irritated)
Jesse:	Oh yeah, put 1 right. (laughs)
Jake:	No, I'll put— (devious)
Jesse:	Zero right. (laughs)
Jake:	Yeah. (Jake scratches out the number 5 and puts the paper away.)

Later in the morning, when Sonia shows her paper to me, Jake grabs it.

Jake	Give it here. (grabs paper)
Sonia:	No.
Jesse:	Oh, yeah. Give it here.
Sonia:	No ooo. Give it to me, Jesse.

Margaret comes over to the table and retrieves Sonia's paper. Sonia, looking frustrated and close to tears, folds up her paper and stuffs it into her pocket. Jake giggles:

Jake	We got her.
Jesse:	Yeah.

In previous examples, Jake and Sonia displayed their friendship; they were consistently interested in and supportive of each other's efforts. (Recall that Jake did not tease Sonia over her inability to ride a two-wheeler; see Example 7.) Both children defended others whose competence was under attack by peers, as has also been seen in previous examples. Yet, in this example, they are set apart from each other because Sonia performed well on a spelling test. Jake and Jesse resorted to peer group play to "get" the child who had done so well, and Sonia received a vivid demonstration of how performing well in school can isolate one from one's friends. Ironically enough, all of the children valued the ability to spell; in fact, both Jake and Jesse were better spellers than Sonia in the children's spelling duels. It was the evaluation of performance on the spelling test that caused the tension.

It is not my intention here to criticize spelling quizzes in the primary grades. While the children did discuss spellings and engage in spelling duels before Margaret began the quizzes—and in fact did so the previous year when there were no quizzes—certainly their valuing of spelling was related to its value in the adult world, including the world of school. However, the children's response to the spelling quiz suggests the possible consequences of language arts programs which, like that of the traditional classroom in School A, place all of the children's language use under the evaluative authority of the teacher. One sees here a possible preview of a conflict between the way school may work—to single out the achieving individual, and the way the peer group worked—to allow children collaboratively to work out flexible, face-saving, and, at times, playful ways of displaying and acknowledging competence (See Daiute & Dalton, this volume).

Being Special

The children did not only aspire to be competent; they wanted to be special. "Special" here refers to being distinctive in some way, to rising above the crowd. The observed children were aware of the concept of "famous," as noted earlier. Pop singers Michael Jackson and Boy George, for example, were cited as "famous." Being famous did not involve being particularly competent on social conventions, such as spelling or punctuating. Being famous seemed most associated with being recognized for one's ability to create particular, meaningful objects or acts—or even for the creation of one particularly powerful object:

Example 14
Manuel: I want to be famous.
Sonia: Go on Kids Incorporated. A whole bunch of famous kids—
Jesse: Yeah. . . .

Sonia: You have to be a good singer I mean, like Boy George.
Jesse: No, no. Michael Jackson. . . .
Manuel: I want to be in a movie ( ). I also want to be a famous artist or singer.
Sonia: I think you would be better at the artist.
Manuel: Still, I have a good voice. I wouldn't sing rock stuff.
Sonia: Oooooh. (Gross).

Manuel, as it happened, was recognized by the group as especially artistic—they called him an "artist." Jake even drew a picture of Manuel at the paint easel. Jake himself was considered by at least some children to be a potentially "famous inventor by the time you're 10," because of his invention of the bubble car.

While not all of the children aspired to be famous, all on at least one occasion remarked about a peer's particularly "neat" production or commented on their own "neatness." For example, Manuel, having invented a "magic word" in his story, observed: "God, I don't know how I made up those words. Never heard of them before." Maggie, on having written a story about a circus made of yarn, remarked: "I can't believe what I'm writing. This is so funny." And Sonia, on having drawn and written an entry on a sunset, commented: "Isn't this a good picture? I'm gonna put this story in a tape. It's real good."

Of course, one can also be special by defying convention; the children, for example, were very aware of who had been expelled or suspended from school. And one can be special by associating with people perceived as special. Jesse seemed to seek such specialness by associating with Jake (see Examples 3, 5, 13). He even explicitly commented to me, "I have to do the same what Jake does."

"Doing the same what Jake does" points up a dilemma: to what extent can one borrow another's "specialness"? As noted earlier, the children monitored and copied peers' behaviors. But for most children, particularly for the second graders, there was a clear, qualitative distinction between adopting a peer's technique or procedure and copying line-by-line a written story or a drawn picture. Writing conventions, such as letter formations, spellings, and punctuation marks, could be copied, as could particular literary techniques (e.g., ending parts of stories with "to be continued"). The exact and whole structure of a story or a picture, however, was the individual's—part of what made that person special; even a particular story element (i.e., a particular character or action) could achieve almost "patent" status and, thus, could not be copied (See Hudson, this volume). '

Copying was a particular problem for Jesse. He attempted to copy both Jake and Manuel, whose journals he admired and both of whom drew and wrote much better than he did. Jake had no patience with this behavior. Once when Jesse made a bubble car (Jake's "invention"), Jake was so upset that he would not let Jesse sit by him the next day. Manuel was more patient: he would let Jesse copy, but he made it clear that Jesse's story and picture should somehow be different:

Example 15
Jesse has been trying to make his picture just like Manuel's. He seems to think that Manuel should be pleased by this: "Like it, Manuel?" He repeatedly questions Manuel about how to get particular effects. Manuel thinks this copying behavior is all right, but:

Manuel: Just don't make exactly the same picture.
Jesse: Except not with the garbage can. (Jesse had noted earlier that he doesn't make garbage cans.) Same story?
Manuel: No.
Jesse: I'll make a different story.
Manuel: I don't want people to think I copied off you.
Jesse: Yeah, or I copied off you. I—
Manuel: I know because then we'll both get bad reputations.
Jesse: Yeah. And we don't want that. Right?
Manuel: No.

Being with One's Friends

Beyond—and as a part of—managing resources and collaboratively acknowledging competence and specialness, the children simply enjoyed being with each other, sharing past experiences and playfully creating together new ones. In many of the previous examples, the children shared their common experiences in the "real" world. In the following examples, the children play in imaginary worlds. That is, to use Garvey's (1977) definition of play, the children are shown participating in spontaneous, nonliteral, pleasurable, and engaging activity that is its own reward. The children's play could involve writing tools, as when pencils become swords, or, more often in this context, simply language itself, as in the following age/grade play:

Example 16
Max: How much old are you?
Jesse: Six.
Max: Me too. So we're sixth grade.
Jake: I'm seventh grade.
Jesse: I'm 100th grade.
Jake: You're not even 100.

Sometimes the children engaged in dramatic narrative play, in which elaborate stories would be collaboratively spun. Oral stories sometimes evolved as an accompaniment to and support for a child's drawing and writing. However, in these instances, the desire for a unique—special—content was clear: The author had the final say in whether or not an idea was incorporated into the narrative. (See Pellegrini & Galda, this volume, for an analysis of the conditions under which one child's narrative line is taken up by a play partner.)

Jake's narrative play is particularly interesting, as he consistently engaged in a great deal of such play during journal time and because the nature of his play changed over the 2 years of observation. During the previous year in the first grade, Jake's narrative stories had evolved during drawing as he interacted playfully with his friends. He consistently drew and talked about the actions of powerful vehicles, especially jets, and adventurous men. His peers' amused laughter and comments led to more elaborate plots:

Example 17
Jake: I'm gonna make a mechanical man.
Manuel: A mechanical man? You mean a robot man?
Jake: Yeah. I'm gonna make a robot man. You got it, Manuel. . . .
           Here's a bomb head. (The "mechanical/robot" man's head has two
           lines extending from it.) It's gonna explode. It hasn't even exploded
           yet. When it does—
Manuel: I hope it explodes in the next century.
Johnny: It's not going to be for real.
Manuel: Well, in the future it is.
Jake: Yeah, in the future it is.

           . . .
           Here comes the bomb explosion! There is the fire, a little smoke.
           (Jake is making quick back and forth motions with his marker.)
           . . .
           I'm gonna make a flying earthling.

Although Jake told dynamic narratives while drawing, his actual written stories simply described his pictures. For the above journal entry, in which Jake had drawn and talked about a robot man and a flying earthling, Jake wrote: "Once upon a time there were two men. One was flying up in to the clouds. The other man was staying on the ground. The and"

During his second-grade year, Jake's lively narrative play began to accompany his writing as well as his drawing, and only then did it begin to appear as well in his written text. For example, in the following event from the second grade, Jake was writing about Manuel:

Example 18
Manuel notices his name in Jake's journal:

Manuel: What are you writing about?
Jake: You.
Manuel: What do you know about me?
Jake: I'm not gonna talk about you. I'm just gonna make sure you get blown to pieces.
Manuel: Blown to pieces?

Soon Jake was ready for the fateful event:

Jake: Watch out, Manuel (writes *blow up*).

Later, Jake relents and has Manuel survive:

Jake: I think I'm gonna write—I already wrote about you and you're OK.
Manuel: Thanks for that.
Jake: Here I'll tell it to you from the beginning.
Jake's story read as follows:

Once there was a boy that is named Manuel. Manuel is going to fly the fastest jet and I am going to fly the jet too. But Manuel's headquarters is going to blow up But I am OK. But I don't know about Manuel but I am going to find Manuel. But when I find him I like him. But I think I see him. He is in the jet. Manuel are you OK? Yes I am OK. you are being attacked. I will shoot the bad guys out of the universe. OK yes shoot them now. The end.

Jake's texts, as in the above excerpt, broke free of the static time frame of a picture and now contained the dynamic movement of a movie screen. (For a discussion of time/space distinctions in children's pictures and texts, see Dyson, 1986.)

As did their critiques of product content, dramatic narrative play confronted the children with the distinction between the real and the pretend—but in play surrounding journal production the distinction became more complicated. There was the enacted real world, the imaginative world of living, three-dimensional players, the imaginary world of two-dimensional graphics, and the world created through linear strings of words:

Example 19
In a later journal story event, Jake has Manuel meet Buck Rogers. Jake tells Manuel to be careful because if he doesn't do what Buck Rogers says, he will get blown to pieces when Manuel and Buck take on the bad guys. Then Marcos (Manuel's brother) "wouldn't see your brother again, Marcos. You would never see him in a story again."

Manuel: Oh God. Oh, well. It's been fun having adventures with you. Um, but I'm gonna get blown to pieces.
        . . .
Jake: You might get your butt saved by Buck Rogers. You want your butt saved by Buck Rogers?

Manuel: What I want is my body saved. I don't wanna die. I don't wanna—. . .

Jake: You want your whole body saved by Buck Rogers?

In Jake's story, Buck does teach Manuel how to take on the bad guys—his existence in the text world is secure. In a similar event, Maggie announced that she was going to erase her "running princess," a drawn figure that turned out rather poorly. Sonia objected: "Sonia means princess. . . . I am a princess who runs. Maggie! You're going to kill me." And, alas, the two-dimensional player died—but the three-dimensional one just laughed.

THE CHILDREN'S ACTIVITIES AS UNINTENTIONAL HELPING

In this chapter, I have argued for recognition and appreciation of young children's social concerns in school. While they admire and aspire to the adult world, children also resist the adult world in an effort to define themselves as "children" (Corsaro, 1985, who builds on the ideas of Goffman, 1961). Moreover, within the child collective, early school-age children both bind themselves together as a group and also seek to define themselves as competent but unique individuals.

In the previous section, we have seen the social networking of a group of young children—their displays and admiration of competence, their critiques of themselves and others, their desire to both rise above and enjoy each other's company. We have also seen that written language was a part of the knowledge and skill valued by the children and, in addition, that it was a social tool that helped them to connect with, and distinguish themselves among, their peers.

While these children were in a nontraditional classroom, they and their age mates on the other side of the country, in School A, were similar in that they valued and made use of literacy in their own social worlds. The observed social networking about and through written language seems an invaluable support for literacy development. From a broad developmental perspective, becoming competent in the written language symbol system involves distinguishing the unique symbolic nature of written language from other symbol systems (Dyson, 1986). This differentiation includes understanding the relationship between speech and print (i.e., encoding or spelling), between lived experience and experience transformed into and through print, between the perspective of the writer and that of the potential readers. And it was just this sort of poking and pulling at written language and at each other that the children engaged in (See Fontaine, this volume; Rafoth, this volume).

With their "How do you spell?'s" the children pushed words at each other—and, of course, they helped each other spell those words. But in their quest for specialness, they exhibited what some adults never do—a discrimination between what is social convention and what is individual creation in writing. Those individual creations, though, were clearly supported by the group. Narrative play helped some children, like Jake, formulate tales and begin to figure out how one achieved dynamic movement in static words. Critiques—their "Who's them?'s"—caused reflection about the distinction between writer and reader, "creator" and "re-creator." The children's continual movement between pretend and "real" worlds forced them to confront the essence of good literature—"lies" that ring true. And their "Look at me's" and "Look at you's" highlighted particular literary techniques and procedures that made written text appealing to a reader.

Indeed, the children were providing for themselves much more sophisticated lessons than adults could ever hope to. In Britton's words:

> In taking part in rule-governed behavior—and that might be a wine-and-cheese party, a debate, a game of volley-ball [or story writing]—the novice, the individual learner, picks up the rules by responding to the behavior of others, a process precisely parallel to the mode by which the rules first came into existence. (1985, p. 74)

Observations of the children illustrated too, as did the observations of School A children, that the potentially positive relationship between the children's social world and the academic world is a fragile one. If children are not allowed to communicate with each other in school, then their networking may go underground. That underground social world may still involve literacy—in fact, it may involve a wide variety of types of literacy—but the degree to which children can collaboratively probe the nature of written language will be limited by the clandestine nature of that world. Moreover, when writing becomes subject to the rigid and hierarchical evaluation of the institution of schooling, written language in the official school world may no longer be a tool to bind children together, but a divisive force in the children's social lives.

IN CONCLUSION, SOME DISCLAIMERS

I am suggesting here the potentially positive power of the children's social world to support written language growth. However, I wish to stress here what I am not suggesting.

First, I am not suggesting that children need to be turned "loose" or that an organized and organizing teacher—a structuring of the language arts curriculum—is unnecessary. Obviously there was a very definite structure in the observed classroom in School 0 and that structure was heavily dependent on the children's teacher, Margaret. The children were concerned about the journal task at least partly because Margaret expected them to accomplish something in that journal. Her admonitions to stay on task, her queries about their progress, her "celebrations" of their efforts, all provided the academic structure that the children were reacting to in forming their own social world (Corsaro, 1985). If there is no structure, the children have nothing to gather together within—and, as any experienced teacher knows, chaos often results.

Second, I am not suggesting that children's work should not be evaluated. The children evaluated themselves and each other continually. Moreover, Margaret evaluated their journal writing regularly, and that evaluation caused no difficulty. She pointed out to individuals what she thought they were doing well—and she had them erase and do over things she thought were not up to an individual's standard. However, no one else was being praised when that individual was being critiqued. The evaluation was private. In addition, Margaret and the whole group celebrated individual children's completed journals. And the children clapped for and spontaneously praised that work while it was shared. But no one was being put down when one child was being celebrated. The problem came with the inflexible evaluation entailed by the written mark, as in the official spelling quizzes. Unlike Margaret's proofreading notes, that mark could not be erased and the error fixed. Further, the written mark was institutionalized gloating—putting one child up and others down. And gloating was not tolerated in the children's world. I question, then, whether publicly comparative evaluation, particularly evaluation capsuled in fixed scores, has a place in the early school years, when children are in the process of defining themselves as peers and as scholars.

Finally, I am also not suggesting that the children's social world causes no problems. Clearly it does. Jesse was a good example. He was so caught up with being like someone else in the first grade that his style of creating, which had been so dynamic in kindergarten (see Dyson, 1986), was lost. There will undoubtedly be children who will need support from the teacher and, perhaps, some manipulation of the social group—of the peer groups with whom individual children write, for example—in order to find a comfortable and productive writing situation.

However, this problem of finding self and group—the "I," the "you," and the "we"—is a problem worth dealing with. It is the problem we all face as people and, of course, as writers. When we move beyond utilitarian writing such as the grocery lists, the paperwork, writing has to do with wanting to appear competent—knowledgeable about the social conventions of writing—and yet also wanting to say something special, something unique, that will be judged valuable by others. There is no reason to assume that writing is any different for school children. To pull writing out of the network of peers is to deny children the opportunity to experience the tension between individual expression and social communication that is the living tension of language use.

Appendix: *Transcript Conventions*

The following conventions are used in the presentations of transcripts:

( ):   notes, usually about nonverbal information; when inserted into speaker's transcribed utterance, refers to inaudible speech for which a tentative transcription may be offered, e.g.,
(Gross)   [Child may have said, "Gross."]

[:   overlapping speech turns, e.g.,

Regina: ⌈My training wheels was took off when I was 6.
Jake: ⌊I saw a 7-year-old—

—:   interrupted speech

ME: word emphasized through vowel elongation and raising of pitch and volume

N-O: letters spelled by the speaker

. . .:   generally, speaker pause between words; when inserted in the middle of a blank line, refers to omitted data

REFERENCES

Britton, J. (1985). Research currents: Second thoughts on learning. *Language Arts, 62,* 72–77.

Cazden, C. (1986). Classroom discourse. In M. C. Wittrock (Ed.), *Handbook of research on teaching* (3d ed.). New York: Macmillan.

Clay, M. (1975). *What did I write?* Auckland, New Zealand: Heinemann.

Cooper, C. R., Marquis, A., & Ayers–Lopez, S. (1982). Peer learning in the classroom: Tracing developmental patterns and consequences of children's spontaneous interactions. In L. C. Wilkinson (Ed.), *Communicating in the classroom*. New York: Academic Press.

Corsaro, W. (1985). *Friendship and peer culture in the early years*. Norwood, NJ: Ablex.

Dewey, J. (1916). *Democracy and education*. New York: Macmillan.

Dyson, A. H. (1981). Oral language: The rooting system for learning to write. *Language Arts, 58*, 776–784.

Dyson, A. H. (1984). Research currents: Who controls classroom writing contexts? *Language Arts, 61*, 618–626.

Dyson, A. H. (1985a). Second graders sharing writing: The multiple social realities of a literacy event. *Written Communication, 2*, 189–215.

Dyson, A. H. (1985b). Research currents: Writing and the social lives of children. *Language Arts, 62*, 632–639.

Dyson, A. H. (1986). Transitions and tensions: Interrelationships between the drawing, talking, and dictating of young children. *Research in the Teaching of English, 20*, 379–409.

Ferreiro, E., & Teberosky, A. (1982). *Literacy before schooling*. Exeter, NH: Heinemann.

Flavell, J. H. (1985). *Cognitive development* (2d ed.). Englewood Cliffs, NJ: Prentice-Hall.

Gardner, H. (1982). *Developmental psychology* (2d ed.). Boston: Little, Brown.

Garvey, C. (1977). *Play*. Cambridge, MA: Harvard University Press.

Garvey, C. (1984). *Children's talk*. Cambridge, MA: Harvard University Press.

Gilbert, S. H., & Gay, G. (1985). Improving the success in school of poor black children. *Phi Delta Kappan, 67*, 133–137.

Gillmore, P. (1983). Spelling "Mississippi": Recontextualizing a literacy-related speech event. *Anthropology and Education Quarterly, 14*, 235–256.

Goffman, E. (1961). *Asylums*. Garden City, NY: Anchor.

Goodlad, J. I. (1983). *A place called school*. New York: McGraw–Hill.

Gundlach, R., McLane, J. B., Stott, F. M., & McNamee, G. D. (1985). The social foundations of children's early writing development. In M. Farr (Ed.), *Advances in writing research: Vol. 1. Children's early writing develoment*. Norwood, NJ: Ablex.

Heath, S. B. (1983). *Ways with words: Language, life, and work in communities and classrooms*. Cambridge, England: Cambridge University Press.

Korzenik, D. (1977). Saying it with pictures. In D. Perkins & B. Leondar (Eds.), *The arts and cognition*. Baltimore: Johns Hopkins University Press.

Labov, W. (1982). Competing value systems in inner-city schools. In P. Gilmore & A. A. Glatthorn (Eds.), *Children in and out of school*. Washington, DC: Center for Applied Linguistics.

Nelson, K. (1985). *Making sense: The acquisition of shared meaning*. Orlando, FL: Academic Press.

Ogbu, J. (1985). Research currents: Cultural-ecological influences on minority school learning. *Language Arts, 62*, 860–869.

Philips, S. U. (1972). Participant structure and communicative competence: Warm Springs children in community and classroom. In C. Cazden, D.

Hymes, & V. John (Eds.), *Functions of language in the classroom*. New York: Teachers College Press.

Piaget, J., & Inhelder, B. (1969). *The psychology of the child*. New York: Basic Books.

Rubin, Z. (1980). *Children's friendships*. Cambridge, MA: Harvard University Press.

Schickedanz, J. A., & Sullivan, M. (1984). "Mom, what does U-F-F spell?" *Language Arts, 61*, 7–17.

Steinberg, Z., & Cazden, C. (1979). Children as teachers—Of peers and ourselves. *Theory into Practice, 18*, 258–266.

Tizard, B., & Hughes, M. (1984). *Young children learning*. Cambridge, MA: Harvard University Press.

Tharp, R., Jordan, C., Speidel, G. E., Au, K., Klein, T., Calkins, R., Sloat, K., & Gallimore, R. (1984). Product and process in applied developmental research: Education and the children of a minority. In M. E. Lamb, A. L. Brown, & B. Rogoff (Eds.), *Advances in developmental psychology*. Hillsdale, NJ: Erlbaum.

Vygotsky, L. S. (1962). *Thought and language*. Cambridge, MA: Harvard University Press.

Vygotsky, L. S. (1978). *Mind in society*. Cambridge, MA: Harvard University Press.

Chapter 11

"Let's Brighten It Up a Bit": Collaboration and Cognition in Writing

Colette Daiute and Bridget Dalton
Harvard University

While collaborating on a story-writing task, 9-year-old Bruce said to his partner, John, "Let's brighten it up a bit." John immediately suggested a change that Bruce thought was just right. Even though the comment "Let's brighten it up a bit" did not indicate precisely what Bruce thought was wrong with the story or how it should be improved, John understood what he meant. This chapter explores how such subtle but powerful exchanges between children can help them learn about writing. The chapter presents results from a study on collaborative writing and discusses the role of subtle negotiating and language play in the development of writing abilities. The results of this study suggest that subtle and playful language activities are as important as explicit planning and revising strategies.

BACKGROUND

According to Vygotsky (1978), social interaction is essential for cognitive development. Development first occurs socially as an interpersonal experience and then psychologically as an intrapersonal experience. Vygotsky's idea that cognitive development involves the internalization

* Author Note: An earlier version of this chapter was presented at the American Educational Research Association Convention, April 17, 1986, in San Francisco. The research was sponsored in part by the Spencer Foundation. The authors also thank Sheri Offerman and Joan Gerster for their participation running the study and coding many hours of transcripts. In addition, Carolee Matsumoto, John Benjamin, Lorita Brockington, David Crump, John Kruidenier, Jodie Yelon, Chris Unger, and Larry Poneman offered critical assistance at various stages of the research. We are also indebted to Shirley Brice Heath and David Perkins for insightful comments on the research and an earlier draft of this paper.

of social interactions differs from Piaget's claim that children must achieve a certain level of cognitive development before they can interact in truly collaborative ways (Piaget, 1959). The importance of the social foundations of thought in Vygotsky's theory is evident in his notion "zone of proximal development." According to Vygotsky, a child's cognitive development should be described in terms of the difference between his or her actual and potential performance, which is revealed through interaction with an adult or more able peer. The conversations that occur during social interaction establish concrete markers in mind that serve as the foundation for abstract thought. Although Vygotsky offered appealing theory, many details of the nature of social-cognitive interaction and the relationship of social interaction to cognition and performance have yet to be defined (Wertsch, 1985).

Research on collaborative learning appears to support Vygotsky's general claims. Studies comparing pre- and post-collaboration gains have offered considerable evidence that collaborative learning activities lead to individual subject mastery (Daiute, 1986a; Johnson, Johnson, Holubec, & Roy, 1984; Slavin, 1983). In addition, researchers have recently begun to understand how children collaborate and why collaboration leads to learning (Forman & Cazden, 1985; Mugny & Doise, 1978; Mugny, Perret–Clermont, & Doise, 1981; Perret–Clermont, 1980; Petitto, 1986).

Researchers who have studied problem-solving and academic activities in school-aged children do not find the sophistication of social skills that are expected. Forman and Cazden studied fourth- and fifth-grade children solving problems based on their analysis of physical data in chemical experiments: "What do you think makes a difference in whether it turns purple or not?" (Forman & Cazden, 1985, p. 332). They found that at first children interacted in "parallel"; they worked on problems side by side but not interactively. Some children referred to each other's efforts in an "associative" manner, and only over time did children engage in "cooperative" problem solving by dividing, coordinating, and relating their efforts. Similarly, Petitto (1986) found that second graders playing a number line estimation game in collaborative, versus turn-taking, conditions engaged in simple arguments, but they were unable to resolve conflicts through justification or explanation. These studies indicate that children's collaboration on difficult tasks is not as elaborated or reflective of "higher level" cognitive processes as Vygotsky's theory suggests. On the other hand, researchers who study salient everyday events, such as trading snacks (Mishler, 1979) and playground power struggles (Brenneis & Lein, 1977) report that children as young as 6 master complex skills of social interaction such as negotiation (see Dyson, this volume; Pellegrini & Galda, this volume). Such mixed results on the explicitness and value of collaboration by children indicate that specific issues about the role of collaboration in cognitive development are yet to be resolved.

Even though process studies of collaboration reveal different specific patterns, the results are consistent with the idea that social interaction supports cognitive development because interaction leads to cognitive conflict. Cognitive conflict is the realization that one's perceptions, thoughts, or creations are inconsistent with new information or another person's point of view. Cognitive conflict may arise from a sense that "something is not right," or from a full-blown argument with another person (Genishi & Di Paolo, 1982). Piaget (1959) found that the ability to consider and to reconcile other points of view with one's own—to decenter—is a key factor in cognitive development. It has been also suggested that explicit cognitive conflicts may provide guidelines for guiding and regulating one's own thought (Brown & DeLoach, 1978; Brown, Bransford, Ferrara, & Campione, 1983; Flavell, 1976; Flavell & Wellman, 1977).

Talking about intellectual tasks may aid cognitive development because each member of a team offers different ways of defining and solving problems (Johnson & Johnson, 1979; Mugny & Doise, 1978). Each child attempts to reconcile his or her approach to an alternative offered during collaboration and via this reconciliation process achieves new understanding (see Pellegrini & Galda, this volume). The consistent success of heterogeneous collaborative groups over collaborative groups including students similar in ability, race, or ethnicity (Johnson & Johnson, 1979; Slavin, 1983) underscores the value of considering different points of view for learning. The details of the nature and value of cognitive conflict still have to be determined, but there appears to be a consensus that becoming sensitive to conflicts in thought and eventually learning to reconcile them are important steps in cognitive development. Moreover, it has been suggested that explicit verbal conflicts that occur when children collaborate may serve as models for the more difficult inner dialogue (Daiute, 1986a; Wertsch, 1985).

Since writing—in contrast to speech—involves making sure that one's ideas are expressed clearly without the aid of listeners, it requires being able to take alternate points of view. In fact, the single factor that related to college freshmen's abilities to write persuasive essays was the ability to recognize or reconcile divergent traits in others (Rubin & Rafoth, 1986). Collaborative writing experiences offer writers the chance to act as writer and reader out loud with the aid of a partner. When children compose texts together, they are likely to have some different ideas and occasionally to express them. The expression of divergent plans or the failure to understand another's plan offers children the opportunity to confront other points of view. In such settings, cognitive conflict may simply be a matter of expressing differences, or the conflict may be more elaborated if the children negotiate and reason over differences together to resolve them. Such explicit cognitive conflict may lead children to engage in more of the self-regulative planning and revising activities that expert writers use (Flower & Hayes, 1981).

Since children tend to engage in a one-step composing process, considerable research has been done to guide them in planning and revising activities (Bereiter & Scardamalia, 1982; Calkins, 1983, 1986; Daiute, 1985; Daiute & Kruidenier, 1985). Children improve certain aspects of their writing when researchers have suggested that they use explicit planning and revising strategies (Bereiter & Scardamalia, 1982; Daiute & Kruidenier, 1985), but evidence has also suggested that training on using such strategies may interfere with children's composing processes (Woodruff, Bereiter, & Scardamalia, 1981–1982). Collaborative writing could be a better method for learning the value and the strategies for planning and revising than teacher or researcher prompts if peers intuitively develop goals and techniques appropriate to their own developmental level. Peer collaboration may also release important playful energies (Bruner, 1985), which have not been discussed much in writing research (but see Dyson, this volume).

One study of collaborative writing provides a link between the research on collaboration and the research on writing development. As discussed elsewhere (Daiute, 1986b), children who collaborated on four story-writing tasks and children who did not collaborate made different types of gains on individual writing samples. Collaborators became more fluent and used more story elements, such as dialogue. On the other hand, children who did not collaborate increased their editing more than did the children who collaborated. As with other pre- and post-test study designs, a careful analysis of the children's activities during the intervention process is required for understanding these results. This chapter explores the nature of the children's interactions as they coauthored stories. We focus on the nature and function of cognitive conflict during collaboration. Analyses of the children's talk and writing during collaboration reveal differences in the interaction patterns of writers who benefited from collaboration and those who did not. This chapter discusses the young coauthors' talk in detail and suggests that collaboration is successful when it engages children in playful as well as evaluative language experiences.

Goals of the Study

The goal of this study was to identify relationships between collaboration and individual development in writing. The talk of fourth- and fifth-grade coauthors was analyzed to find out whether collaboration involves cognitive conflict, such as negotiation, and if so, whether this cognitive conflict leads to increases in explicit planning and analysis activities in collaborative and individual writing tasks. This study addressed three questions: (1) What is the nature of children's talk during collaboration? (2) Does collaboration lead children to engage in explicit planning and revising activities? and (3) What role do specific types of talk have in individual learning?

Methods

This study was built around school-based writing activities in fourth- and fifth-grade classrooms in two suburban Boston public schools. The experimental intervention involved randomly assigning children to different orders of activities so that groups of collaborators could be compared with each other and to groups who did not collaborate.

Two groups of 43 fourth and fifth graders wrote six stories about animals over a 5-week period. One group of students wrote six stories on their own at about 4- to 5-day intervals across the 5 weeks. The other group of students wrote the first and sixth stories individually and coauthored the second through the fifth stories. Assignment to group and the order of story topics was random, but students chose their own partners for collaboration. Students in the control group were told that they would collaborate during the next month, which they did.

Academic expression and thinking skills are stressed in this school system. The teachers had attended "writing process" workshops (Graves, 1983; Calkins, 1983,1986), so they encouraged peer conferencing and revising. The teachers also encouraged collaboration, particularly for computer-programming activities. The students used computers for much of their writing. Students had used the Quill Writer's Assistant on the Apple IIe microcomputer and other Quill programs for some of their writing every week for 7 months; some of the fifth graders had used Quill for over a year. The teachers and researchers together designed the writing tasks and activities so that the experiment would fit within a typical class day.

There were three computers, two printers, word-processing software, and three tape recorders in each classroom for this study. Children worked at the computers throughout the day as they had all year. Just before beginning to write, collaborators turned on a tape recorder at the desk, and after writing, made several printouts of their texts. At the end of the day, the researcher collected a copy of each writing sample, printed out and retained a computer keystroke record of each composing session, and collected audiotapes of the collaborative sessions.

The story-writing task involved information students had been studying in science and was developed in collaboration with the two teachers. The tasks were designed to be appropriate for individual as well as collaborative writing. Pilot testing indicated that providing a set of related facts about animals in their habitats served as a good basis for collaboration. In this creative science-writing task, all children began from a common, objective reference point for their collaboration.

Facts about six animals were presented in "minibooks" prepared for the experiment. Each minibook included four pictures and sentences about the animal's description, habitat, and conflicts, such as predator/prey relationships. The animal protagonists were the frog, owl, beaver, otter, llama, and crocodile. Sentences in the minibooks were controlled for content and readability. Factual content was controlled to include one sentence and picture about the important aspects of the animal's description; one sentence and picture about the animal's habitat; one sentence and picture about the animal as prey; and one sentence and picture about the animal as predator. The pictures had approximately the same number of major visual elements, and each four-sentence text was controlled for sentence structure (all simple declaratives or compound sentences deviating no more than two words with respect to the ratio of function words to content words). The Dale/Chall (1948) and Fry (1968) readability formulas were used to determine and control readability at the third-grade level.

Students were asked to write a series of six stories showing that animals' lives, like people's, can be difficult. For each task, the researcher asked the students to write a story about the animal using some of the facts, but also using their imaginations to create an interesting story. The researcher read the facts to the students, while pointing to the picture and accompanying sentence. The booklets were available to the students as they wrote. The students had as much time to write as they wanted, although after 45 minutes the researcher suggested that they begin to think about completing the task. When the students said they were finished, the researcher asked them to "Pretend you are someone else, and read over your story. Make sure that the story is clear and complete, and make any necessary changes."

ANALYSES OF CHILDREN'S TALK DURING COLLABORATION

The study yielded 48 collaborative composing sessions. Audiotapes for two of the four collaborative sessions by 12 pairs of students were transcribed. This chapter focuses on detailed analyses of 16 transcripts by two groups of 8 pairs of children: the students in 4 pairs received the same or higher holistic writing scores on individual samples after collaborating, and the students in the other 4 pairs received lower holistic writing scores after collaborating.

Since the goal of this analysis was to describe the complete range of talk, the taxonomy was developed from the data; no categories were established ahead of time. The principal investigator and two research assistants participated in the tape transcription process and thus became familiar with what the children were saying. These three researchers then read over all the transcripts and met several times to talk about "the kinds of things the kids talked about." Although patterns of dominance appeared to vary among the pairs, we decided to separate the content analysis from what we called the "tone" analysis. This study focuses on the content analysis because it directly addresses the relevant questions.

A preliminary list of content codes was merged from lists kept by each researcher during second readings of the transcripts. One guideline for identifying categories was that coding should require no inferences or assumptions about the speakers' intent. The list of codes was refined by doing reliability checks of codings of several transcripts over several weeks. The list of categories was set when the three researchers reached 85% agreement on two transcript codings. Categories were grouped according to cognitive processes, such as monitoring, when this was possible. The basic coding procedure was to read a transcript several times and to code each speaker's turn. Thus, one utterance such as "Sleepy goes cold turkey or something like that. Let's say he turns over a new leaf," might be assigned two codes. The first sentence is an example of gisting, and the second involves suggesting an alternative. A single sentence could also be assigned two codes.

Two categories that appeared in preliminary analyses were eliminated: off-task talk and unclear utterances. Preliminary codings of four transcripts indicated that about 13% of all codings were about subjects unrelated to the task, such as "What do you think about Doug Flutie?" Such off-task talk was striking because it was typically done by students who the researchers felt were "good collaborators," and because children showed a remarkable ability to maintain a train of thought about the story around such interjections. Even though the off-task talk appeared to be interesting, subsequent analyses were limited to task-related talk. Off-task talk will be addressed at a later time with analyses of the collaboration tone. Uncodable utterances, which were sometimes as much as 20% of a tape, are also not considered in this analysis. The young coauthors' talk was also examined in relation to other data from the study, including text analyses (holistic quality ratings and text fluency measures) and keystroke records of changes made during composing, and interviews.

Results

The results of this study include a taxonomy of categories that accounts for the children's talk during collaboration, frequencies of each type of talk across collaborators, contrasts between frequencies of talk categories by two groups of collaborators, and analyses of two types of talk that reveal the occurrence of cognitive conflict: negotiating and suggesting alternatives.

THE NATURE OF CHILDREN'S TALK DURING COLLABORATIVE WRITING

Like children in many other studies on composing processes (Hillocks, 1986), the young collaborators in this study did not engage in much explicit planning or revising. Rather, as shown on Table 1, the major activities that emerged from transcripts of collaboration sessions were composing, monitoring/clarifying, evaluating and explaining, discussing procedures, and several conversation directives, such as confirming and disconfirming. Table 1 shows the types of collaborative talk, examples of each type, and the mean percentage of occurrence for each type of talk in the 16 transcripts studied in detail.

Most of the children's talk was oral composing (37.2%). There were seven forms of oral composing, but the most typical (15.0%) was literal suggesting of text content, such as saying "Sleepy was a llama." In some cases, a student orally composed while typing; sometimes, a student dictated to his or her partner, and sometimes, the sequence was a suggestion. The next most frequent (8.4%) category of oral composing was the posing of alternatives. For example, one student would say "Sleepy has soft black fur," followed by "brown fur," then the other student would say "black fur." Alternatives were posed without discussion of their merit. The negotiation category described below covered discussions about alternatives. Another form of oral composing was exact repetition of a story segment (5.0%), such as "Sleepy is a llama; Sleepy is a llama." The types of oral composing that most suggest planning are the gisting category (4.2%), including segments that are marked as suggestions such as "Sleepy goes cold turkey or something like that," and the less frequent (1.0%) category involving requests for text content: "Then what would we write about?" Students' oral composing also included literal spelling or punctuation (2.6%), such as "t-h-e-r-e period," slight rephrasings (1.2%), such as "Davey the Crocodile" following "Davey Crocodile."

After oral composing, the next most frequent general talk category

Table 1.   Categories, Examples, and Mean* Percentages of Occurrence
of Talk by Young Coauthors

Categories of Talk and Examples	Mean Percentage
1. Composing	37.2
1.1 Literal suggesting of text sequences "Sleepy is a llama."	15.0
1.2 Gisting "Sleepy goes cold turkey or something like that."	4.2
1.3 Suggesting alternatives "Black, brown, black"	8.4
1.4 Literal spelling "T-h-e-r-e."	2.6
1.5 Rephrasing slightly "Davey Crocodile" to "Davey the Crocodile."	1.2
1.6 Requesting text content "Then what should we write?"	1.0
1.7 Repeating exactly "Sleepy is a llama. Sleepy is a llama."	5.0
2. Monitoring and Clarifying Form "Put in a comma now." (2.4)	5.8
2.1 Sentence structure	.4
2.2 Vocabulary	0
2.3 Punctuation	.5
2.4 Capitalization	1.4
2.5 Spelling	.7
2.6 Paragraphing	2.0
2.7 Other (format)	.2
2.8 Oops "Whoops, I messed up."	.6
3. Monitoring/Clarifying Content	3.0
4. Rereading	1.6
5. Evaluating, Explaining, Negotiating	8.2
5.1 Expressing rhetorical value "Let's brighten it up a bit."	1.0

5.2 Explaining
     ("Why'd you put in the quotes?")
     "He's still talking."
	.7

5.3 Evaluating "That's wrong."	2.7

5.4 Checking facts
     "What do llamas eat?"
     "When was the Empire State Building built?"
	1.4

5.5 Negotiating
     1: "Well, just say that Laurie Llama has"
     2: "or Laurie had soft"
       "had"
     1: "She has it"
     2: "She's not alive"
     1: "OK"
	2.0

Table 1.   (*Continued*

Categories of Talk and Examples	Mean Percentage
5.6 Stating rules	1.0
"Begin a sentence with a capital."	
6. Talking about procedures	16.2
6.1 Writing processes	5.4
"Let's end now?"	
6.2 Typing and Word Processing	5.6
"Press shift"	
"Do control—C"	
6.3 Division of labor	3.5
"You type."	
"Can I type?"	
6.4 Other	1.9
7. Confirming and Disconfirming:	13.5
"Yes," "OK," "No"	
8. Associating beyond the text:	2.5
Students are writing about two animals who are television news reporters. Then one says to the other "Now to you, Jane"	
9. Making intra/interpersonal comments	10.9
9.1 Judging	3.9
"You're a good speller."	
9.2 Affect	5.2
giggles	
"I don't care"	
9.3 Naming	
Children call each other by name	1.6
10. Off-task talk**	
"What do you think about Doug Flutie?"	
"What are you doing this summer?"	

*Means computed from analyses of talk by eight pairs of coauthors on 16 writing tasks.
**Not computed for this analysis.

(16.2%) was mentioning procedures, including writing processes (5.4%) like "Let's end now," typing/word processing (5.6%) like "Press the shift key," and division of labor (3.5%) like "You type now," and miscellaneous procedures (1.9%) coded under "other."

Talk that is characteristic of social exchanges made up the next two most frequent general categories: confirming and disconfirming (13.5%), mostly instances of "yes" and "no," that were usually associated with another category as well; intra- and interpersonal comments (10.9%), such as "You're a good speller," and "You're terrible."

The next most frequent type of talk was categorized under the general evaluation category (8.2%), including several interesting although infrequently occurring types of talk: evaluating text (2.7%), "That's not good;" negotiating (2.0%; examples in Table 4); checking facts (1.4%),

"What do llamas eat?"; rhetorical value (1.0%; concept from Freedman and colleagues (Freedman, Greenleaf, Sperling, & Parker, 1985); explaining and stating rules (1.0%). The monitoring and clarifying category most frequently (7.0%) involved aspects of text form and less frequently of content (3%). Students tended to note problems with spelling and punctuation over other issues of form, or they simply said "wait" or "uh oh" to note an unidentified problem, noted as "oops" in the taxonomy.

The children's story composing tended to move forward quickly with relatively little looking back, and the talk did not fit neatly into categories of "planning" and "revising." It is not surprising that children spent the majority of time composing orally, but the form of this oral composing is interesting. The text that children typed was often what they were saying at the time, the pair typically functioning as one writer composing "on-line." The children did little checking with each other to find out if the next step was okay with the other person. The assumption seemed to be that composing was like a dance in which the students followed each other by signals in the rhythms of talk rather than by explicit cues. Disagreements were most typically marked by suggestions of alternatives and sometimes by attempts to negotiate. Alternatives were often posed playfully. For example, when one child composed the name of a character, the other would pose an alternative that plays with the sound or meaning in the name. Considering the large amount of playful character naming, plot developing, and dialogue forming that children did without reviewing what they had done, the stories were quite coherent.

The children devoted less verbal energy to checking mechanics than to evaluating and negotiating about the story. When children did discuss mechanics, however, they most often talked about spelling and punctuation. Many of the spelling mistakes noted by partners who were not typing seemed to be typing mistakes, but it was impossible to distinguish these definitively. The focus on punctuation was related to the fact that the children used the six story-writing tasks to experiment with dialogue conventions. The relatively infrequent explaining and stating rules categories, however, reflect the nature of the children's teaching. When one student knew how to use quotation marks and commas for dialogue, he or she taught via demonstration—typing the punctuation in correctly when at the keyboard and noting problems or corrections when not at the keyboard. Since the children's use of dialogue-related punctuation improved, it appears that this method was effective, at least over the short run. An analysis of two groups of collaborators offers information on the types of talk that relate to the major improvements on subsequent individual writing samples.

COMPARISON OF THE TALK BY COLLABORATORS WHO IMPROVED ON INDIVIDUAL WRITING SAMPLES TO TALK BY THOSE WHO DID NOT

To understand better the functions of the various types of talk, we contrasted the talk by two groups of collaborators: those who improved on quality ratings of individual samples (Group A) versus those who did not improve or received lower quality ratings after several weeks of collaboration (Group B). A holistic scoring session was run according to ETS guidelines by a writing researcher who was not associated with this study (Stotsky, 1980). The teachers of the two classes in the study and another teacher from their district who had taught both fourth and fifth grades judged the texts. The texts were presented on computer printouts with all information that would reveal student identities removed from headings or substituted in the text. Two raters scored each paper, using a scale from 1 to 4, and the paper received the sum of the scores. Table 2 includes the holistic quality scores on the individual and collaborative tasks by Group A and Group B students.

The pairs in Group A (students who improved) all received higher or the same (within 1 point) holistic scores on their individually written Task 6 stories than they received on their individually written Task 1 stories. The mean increase in individual quality score for each pair was at least 1.5, and the group mean was a 2.0 increase in quality score at time 6 over time 1. In contrast, of the pairs in Group B (students who did not improve) all but one student received lower quality scores on individually written task 6 stories than on Task 1. The mean decrease of each pair was at least 1 point, and the group mean was a 1.7 decrease, which is significantly different from the Group A mean ($p < .001$ level). As also shown on Table 2, the patterns of scores on collaborative Tasks 2 through 5 differ for the two groups. Although both groups received a range of scores, Group A received more scores of 4 and above, Group B more 3s and 2s. Moreover, while both groups began with a mean score of 4 on Task 2, the first collaborative task, Group A progressed to a 5 on Task 4 and leveled off at 4 on Task 5. Group B's scores, on the other hand, steadily decreased.

Even though holistic quality scores are not always accurate measures of writing ability, they tend to reflect fluency and correctness in texts by beginning writers (Daiute, 1986b; Nold & Freedman, 1977). In brief, quality scores serve here to offer general information about the impact of collaborative writing experiences. Since other objective and subjective data in this study support the trends indicated by the quality scores, using the scores to distinguish groups of pairs is appropriate.

Comparisons of the percentages of each type of talk by collaborators

Table 2. Holistic Quality Scores on Individually
and Collaboratively Written Texts by 2 Groups of Coauthors

		Group A Pairs Who Improved					
		Individually Written Texts Tasks			Coauthored Texts Tasks		
Pair #	Individual	1	6	2	3	4	5
1	CHRIS	1	5				
	ALLEY	2	7	6	4	7	6
3	JOHN	6	6				
	BRUCE	3	6	4	5	3	3
8	MIKE	4	8				
	BILL	3	7	8	2	2	*
9	DAVID	3	7				
	ROY	6	5	5	3	8	3
	MEANS	3.7	5.7	4	3.5	5	4

		Group B Pairs Who Did Not Improve					
		Individually Written Texts Tasks			Coauthored Texts Tasks		
Pair #	Individual	1	6				
6	TOM	5	4				
	ANDY	6	3	2	2	4	3
7	STEVE	3	6				
	PETER	6	4	6	6	3	2
11	ASHLEY	5	4				
	BETTY	5	4	4	5	2	3
12	AMY	4	2				
	TERRI	5	3	4	2	3	2
	MEANS	5	3.3	4	3.8	3	2.5

*File lost because computer was disconnected.

who improved (Group A) and those who did not (Group B) reveal clear differences. Differences in frequency of talk type used by Group A and Group B pairs were examined using *t*-test analyses to determine statistical significance. To reduce the possibility of obtaining chance significance because of testing all the categories, we selected categories for *t*-tests according to two criteria: (1) a difference had to be more than twice as much, and (2) the category had to be related to questions posed for this study. For example, negotiation was included, since one group used it more than twice as much as the other group, and it involves conflict between partners. Naming, on the other hand, occurred six times as much for Group B pairs, but was not included, since it does not address the issues of the present analysis. In all, 11 of the 37 talk categories were tested. Table 3 shows the means, standard deviations, and significances of the 11 categories tested.

Group A did significantly more talking in the following categories: suggesting alternatives; monitoring and clarifying form; evaluating, explaining, and negotiating; specifically the subcategories of negotiating; expressing rhetorical value; explaining; and checking facts. In contrast to the several types of talk predominating by Group A, Group B pairs only did more literal spelling. Group B also did more talking about procedures of typing, word processing, and dividing labor, but these differences were not significant.

The common characteristic among the seven categories that the Group A students engaged in more than the Group B students is the evidence of cognitive conflict. Negotiating involves explicit markers of cognitive conflict, while the other categories such as suggesting alternatives reflect some underlying conflict or difference in point of view. Children's negotiating talk, as shown in Table 4, appears to be cryptic from an adult point of view yet is apparently understood by these young peers.

Negotiating episodes, like those on Table 4, are characterized by four structural elements: initiation, uptake, elaboration, and resolution. Negotiation episodes were initiated when a speaker noted a disagreement with a prior comment. Children disagreed with their own suggestions

Table 3.   Mean Frequency Percentages of Selected Types of Talk by Coauthor Pairs Grouped According to Individual Improvement on Pre-to Post-Writing Tasks

(Code)	Type of Talk	Pairs Who Improved ($n = 4$)		Pairs Who Did Not Improve ($n = 4$)		
		$\overline{X}$	SD	$\overline{X}$	SD	
1.3	Suggesting alternatives	11.8	3.7	5.2	3.9	**
1.4	Literal spelling	1.4	1.1	3.8	.7	**
2.0	Monitoring/clarifying form[1]	9.7	3.5	4.2	1.6	**
2.3	Monitoring punctuation	2.4	2.5	.3	.2	
5.0	Evaluating, explaining[1]	10.7	2.6	5.6	3.5	*
5.1	Expressing rhetorical value	1.5	.7	.5	.4	**
5.2	Explaining	1.1	.7	.3	.3	*
5.4	Checking facts	2.0	.9	.8	.6	*
5.5	Negotiating	2.9	1.1	1.1	.8	**
6.2	Typing, word processing	3.6	2.2	7.6	5.8	
6.3	Division of labor	1.8	.7	4.8	5.3	

1 = Summary categories $*p < .10$
$**p < .05$

Table 4. Examples of Negotiating

Example 1:
  2: no no 2 spaces
  1: who says?
  2: it's just initial typing. just always. giggles. and one space after the comma.
  1: oh.

Example 2:
  2: Wait wait no wait. forget forget it. Chased him to South.
     South America.
  1: Chased him to Venezuela. giggle. chased him to south? They're in South America
     already.
  2: No. they're not
  1: Yes they are
  2: No—they're not. Where?
  1: Yea look. One day him and his troops went to save South America
  2: It doesn't mean they're in South America. laugh
  1: laugh. well they are
  2: OK went to
  1: What's in the middle? What about Brazil
  2: Let's blow up Brazil. laugh
  1: They blow up the whole thing.
  2: I know but they go to Brazil. Brazil's the biggest part. It's right in the middle. the
     middle part. What's the end
  1: Whats in the middle: What's the middle others? others? Brazil's all over the place
  2: No kidding
  1: Chased him to Brazil. Brazil comma.
  2: Wait Brazil.

Example 3:
  2: He and three members . . . Harold . . . Herman . . . and Fred
  1: Come on don't put all those names in. Just have him.
  2: No
  1: But I'll get lonely up there.
  . . . .

Example 4:
  2: Rover and his best friend Fred.
  1: call him the beaver
  2: You have to give him a name.
  1: The beaver The beaver. That's a good name.
  2: Dum de dum dum.

Example 5:
  2: so far let's say it had taken him 8 years
  1: four years
  2: But look how far he's got to go through?
  1: he go to go this far . . .
  2: he's already crossed Mexico
  1: say
  2: so far it had taken leny 8 years
  1: Lenny went a long time without water. wait let me think
  2: it took him three months to fill up
  1: Lenny took a long time . . . Lenny went a long time without water in fact the whole
     distance of Mexico just say it just say it.

as well as with their partner's, and these disagreements were marked by questions, alternatives, words such as "no," "hold it," "wait," and "but," or statements indicating a contrary belief, such as "I thought you meant . . . ." Negotiating also typically involved up-take (a direct response to the point of initiation), with a more or less elaborated continuation of the discussion. Initiated negotiations were occasionally ignored, but typically initiations were elaborated by restatements of concern, explanations, clarifications, and other disagreements. Disagreements were sometimes resolved as in examples 1 and 2 in Table 5, but more often they ended with statements of acknowledgement that fell short of true resolution, such as "OK," "allright," restatements of a suggested alternative, or the more neutral, "well whatever." In spite of such underdeveloped negotiations, these children's writing scores and fluency increased, suggesting that it was valuable.

While negotiating language tended to be vague, the children's suggesting of alternatives was concrete. Table 5 includes several examples of children's suggesting of alternatives.

Children posed alternatives about character names, setting, plot development, and wording, thus using this technique to express and to share their ideas about what stories should be like. This alternative-posing activity implies conflict and evaluation, as in the interchange "Brown, no black, no white," but the disagreement is not expressed directly. The most notable quality of a large number of the alternative-posing interchanges is their playfulness.

Children base their alternatives on alliteration ("Christopher Crocodile. Crissy the Crocodile. Cramped Crocodile") and contrasts (". . . the Atlantic. No, into the Pacific Ocean"). This alternative posing appears to be driven more by exploration and fun than by critical evaluation of prior elements. The range of associations showed that suggesting alternatives was exploratory. The singsong nature of the sound and meaning contrasts and the number of giggles in alternatives suggest that this composing activity was fun. Just as children originally learn language by apparently aimless play with sounds and meanings (Garvey, 1977), these 9- and 10-year-old children played with literary elements such as character names, dialogue, setting, and plot development. Since this type of talk was characteristic of the collaboration pairs who became more fluent writers, we can hypothesize that such playful composing has an important role in the writing process.

INTERPRETATION AND DISCUSSION

This study offers information for answering questions about the nature of collaboration and its role in learning how to write. The talk analysis

Table 5.   Examples of Suggesting Alternatives

1. A: I know. Davey Crockett the Crocodile
    B: How about Christopher Crocodile?
    A: Christopher—(not clear) Crocodile
    B: Crissy the Crocodile
    A: Cramped Crocodile

2. A: Bad Boy Bartie . . . Bartie . . . Bartie . . . Bad Bartie
    B: Bad Bartie. giggle
    A: Bad Boy Bartie . . . Bad Martie . . . no Bad Boy Bart
    B: Bad Bart

3. A: And he flew off into the Atlantic Ocean
    B: The Atlantic?
    A: Yeah, the Atlantic
    B: No, into the Pacific Ocean . . . he swam for a couple of hundred miles

showed that collaboration does involve productive cognitive conflict, but these young coauthors did not sound like a seasoned author reflecting a text or text goals, as portrayed in other research (Flower & Hayes, 1981). The concrete and playful nature of the collaborative talk, specifically by children whose writing improved after collaborating, indicates that collaboration is valuable because it is fun and because it provides experience with questioning one's own point of view. The talk analysis in this study offers some specific information on how play helps young writers. The fun children had with the sounds and meaning of language and literary discourse led to increased fluency and experimentation with story elements such as dialogue. This playful quality of collaboration was complemented by some negotiating and text evaluation. The children were less skilled at negotiating than they were at playing, but the sketchy arguments about story development or wording are also associated with gains in individual writing improvement. Thus, this study shows that collaborative writing is a good context in which to practice these creative and regulative cognitive activities.

The data in this writing study suggest that collaboration involves productive conflict even though the discussions appear to be vague, unresolved, and only implicitly related to planning and evaluating. It appears that child-like talk, such as playing with language and negotiating is important for children in conjunction with, or perhaps even instead of, adult-like talk. In other words, since many children write well even when their composing process is playful rather than planful, we are focusing on the value of childlike talk, rather than the paucity of adult-like planning and revising strategies.

Bruner (1985) has recently discussed the value of play as an enticement into the "zone of proximal development" hypothesized by Vygotsky (1978). We present the results of this study as evidence that playful and immature talk are a foundation for improvement in individual writing skills. These results are not inconsistent with those of Brown and her colleagues (1983), who argue that children need deliberate instruction in cognitive strategies. Indeed, evidence confirms that children benefit from strategic self-guiding activity and teacher's generalizations, but children also benefit from playing with language. Those involved in teaching methods, such as Graves (1983), Calkins (1986), and others who report on children's writing development have urged that we help children perform in developmentally appropriate ways (i.e., by accepting invented spellings), but these prescriptions do not offer explanatory information because they are not based on theory or experimental research. This study suggests that children's playfulness involves cognitive conflict, which may be an early step in decentering as Bruner has suggested.

Language play and subtle negotiation may be valuable to children because they serve as modeling activities. When children play with language as they compose texts on the computer screen and even as they talk around issues, they are sharing experiences as writers. Such concrete experiences in making and talking about text may provide children with the rhythms and feel of literacy as well as with specific techniques and rules. Such modeling has been ignored in recent developmental literature (Bruner, 1985) because an emphasis on modeling processes suggests that learning is simply copying or imitating. These data show that modeling is effective. This experiential form of learning can function in tandem with the more intellectual interventions that have been shown to be important in cognitive development.

This study also suggests that perhaps the adult and the slightly more able peer serve as different types of guides in the "zone of proximal development" as described by Vygotsky. Each of the collaboration pairs who improved in this study included one person who had a higher quality rating on Task 1 than the partner, while the pairs who did not improve began more equally. Thus, this study offers evidence to support the idea that collaboration is most useful when partners differ, if not in ability then in performance. Slightly more able peers talked the same language as their coauthors, which may be one reason why they were successful.

Finally, it is important to note that even though collaboration can be an effective method for individual development, collaborative activities are also valuable because they give children the chance to cooperate toward common goals and to develop collaboration skills. This study has shown that many children are good at collaborating, and they enjoy it. Even though the children were happily unaware of the researchers' notion of "cognitive conflict," they recognized that writing together led to conflicts and that these were difficult. During interviews after the experiment, one of the most successful pairs offered the following indications of productive cognitive conflict. When asked, "Would you rather write with another person or alone?" Roy said, "With another person. Because I collaborate well. I like talking." His partner, whose writing improved 4 quality points after collaborating, said, "Sometimes it's fun. It's more fun to write alone. If you write with someone else sometimes you argue." A classmate, Terri, interjected, "Yeah, you have to argue, but arguing helps you see more."

REFERENCES

Bereiter, C., & Scardamalia, M. (1982). From conversation to composition: The role of instruction in the developmental process. In R. Glaser (Ed.), *Advances in instructional psychology* (Vol. 2, pp. 1–64). Hillsdale, NJ: Erlbaum.

Brenneis, D., & Lein, L. (1977). "You fruithead": A sociolinguistic approach to children's dispute settlement. In S. Ervin–Tripp & C. M. Kernon (Eds.), *Child discourse*. NY: Academic Press.

Brown, A. L., Bransford, J. D., Ferrara, R. A., & Campione, J. C. (1983). Learning, remembering, and understanding. In P. H. Mussen (Ed.), *Handbook of child psychology* (4th ed., pp. 77–166). New York: Wiley.

Brown, A., & DeLoach, J. (1978). Skills, plans, and self-regulation. In K. Siegler (Ed.), *Children's thinking: What develops?* Hillsdale, NJ: Erlbaum.

Bruner, J. (1985). On teaching thinking: An afterthought. In S. Chipman, J. Segal, & R. Glass (Eds), *Thinking and learning skills. Vol. 2: Research and open questions*. Hillsdale, NJ: Erlbaum.

Calkins, L. (1983). *Lessons from a child: On the teaching and learning of writing*. Exeter, NH: Heinemann.

Calkins, L. (1986). *The art of teaching writing*. Exeter, NH: Heinemann.

Daiute, C. (1985). Do writers talk to themselves? In S. W. Freedman (Ed.), *The acquisition of written language: Revision and response*. Norwood, NJ: Ablex.

Daiute, C. (1986a). Do 1 and 1 make 2?: Patterns of influence by collaborative authors. *Written Communication, 3*, 382–408.

Daiute, C. (1986b, May). Physical and cognitive factors in revising: Insights from studies with computers. *Research in the Teaching of English*, 141–159.

Daiute, C., & Kruidenier, J. (1985). A self-questioning strategy to increase young writers' revising processes. *Applied Psycholinguistics, 6*, 307–318.

Dale, E., & Chall, J. S. (1948). A formula for predicting readability. *Educational Research Bulletin, 27*, 37–54.

Flavell, J. (1976). Metacognitive aspects of problem-solving. In L. B. Resnick (Ed.), *The nature of intelligence*. Hillsdale, NJ: Erlbaum.

Flavell, J., & Wellman, M. H. (1977). Metamemory. In R. V. Kail, Jr., & J. W. Hagen (Eds.), *Perspectives on the development of memory and cognition*. Hillsdale, NJ: Erlbaum.

Flower, L., & Hayes, J. R. (1981). A cognitive process theory of writing. *College Composition and Communication, 32,* 365–388.

Forman, E., & Cazden, C. (1985). Exploring Vygotskian perspectives in education: The cognitive value of peer interaction. In J. Wersch (Ed.), *Culture, communication, and cognition: Vygotskian perspectives.* Cambridge, England: Cambridge University Press.

Freedman, S., Greenleaf, C., Sperling, M., & Parker, L. (1985). *The role of response in the acquisition of written language.* Final report to the NIE, NIE–G–083–0065. Berkeley: The University of California.

Fry, E. B. (1968). A readability formula that saves time. *Journal of Reading,* April, 513–516, 575–578.

Garvey, C. (1977). *Play.* Cambridge, MA: Harvard University Press.

Genishi E., & Di Paolo (1982). Learning through argument in preschool. In L. Wilkinson (Ed.), *Communicating in the classroom.* New York: Academic Press.

Gentner, D., & Stevens, A. (Eds.). (1983). *Mental models.* Hillsdale, NJ: Erlbaum.

Graves, D. (1983). *Writing: Teachers and children at work.* Exeter, NH: Heinemann.

Hillocks, G. (1986). *Research on written composition: New directions for teaching.* Urbana, IL: ERIC Clearinghouse on Reading and Communication Skills and the National Conference on Research in English.

Johnson, D., & Johnson, R. (1979). Conflict in the classroom: Controversy and learning. *Review of Educational Research, 49,* 51–70.

Johnson, D., Johnson, R., Holubec, E., & Roy, P. (1984). *Circles of learning.* Washington, DC: Association for Supervision and Curriculum Development.

Mishler, E. C. (1979). "Will you trade cookies with popcorn?" The talk of trades among six year olds. In O. Garcia & M. King (Eds.), *Language, children, and society* (pp. 221–236). Oxford, England: Pergamon Press.

Mugny, G., & Doise, W. (1978). Socio-cognitive conflict and structuration of individual and collective performances. *European Journal of Social Psychology, 8,* 181–192.

Nold, E., & Freedman S. (1977). An analysis of readers' responses to essays. *Research in the Teaching of English, 11,* 164–174.

Perret–Clermont, A. N. (1980). *Social interaction and cognitive development in children.* New York: Academic Press.

Petitto, A. (1986). *Problem-solving in turn-taking and collaborative groups.* Manuscript submitted for publication.

Piaget, J. (1959). *The language and thought of the child.* New York: Harcourt Brace Jovanovich.

Rubin, D., & Rafoth, B. (1986). Social cognitive ability as a predictor of the quality of expository and persuasive writing among college freshman. *Research in the Teaching of English, 20* (1), 9–22.

Slavin, R. (1983). *Cooperative learning.* New York: Longman.

Stotsky, S. (1980). Evaluation of the writing program at William M. Trotter School, Boston: Sept. 1978–Jan. 1980. Report prepared for Boston Public Schools and Curry College. ERIC Document # 196011.

Vygotsky, L. (1978). *Mind in society.* Cambridge, MA: Harvard University Press.
Wertsch, J. (1985). *Culture, communication, and cognition: Vygotskian perspectives.* Cambridge, England: Cambridge University Press.
Woodruff, E., Bereiter, C., & Scardamalia, M. (1981–1982). On the road to computer compositions. *Journal of Educational Technology Systems, 10*(2), 133–148.

Part Four

Assigning Social Values to Writing

Chapter 12

Ethnocultural Issues in the Creation, Substitution, and Revision of Writing Systems

Joshua A. Fishman
Yeshiva University

INTRODUCTION

Like all oral language, the world's writing systems are subject to influences related to various historical junctures and sociocultural milieus. Important dimensions of such interrelationships are well recognized in the sociocultural impact of writing/reading per se and in the psycholinguistic-psychoeducational (Augst, 1986) and econotechnical (Ferru, 1986) involvements of new and revised writing systems. Other relationships between writing systems and their societal contexts now deserve to be highlighted. Accordingly, this chapter will focus on a number of ethnocultural issues in the development of writing systems, particularly on the sense of authenticity, of self-regulated indigenousness and of relative autonomy in the rate and direction of sociocultural change. In short, this chapter considers the development of writing systems within the total realm of intergenerational ethnic identity and continuity (see Irvine & Elsasser, this volume).

Our attention to writing systems will focus upon three different stages of ethnocultural involvement: (a) the stage when the first writing system (FWS) is introduced, that is, when a speech community that has not hitherto had any writing system at all is faced with the creation and adoption of such a system; (b) the stage when a previously established writing system (EWS) is a candidate for total replacement by a newly advocated rival system, for example, the substitution of an ideographic writing system by an alphabetic one, or the replacement of a Cyrillic writing system by a Latin one; and finally, (c) the stage when partial modifications of a current writing system (CWS) are on the agenda. Although these three different stages (creation, substitution, and revision) differ greatly from one another in terms of the overall complexity and scale of the social change and social dislocation that they imply, they are also instructively similar in many respects. Although they tend to occur in sociocultural entities that are at vastly different stages of econotechnical and sociocultural development they can, nevertheless, be viewed as differing more in the degree than in the kind of basic ethnocultural issues that surround them.

THE CREATION AND INTRODUCTION OF FIRST WRITING SYSTEMS

By this time in human history there are relatively few and mainly small and isolated ethnocultural communities for whom first writing systems (FWSs) are now being considered or remain to be determined. Since such communities are, by now, rarely characterized by full-scale self-regulation in their economy or the nature of their intergroup contacts, it can come as no surprise that the introduction of FWSs is usually under some sort of outside auspices or arises as a result of implicit or explicit pressures from outside their own ethnocultural networks. As a result, the larger context of intergroup interaction, and the intergroup as well as intragroup tensions that surround it, necessarily influence (and may even dominate) the entire consideration of whether or which FWSs should be adopted. Although explicit consideration may be given to matters of visual form (i.e., the particular physical shapes selected for graphemes, ideographs, or pictographs) and notational complexity, cultural self-regulation (autonomy) and authenticity, on the one hand, and accompanying social change and the distribution of social rewards with respect to literacy, on the other hand, are more likely to be the determining factors in the development and adoption of particular FWSs (Fishman, 1977; Sjoberg, 1966), whether this is admitted and recognized or not.

Visual forms and degrees of notational complexity of FWSs associated with (if not imposed by) authorities from outside the indigenous ethnocultural system constantly evoke their outside regulatory and punitive origins. Those individuals or social strata who utilize these FWSs are, therefore, by implication, perceived as collaborating to one degree or another with such outside powers. Accordingly, the creation and introduction/imposition of FWSs are never viewed as ethnoculturally dispassionate or apolitical acts, neither by those who foster them nor by those upon whom they are imposed. Above and beyond the issue of purported material advantage (e.g., when Amerindian FWSs are Latin alphabet-based [Holm, 1972; Young, 1977] or when Soviet Inner Asian FWSs are Cyrillic alphabet based [Henze, 1977], there is the issue of internal ethnocultural self-regulatory capacity and continuity. Thus, while outside authorities tend to point to the advantages of exonormative ("imported") FWSs, doing so in terms of the greater availability and lower cost of modern printing/typing equipment and in terms of easier acquisition of the "obviously appropriate and inevitable" language of wider communication, many endonormative ("native") authorities and traditional cultural elites are concerned with the continuity of their own status position and with their collectivity's ability to maintain cultural autonomy and authenticity.

Exonormative considerations are also evident in connection with the notational complexity of many newly created FWSs, over and above the issue of visual form per se. Thus, it is probable that the indication of vowel length and tone in modern Navajo orthography is primarily an aid to outside linguists and teachers whose mother tongue is English, rather than an aid for Navajo mother tongue readers and writers. The latter have generally been fully socialized to vowel length and tone before their literacy exposure begins. Both vowel length and tone are, therefore, contextually regulated for them and are not really necessary at the visual level in order to "clarify meaning." For nonnative language users, however, their control of Navajo being more recent and more marginal, the complex conventions of indicating vowel length and tone are quite important guides to correct meaning. Thus, while it is true that Navajo "looks less like English" when all tones and vowel length indications are inserted—and that such insertions may, therefore, come to have a certain authenticity appeal which can be ideologically activated and cultivated—these indications may, nevertheless, be deleted, minimized, or ignored entirely in most intragroup reading and writing in which authenticity is not at issue. Literate native speakers of Navajo just tend to leave out these indications when they are writing, particularly those in the younger generation who have been raised with Navajo literacy, and the recipients and readers of their letters never even miss these indications since their knowledge of the language is eminently good enough to get along without most tone and vowel length reminders of meaning.

The above example indicates that exactly what will be considered exonormative or endonormative in the visual form/notational complexity of FWSs cannot be fully predicted in advance, precisely because such considerations are, in part at least, matters of socially patterned and politically motivated interpretation. Borrowed forms may be so thoroughly reworked or integrated as to lose foreign markedness. Conversely, internally derived forms may, nevertheless, be nontraditional and, therefore, interpreted as intrusive or foreign. Long-accepted and seemingly integrated material of foreign origin may ultimately be rejected as foreign because of newly discovered (or newly exploited) associations with disfavored ideological, economic, or political factions, just as recently imported innovations may come to be interpreted as "really indigenous" through the fanciful sociologies of knowledge that arise in all social struggles. Thus, for example, the "great sun" theory in the late 1920s interpreted all Europeanisms in Turkish as ultimately derived from Turkish. What is endonormative or exonormative in a particular context is not so much a question of verifiable origins (which are not always accurately ascertainable at any rate) as a question of convinced belief and convincing argumentation. This is true not only with respect to FWSs but with respect to writing systems as a whole, and even with respect to orthographic revisions that may seem to be quite minor to the disinterested outsider but that excite extreme passions within the speech-and-writing community. More than rational considerations are at issue: self-regulated authenticity (who we are, what is ours, who controls us, what loyalty to tradition and past generations we desire, what kind of future we wish to pursue) often assumes major proportions.

Given the foregoing influences and considerations (ideological, political, and pragmatic) in connection with FWSs, it is quite apparent why so few of them have been endonormatively governed with respect to visual form and complexity of notation, and why, instead, they have generally gravitated inexorably toward the writing conventions of one big brother or another (usually English, French, Spanish, Russian, Chinese, or Hindi) even where endonormative ethnocultural self-regulation initially obtains. It is virtually impossible for smaller ethnocultural establishments to remain self-regulating in the cultural domain when they enter or are forced into intense interaction with their surrounding or engulfing protectors. In the absence of such ethnocultural self-regulation, FWSs are likely to play interstitial contributory roles en route to language spread via second-language literacy or even en route to mother tongue shift as a whole. Missionaries, capitalists, and commissars alike have utilized newly created FWSs to introduce their own ideologies and texts to cultures in which these were previously generally unknown.

As a result, it is not only that the visual forms and notational complexities of FWSs are commonly exonormatively determined but also that the very social functions of these FWSs are under similar outside regulation. Members of indigenous societies that adopt and master these systems are exonormatively rewarded, new positions and statuses being made available to them differentially by authorities whose power base is ultimately outside the indigenous culture. Such rewards are likely to be far greater, at least materially, than those available under traditional and authentic endonormative control. Accordingly, the transition to second-language literacy is hastened while native language literacy, the ostensive reason for FWSs, may become little more than an esoteric affectation (Garvin, 1954, and many accounts of the spread of English, French, and Russian literacy into areas where these languages are not mother tongues). Thus while the spread of FWSs may be facilitated or delayed by intrasystem characteristics such as those discussed above, their ultimate stability and maintenance depends on whether the social functions and rewards associated with them are sufficient to (a) compensate for the time and effort required to master them, (b) overcome the opposition of those whose preliteracy status might be threatened by the advent of literacy, and (c) compete with the rewards dispensed (by exonormatively based authorities) for second-language literacy rather than for first-language literacy, at least in a few important endonormative ethnocultural domains, for example, religion, traditional folk medicine, traditional celebrations, and so forth.

Every ethnocultural entity has an established system of recognized and rewarded statuses. These exist prior to the introduction of FWSs; the FWSs cannot but have consequences for the status systems every bit as much as the status systems seek to influence use of the FWSs. Indeed, the very adoption of FWSs is a function of their probable consequences. However, where no consequences are foreseeable, the adoption process has no social dynamic. Where such consequences *are* foreseeable they will inevitably not be universally interpreted as desirable (Winter 1983). Indeed, endonormative preliteracy status systems are likely to be threatened by the introduction of FWSs, whether or not that introduction is under exonormative sponsorship. When such sponsorship does exist (as is typically the case), it tends to add considerations of loyalty and authenticity to what would generally have been considered by at least some indigenous elites as a status-threatening innovation, even had it been entirely endonormatively sponsored.

The FWS per se (as well as the replacement or revision of such systems later, as we will note below) is a problematic issue. Both acceptance and rejection are sociopolitical statements and advocates and opponents will react to them as such (Burns, 1953; Ehlich, 1983; Goody & Watt, 1963). FWSs face a two-front war. They are attacked not only by those who fear their exonormative tendencies but also by those who fear status erosion even when the FWSs are under strong endonormative auspices. When we turn to the replacement and revision of writing systems we will again find the same double opposition from those who fear the direction of probable social change as well as from those who fear any and all social change.

It is not just individual lives that are changed by FWSs, but ethnocultural systems as a whole. However, the basic dynamic of change at the societal level is located well outside of the writing system, no matter how ideologized the latter may become in the process of social change. When exonormative influences are paramount, then the indigenous self-regulatory capacity may be exposed to outside military, economic, political, cultural, and philosophical control. Under such circumstances much more than a FWS will be introduced and the FWS will be reacted to, positively and negatively, much as its accompanying larger scenario is reacted to. This is equally true when the FWS is endonormatively sponsored and regulated. In these circumstances the "abstand" nature of the FWS (i.e., the extent to which it is actually distinctively and authentically in accord with traditional endonormative visual conventions) is not the only issue of concern. Increased access to hitherto limited-access rewards and statuses, even in the context of endonormatively controlled modernization, will result in conflict and lead to both negative and positive evaluations of FWSs.

The FWS is always only part of a complex process of social change. Whether conducted under exonormative or endonormative sociocultural and econotechnical control, it is, in varying degrees, dislocative and, therefore, likely to be resisted by those who have more to lose than to gain by change in the status quo. The ensuing struggle for and against social change more broadly conceived (or for a controlling role in the regulation of such change) will determine the fate of any particular FWS. The ubiquity of writing systems in the world today is itself an indication of the extent to which social change has engulfed the world. Even when hitherto isolated and insulated smaller ethnocultural units adopt FWSs under their own regulatory authorities, they generally do so as last-ditch efforts to cope with problems of cultural dislocation that are usually already far advanced (Walker, 1981; 1984). In a sense, they are fighting fire with fire, a distinctly modern dilemma, and are likely to be transformed in the very process of resisting transformation.

THE SUBSTITUTION OF ESTABLISHED WRITING SYSTEMS

By far most writing system planning today is concerned with systems that are already in widespread use. As a result, it is not so much the advantage of reading/writing per se that needs to be justified and rewarded as it is the writing system—through which both reading and writing are engaged in—that needs to be either modified, replaced, or defended. Nevertheless, efforts to alter ongoing writing systems are largely subject to similar stresses and dynamics as those we have just discussed in conjunction with FWSs. The alterations proposed for estab-

lished writing systems (EWSs) may be under endonormative or exonormative sponsorship, and, in the latter case, may well be associated
with colonization, conquest or spread of "sphere of influence." Once
again, the gains associated with the proposed revisions must authorita-
tively and effectively outweigh the costs for those who have already
mastered and benefited from the prior system. Finally, the large-scale
sociosymbolical significance of the revisions must coincide with social
change processes and ideologies that are positively regarded, the latter
being particularly crucial when writing system revision is contemplated
within relatively self-regulating ethnocultural entities which, by definition, have a vested interest in perpetuating their perceived autonomy
and authenticity.

Changing one system for another is even rarer in recent times than
the introduction of FWSs. This is testimony to the ability of writing systems to attain sanctified symbolic and pragmatic statuses within ethnocultural entities. Their complete replacement becomes well nigh impossible without compelling force. The major exonormative examples of
such changes are those pertaining to the many initially Latin alphabet
systems of Soviet Inner Asia that were changed to Cyrillic in the late
1920s and early 1930s (Quelquejay & Bennigsen, 1961). The major endonormative example of politically/philosophically motivated substitution
of an EWS is Kemal Pasha Ataturk's replacement of Perso–Arabic by
Latin letters for writing Turkish (Heyd, 1954) at about the same time.
Clearly, both of these replacements were effected under authoritarian
auspices. Indeed, this may be a necessary contextual characteristic for
the replacement of EWSs, whether in recent (Macedonian, Moldavian)
or in former (Czech, Slovak) times. On the other hand, authoritarian
rule is hardly a sufficient contextual characteristic for the substitution of
one EWS by another. Even totalitarian regimes must consider whether
the dislocation involved, including indigenous opposition for reasons of
ideology and self-interest, is worth the price of replacement. Yugoslav-
ian efforts to romanize Serbian (Kalogjera, 1985) and Chinese efforts to
romanize Mandarin (De Francis, 1977b, 1984; Seybolt & Chiang, 1979)
reveal that even authoritarian regimes may have to accept only limited
success when the price of complete victory is too high. It should also be
noted that romanization is actually very far from the unmixed blessing
at a purely technical level that Westerners often believe it to be (discussed by Coulmas, 1983; De Francis, 1977a) because of problems with
tone, vowel length, visual similarity between letters, the variety of different type faces, uppercase and lowercase letters, the greater need to
specify one dialect or another as a guide to spelling, the problem of homonyms, and so forth. In the absence of compelling force, all efforts to
replace endonormative EWSs with exonormative romanized systems

have failed. In this category we may enumerate various efforts to romanize India's various Devanagari scripts (James, 1985; Pattanayak, 1981) and Japan's traditional ideographic and syllabic scripts (De Francis, 1947), as well as the less focused efforts to romanize Arabic (Mahmoud, 1981), Hebrew (Avinor, 1977) and Amharic (Demoz, 1986).

Replacement of a writing system threatens to dislocate indigenous intellectual authority structures. The longer the prior writing system has functioned as an indigenous marker of authenticity and status in association with other indigenous symbols of identity, sanctity, and attainment, the less likely it is that this established system will be completely replaceable without extreme dislocation under exonormative auspices. Instead, bilateracy patterns often arise (different writing systems being utilized by the very same writers/readers in conjunction with different languages) that are in complementary functional distribution. Thus, the autochthonous scripts of West Africa (Kotei, 1977) and Western Apache writing (Basso & Anderson, 1977) have their specific functions. In their limited traditional spheres they are not necessarily threatened by the Latin scripts that surround them. However, should their traditional functions undergo serious erosion, the traditional scripts would probably be replaced quickly, as was the Gaelic type face in the case of all-encompassing Irish literacy aspirations (O'Murchu, 1977), or the *vaybertaytsh* type face in the case of early 19th century Yiddish (Fishman, 1985), or the now marginal (that is, merely decorative) "Basque font."

MODIFYING CURRENT WRITING SYSTEMS

Modifying a current writing system (CWS) without attempting to replace it by a totally different system is, by all odds, the least difficult of the three types of popular ethnocultural concern for writing systems. Of the three, it is the one most likely to be endonormative in inspiration and enforcement and, accordingly, least likely to arouse fears of disloyalty and inauthenticity. It is also the one that is least disruptive of established authority systems, established symbolic linkages and established roles and statuses. Although the revision of CWSs, like the introduction of FWSs and the substitution of EWSs, is related to ongoing social change, it is far less likely to imply far-reaching or uncontrolled change. Finally, of all three types, it is the one that is most directly and genuinely concerned with intra-writing-system efficiency rather than with symbolizing social processes. Nevertheless, like all change in writing systems, it does not occur in a social vacuum and, therefore, it is by no means devoid of the social complications mentioned above.

The primary internal rationale for modifying CWSs is simplification.

Certain aspects of the current system are considered to be disturbingly difficult (take too much time, yield too many errors even after many hours of instruction, slow the reading/writing process, present difficulties for keyboards and other modern typesetting or type-processing equipment, and so forth [viz. Siromoney, 1978]) and, therefore, become candidates for simplification. Simplification takes many paths, all of which are philosophically/ideologically encumbered. In ideographic/logographic systems simplification aims to decrease the number of strokes. In grapheme–phoneme correspondence systems, simplification drops silent letters, redundant letters, foreign letters or letters whose orthographic "function" is etymological rather than phonemic. In modern, democratic circles, where popular, all-encompassing literacy not only has participatory but philosophical value, simplification rationales often aim at moving the written language closer to spoken pronunciation. The view is advanced that native speakers should not have to devote undue time to learning how to spell or read their own language. Since speech is normally acquired well before reading or writing, it should be given priority in determining the spelling of the mother tongue in written and printed form. As spoken pronunciation changes over time, spelling should be adapted accordingly. Spelling conventions should not be hostage to the past but, rather, fully attuned to the present. The Western language that has been most frequently adjusted along these very lines is Dutch (Geerts, van den Broeck, & Verdoodt, 1977). Since the spoken language normally exists in a variety of different regional and social lects, one of these may be designated as "standard"; alternatively, a series of vowel transformation rules obtains, such that certain vowels are pronounced differently but written uniformly in various regional and social circles. This solution does not iron out lexical and morphosyntactic differences between lects, but such differences are not susceptible to writing system solutions in any case.

As with issues of "endonormativeness/authenticity/indigenousness," so "simplification" is not an uncontroversial issue, but one that requires interpretation in order to provide it with direction. Phonological simplification for writers may run counter to morphological or etymological principles that many readers find helpful. "Simplification" efforts are rarely grounded in solid least-effort evidence and even where such evidence *is* available (Rabin & Schlesinger, 1974) it is convincing only from a particular value perspective rather than equally so for all vested interests, for all contexts or for all stages in the literacy acquisition process. Finally, "simplification" cannot be totally separated from the "Ausbau" needs of languages that function within the shadow of vastly stronger languages of the same "genetic family." By spelling Dutch more and more as it is spoken it also begins to look more and more different than (independent of) German. It is not unusual, therefore, for various opposing parties to be arguing on behalf of the "simpler solution," although they disagree vehemently as to which solution is the simpler one, given that vastly different criteria and criterion groups are preferred by different advocates of "simplicity."

Almost all CWSs have experienced a degree of modification within the past century, foremost among them German, Norwegian, American English, Hausa, Irish, Yiddish, Tamil, and Israeli Hebrew. The very absence of authoritarian compulsion, on the one hand, or of rapid and all-encompassing social change, on the other hand, often makes such modification difficult to enforce. As a result, texts in several of the above languages exhibit modified and unmodified spelling side by side, not only in different contemporary publications but, at times, within one and the same publication as well (James, 1985). The inertia of older readers and writers is particularly difficult to overcome, given that no dramatic change in social function, ethnic identity, or social status is usually available (or attributed) to foster conformity with the modified system. The substitution of a totally different EWS or the introduction of FWS, for all the serious social conflict that each reflects and engenders, nevertheless usually results in the clear-cut victory or defeat for the newly proposed systems. Organized social forces are marshaled for or against them and it becomes clear, often soon enough, which has won and which has lost. In conjunction with the modification of a CWS, particularly when such modification is attempted under decentralized democratic auspices, a long period of drift may ensue, with the final outcome depending largely on natural processes of generational replacement. Ideological appeals on behalf of distinctiveness and cultural continuity and in opposition to actual or suspected outside influences may, to some extent, be effective determinants of support as well, although usually not to the extent that they are in connection with FWS and EWS problems. The young became the natural, unideologized carriers of CWS modifications, being socialized accordingly by the schools, civil service, armed forces and other "official" institutions, whereas the old, being safely past the reach of such institutions, generally remain with the conventions to which they became accustomed during their own youth. A three-generational lag may transpire before CWS modifications are widely implemented. Although the Dutch case may indicate that it *need* not necessarily take this much time, it is the Dutch case which is the exception in the CWS-revision literature and, therefore, it needs to be explained in terms of its own possibly nongeneralizable dynamics rather than in terms of the generality of cases of this kind. More typical are the cases of spelling reform in German or in English where change has required two to three generations to become widely implemented, given noncentralized enforcement patterns, or, in the case of more centralized enforcement, a full generation, as in the case of Norwegian or Yiddish.

A final variation on the theme of endonormative–exonormative lability is the possibility of cross-national agreement on a commonly shared CWS. Such agreements currently obtain with respect to orthographic revisions in German (between various German mother-tongue polities), Netherlandic (between Holland and Belgium) and Malay–Indonesian (between Indonesia, Malaysia, and Singapore). In these instances, the larger, collective language community (rather than the individual polities that exist within such referential communities) can be the basis, at least temporarily, of endonormative interpretation, although such interpolity harmony may be short-lived if other, more urgent political considerations come to the fore. Needless to say, many languages that cross national boundaries have not yet benefited from joint orthographic planning (note the host of zealously protected minor differences that separate American and British spelling of English (e.g., airplane/aeroplane, curb/kerb) and French and Quebecois spelling of French, thus revealing again that orthographic change and endonormativeness are both by-products of much larger and more powerful social forces.

CONCLUSIONS

Several dimensions of ethnocultural import have cropped up in each of the writing system change-contexts that we have examined. The issue of internal authenticity or distinctiveness *vis-à-vis* outside ethnocultural systems invariably arises. This issue is the other side of the coin of competing drives toward modernization and intertranslatability (with particular languages of wider communication). This pair of concerns inevitably confronts disadvantaged and late-modernizing ethnocultural entities. The more modernity imposes a similar life-style and value system on us all, the more societies which are also striving for authenticity and indigenousness seek symbolic satisfactions. The writing system is often one arena in which such satisfaction can be approximated, but the more such satisfactions are indulged in, the more the goals of modernization and intertranslatability may need to be compromised. All ethnocultural entities have elites of their own and these are often the most reluctant to change the status quo *vis-à-vis* writing systems. Like all policy matters relating to literacy, writing system changes must be linked to social functions and to desired social mobility if they are to be widely implemented. The planning of writing systems is an activity within the larger field of social planning in general and of identity and opportunity planning in particular. All such planning follows the conventions of the local "culture of planning" as a whole (economic, family, educational, cultural, agricultural, etc.). Writing system introduction, substitution and revision must be seen as part of a much larger constellation of goals and distinctions within and between ethnocultural units.

Clearly, sociolinguistic analysis can help the writing system specialist become aware of additional problems and dimensions, above and beyond his or her own areas of technical competence, rationality and efficiency. Technical competence, rationality and efficiency in the design, improvement and propagation of writing systems depend on ethnocultural goals and directions. These goals are derived from the ideologies, philosophies, traditions, and cross-purposes of nations, cultures and societies and the elites that lead them. A clearer realization of the complexity and conflict that characterize the real-life contexts in which writing systems function should also help make the writing system specialist more aware that cooperation with other social researchers outside the usual linguistic and psychoeducational specializations (e.g., with sociologists, political scientists, economists, anthropologists) is absolutely necessary if the creation and revision of writing systems is to be understood more completely or achieved more humanely in the future than it has been in the past.

REFERENCES

Augst, G. (Ed). (1986). *New trends in graphemics and orthography*. Berlin: de Gruyter.

Avinor, M. (1977). *Briyat ha-olam v-shear yirakot*. Tel Aviv: Eked.

Basso, K. H., & Anderson, N. (1977). A Western Apache writing system: The symbols of Silas John. In J. A. Fishman (Ed.), *Advances in the creation and revision of writing systems* (pp. 3–16). The Hague: Mouton.

Burns, D. (1953). Social and political implications in the choice of an orthography. *Fundamental and Adult Education, 5*, 80–85.

Coulmas, F. (1983). Writing and literacy in China. In F. Coulmas & K. Ehlich (Eds.), *Writing in focus* (pp. 239–253). The Hague: Mouton.

De Francis, J. (1947). Japanese language reform: Politics and phonetics. *Far Eastern Survey, 16*, 217–220.

De Francis, J. (1977a). *Colonialism and language policy in Viet Nam*. The Hague: Mouton.

De Francis, J. (1977b). Language and script reform in China. In J. A. Fishman (Ed.), *Advances in the creation and revision of writing systems* (pp. 121–148). The Hague: Mouton.

De Francis, J. (1984). *The Chinese language: Fact and fantasy*. Honolulu: University Press of Hawaii.

Demoz, A. (1986). Language, literacy and society: The case of Ethiopia. In J. A. Fishman, et al. (Eds.), *The Fergusonian impact: In honor of Charles A. Ferguson; Vol. I: From phonology to society* (pp. 343–366). Berlin: Mouton de Gruyter.

Ehlich, K. (1983). Development of writing as social problem solving. In F. Coulmas & K. Ehlich (Eds.), *Writing in focus* (pp. 99–130). The Hague: Mouton.

Ferru, J. (1966). Possible repercussions of a technical and economic nature of the adoption of particular letters for the standard transcription of West African languages. In *Bamako Meeting on the Standardization of African Alphabets, Feb. 28–March 5, 1966*, pp. 435–457. Paris.

Fishman, J. A. (1977). Advances in the creation and revision of writing system. In J. A. Fishman (Ed.), *Advances in the creation and revision of writing systems*, pp. xi–xxviii. The Hague: Mouton.

Fishman, J. A. (1985). Why did Yiddish change? *Diachronica, 2*, 67–82.

Garvin, P. L. (1954). Literacy as a problem in language and culture. *Georgetown University Monograph Series on Languages and Linguistics, 7*, 117–129.

Geerts, G., van den Broeck, J., & Verdoodt, A. (1977). Successes and failures in Dutch spelling reform. In J. A. Fishman (Ed.), *Advances in the creation and revision of writing systems* (pp. 179–246). The Hague: Mouton.

Goody, J. R., & Watt, I. P. (1963). The consequences of literacy. *Comparative Studies in Society and History, 5*, 304–345.

Henze, P. (1977). Politics and alphabets in Inner Asia. In J. A. Fishman (Ed.), *Advances in the creation and revision of writing systems*, pp. 371–420. The Hague: Mouton.

Heyd, (1954). *Language reform in modern Turkey*. Jerusalem: The Israel Oriental Society.

Holm, W. S. (1972). *Some aspects of Navajo orthography*. Unpublished dissertation, University of New Mexico, Albuquerque.

James, G. C. A. (1985). The Tamil script reform: A case-study in folk linguistic standardization. In J. D. Woods (Ed.), *Language standards and their codification: Process and application* (pp. 102–153). Exeter: University of Exeter.

Kalogjera, D. (1985). Attitudes toward Serbo-Croatian language varieties. *International Journal of the Sociology of Language, 52*, 93–110.

Kotei, S. I. A. (1977). The West African autochthonous alphabets: An exercise in comparative palaeography. In J. A. Fishman (Ed.), *Advances in the creation and revision of writing systems* (pp. 55–75). The Hague: Mouton.

O'Murchu, M. (1977). Successes and failures in the modernization of Irish spelling. In J. A. Fishman (Ed.), *Advances in the creation and revision of writing systems* (pp. 267–289). The Hague: Mouton.

Mahmoud, Y. (1981). The Arabic writing system and deliberate orthographic change. *Al-'Arabiyya, 14*, 79–84.

Pattanayak, D. P. (1981). The problem and planning of scripts. In D. P. Pattanayak (Ed.), *Multilingualism and mother tongue eduction*, pp. 94–109. Delhi: Oxford University Press.

Quelquejay, C., & Bennigsen, A. (1961). *The evolution of the Muslim nationalities of the USSR and their linguistic problems*. London: Oxford.

Rabin, C., & Schlesinger, I. M. (1974). The influence of different systems of Hebrew orthography on reading efficiency. In J. A. Fishman (Ed.), *Advances
in language planning* (pp. 555–571). The Hague: Mouton.

Seybolt, P. J., & Chiang, G. K. K. (Eds.). (1979). *Language reform in China*. New
York: Sharpe.

Siromoney, G. (1978). Computer recognition of printed Tamil characters. *Pattern
Recognition, 10,* 107–120.

Sjoberg, A. F. (1966). Socio-cultural and linguistic factors in the development of
writing systems for preliterate peoples. In W. Bright (Ed.), *Sociolinguistics*
(pp. 260–276). The Hague: Mouton.

Walker, W. (1981). Native American writing systems. In C. A. Ferguson & S. B.
Heath (Eds.), *Language in the USA* (145–174). Cambridge, England: Cambridge University Press.

Walker, W. (1984). The design of native literacy programs and how literacy came
to the Cherokees. *Anthropological Linguistics, 26,* 161–169.

Winter, W. (1983). Tradition and innovation in alphabet making. In F. Coulmas
& K. Ehlich (Eds.), *Writing in focus* (pp. 239–253). The Hague: Mouton.

Young, R. W. (1977). Written Navajo: A brief history. In J. A. Fishman (Ed.),
Advances in the creation and revision of writing systems (pp. 459–470). The
Hague: Mouton.

Chapter 13

An Analysis of Oral and Literate Texts: Two Types of Reader–Writer Relationships in Hebrew and English

Michal Zellermayer
Tel–Aviv University

Recent research efforts to establish connections between the processes of reading comprehension and composing have attempted, as Louise W. Phelps explains, "to build up a unified theory of composition from already integrated concepts, instead of trying to reconcile separate theories of composing, reading, texts, and social action in context" (1985, p. 14). In this chapter I will compare two types of reader–text–writer relationships. I will attempt to show how readers and writers of two rhetorical communities meet certain conditions for negotiated meaning in order to achieve what Phelps calls "the overarching process" or "the cooperative enterprise whereby writers and readers construct meanings together, through the dialectical tension between their interactive and interdependent processes" (1985, p. 14).

The most obvious connection between reading and composing is the fact that the two processes include the same components: writer, reader, and text. It has also been established that both of the processes actually include the other one. In the comprehension process the reader must not only read like a reader, he must also read like a writer and recognize the author's plans in composing the text. The successful composer, on the other hand, devotes much of his or her composing time to reading in the course of reviewing and revising. Accordingly, two conditions that both reader and writer must meet in their negotiation for meaning through the medium of the text are *thoughtfulness* and *considerateness*.

THOUGHTFULNESS AND CONSIDERATENESS
IN READING AND WRITING

According to schema theory (Rumelhart, 1980), reading comprehension is a process in which the reader brings prior knowledge and expectations to a text. Extreme interpretations of schema theory such as Anderson's (1977) and Louise Rosenblatt's (1978) insist that the text gains meaning only through the reader's interpretation. Following this line of thought, metacognitive theorists of reading (Baker & Brown, 1984) explain that the successful reader is a thoughtful one. This reader sorts through existing knowledge and activates whatever is relevant to the comprehension of the text, identifies what must still be learned, and discovers the most useful way to do it. However, Bruce (1980) and Widdowson (1984) insist that the thoughtful activation of a schema is not enough for reading comprehension, since the good reader must also be considerate and empathize with the author's plans and intentions for writing the text. Pearson and Tierney (1984) call the reader's considerateness of the writer's plans an "alignment" with the author. They claim that alignment has a powerful effect on comprehension and memory. In support of their theory, they cite a study by Tierney which found that students who made a decision about how to align themselves with an author and his intentions were better able to figure out how to follow a complex set of directions for putting together a model water pump.

Current theories of composing combine heuristics and rhetoric to describe composing as a two-dimensional process. Heuristics treat composing as an act of inventing in which the thoughtful writer must find out what to write about and how to express it. In rhetoric, writing is viewed as a social act in which the writer confronts an audience and acknowledges its expectations.

Much has been written about the way writers appropriate their texts to conform with the implied readers' knowledge or schemata. Summarizing the research done on this issue, Rubin, Piché, Michlin, and Johnson (1984) explain that "competent writers engage in social cognition, representing to themselves their audiences' interests, values, prior knowledge, and experiential associations, as well as readers' linguistic skill and ongoing information-processing operations" (p. 297; see also Rubin, this volume; Rafoth, this volume). Building upon this perspective, this chapter addresses the way writers deal with readers' thoughtfulness. But rather than beginning with the writers' intentions, I will describe the reader–writer relationship by beginning with the text. I will argue that the text reflects a writer's considerateness of the reader's expectation to invest a certain amount of mental effort or thoughtfulness in the reading process. To illustrate this claim I will provide examples from two types of written texts—*oral* and *literate*—which are products of two different literacies and two different conventions for reader–writer relationships.

LITERACIES AND THEIR DIFFERENT VIEWS
OF THOUGHTFULNESS IN READING AND WRITING

The place of thoughtfulness and mental effort in the relationship between reading and writing is quite problematical. This issue is part of a broader controversy concerning learning with or without awareness. There are two views concerning thoughtfulness and mental effort in learning. The first view focuses on automatization as the major component of skill acquisition in the cognitive domain (Shiffrin & Dumais, 1981). For these theorists the first condition of learning is not mental effort. Mental effort, or mindfulness, it is thought, can only be achieved where automatic activities take place. And the mastery of automatized activities is a prerequisite for the learning of higher order cognitive skills. Salomon (1983) exemplifies the second view, claiming that "learning is strongly influenced by the amount of mental effort learners invest in processing the material—that is, the 'depth' or 'thoughtfulness' with which they process it" (p. 42).

Just as there are two views of thoughtfulness in learning, there are two different ways that cultures view the place of mindfulness or thoughtfulness in reading and writing. These differences become apparent both through studies of the development of Western literacy as compared with non-Western literacies, and through studies which compare oral and written language.

Historical studies of the evolution of modern consciousness (Innis, 1951; McLuhan, 1962) conceive Western literate history as a series of symbolic transformations in which notation systems are internalized. Goody and Watt (1963), Goody (1977), Havelock (1976), and Olson (1977), as well as Innis (1951) and McLuhan (1962), believe that when mediation of one type of symbols becomes automatic, the mind becomes able to manipulate yet a new system of signs. This new system is not only able to communicate newer and more complex information, but its messages are also more specific, more explicit and less context-dependent. The more automatic its decoding process, the more accessible the system is to new information and its elaboration. The phonetic alphabet and print have made the task of decoding both automatic and explicit and have helped readers to move from mere decoding to relatively more complex comprehension.

Ong (1982) and Olson (1977) emphasize that a phonetic/alphabetic system of signs, which allows for almost automatic decoding, is important for the production of explicit and autonomous texts. Olson argues that in the Western literate tradition the autonomous essay is seen as the ideal text, because the locus of meaning is in the text rather than in the reader's mind. The way in which essayist literacy conveys meaning differs sharply from the way meaning is typically conveyed in oral communication.

Ong (1982) explains that *orality* and *literacy* are not merely terms which describe nonliterate vs. literate cultures, but that they also designate different modes of communication like speech and writing, which exist simultaneously in the same culture. His ideas on orality and literacy are further developed by Tannen (1982, 1985), who explains that orality and literacy are not simply products of communication systems which use speech or writing for their chief means of expression, but that they are a function of the degree of contextualization or decontextualization cues their spoken or written texts include. According to Tannen (1982) we can use the term *oral text* for a written text which is based on speech-like communication and is context dependent, while the term *literate text* may be applied to a planned speech which is given orally but has the autonomous qualities of a written text. Tannen (1982) devises an oral/literate discourse continuum, in which written or spoken texts may be compared according to their relative reliance on contextualization or decontextualization cues. The more that texts depend on contextual cues (which, like the paralinguistic cues in speech, focus on involvement between the parties), the closer they are to the oral pole of the continuum. The more texts depend on decontextualization cues (which focus on independence from immediate context and on establishing distance between the participants), the closer they are to the literate end.

That contextualizing and decontextualizing cues are indicative of the amount of involvement or distancing between the participants has already been shown in the work of discourse analysts such as Gumperz (1982), Labov (1972), and Chafe (1982, 1985). Gumperz (1982) and Gumperz, Kaltman, and O'Connor (1984) focus on the use of cohesive markers in discourse and show how transitions and references to information in the text replace paralinguistic cues in decontextualizing language. Labov (1972) points out the significance of intensifiers in channeling the reader's attention to important information in the text. Chafe (1982) claims that the literate text is characterized by syntactical structures such as nominalization, subordination, and modification. Like cohesive markers and intensifiers, these syntactical structures serve as decontextualization cues because they pack many idea units into sentences and thus prepare the information for storage in compact units in the reader's long-term memory. But decontextualization cues are important not only because they explicate and integrate information. Such cues are also important, according to Phelps (1985), because they enhance automaticity, and establish a linear and climactic flow of energy for readers who may then integrate information cumulatively and effortlessly.

My claim is that contextualization or decontextualization cues in written texts are indicative of the writer's considerateness of reader's expectations to invest a certain amount of mental effort or thoughtfulness in the reading process, and that such expectations vary in different rhetorical communities. Purves and Purves (1986), who discuss the cultural aspect of such expectations, raise the following questions for cross-cultural research:

> Do different communities view text and textuality in similar ways? How do their views, if they differ, affect each other? Do tendencies and trends concerning the writing activity and associated issues of each community affect each other and, if so, how? (p. 192)

ORAL AND LITERATE TEXTS

Intrigued by questions such as these, as well as by notions of the significance of the phonetic alphabet to the development of the literate text and literate culture, I decided to look at contextualization and decontextualization cues in specific *oral texts* and *literate texts*. These are actually two groups of written texts composed by contemporary Jewish writers in the same genre—the novel. Within each novel, the passages selected served the same function—exposition. What distinguishes them is that they were conceived within two different literacies for two different audiences. The *oral* group of texts, which are composed by writers whose first literacy and schooling has been attained in Hebrew, is aimed at an audience of the same rhetorical community—readers whose first literacy and schooling is Hebrew; the *literate* group written in the Western literate tradition is written for an audience whose concept of literacy has been shaped by the essayist tradition and the model of the explicit text.

Hebrew literacy has for 2,000 years resisted all attempts to adopt a phonetic writing system and thus distance itself from its oral roots. In spite of several attempts to impose a fully phonetic alphabet on the culture, Hebrew writing still adheres to a consonantal system. It is a context-dependent writing system in a sense that one has to infer the vowels from the context of the utterance. In a Hebrew text a full sentence may be ambiguous because of the lack of vowels. The sentence *sm avi hyh rv*, for example, could be decoded in two ways: *šam avi hayah rav*—my father was a rabbi there, or *šem avi hayah rav*—my father's name was Rav. Readers must use previous information in the text to make the right choice. Moreover, complete mastery of the writing system is not sufficient for the reader of Hebrew. Rosen (1977) and Rabin (1975) insist that the reader of Hebrew texts must also be acquainted with the repertoire of canonical texts shared by members of the culture, since the repertoire forms a significant part of the body of shared knowledge necessary for reading comprehension. Schooling in Israel does not only teach the skill of decoding texts written in a vowelless system, but attempts to supply the necessary repertoire for comprehending such texts. Second graders in Israel already read and recite segments of the Hebrew Bible. Moreover, their acquaintance with such texts begins even before they learn to read since contextual cues in the form of archaic structures taken from ancient texts can even be found in books written for preschool children. So from a very early age, children accept the dependence of written texts on contextual information. The important message conveyed from early childhood on is that a written text can be vague and ambiguous and that the reader must carry the burden of elaborating its information.

When Havelock (1976) describes the development of Western literacy, he makes the radical argument that non-Western writing systems, such as Hebrew, which have not adopted the fully phonetic alphabet, developed a literacy which is inefficient in contrast to Western literacy. Among the consequences of such literacy, according to Havelock, is the insufficient development of higher cognitive skills. Havelock's claim has since been tempered by Scribner and Cole (1981), who showed that literacy alone cannot form cognitive aptitudes, but that the combination of literacy and schooling shapes a culture's style of conceptualization. There is now a general agreement among writers on literacy that different societies make different uses of literacy and that these uses have different cognitive implications.

Both the context-dependent writing system of Hebrew and the school's emphasis on the mnemonic recitation of canonical texts are, according to Ong (1982) and Scribner and Cole (1981), very important indications for a strong oral tradition. Thus I am claiming that the original Hebrew texts constitute *oral texts* constructed within an oral tradition. The original English texts I am taking to be *literate texts* constructed within a literate tradition. A comparison of *oral* texts and *literate* texts along with their translations to the respective audiences provides an excellent opportunity to identify systematic additions or deletions of contextualization and decontextualization cues. At the same time, the cues provide information about the differences between reader/writer expectations existing in the two literacies and the way that the different rhetorical communities view textuality.

The comparison in this study focuses mainly on such decontextualization cues as (1) cohesion, (2) elaboration, and (3) integration in eight texts and in their translations, while a subsidiary analysis examined order of information and metaphorization. Specific stylistic variables tabulated are: (1) the use of cohesive ties such as personal and demonstrative references, additive connectors, simple conjunctions (which, who, that, when), and logical conjunctions in Hebrew and English source texts and their translations; (2) the proportion of intensifiers (modifiers and qualifiers) in relation to the number of nouns in the texts; (3) the ratio of numbers of propositions to clauses as an indication of the extent of syntactical integration in the text.

Table 1 summarizes quantitative indexes of cohesion, intensification, and integration. It demonstrates in a gross manner how—by adding contextualization or decontextualization cues—translations change the direction of information processing in the text from a recursive direction to a more linear one in which information can flow more automatically (Hebrew to English); or from a linear direction to a more recursive one (English to Hebrew). Thus the reader–writer relationship changes from one which demands reader elaboration to one in which the writer supplies elaboration in the text (Hebrew to English); or from a text-based elaboration to a somewhat vague and more implicit text demanding more mental investment (English to Hebrew). Naturally, each of the texts included in this study has its own idyosyncratic characteristics and cannot in every aspect be compared directly with others. I found, however, that what each of these groups of oral and literate texts did have in common was the fact that texts shifted in certain directions during translation to the opposite language. Excerpts from the corpus illustrate more specifically these patterns of rhetorical/cultural transformations.

Table 1.   Comparisons of Cohesive Ties, Intensifiers, and Integrative Devices in Hebrew and English Source Texts and Their Respective Translations

Categories		Hebrew Source Texts	English Target Texts	English Source Texts	Hebrew Target Texts
Cohesive ties	Personal reference	139.75	141.25	124.5	127
	Additive connectors	37.75	26.75	25	36
	Which, who, that, when	25.5	19.5	10	25.5
	Logical conjunction	17.25	19.25	31.5	26.25
Intensifiers	Modifiers and qualifiers:nouns	2.05	2.44	1.87	1.44
Integrative devices	Propositions:clauses	3.86	3.06	3.01	3.37

SHIFTS IN COHESION

Hebrew to English

Gumperz (1982), Tannen (1982), and Phelps (1985) emphasize the significance of cohesive ties for both decontextualization and integration of information in a written text. My study has found that all English translations of Hebrew texts add cohesive markers, such as personal and demonstrative reference and logical conjunction. These markers have a double function: They establish a tighter connection between new and given information, and they also give the readers cues about the global arrangement of information. These cues help readers categorize texts into known logical schemata, such as comparison, cause and effect, or problem/solution. Here is a selection from the English translation of *With His Own Hands* by Moshe Shamir (1970, p. 1), in which the added personal pronouns are underlined, while the lexical item deleted from the Hebrew source text (1957, p. 1) is in square brackets:

> Elik was born of the sea. That's the way that father used to tell it when we would be sitting on the verandah of [the] our little house on summer evenings.

The following passage from Kaniuk's *Rockinghorse* (1974, p. 7) shows how the addition of conjunctives, such as "if" as well as the temporal reference "then" and "now," rearrange information for the English translation (1977, p. 1) in a clearer compare/contrast schema than that which appeared on the Hebrew source text. (For present purposes I compare the translated version with a literal rendition of the original Hebrew.):

Hebrew Source Text	English Target Text
(Literal translation)	(Published translation)
What has not yet been finished is finished now.	If I had anything in me then there is nothing now.

The English translation of this passage is clearly more explicit, more decontextualized, and more integrated than the Hebrew original.

English to Hebrew

Although translation theory claims that all translations shift toward greater explicitness (Blum–Kulka, 1986), my studies show that this is not always the case in English–Hebrew translation. The following passage demonstrates that Hebrew target texts often opt for a rendition that is rather redundant and in some sense disorderly. The shift toward a more oral style satisfies the Hebrew reader's expectation to participate in a more involved manner in processing the text. Where the English source text uses personal reference or ellipsis—a relatively "tight" way of integrating information—the Hebrew target text offers lexical repetition of words constituting the given information. In these examples I follow the convention of underlining items added in translation and bracketing items deleted from the source text.

> Herzog scarcely knew what to think of this scrawling. He yielded to the excitement that inspired it and suspected that [it] the scrawling might be a symptom of disintegration. (Bellow, 1961, p. 9 & 1965, p. 7).

> I hate funerals—I hate funerals passionately because there is always something morbid about them and I do my best to avoid going to any (especially my [own] funeral). (Heller, 1975, p. 5, & 1979, p. 10).

The lexical repetition in the Hebrew target text functions here more as a contextualization cue rather than a decontextualization cue because the relationship between new and old information is not signaled by the immediate syntactical environment. One has to draw on linguistic context and decide whether the repeated item has or has not been mentioned previously (i.e., more remotely) in the text.

SHIFTS IN INTENSIFICATION

Hebrew to English

Texts, especially written texts, work to direct the reader to important information. Discourse markers which help maintain the attention of the reader function as evaluative devices which point out relationships among ideas, highlight relative importance, and so on. Among the evaluative devices which Labov (1972) mentions are logical conjunctions, repetitions, and demonstrative reference. As shown in the preceding section, these evaluative devices function also as cohesive ties providing transitions and connections. A comparison of Hebrew source texts and their English translations shows that the addition of such cohesive ties not only helps integrate information in a more compact arrangement but also adds important intensification and salience to the information in the text. Here are some examples from English translations of Hebrew source texts where the evaluative devices added in translation are underlined:

> I have written somewhere in these pages. (Oz, 1968, p. 195, & 1972, p. 283)

A woman of thirty is not <u>quite the same as</u> a girl of twenty. (Oz, 1968, p. 195, & 1972, p. 283)

<u>What</u> wonderful colors <u>that</u> kingfish. (Shamir, 1957, p. 12, & 1970, p. 2)

The sea was <u>right</u> next to our house, a <u>mere</u> couple of steps away. (Shamir, 1957, p. 12, & 1970, p. 2)

In the above illustrations the relative vagueness of the Hebrew source text becomes apparent when the underlined evaluative information is deleted.

English to Hebrew

When translating into Hebrew and attempting to accommodate a reader who expects to deal with a certain amount of vagueness, the translation process shifts away from explication rather than toward it. Many translations into Hebrew have been found to drop evaluative devices provided in the original English texts, as in the following passages from Malamud (1973, p. 7, & 1973, p. 10) and Potok (1967, p. 11, & 1968, p. 15):

English Source Text	Hebrew Target Text
<u>Just</u> enough to be cold	Enough to be cold
You saw <u>your</u> inspired breath. (Malamud)	The inspired breath can be seen.
I had become <u>quite</u> adept at second base. (Potok)	I had become adept at second base.

SHIFTS IN INTEGRATION

Hebrew to English

I have shown that English texts are relatively more cohesive and explicit in the way they connect information, both locally and globally, than their Hebrew counterparts. Chafe (1982, 1985) points out that syntactical structures serve an important function in the integration of information in a written text. In writing, more so than in speech, we tend to pack information into compact units which are smaller than clauses. Constructions which integrate information in this fashion include nominalizations, attributive adjectives, gerundive and participial phrases, as well as series and conjoined phrases.

In the Hebrew source texts there are about three propositions to each clause, while in their English translations the relationship of propositions to clauses moves closer to four propositions per clause. For example, in the following sentence from Shamir (1957, p. 12), the English translation (1970, p. 2) transforms a coordinate/subordinate structure of six clauses into a single clause unit without deleting any of the information:

Hebrew Source Text	English Target Text
The senses sharpen, and only now the boy realizes that night [is] above him—but the sea glimmers behind and the waves pound heavily as if they become black oil.	Your senses sharpened, only now do you become aware of the night spread out above you with only the sea glimmering behind you and waves, oily black, pounding heavily.

English to Hebrew

Translations into Hebrew often transform sentences in the opposite manner and replace phrases by clauses. In the following citation from Heller (1975, p. 6), a one-clause sentence in English disintegrates into a coordinate/subordinate structure of three clauses in Hebrew (1979, p. 11):

English Source Text	Hebrew Target Text
It bothered me to have my family around me staring at me.	It bothered me that my family was standing around and [it] was staring at me.

If integration is one of the main characteristics of a literate text, Hebrew texts are clearly more oral. Their relatively strung-along sequencing of information brings them closer to a sort of episodic unfolding. This kind of sequence mirrors the process by which writers envision information in their creative process. On the other hand, more highly integrated units presumably can be stored more efficiently in the reader's long term memory.

SHIFTS IN LINEARITY

Hebrew to English

Ong (1982) and Olson (1977) emphasize the linear nature of literacy in which information is arranged climactically with minimal repetition, redundancy, or ambiguity. One of the chief concerns of translators from Hebrew to English is to eliminate potential ambiguities. One of the most common ways of doing so is by reordering information so that relationships between constituents become clearer. In the original sentence from Oz (1968, p. 196) presented below, the reader must decide whether the temporal adverbial "once, many years ago" modifies the main clause ("Have you forgotten, Michael") or the subordinate one ("when we sat together in Cafe Atara"). The English translation (1972, p. 285) places that phrase in a position which clearly modifies only the subordinate clause:

Hebrew Source Text	English Target Text
Have you forgotten, Michael, many years ago, when we sat to-gether in Cafe Atara that . . .	Have you forgotten, Michael, how you said once, many years ago when we were sitting together in Cafe Atara that . . .

Another type of shift in linearity is evident in that exercise of topic control. Translators into English seem to be bothered by the fact that consecutive clauses have different topics, probably because this diffusion of information puts an extra burden on the reader. Thus sentences which have served different topics, like the following one from Shamir (1957, p. 12), are transformed into a single topic sentence. In this case the English translation (1970, p. 3) interposes an indeterminate "you" as unifying topic.

Hebrew Source Text	English Target Text
Of course—barefoot always. And first thing—the dipping of the feet: and since above a certain height in the leg starts that bothersome thing which is called trousers—one rolls them up as much as possible, until the heavy pockets are exposed hanging heavily (marbles, bottle caps, a penknife, a bicycle spanner) and until it simply does not work any more.	You're always barefoot, of course. And the first thing you do is dip your feet in: but since at certain height up your legs you come against that bothersome and totally unnecessary encumbrance called trousers, you roll them up as far as they go, exposing heavily laden pockets (marbles, bottle-caps, a key, a penknife, a bicycle spanner) which sag down limply, and they just won't go any higher.

The Hebrew source text cited above appears similar to what Linda Flower (1979) calls "a writer-based prose." Considered from the perspective of academic expectations in a literate society, writer-based prose is not sufficiently developed and is not considerate enough of audience expectations. Yet the passage was written by one of the most prominent contemporary Hebrew writers; it conforms to the expectations of readers versed in a more oral-based culture.

English to Hebrew

Perhaps because they do not consider linearity a significant expectation of Hebrew readers, translators of the English source texts to Hebrew often neglect to maintain the uniformity of topic found in the original texts. For example, in the following sentence from Heller (1975, p. 7), the original English version has a single topic in two conjoined predicates. It is translated in Hebrew (1979, p. 12) into a sentence which has different topics in two adjacent independent clauses.

English Source Text	Hebrew Target Text
But they gave my wife the creeps and kept her in a constant state of fright.	But they gave my wife the creeps and she was in a state of constant fright because of them.

Notice that the diffusion of topics in the Hebrew target text invites the redundant clause "because of them."

SHIFTS IN METAPHORIZATION

Metaphorization is a well-known problem for translation because metaphors cannot be readily translated. Good translators tend to replace a metaphor in the source language by another one in the target language so that the poetic-figurative effect of the metaphor is not lost. Hebrew texts typically contain two types of metaphors: new metaphors created by the writer for the purpose of that particular text, and metaphors created by the introduction of archaic structures into a new environment. The dependence of Hebrew literacy on knowledge originating in canonical texts has already been mentioned. The creative element in such a metaphor lies in the new relationship drawn between the text and the canonized text. In English, metaphors are made original by design; they do not bind the relevance of the utterance to an old context. (Indeed, we refer disparagingly to "dead" metaphors as clichés.) The use of figurative speech in live metaphors introduces only new information.

A literal English translation of the Hebrew way of referring to archaic structures is practically impossible because contemporary English writing has no counterpart practice. Consider, by way of illustration, what happens to a sentence from the English source text written by Malamud (1973, p. 3) when translated into Hebrew (1973, p. 7):

English Source Text	Hebrew Target Text
He wrestles to sleep again but can't, unease like a horse dragging him by both bound legs out of bed.	He tries to return to sleep again but can't; his soul's unease drags him like a horse in his bound legs. (The verb "bound" appears here in its archaic form, the way it is used in the Biblical story of Isaac's sacrifice.)

The sentence in the English source text opens with the metaphor in the first verb—"he *wrestles* to sleep," which immediately evokes the strong effect of a contrast between the active verb "wrestle" and the static complement "to sleep." The same contrast is developed in the second part of the sentence in the description of the way the writer is being forcibly dragged out of bed by a mere feeling of unease. The description of being acted upon by stronger forces is reinforced by the comparison at the end of the sentence with a horse dragging the writer, whose legs are bound. In the Hebrew target text the opening metaphoric verb "wrestles" is replaced by a simple verb "tries." However, the complement "to sleep" is manipulated in an archaic style in the collocation "to return and to sleep," which implies a repetitive effort on the part of the writer to go back to sleep. Still, the translation is less metaphoric and less vivid in this part of the sentence. However, this difference is compensated for at the very end of the sentence where the simple comparison with a horse dragging the unwilling bound-legged writer is further compared, through the use of the archaic version of the verb "bound," to the historical incident of the sacrifice of Isaac by his father, Abraham.

CONCLUSION

In this chapter I have discussed various ways in which texts written for two different rhetorical communities demonstrate considerateness to their respective audience's thoughtfulness. Hebrew texts (especially the source texts) adjust their coherence to an audience that expects to participate quite actively in the processing of information. English texts accommodate readers who expect a more effortless flow of comprehension through a tighter, more logical, more integrated, and more explicit textual scheme, which enhances a simultaneous grasp of the text's design and its ideas.

These differences between two types of rhetorical expectations become apparent when we compare each group of texts with their translations in the respective language and follow the shifts made consistently in the published translations. I have shown how English target texts add decontextualization cues, such as cohesion markers, intensifiers, integrative devices, and adjustments of information ordering. These features help transform the text into a more *literate* or *writing-like* medium elaborated by the translator to allow a smooth and automatic processing by the reader. Conversely, I have shown that Hebrew target texts translated from English source texts delete some of these decontextualization cues and add some references to information in Hebrew canonical texts as a way of providing additional contextualization cues for the Hebrew reader and to transform the text into a more *oral* or *speech-like* medium, probably in order to satisfy the expectation of Hebrew readers to take a more active part in text processing.

Reder (1985) ponders the question of whether elaboration by reader or elaboration by writer is more effective for comprehension. Each type of elaboration has proven, according to her, to be more effective for certain types of readers and different types of reading tasks. It seems from the description of these two different types of text—the oral and the literate—that the main difference between them is that, indeed, they are designed for two different types of readers and two different reading tasks.

These two different reading tasks have been described by Rosenblatt (1985) as demanding different stances by the reader. The first stance, which she calls the "aesthetic stance," demands mindfulness of the aesthetic transaction, in which the reader's attention is focused on what he is living during the reading event. The text comes into being through the reader's awareness of what it activated within him. The other type of reading is described by Rosenblatt as an "efferent stance," in which the reader's attention is centered on what is retained as residue after the actual reading event. Rosenblatt claims that any reading transaction will fall somewhere along the continuum between the aesthetic and the efferent.

My study examined texts of two rhetorical communities. From the differences between the texts I inferred the varying expectations of two rhetorical communities as to how close they should place their reading transaction to either end of the continuum. The rhetorical community of *oral texts*—like the Hebrew community—places its reading process close to the aesthetic stance, which requires a great deal of thoughtfulness on the part of the reader. The community of more *literate texts*—like the English community—is closer to the efferent stance of reading, which requires less thoughtfulness on the part of the reader and more considerateness on the part of the writer. Both methods work for the different communities. As Bruner (1985, p. 599) writes,

> Perhaps style is, after all, just a specification about strategy preference. There is some sort of stylistic balance operating in strategy construction about which we know very little. We had better know more about such matters.

REFERENCES

Anderson, R. C. (1977). The notion of schemata and the educational enterprise. In R. C. Anderson, R. J. Spiro, & W. E. Montague (Eds.), *Schooling and the acquisition of knowledge*. Hillsdale, NJ: Erlbaum.

Baker, L., & Brown, A. L. (1984). Cognitive monitoring in reading. In J. Flood (Ed.), *Understanding reading comprehension*. Delaware: International Reading Association.

Bellow, S. (1961). *Herzog.* New York: Avon Books. Translated into Hebrew by Eliyahu Porat (1965). Tel Aviv: Sifriat Poalim.

Blum–Kulka, S. (1986). Shifts in cohesion and coherence in translation. In J. House–Edmondson & S. Blum–Kulka, (Eds.), *Interlingual and intercultural communication: Discourse and cognition in translation.* Tubingen: Gunter Narr Verlag.

Bruce, B. C. (1980). Plans and social action. In R. J. Spiro, B. C. Bruce, & W. F. Brewer (Eds.), *Theoretical issues in reading comprehension.* Hillsdale, NJ: Erlbaum.

Bruner, J. (1985). On teaching thinking: An afterthought. In S. F. Chipman, J. W. Segal, & R. Glaser (Eds.), *Thinking and learning skills, Vol. 2.* Hillsdale, NJ: Erlbaum.

Chafe, W. L. (1982). Integration and involvement in speaking, writing and oral literature. In D. Tannen (Ed.), *Oral and written language.* Norwood, NJ: Ablex.

Chafe, W. L. (1985). Linguistic differences produced by differences between speech and writing. In D. R. Olson, N. Torrance, & A. Hildyard (Eds.), *Literacy, language and learning: The nature and concequences of reading and writing.* New York and London: Cambridge University Press.

Flower, L. (1979). Writer-based prose: A cognitive basis for problems in writing. *College English, 41,* 19–37.

Goody, J. (1977). *The domestication of the savage mind.* Cambridge, England: Cambridge University Press.

Goody, J., & Watt, I. (1963). The consequences of literacy. *Comparative Studies in History and Society, 5,* 304–345.

Gumperz, J. J. (1982). *Discourse Strategies.* New York and London: Cambridge University Press.

Gumperz, J. J., Kaltman, H., & O'Connor, M. C. (1984). Cohesion in spoken and written discourse: Ethnic style and the transition to literacy. In D. Tannen (Ed.), *Coherence in spoken and written discourse.* Norwood, NJ: Ablex.

Havelock, E. (1976). *Origins of Western literacy.* Toronto: The Ontario Institute for Studies in Education.

Heller, J. (1975). *Something Happened.* New York: Ballentine Books. Translated into Hebrew by Ophira Rahat (1979). Tel Aviv: Zmora, Bitan, Modan.

Innis, H. A. (1951). *The bias of communication.* Toronto: University of Toronto Press.

Kaniuk, Y. (1974). *Rockinghorse.* Tel Aviv: Sifriat Poalim. Translated into English by Richard Flantz (1977). New York: Harper & Row.

Labov, W. (1972). The transformation of experience in narrative syntax. In W. Labov (Ed.), *Language in the inner city.* Philadelphia: University of Pennsylvania Press.

Malamud, B. (1973). *The Tenants.* New York: Farrar, Straus & Giroux. Translated into Hebrew by Baruch Modan (1973). Tel Aviv: Am Oved.

McLuhan, M. (1962). *The Guttenberg galaxy: The making of typographic man.* Toronto: University of Toronto Press.

Olson, D. R. (1977). From utterance to text. *Harvard Educational Review, 47(3),* 257–281.

Ong, W. (1982). *Orality and literacy*. London: Methuen.

Oz, A. (1968). *My Michael*. Tel Aviv: Am Oved. Translated into English by Nicholas de Lange (1972). New York: Knopf.

Pearson, D. P., & Tierney, R. J. (1984). On becoming a thoughtful reader: Learning to read like a writer. In A. C. Purves & O. Niles (Eds.), *Becoming readers in a complex society*. Chicago: National Society for the Study of Education.

Phelps, L. W. (1985). Dialectics of coherence: Toward an integrative theory. *College English, 47*(1), 12–29.

Potok, C. (1967). *The Chosen*. New York: Alfred A. Knopf. Translated into Hebrew by Abraham Oren (1968). Tel Aviv: Zellikovitz.

Purves, A. C., & Purves, W. C. (1986). Viewpoints: Cultures, text models, and the activity of writing. *Research in the Teaching of English, 20*(2), 174–197.

Rabin, C. (1975). The ancient in the modern: Ancient source materials in present day Hebrew writing. In H. H. Paper (Ed.), *Language and texts: The nature of linguistic evidence*. Ann Arbor: University of Michigan Press.

Reder, L. M. (1985). Techniques available to author, teacher and reader to improve retention of main ideas of a chapter. In S. F. Chipman, J. W. Segal & R. Glaser (Eds.), *Thinking and learning skills, Vol. 2*. Hillsdale, NJ: Erlbaum.

Rosen H. (1977). *Contemporary Hebrew*. The Hague: Mouton.

Rosenblatt, L. M. (1978). *The reader, the text, the poem: The transactional theory of the literary work*. Carbondale: Southern Illinois University Press.

Rosenblatt, L. M. (1985). The transactional theory of the literary work: Implications for research. In C. R. Cooper (Ed.), *Researching response to literature and the teaching of literature: Points of departure*. Norwood, NJ: Ablex.

Rubin, D. L., Piché, G, Michlin, M. L., & Johnson, F. L. (1985). Social cognitive ability as a predictor of the quality of fourth-graders' written narrative. In R. Beach & L. S. Bridwell (Eds.), *New directions in composition research*. New York: Guilford Press.

Rumelhart, D. E. (1980). Schemata: The building blocks of cognition. In R. J. Spiro, B. Bruce, & W. Brewer (Eds.), *Theoretical issues in reading comprehension*. Hillsdale, NJ: Erlbaum.

Salomon, G. (1983). The different investment of mental effort in learning from different sources. *Educational Psychologist, 18*(1), 42–50.

Scribner, S., & Cole, M. (1981). *The psychology of literacy*. Cambridge, MA: Harvard University Press.

Shamir, M. (1957). *With his own hands*. Tel Aviv: Sifriat Poalim. Translated into English by Joseph Schachter. (1970). Jerusalem: Hebrew University Press.

Shiffrin, R. M., & Dumais, S. (1981). The development of automation. In J. R. Anderson (Ed.), *Cognitive skills and their acquisition*. Hillsdale, NJ: Erlbaum.

Tannen, D. (1982). The oral/literate continuum in discourse. In D. Tannen (Ed.), *Oral and written language*. Norwood, NJ: Ablex.

Tannen, D. (1985). Relative focus in involvement in oral and written discourse. In D. R. Olson, N. Torrance, & A. Hildyard (Eds.), *Literacy, language and learning: The nature and consequences of reading and writing*. London and New York: Cambridge University Press.

Widdowson, H. G. (1984). *Explorations in applied linguistics II*. London: Oxford University Press.

Chapter 14

The Ecology of Literacy: Negotiating Writing Standards in a Caribbean Setting

Patricia Irvine
Nan Elsasser
Working Classroom, Inc.
Albuquerque, New Mexico

Until recently, *campesinos* on the small peasant farms of Panama planted their rice using the same slow, back-breaking method their great grand-parents used. They carried seeds in a flour sack slung over a shoulder. One hand held a pointed stick used to puncture the earth while the other hand carefully removed a seed from the bag and deposited it in the hole. The farmer moved forward slowly, repeating the one–two movement of hands, the bending and straightening, all through the weeks of planting.

This grinding routine was changed when Lalo Mendez, a young stu-dent who would later become the governor of Darién Province, filled a hollow stick with seeds and added a simple mechanical catch at the bot-tom. Farmers could plunge one end into the soil, press the catch, and release a seed into the hole.

Hailed by local farmers, the young inventor was awarded a trip to the United States. His North American hosts were rice growers whose fields were almost as wide as Panama. They invited the young student to tour their farms. Lalo Mendez, whose hollow stick had just halved the mis-ery of planting and doubled potential production in his own country, watched as a Cessna droned over acres of fields, scattering rice seeds in its wake (M. Collela, personal communication, June 7, 1986).

We don't know how young Lalo felt when presented with the con-trast between his invention and aerial seeding, but the importance of his invention was in no way diminished; it was a major technological ad-vance for the villagers who worked small, subsistence plots and had no access to airplanes.

The inappropriateness of seeding by Cessna does not imply that Panamanians remained dependent on the hollow stick because each change in technology ultimately affects layer upon layer of social and physical ecology. The increased production resulting from innovations in technology may necessitate the construction of roads linking the village to towns. Accessible markets may expand production, which would require tractors. The cost of the machinery and fuel could lead to cooperatives, bank loans, or the sale of small plots to wealthier individuals. Whatever happens, the social and economic relations of campesino society would be altered.

We believe literacy curricula, like technology, impact significantly on delicate human ecologies. The kind of curriculum that works best in one society may not be appropriate for another. Some researchers have recognized that literacy shapes and is shaped by the larger socioeconomic and political ecology (Fishman, this volume; Heath, 1983; Hymes, 1980; Scribner & Cole, 1981). However, few educators have found effective ways to use this premise in their classroom teaching. Although we ourselves had worked assiduously to incorporate Freirian principles (e.g., Elsasser & John–Steiner, 1977; Freire, 1970) into our curricula, we realized with chagrin that we were victims and perpetrators of the race, class, and geopolitical biases which structure the practice of advanced literacy. As English professors at the College of the Virgin Islands, a public institution in a U. S. colony, we found ourselves delivering "Cessnas."

We ignored the fact that writing systems, genres and conventions which we take for granted evolved to meet the needs of particular societies at particular times. Thus, when teachers assign term papers or essay exams, subtract points for spelling or subject–verb agreement errors, or use standardized tests, they impose forms and social functions of written English that developed in England or North America and that do not necessarily meet the needs of other communities throughout the world. In fact, the proliferation of regional varieties of written English (Bailey & Gorlach, 1982; Collins, 1968; Obeichina, 1972; Platt, 1980) attest to the interaction between linguistic forms and functions and belie the concept of a single, universal criterion of "good" writing. Yet, as in the story of the emperor's new clothes, educators cling to a pretense of academic rigor which hinders the development of realistic and useful indigenous models.

EXAMINING THE WRITING CRISIS

Our search to penetrate this mirage began at the College of the Virgin Islands in response to a "crisis." Students were failing the Writing Proficiency Exam, a 400-word narrative-descriptive essay required for graduation, at a rate exceeding 60%. The results caused alarm, since those who failed had completed two to five semesters of English and 30 to 120 other credit hours of coursework.

Not surprisingly, the alarm was followed by a round of finger-pointing and recrimination. Students said the test was too hard and graded too strictly. English faculty claimed that other faculty did not require enough writing, while faculty in other disciplines countered that students hadn't been taught the rudiments of academic writing in composition classes. Both groups of faculty blamed students for coming from an "oral" culture and from homes which did not encourage reading and writing.

We undertook our investigation of the high failure rate determined, like everyone else, to find a culprit. But each time we thought we had an answer, we found we had only unraveled another small knot in a tangled ball of string. We tested and rejected one possibility after another, finally discovering what we should have known all along–that vague words like *college-level writing, remediation,* and *standards* mask the profoundly diverse educational experiences of college students and perpetuate the pretense that we as instructors adhere to uniform criteria of instruction and evaluation. This jargon blinded our imagination and kept us searching for simple answers. We looked past the obvious: Most of our students, unlike us, were writing in a language other than their own, a language laden with the legacies of class and colonialism. They were writing papers assigned by members of an alien and dominating society and reading texts written by and designed for other communities.

Writing Quality on the Proficiency Test

Initially, we doubted whether a 90-minute test was a valid or reliable indicator of writing ability, particularly since the composition program stressed leisurely rewriting. We therefore expected to find that the essays were graded too stringently. Our first shock came when we actually looked at samples of passing essays. One which received 9 out of 10 possible points opened as follows (all samples appear as in the originals):

THE TEACHER WHO TAUGHT ME HOW TO BE RESPECTFUL
AND GAIN RESPECT

Memories are treasured by all human beings. It maybe some good that have happened to us long ago as children or even as adults. Sometimes we maybe feeling depressed and just by recalling something that happened a long time ago an instant smile is brought to our face or a tear to our eye. Right down I going to take a walk down memory lane.

I the British islands you are not exposed to many of the other things that are in the other parts of the world. For instance, in elementary school there is no big fancy classrooms with individual desk and chair. Instead, there is one large room with no petitions dividing the class rooms and some long benches that are shared by six or seven classes with one teacher assigned to a particular class. . . .

The introduction to this essay failed to allude to the assigned topic and contained several grammar and diction errors; the second paragraph lacked organization, unity, and coherence. Neither this nor other passing essays struck us as good examples of college-level writing. Indignant, we reversed our stance: The test was too easy and the English faculty's standards were inexcusably slack. We switched from lamenting the high failure rate to wondering how so many essays had passed.

Our indignation grew when we read the *prescriptives*, postmortems which English faculty attached to failing essays. In a hopelessly disorganized and underdeveloped essay, the following errors were singled out:

The main problem is *verb usage*:

wrong tenses = past years . . . teachers asks
shifts in tense = present and past tenses mixed
endings omitted = He never pass me by . . .
        If he *ask* me a question . . .
noun endings omitted = all my decision
spelling - thought for taught/quotes misused
Content could be more specific; it's not clear at the top of page two.

We were jolted by the disparity between these superficial comments, the text itself, and the stated criteria for the test, which emphasized logical organization and concrete details:

1. Read the topic carefully. Your treatment of the subject must be relevant and thorough.
2. Organize your ideas logically and support your generalizations with specific references and concrete examples.
3. Your paper will be evaluated for its content and organization as well as sentence structure, punctuation, diction, grammar, and mechanics.
4. Write in ink. You may make corrections if you take care to keep your writing legible. '

At this point, we were convinced that no standards existed and that grading was entirely capricious. In order to substantiate this conclusion, we examined the first paragraph, a middle paragraph, and the last paragraph of six passing and six failing papers on the same topic: "Describe a teacher who made an impression on you and tell why."

We were wrong again. Although exam graders did not adhere strictly to traditional canons as reflected in the stated criteria, neither did they capitulate to immature writing. Standards indeed existed at the College of the Virgin Islands, but they were neither as stringent nor as lax as we once believed.

No essay passed if it did not address the assigned topic, contain at least 350 words and include an introduction, a conclusion, and at least two intervening paragraphs. Moreover, many papers which met these minimum requirements still failed.

Surprisingly, the features which actually distinguished passing from failing essays did not match those articulated by faculty in the prescriptives, the stated criteria, or even our own conceptions of what would be important. This discovery was our first insight into the negotiation process which ultimately determines standards within a particular context.

Several features which never appeared in the formally stated guidelines turned out to differentiate passing and failing papers: *introductory paragraphs, vocabulary, spelling,* and *variety of sentence structure.*

Papers judged college-level often contained pertinent anecdotes in the introductory paragraphs, precise vocabulary, and a variety of sentence structures, as the following paragraphs from two passing essays illustrate:

1. Until a few years ago, I hated teachers. I thought of them as people who took pleasure in making my life miserable. They were always beating me whenever my homework was not done, and at the end of the school term, they would write low grades on my grade report which would always make my parents angry. I remember, about five years ago, when I got an "F" for my mathematics exam, my father beat me, until I began to bleed. Naturally, I blamed the teacher for my beating and grew to hate him and all the others even more than before.

2. During the course of my life as a student, beginning with my years in elementary school to my present year in college I have interacted with many professors of varying interests, qualifications, intelligence and dedication to teaching. They have all influenced my life in different respects, whether positively or negatively; however, my interaction with professor x, who taught me Speech 116, has made such an impact on my life that it is worth mentioning.

On the other hand, failing essays, as the following paragraphs from two different papers demonstrate, opened with introductions which repeated the essay question and/or proceeded from a general observation to the particular event to be discussed, often with irrelevant information interspersed. They were also characterized by limited vocabulary and repetitious sentence structure:

1. I attended the Julius E. Sprauve school from first grade to ninth grade. Upon my ninth grade graduation I attended the Nazareth Bay High School, now known as Eudora Kean High School, form ten thru twelve grade. During my junior year at nazareth, I signed up for a Speech and Drama class. When I got to the class there was a teacher by the name of Mr. Donovan.
2. He gave me a great sense of self-confidence. He told us that each of us has unique qualities, and we should always feel proud of our selves. His advice gave me a propitious insight on life. He told us that "life has its ups and downs." He said that we have to be strong, so that. . . .

Although one of the stated criteria was the use of concrete examples, details did not distinguish passing papers. Some failing essays abounded in detail:

> As long as I knew Mrs. Penn, she was never a day absent or late from her classroom. She was always neatly dressed, her milky white hair in place, and her freshly low heel polished shoes never wore signs of unevenness, a run in her off-greyish stockings, would be an embarrassment to her.

In contrast, some passing papers lacked detail:

> To describe him, the first thing I would say is that he is prejudiced. I noticed this about him during the first couple of weeks of that particular semester. Not meaning to get into his personal life, but I never really understood why because his wife is black.

Nowhere in the paper did this writer document the teacher's alleged racist behavior.

Furthermore, different types of grammar and mechanical errors characterized passing and failing papers. Errors of omission, such as failure to insert a comma where required, occurred often in passing papers. Inserting unwarranted punctuation, however, was typical in failing papers, as in the following example: "I was upset when I found out that, I had to take one of my English classes. I wondered why, I was not informed of this before since, I took that class over six years ago. . . ."

Since 60% of the students who take the Writing Proficiency Exam fail to meet what appear to be rather minimal standards, one might conclude that no standards were enforced previous to the exit exam. Such was not the case. The fact that only 20% of all freshmen are exempted from remedial coursework attests to the college's commitment to writing standards which most of the region's high school graduates are unable to meet. How this sorting operates is illustrated by the following placement essays. The first was judged *college-level*, its numerous errors notwithstanding. The writer demonstrates knowledge, if not control, of essay structure, and includes such vocabulary as *integral, consequently, matriculation, ultimate goal*, and *pursue*:

ME AND MY INSTRUMENT

From the time I knew myself, I always loved music and instruments. I'm seventeen years old now and I still love music; consequently, I especially fell in love with the guitar.

It all started about 7 years ago when I went to Antigua for a summer vacation. One of my cousin there, Played the guitar Very well. He also played in a band. Whenever the band had practice, I always attended it earlier than the scheduled time to strum a few strings before the band officially started to practice. All of a sudden guitar had become an integral part of my life.

When I returned to St Thomas, I ask my mother to buy me a guitar. she took me for granted so I had to press her until she bought me one.

I started to take lessons and before I knew it, I was a pretty good player. In my Junior year at charlotte Amalie High School, I played guitar In the school's jazz band. Because of my superb playing I was given A trophe labeled (outstanding guitarist). In my Senior year in the Jazz band my playing leaped and I was given a trophe for being an outstanding soloist and another for outstanding membership.

Presently I am accepted for matriculation at Texas Southern University where I will persue a Career in music. My ultimate goal is to maintain A PHD in performance. That is, performing on my Guitar.

Guitar has become an intergral part of me and me and the guitar will never part,

In another context the previous essay might not be judged college-level. However, it differs markedly from the following failing essay, which shows a lack of knowledge of essay organization and little control of sentence structure:

THE WONDERFUL WORLD OF SNORKELING

I like snorkling. Snorkling is a world all it's own. On a warm Saturday morning with the sun shining bright in the sky, is a good time to go snorkling. I like snorkling for many reasons, one those reasons is the quiet, huge, speacey world down beneath the noisey serface of the passing, Hurried to be exact, world. when your down there it's like a totally different world which you control, except for one barrer, your snorkle hose, in other words your breath. Crusing slowly, more like flying, over a speacey world where everything takes their time, except for some road-runners. Big and small they all learn to be. Its like a chain, the huge eats the big, the big eats the small and the small eat what's left. It's amazing to see how they go about their lives undisturbed by whats above. There are times when I wished I was one of them, big or small, it really doesn't matter because they all swim so happy They all have different ways of living in their liquid home. Some live in groups while others live alone its fun to see some hundred or more of them swooping beside you. Snorkling as I said before is a world all its own which which to me there is no comparison. I will always enjoy snorkling for as long as I can. Besides snorkling, well, I realy dont know. Maby someday you can go snorkling with me. Huh.

Once out of the basic skills program, students proceed through an English curriculum copied from U. S. mainland universities. The first of the two-semester sequence covers description, narration, comparison/contrast, and definition while the second introduces persuasion, analysis, and the rudiments of research writing. The model of good writing is imported from the United States via the *Harbrace Handbook*, Educational Testing Service's *Sequential Test of Educational Progress*, the workbooks in the tutoring center, textbooks on the bookstore shelves, and the academic journals to which faculty subscribe.

LOOKING BEYOND THE TEST

Although conceding that students' writing improved during four years at the college, we still believed it was not *college-level*. Our next move was to show that students wrote so poorly because they weren't assigned enough writing in non-English courses and therefore lacked practice. After all, at the time students wrote their exit essays, they would have taken only two (or perhaps three) English courses. If expository writing skills were not reinforced and expanded in other courses, backsliding could be expected.

In anticipation of finding the non-English faculty culpable, we obtained syllabi from introductory and advanced courses in each department and listed the kinds of writing that students were required to produce. We were surprised that students were assigned essay tests, lab reports, book reviews and/or term papers in every course.

Since lack of writing assignments did not explain poor performance on the Writing Proficiency Exam, the question of standards loomed again: What quality of writing was acceptable? As term papers traditionally typify undergraduate writing assignments, we chose to examine "A" and "B" papers for content, organization, grammar, and mechanics.

We were dismayed by what we found. At the College of the Virgin Islands, term papers in freshman and sophomore courses averaged only 6–7 pages; upper-level and senior seminar papers averaged only 11. In lower-level courses, papers contained 2–3 bibliographical sources, one of which was often the course textbook. Supplementary sources were often weekly news magazines or the *Random House Dictionary*. Of the four to five citations, most (and sometimes all) were to the textbook. Papers in upper-level courses usually increased to six to eight sources, but problems with citation abounded. Yet instructors' responses to glaring weaknesses were often limited to capitalization or underlining.

The following paragraphs from a B+ paper in a sophomore business course typify the poor writing we encountered:

> The only theroy behind why Virgin Islands' managers don't plann is because it requires thinking, and we usually perfer to take spontaneous centric action, rather than go through the frustrating and and demanding labour of moving to the rational mode.
> Organizing is essential to a project. Without this, one would not know what kind of resources to use. Organizing is defined as qw 50 r04m qw or into a whole for united action. Organzing take the coorination of people, money, techinology, and other resorces. The Virgin Islands Government has gone through decades of disorganizing within departmemnts. For instance, they have mismanaged funds for local schools and had to go back to congress to asks for an extension of additional funds. Also, many times roads were rebuilt or rereparied because there were funds left over in *that budget*. The governmnet dug up the roads make sure the money was spent. Isn't this a waste of *taxpayer's money*? Also, a sure sign of disorganization.

The instructor's comment on this paper was "an excellent paper but lacked a good finishing 'touch' e.g. no title, heading; too many spelling and typing errors."

This sloppiness persisted through the senior seminar, a compulsory two-semester course which was the culmination of students' education in their major fields. Students worked individually with professors, wrote term papers, presented them orally, and defended them before peers and division faculty members. In the humanities division, these papers averaged only 10 pages and contained 5 to 10 references, often almost exclusively to textbooks and popular magazines.

Form was not the only problem. Some (but not all) papers showed little depth or sophistication of analysis. The following excerpts from an eight-page seminar paper passed without comment by the advising faculty member:

It appears to me that European or American music has only one steady rhythm, where as, African music has a variety of rhythm levels. A piece of African music could have two, three, or more levels of music playing at the same time. The rhythm is closely tied to drumming.

In addition, rhythm in the African music causes certain body responces which European or modern American music doesn't cause. However, this rhythm is used still today in modern kind of African music known as reggae music.

The paper also included such statements as: ". . . the romantic reggae songs are songs of romance," and "However, one of the people who is in my opinion a contributer to reggae music is Bob Marley."

In the social science division, passing senior seminar papers were slightly longer—15 to 20 pages—and contained bibliographies. However, many citations in the text did not appear in the references at all, and the bibliographic entries did not conform to any style manual or to each other.

In our outrage at the apparently laissez-faire attitude toward writing skills, we scheduled interviews with non-English faculty. All seven professors expressed their exasperation with poor grammar and mechanics, but only two penalized students for such errors. The others felt that grammar instruction was the province of the English department, though some marked errors "for students' awareness." One professor stated that he did not demand correct grammar because he would then be forced to fail most students. Another did not correct subject–verb errors or diction because he felt the community tolerated such errors.

All stated that the quality of content was their major concern in evaluating term papers. However, we observed few, if any, comments addressing scope of topic, numbers of references, and evidence. A gap existed between faculty members' stated criteria for term papers and those we observed. The greatest number of comments referred to formal conventions of the genre: title page format, outlining, capitalization, reference form, spelling, and typographical errors. Often ignored were the myriad problems with content, organization, grammar, and vocabulary.

Our ire abated somewhat as faculty revealed their frustration with students' writing. In despair, several professors had dropped the research writing assignments entirely; others had lowered the number of required papers. Some resented the English faculty for failing to teach term-paper skills. They reported feeling overwhelmed by the time needed to explain the assignment in class, help students individually, and evaluate term papers when there were so many severe shortcomings.

LOOKING BEYOND THE COLLEGE

Our inability to pinpoint a culprit for what we stubbornly insisted were "low standards" compelled us, finally, to extend our inquiry beyond the college boundaries. We came to understand that standards do indeed exist at the College of the Virgin Islands. But, like everywhere else, they emerge from the dynamics among economic, social, cultural, and linguistic circumstances and are reified in the faculty and students.

At the college, the ecology of literacy derives from at least two, often conflicting, systems. The first, imported from the United States, is the formal institutional structure, which includes administrative organization, curricula, most textbooks, and more than half the faculty. It is superimposed on a local and regional system deformed by colonialism.

We believe the historical clash between dominating outside forces and colonized Caribbean societies not only explains but actually spawns the academic standards at the College of the Virgin Islands. Woven into the texture of daily life are the answers to our original questions: Why do so many students fail the Writing Proficiency Exam? Why are even the passing essays full of mistakes? And answers to the larger questions: What are academic standards? How are they created and maintained?

Negative Attitudes Toward English Creole

Central to the ecology of literacy at the College of the Virgin Islands is the cumulative negative attitude toward students' first language, English Creole (Elsasser & Irvine, 1985). At home and in school Eastern Caribbean students grow accustomed to hearing their language referred to as *broken English, dialect*, or *calypso* and to being constantly admonished to speak "proper English" by adults who themselves are often speaking Creole.

In school, language instruction proceeds as if Creole did not exist. There are no bilingual programs, English as a Second Language materials, or contrastive analyses. With the exception of Grenada under the People's Revolutionary Government of Maurice Bishop (Kephart, 1983; Searle, 1984; Torres, 1984) and to a lesser extent St. Lucia (Anthony, Charles, Compton, Louisy, & Tobias, 1981; Bernabe, et al., 1983), all reading and writing instruction from the first day of primary school to the last day of university is in English. The cumulative effect of present language policy is the belief among Eastern Caribbean people that they don't have a language. In essence, Eastern Caribbean students are linguistic orphans, expected to deny the existence of their first language and to read and write in a second one.

Despite this negative attitude, primary and secondary school teachers, victims of their own limited language education, use acrolectal forms of Creole unwittingly in the classroom. Consequently, constructions like the following, which were written by a secondary schoolteacher from St. Kitts and an elementary school teacher in St. Thomas, are perceived as Standard English: *Why then their children don't know? Why less competitive crops are not implement?*

Recently, West Indian linguists and writers have attacked the negative attitude toward Creole and limited concessions have been gained. The Caribbean Examination Council, which designs and evaluates standard exams for all independent English-speaking islands, now permits the use of "dialect" in creative writing. Purely linguistic concessions, however, only scratch the surface. Differences between Creole and English extend beyond syntax, phonology, morphology, and lexicon.

Even for those of us whose first language is English, developing a written voice is extremely difficult work. Like jazz, writing depends on conscious variations on a theme. Students at the College of the Virgin Islands don't control the basic code, yet they are expected to manipulate sentence structure, organizational patterns, levels of formality, and vocabulary. They can't. Preoccupied with the code itself, they turn in papers which are either correct but empty, or interesting but hopelessly tangled.

Each language has its own norms and forms for organizing verbal expression, and whether and to what extent these are separable is at present an unanswered question (Hymes, 1980). In the Eastern Caribbean, for example, calypso is the traditional form for critical social and political commentary. Composed in Creole, calypso treats serious subjects with a dose of humor. When students are liberated from the confines of English discourse, they borrow rules from calypso, as in the following essay on teen-age pregnancy. The writer weaves humor, dialogue, allusions, double entendres, and metaphors deftly through a Creole narrative in which the adolescent mother loses her premature baby and almost dies, due to limited availability of medical services:

> I blame John father, Sam. . . . Since the boy small, he use to carry him up when he going go drink with he friend them. He not only carrying him, but he giving him beer and rum to drink. When I find out what he wass doing and tackle him about it, he telling me stupidness about how rum does kill worm and get rid of gas. . . .
> Well when I see he and Miss Thomas daughter Sheila looking real chummy, I beg him hard not to get heself nor the girl in no trouble. He tell me I must take it easy, how he got everything under control.
> Well, up to now I don't know what he had under control for the next thing I know, the girl breeding for John. Now he pull he chin till he force couple strawn of beard to grow and he got some funny talk about Babylon say is

Rasta talk. On top of that, he now walking with he leg them wide apart like he got piles come tell me how he skanking. . . .

The sociolinguistic norms this student applied to the task of addressing Caribbean youth about teen-age pregnancy differ markedly from those expected in the five-paragraph essay or a library research paper, two typical imported academic assignments.

Literacy in the Caribbean

Middle-class college students from the mainland United States tackle such assignments after 12 years of exposure to similar discourse, beginning with *Weekly Readers* and encyclopedia assignments in elementary school. By the time students enter high school, *Time* and *Newsweek* often appear as assigned reading material. Even small towns have daily newspapers. Thus, when these students enter college, professors may be justified in expecting familiarity with research and expository writing and demanding that students progress from popular magazines to academic journals, from tertiary sources, such as an encyclopedia, to secondary or primary sources of information. Students from the Eastern Caribbean, however, do not have the same experience.

The U. S. and British Virgin Islands and Barbados are the only Eastern Caribbean islands where daily newspapers are published. The three papers from the Virgins devote 1 to 3 pages to regional, national, and international news; the remaining 15 to 20 pages are filled with local news, social events, and sports coverage. Only Barbados boasts two competing newspapers that analyze regional and international issues. On some islands, like Dominica, a weekly paper focusing on local affairs circulates, but on many, like St. Kitts, the only available papers are political broadsheets published by competing parties.

Economic scarcity in the Caribbean limits educational resources. Governments strain their budgets in order to provide minimal educational opportunities for all children. Few schools boast the libraries, educational technology, and scientific equipment which the North American public takes for granted. The social and economic plight of the schools is mirrored in students' homes. Living space is cramped and precludes the solitude usually associated with reading and writing. Many families lack extra money to spend on books, which are imported and expensive. For some, even electricity is an expensive luxury. One of our students wrote an essay recounting her delight at receiving a kerosene lamp to read by:

My grandmother is a very old fashion woman, and she hated to see the lights on for two hours without been turned off. She always said to me, "child, please turn the lights off, you know you are wasting current!" But I love to read so she was always having a hard time getting me to do it. One night I was lying down on my bed, when I heard her foot-steps coming towards my door. I jumped up quickly and turned off the lights, then I heard her knocked on the door, my heart started thumming. I got up and opened the door expecting to see grandmother with a long face and to hear her say, "turn off the light!" but instead of that; she had the most beautiful Kerasine lamp I have ever seen in her hand. then she said to me, "darling I brought you this lamp so that you would not have to turn the light on, and have me arguing with you."

From then on, everytime I wanted to read late in the night I would just light my lamp and I would started reading. the glow from it use to make me feel so warm inside. . . .

These economic constraints do not preclude familiarity with and respect for literacy among West Indians. With the exception of St. Lucians and Dominicans, most people in the Eastern Caribbean attend Protestant churches where Bible reading and interpretation are important activities. Letter writing is also a common activity in West Indian homes because of generations of migration caused by economic hardship. Finally, political independence has expanded opportunities for economic and social mobility. These, in turn, have increased the desirability and importance of education, as well as its availability.

Those students from the independent islands who attend college have survived in an extremely competitive educational system. Furthermore, they are all too aware of the economic hardships their families endure in order to pay their tuition. Consequently, the diligence and ambition of many students compensate for the gaps in their educational backgrounds.

Yet at the college, students' opportunities to acquire the intellectual knowledge associated with advanced literacy are restricted by rigid class and racial divisions. The social legacies of colonialism are evident in the absence of a faculty lounge or any space designated for informal faculty or student–faculty interaction. In fact, contact between black and white faculty or between students and faculty, whether white or black, is emotionally loaded behavior subject to critical comment and gossip, a powerful inhibitor on a small island.

IMPORTED VS. INDIGENOUS LITERACIES

When we use imported terminology like *remediation* to discuss imported issues like *standards* in an imported system, the subterranean differences between the College of the Virgin Islands and the mainland universities on which it is modeled are obscured. Yet many faculty explain students' poor performance within the framework of the class and racial folklore of the U. S. Convinced that the essays and term papers they receive reflect the "decline of standards" or the "literacy crisis" they read about in *Time* or *Newsweek*, they respond in several counterproductive ways. West Indians and North Americans alike adjust to the overwhelming problems which they confront by compromising their expectations. In extreme cases, they simply stop requiring term papers. Others ignore grammar and spelling errors. A second group clings to the rhetoric of "high standards," while distributing the same inflated grades as those who have given up.

These misguided responses only exacerbate the situation: By importing a curriculum and applying it as if West Indian students had practiced the forms of writing integral to a North American education, we contribute to confusion and lack of learning. Students fail to master the imported functions and never even study local functions. Many graduate unable to meet the literacy needs of their own communities. As long as this imported model prevails, little discussion is devoted to the kinds of writing skills graduates of the college actually need or which standards are feasible within the larger social context. Thus, what is most wrong with the present approach to writing at the College of the Virgin Islands is that failing to recognize how actual standards were created makes change difficult (see Fishman, this volume). To improve writing qualitatively at the college, we must stop relying exclusively on imported "Cessnas" and incorporate the social, economic, and political realities in bold, innovative curricula.

Directions for Change

Options for changing the model of education could grow out of ethnographic descriptions of advanced literacy in the Eastern Caribbean. For example, the College of the Virgin Islands could, like Yale, Oxford, or the University of the West Indies, cater to an educational elite. Or like American junior colleges, writing skills could be limited to the functional literacy required in vocational training. Another alternative, the one to which we are committed, is for the college to become an institution where the curriculum emerges from and serves the needs and aspirations of an independent Eastern Caribbean. Since no such institution exists, we can only guess what it would look like.

Perhaps students would learn to write in their native Creole. Alternatively, they might contribute to the creation of a distinctly West Indian Standard English and discourse styles which reflect regional values. Rather than penalizing students for the traces of Creole discourse features which appear in their writing, faculty could encourage mutual exploration of ways to incorporate West Indian humor, imagery, and dialogue into expository genre.

Instead of settling for poor approximations of the five-paragraph essay, the college could foster the growth of a regional literary language (Joseph, 1984). Furthermore, instead of *Time* and *Newsweek*, *Caribbean Contact*, a monthly review published in Barbados by the Caribbean Council of Churches, could serve as a model of expository writing.

Term paper assignments might focus less on library research and more on concrete fieldwork assignments. Since library resources are scant and cannot in all practicality serve as the cornerstone for first-rate research, a good case can be made for emphasizing primary instead of secondary research. Properly guided, university students can contribute to the basic knowledge of their societies while learning to design, administer, and interpret questionnaires; to analyze data; and to report research.

Universities should serve their societies' unique creativity. In the type of program we advocate, curriculum would be built on indigenous models of the region's abundant literary and expository prose. The study of West Indian literature could be the window on the whole question of language use in the region. To understand and appreciate the pioneering nature of Caribbean authors' styles, students would need to study the linguistic structure and social history of their language, which is a major cultural characteristic of the Eastern Caribbean. A generation of writers (Paul Keens–Douglas, Derek Wolcott, Edward Braithwaite, Michael Anthony, and Samuel Selvon) has struggled to create a regional literary language. Universities could support their work by providing a critical audience, standardizing orthographies, and publishing dictionaries and handbooks of usage.

In addition to the study and creation of fiction and exposition, the curriculum might incorporate calypso and poetry, two forms of writing that educated people in the Eastern Caribbean produce for pleasure and entertainment. Since calypso provides political and social commentary, training bright, critical calypsonians might be a responsibility of the college.

None of this precludes studying American, British, African, or Canadian writing styles. Their wholesale importation, however, violates indigenous ecology and retards the struggle to build an independent Eastern Caribbean (see Fishman, this volume). Paulo Freire (1970) has stated, ". . . the fundamental theme of the Third World . . . is the conquest of its right to a voice, of the right to pronounce its word. . . ." (p. 4). In the first world or the third, our responsibility as educators is to support students' efforts to regain that right.

REFERENCES

Anthony, P., Charles, P., Compton, P., Louisy, P., & Tobias, E. (1981). *Language and development: The St. Lucian context* (Final Report of a seminar on an orthography for St. Lucian Creole held January 29–31, 1981). Castries, St. Lucia: Caribbean Research Centre and Folk Research Centre.

Bailey, R., & Gorlach, M. (1982). *English as a world language.* Ann Arbor: University of Michigan Press.

Bernabe, J., Carrington, L. Charles, P., Henderson, F., Hippolyte, K., & Louisy, P. (1983). *The development of Antillean Kweyol: Report of the second creole orthography workshop held in St. Lucia* (Report Series No. 1). Castries, St. Lucia: National Research and Development Foundation of St. Lucia and Folk Research Centre.

Collins, H. R. (1968). *The new English of the Onitsha chapbooks.* Athens, OH: Ohio University Center for International Studies Africa Program.

Elsasser, N. & Irvine, P. (1985). English and Creole: The dialectics of choice in a college writing program. *Harvard Educational Review, 55,* 399–415.

Elsasser, N., & John–Steiner, V. (1977). An interactionist approach to advancing literacy. *Harvard Educational Review, 47,* 355–369.

Freire, P. (1970). *Cultural action for freedom* (Monograph Series No. 1). Cambridge: Harvard Educational Review and Center for Study of Development and Social Change.

Heath, S. B. (1983). *Ways with words.* London: Cambridge University Press.

Hymes, D. (1980). *Language in education: Ethnolinguistic essays* (Language and Ethnography Series). Washington, DC: Center for Applied Linguistics.

Joseph, R. (1984). *Pan-Caribbean Creole—A need.* Unpublished manuscript, College of the Virgin Islands, St. Thomas.

Kephart, R. (1983). *Kom le we rid!* Unpublished manuscript, University of Florida, Department of Anthropology, Gainesville.

Obiechina, E. N. (Ed.). (1972). *Onitsha market literature.* London: Heinemann.

Platt, J. T. (1980). *English in Singapore and Malaysia: Status, features, functions.* Kuala Lumpur: Oxford University Press.

Scribner, S., & Cole, M. (1981). *The psychology of literacy.* Cambridge, MA: Harvard University Press.

Searle, C. (1984). *Words unchained: Language and revolution in Grenada.* London: Zed Press.

Torres, R. M. (1984). *Educacion y democracia en la Grenada revolucionaria* [Education and democracy in revolutionary Grenada]. Managua, Nicaragua: Instituto de Investigaciones Economicas y Sociales.

Author Index

Subject Index